Computer Security, Privacy, and Politics:
Current Issues, Challenges, and Solutions

Ramesh Subramanian
Quinnipiac University, USA

IRM Press
Publisher of innovative scholarly and professional
information technology titles in the cyberage

Hershey • New York

Acquisition Editor:	Kristin Klinger
Development Editor:	Kristin Roth
Senior Managing Editor:	Jennifer Neidig
Managing Editor:	Jamie Snavely
Assistant Managing Editor:	Carole Coulson
Copy Editor:	Jennifer Young
Typesetter:	Larissa Vinci
Cover Design:	Lisa Tosheff
Printed at:	Yurchak Printing Inc.

Published in the United States of America by
 IRM Press (an imprint of IGI Global)
 701 E. Chocolate Avenue, Suite 200
 Hershey PA 17033-1240
 Tel: 717-533-8845
 Fax: 717-533-8661
 E-mail: cust@igi-global.com
 Web site: http://www.irm-press.com

and in the United Kingdom by
 IRM Press (an imprint of IGI Global)
 3 Henrietta Street
 Covent Garden
 London WC2E 8LU
 Tel: 44 20 7240 0856
 Fax: 44 20 7379 0609
 Web site: http://www.eurospanonline.com

Library of Congress Cataloging-in-Publication Data

Computer security, privacy, and politics : current issues, challenges and solutions / Ramesh Subramanian, editor.
 p. cm.
 Summary: "This book offers a review of recent developments of computer security, focusing on the relevance
and implications of global privacy, law, and politics for society, individuals, and corporations.It compiles timely
content on such topics as reverse engineering of software, understanding emerging computer exploits, emerging lawsuits and cases, global and societal implications, and protection from attacks on privacy"--Provided by
publisher.
 Includes bibliographical references and index.
 ISBN-13: 978-1-59904-804-8 (hardcover)
 ISBN-13: 978-1-59904-806-2 (e-book)
 1. Computer security. 2. Computer networks--Security measures. 3. Computer security--Government policy.
I. Subramanian, Ramesh.
 QA76.9.A25C6557 2008
 005.8--dc22
                              2007037717

British Cataloguing in Publication Data
A Cataloguing in Publication record for this book is available from the British Library.

Computer Security, Privacy, and Politics:
Current Issues, Challenges, and Solutions

Table of Contents

Section V
Security and Privacy: Emerging Issues

Preface

The last decade of the 20th century was the decade of the Internet. The invention of the World Wide Web (Web) by Tim Berners-Lee, who built the first Web site in 1991 while working at the European Organization for Nuclear Research (or CERN) in Geneva, Switzerland, started a world-wide trend in developing Web sites not only for personal and research purposes, but for disseminating governmental information and for engaging in global electronic commerce. Thus the Internet, with its "killer application," the Web, heralded the furious pace of globalization in the 1990s.

Today, as the Internet and the Web continue their furious growth and global spread, they have filtered down to encompass every aspect of society. Nowadays it is rare to see an aspect of domestic or public life that is not in some way touched by the Internet. This situation is not restricted only to the technologically developed countries, but is becoming increasingly prevalent in developing countries too. As a result, new terms and phrases such as "virtual world," "cybercrime," "computer virus," "data privacy," "identity theft," and "data mining" have entered the everyday vocabulary. Debates have ensued on the virtues and vices of the Web and the consequent large scale digitization that it has heralded.

While many have argued that the pace of the growth of the Internet, the Web, e-commerce, and digitization should continue without any curbs or governmental restrictions, others have argued the exact opposite—that these should be actively regulated and controlled through laws both domestic and international. The latter group has argued that unregulated and unmitigated growth of the Web coupled with the current pace of digitization of almost all data belonging to individuals could cause an erosion of privacy and cause them to become exposed to malware and identity theft. This would, they argue, curb e-commerce and seriously affect global economic development and growth. Indeed, in the 1990s the Internet was considered to be a virtual world that was ungovernable and thus could not fall under the purview of any government. Proponents of this view felt that the users of the Internet would somehow govern themselves and make it into a global vehicle of commerce and information outside of any governmental influence. However, in recent years, realizing the importance of the Internet, governments also have stepped in to flex their muscles in an attempt to gain control of the Internet through regulations and laws. Predictably, increasing government regulation of the Internet has its detractors who believe that certain fundamental rights such as the freedom of expression may be lost if the government controls the Internet.

These developments and trends have, inevitably, led to a four-way tussle: between the public, governmental policy makers, the technology industry, and the businesses that use the technologies. This intersection of politics, law, privacy, and security in the context of computer technology is both sensitive and complex.

As we are all aware, computer viruses, worms, Trojan horses, spy-ware, computer exploits, poorly designed software, inadequate technology laws, politics, and terrorism all have a profound effect on our daily computing operations and habits. Further, new technological innovations such as file-sharing software and location-based tracking tools also have major privacy-related, political, and social implications. In such an environment, various questions arise, such as: Can there be global laws to preserve security? How will such laws affect privacy? What are the politics of security and privacy? What is the role of legal systems in the way privacy is addressed in various nations? What is the connection between privacy and democratization in various countries? How do organizations tackle the issue of privacy? What are the implications of file-sharing software, peer-to-peer systems and instant messaging in autocratic societies? What are the global effects of file sharing? Are there cultural differences that account for differences in perceptions of security and privacy? Does national or regional culture play a role in shaping the political arguments pertaining to security and privacy? If yes, to what extent?

Unfortunately, basic knowledge and understanding of computer security, *especially the legal, political and social underpinnings* concerning the use of security technologies within organizations and in the society at large is generally lax. There is a general sense that while security has not improved, privacy has been lost. There is concern about the misuse of information by companies and governments. There also is a general sense that the problems are only getting worse—new developments including electronic voting, Radio Frequency Identification (RFID) tags, location-based tracking technologies, and the Digital Millennium Copyright Act (DMCA) only add to the confusion and concern about security and privacy. In addition, national and international politics play a very important role in shaping the discourse on privacy and security.

This book aims to provide a window to academics and practitioners to view and understand the ties that bind computer technology, security, privacy, and politics. In addition to chapters on the above topics, the book will also include chapters that delve into emerging lawsuits and cases, global and societal implications, and how an individual can protect herself from attacks on privacy.

The 14 chapters of this book offer:

- A point-in-time review of the new developments and thought in the field of computer security, with a special focus on privacy, law, and politics in a global context
- Its implications on people, business, and law
- The evolution of security and privacy laws and their relevance to society, individuals, and corporations
- An examination of security and privacy communities: the practitioners of the art
- Provide a vision for the future of security and privacy in the context of global politics.

The audience for the book would be anyone from advanced-novice to expert in the fields of security, privacy, law, and politics; academics, technology managers, social, and political scientists, CIOs, and information security officers.

Organization of the Book

The book is organized into five sections, with a total of 14 chapters. The **first section** briefly introduces the notions of security and privacy in a global context, setting the tone for the rest of the book. In the only chapter **(Chapter I)** in this section, Alok Mishra gives a nice overview of the theme of the book by assessing various issues related to individual privacy on the Web, growing concerns among the Web users, technologies employed for collecting and protecting information on the Web, privacy-enhancing technologies and the legal provisions to curb the Web privacy. This chapter also provides a detailed discussion on the Platform for Privacy Preferences (P3P), its structure, present scenario of its implementation, and its future success.

The **second section** quickly takes the reader into a major aspect of the implementing computer security and personal privacy across various nations—namely privacy and security laws. In **Chapter II**, John Thomas traces the development in the United States of legal protections of the right to privacy. The chapter begins with the common law "right to be let alone" in the early 1900s and proceeds through the enactment of the U.S. Patriot Act in 2001 and the National Security Administration's warrant-less wire tapping program revealed to the public in 2005. It concludes with a discussion of emerging electronic threats to the security of privacy of the public and concomitant challenges to law makers and law enforcers.

In **Chapter III**, Sushma Mishra and Amita Goyal Chin discuss some of the most significant of the governmental regulations recently mandated of the IT industry and their considerable impact and implications on information technology, both from a technical and managerial perspective. Employing neo institutional theory as the guiding framework for analysis, they suggest that the plethora of regulations being imposed on the IT industry are migrating organizations in the IT industry to conform and implement standardized processes and practices, resulting in the industry wide commoditization of IT.

In **Chapter IV**, Bernd Carsten Stahl presents the current state of legal protection of privacy in the United Kingdom. He argues that there are different philosophical concepts of privacy that underpin different pieces of legislation and explores what this may mean for the justification of privacy protection. He then speculates on where the future development in this field may be heading.

The **third section** focuses on emerging privacy technologies, their uses, and implications.

This section starts with **Chapter V**, discussing a taxonomy of existing data mining techniques, by Madhu Ahluwalia and Aryya Gangopadyay. Their chapter gives a synopsis of the techniques that exist in the area of privacy preserving data mining. Privacy preserving data mining is important because there is a need to develop accurate data mining models without using confidential data items in individual records. In providing a neat categorization of the current algorithms that preserve privacy for major data mining tasks, the authors hope that students, teachers, and researchers can gain an understanding of this vast area and apply the knowledge gained to find new ways of simultaneously preserving privacy and conducting mining.

In **Chapter VI**, Yue Liu discusses some rational security and privacy concerns about biometric technology. The author gives a critical analysis of the complexities involved in using this technology through rational discussions, technology assessment and case examples.

In **Chapter VII**, Roger Clarke addresses the multiple issues of threats to privacy through privacy-intrusive technologies, which have led to a widespread distrust of technology, causing e-businesses to under achieve. He then discusses privacy enhancing technologies (PETs), their technical effectiveness and ways by which several constituencies can harness PETs. Clarke's chapter thus examines PETs, their application to business needs, and the preparation of a business case for investment in PETs.

The **fourth section** focuses on how privacy and security are handled in the organizational context. In **Chapter VIII**, Ian Allison and Craig Strangwick discuss how one small business planned for, and implemented, the security of its data in a new enterprise-wide system. The company's data was perceived as sensitive and any breach of privacy as commercially critical. From this perspective, the chapter outlines the organizational and technical facets of the policies and practices evidenced. Lessons for other businesses can be drawn from the case by recognizing the need for investments to be made that will address threats in business critical areas.

In **Chapter IX**, Richard McCarthy and Martin Grossman examine the connection between Privacy, Security and the Enterprise Architecture Framework. Enterprise Architecture is a relatively new concept that has been adopted by large organizations for legal, economic and strategic reasons. It has become a critical component of an overall IT governance program to provide structure and documentation to describe the business processes, information flows, technical infrastructure and organizational management of an information technology organization. The chapter describes two of the most widely used enterprise architecture frameworks (the Zachman Framework and the Federal Enterprise Architecture Framework) and their ability to meet the security and privacy needs of an organization.

In **Chapter X**, Frederick Ip and Yolande Chan turn to the ever-important business issue of information security in organizations by researching these issues in the context of Canadian financial firms and educational organizations. Taking a resource-based view of the firm, they examine relationships between the following organizational variables. The organization's appreciation of the strategic value of its knowledge bases, the information systems security resources, the number and nature of security breaches experienced, and the organization's customer capital and human capital are studied. Relationships between various variables are tested and a managerially-friendly information security model is validated.

The **fifth section** discusses some important, interesting, emerging topics and issues in the arena of security, privacy and politics. In **Chapter XI**, Sue Conger comprehensively discusses emerging technologies and emerging privacy issues. With each new technology, new ethical issues emerge that threaten both individual and household privacy. Conger's chapter investigates issues relating to three emerging technologies—RFID chips, GPS, and smart motes—and the current and future impacts these technologies will have on society.

In **Chapter XII**, Anza Akram provides a window into the emerging world of tele-democracy in developing countries. Her chapter discusses the effects of information and communication technologies on democracy and focuses on the driving forces, citizen and technology, to understand the effects and future implications. The research is based on literature review and uses informative approach to analyze the existing practices in electronic democracy. It inquires the relationship between the theories in communications and democracy, and analyzes the interaction with the citizens from Athenian and the Orwellian perspectives in Politics. It proposes a framework to identify and analyze the driving forces and the issues related to the digital democracy.

In **Chapter XIII**, Zheng Yan and Silke Holtmanns introduce trust modeling and trust management as a means of managing trust in digital systems. They state that trust has evolved from a social concept to a digital concept, and discuss how trust modeling and management help in designing and implementing a trustworthy digital system, especially in emerging distributed systems.

Finally, in **Chapter XIV**, Dan Manson brings a pedagogical focus to the theme of the book. His chapter introduces the interrelationships of security, privacy and politics in higher education. University curriculum politics are ingrained through organizational structures that control faculty hiring, retention, tenure, and promotion, and self-governance policy bodies such as academic senates and faculty curriculum committees that control curriculum approval and implementation. Compounding the politics of curriculum are different constructs of security and privacy, with security viewed as a technical issue versus privacy as a legal and organizational issue. Manson believes that multiple disciplines must learn to work together to teach the constantly changing technical, scientific, legal, and administrative security and privacy landscape. While university "ownership" of security and privacy curriculum may create new political challenges, it has the potential to help limit competing faculty, department and program politics.

Editing this book has been an enlightening and thought-provoking experience to me. I hope that you enjoy reading this book, and that your interest in the field of security, privacy and politics are further aroused through reading the varied perspectives presented by the authors of the various chapters.

Ramesh Subramanian
Hamden, Connecticut, USA
December 2007

Acknowledgment

Two years ago I was searching the Web, looking for teaching materials in the intersection of computer security, policy, and privacy. To my pleasant surprise, I came across Ming Chow's course on *Security, Privacy, and Politics in the Computer Age,* an experimental course he was teaching at Tufts University, Boston. Thrilled by this coincidence, I wrote to Ming and soon an exchange of e-mails followed. I sounded the idea of jointly editing a book on the topic with him. Unfortunately, time constraints precluded Ming from co-editing this book, and I ended up working on this project alone. I would like to use this opportunity to acknowledge and thank Ming. This book was inspired by his course at Tufts.

This project began in early 2006 in Connecticut, USA, and moved to Chennai, India in early 2007—a change that caused many logistical challenges and required tremendous personal adjustment. I was fortunate in having a great set of authors, reviewers, and colleagues, for without their active and prompt participation this book would not have been possible. My sincere thanks to all of them.

I would also like to thank Mehdi Khosrow-Pour, DBA, Information Resources Management Association, and Jan Travers, vice president editorial of IGI Global for inviting me to develop this book; Kristin Klinger for handling the contract details; Kristin Roth for overseeing the development process of the book; Deborah Yahnke, the editorial assistant; and finally, the two development editors of the project, Meg Stocking and Jessica Thompson—whose unstinting and cheerful assistance throughout the project made it an enjoyable experience.

And last but not least, I would like to thank my wife Ramya for her constant encouragement and understanding during the various stages of development of this book.

Ramesh Subramanian
Chennai, India
December 2007

Section I

Security and Privacy: Global Concepts

Chapter I

Web Privacy:
Issues, Legislations, and Technological Challenges

Alok Mishra, Atilim University, Turkey

Deepti Mishra, Atilim University, Turkey

Abstract

People all over the world increasingly are concerned about the privacy issues surrounding the personal information collected by private organizations, governments and employers. Privacy relates to issues regarding collection, secure transmission, storage, authorized access, usage, and disclosure of personal information. This information is used for commercial gain by many organizations. Individual privacy concerns significantly affects consumer willingness to engage in electronic commerce over the Internet. The increased use of the Internet and Web for everyday activities is bringing new threats to personal privacy. This chapter assessed various issues related to individual privacy on the Web, growing concerns among the Web users, technologies employed for collecting and protecting information on the Web, privacy-enhancing technologies and the legal provisions to curb the Web privacy. This chapter also reported detailed discussion about Platform for Privacy Preferences (P3P), its structure, present scenario of its implementation and its future success. Global consistency on Internet privacy protection is important to promote the growth of electronic commerce. To protect consumers in a globally consistent manner, legislation, self-regulation, technical solutions and combination solutions are different ways that can be implemented

Introduction

The Internet is proliferating in an exponential way all over the world. It has the potential to change the way people live. With only a few mouse clicks, people can follow the news, look up facts, buy goods and services, and communicate with others from around the world (Chung & Paynter, 2002). People can provide information about themselves if they are not careful. This raises concerns regarding threats to their personal privacy whilst online. Information privacy has been recognized as an important issue in management, and its significance will continue to escalate as the value of information continues to grow (Mason, 1986; Raul, 2002; Rust, Kannan, & Peng, 2002). Therefore personal privacy in information systems is becoming increasingly critical with widespread use of networked systems and the Internet (Earp, Anton, Aiman-Smith, & Stufflebeam, 2005). These technologies provide opportunities to collect large amounts of personal information about online users, potentialy violating those users' personal privacy (Bellotti, 1997; Clarke, 1999). Web users are becoming increasingly concerned about what personal information they may reveal when they go online and where that information might end up. It's common to hear about organizations that derive revenue from personal information collected on their Web sites. Information you provide to register for a Web site might later be used for telemarketing or sold to another company. Seemingly anonymous information about your Web-surfing habits might be merged with your personal information. Web sites might e-mail you to say that their privacy policies are changing, but most of us find it difficult and time-consuming to read and understand privacy policies or to figure out how to request that the use of our personal information be restricted. Privacy concerns are making consumers nervous about going online, but current privacy policies for Web sites tend to be so long and difficult to understand that consumers rarely read them.

Although there is no universally accepted definition, privacy can be articulated as the need to secure for the individual "the right to be left alone" or as the "state or condition of limited access to a person" (Schoemann, 1984; Warren, & Brandeis, 1980). Alan Westin's well known definition of privacy describes privacy as the claim of individuals, groups, or institutions to determine for themselves when, how, and to what extent information about them is communicated to others (Westin, 1967). While Warren and Brandeis (1980) defined privacy as the "right to be left alone." Information privacy exits when the usage, release and circulation of personal information can be controlled (Culnam, 1993). Three key elements of information privacy includes separateness, restricted access, and benefical use. Separateness is defined as the ability to describe the boundaries and ownership or access rights to information. Restricted access refers to the ability to protect the identified data, and beneficial use implies that only data owners or parties explicitly authorized to receive the information are able to benefit from its use (Toscana, 2001).

There are three technical barriers to the continued widespread adoption of electronic commerce on the Internet, including ease of use, access to the hardware needed to participate, and privacy (Chaum & Chaum, 1997). Privacy concerns remain a significant inhibitor preventing more extensive use of the Internet for conducting business-to-consumer (B2C) e-commerce. Privacy pertains to the protection of information about individuals, transactions, or organizations. Web user information is a valued commodity that provides business organizations with a means to more effectively target and segment its market. Sellers of information goods find it advantageous to segment their markets based on observable characteristics or revealed consumer behaviour that can be used to increase profits (Bakos & Brynjolfsson, 1999).

U.S. Congressional hearings in the 1970s, where privacy advocates sought to ban credit bureaus from using centralized computer databases, lead to the recoginition that organizations have certain responsibilities and individuals have certain rights, regarding information collecton and use. Since 1973, the Fair Information Practice (FIP) principles (The code of FIP, 1973) have served as the basis for establishing and evaluating U.S. privacy laws and practices. The FIP principles consist of : 1) notice/awareness; 2) choice/consent; 3) access/participation; 4) integrity/security; and 5) enforcement/redress (The code of FIP, 1973). U.S. government agencies, Internet users, and industry leaders all agree that organizational privacy policies—particularly those belonging to organizations using electronic transactions—should reflect the FIPs [18-20]. Several studies, however, have found that often they do not (Anton, Earp, & Reese, 2002; Culnan, 1999; Electronic Privacy Information Center, 1999). In 1980 the Organization for Economic Cooperation and Development (OECD), an international organization, issued Guidelines on the protection of privacy and trans-border flows of personal data (OECD, 1980). The OECD guidelines are the current best-practice global standard for privacy protection and are the recommended model for legislation in member countries. Although not legally binding, the guidelines are recognized by all OECD members, including the European Union (EU) and the U.S. They are implemented differently among individual nations, suggesting privacy views differ between countries (Baumer et al., 2005). The US FIPs do not include all of the OECD guidelines, but reflect a subset of them. The EU directives are even more comprehensive with respect to privacy, and provide the legal foundation for those countries. In making online consumer privacy recommendations to the U.S. Congress, the Federal Trade Commission (FTC) has relied on four studies assessing organizational awareness of and adherence to the U.S. FIP principles (Adkinson et al. 2002; Culnan, 1999; FTC, 1998; FTC, 2000). FTC conducted a study in March 1999 (Anton, Earp, Potts, & Alspaugh, 2001) which discovered that 92.8 percent of Web sites were gathering at least one type of identifying information (name, e-mail address, postal address) while 56.8 percent were collecting at least one type of demographic information (gender and preferences). The monetary value of this information explains why so many Web sites gather personal information. This raises consumers' concern about their privacy rights. Consumers worry about the security of their personal information and fear that it might be misused (Chung and Paynter, 2002).

In 1999, DoubleClick Inc. became a target of privacy advocates and lawsuits for collecting and selling information on individual Web surfing habits merged with information from other databases to identify users by name and create online customer preference profiles (Straub & Collins, 1990). In 2002, U.S. Bancorp paid a $7.5 million fine to settle one lawsuit, agreed to stop sharing customer account information, including credit card numbers, account balances, and Social Security numbers with unaffiliated, nonfinancial third parties to settle yet another suit, and still has other privacy lawsuits pending (Joss, 2001). Users of the Internet are getting lots of unwanted e-mails from even those companies with whom they have not had a previous business relationship. A year 2000 poll shows that 63 percent of U.S. online users who have never made a purchase were very concerned about the use of personal information and 92 perecent were not very comfortable with having their information shared with other organizations (Business Week-Harris Poll, 2000).

With references to public concerns various countries have implemented varying degrees of privacy legislations designed to regulate how companies access and utilize information on potential customers. The United States to date has had a relatively business-friendly, minimal intervention approach encouraging organizationas to provide self-regulated privacy protections. By contrast, the European Union (EU) has taken a pro consumer approach with stringent regulations banning the use of personal information until consent is received (Turner & Dasgupta, 2003). The effective mitigation of privacy issues will improve consumer willingness to shop on the Web, thus improving revenue for online business initiatives and facilitating future growth in the international e-commerce market place. Information technology will continue to redefine organizational practices and business models with respect to privacy (Payton, 2001). Research conducted by Straub and Collins provides a comprehensive discussion of the privacy implications of unauthorized access to personal information resulting from a security breach (Straub & Collins, 1990).

Privacy Transition Stages

The advent of mainframe data processing in the 1960s provided mostly large organizations with a means to obtain, store, and manipulate information in a centralized manner that up until that time was not possible (Westin, 1967). As mainframe computer technology was assimilated into mainstream business and governmental organizations, users of the technology began exploiting the massive computing and storage capabilities to create databases of information on individuals, much of it considered personal. The explosive growth of the multibillion dollar direct marketing industry, for example, was facilitated by the availability of large commercial databases compiled from the public information, including motor vehicle and real estate records, telephone and other directories, or from responses supplied by consumers on warranty cards and other surveys (Turner & Dasgupta, 2003). The new capabilities also allowed profiles of individuals to be created to assist firms in credit decisions. The resultant public anxiety led to the passage of the Fair Credit Reporting Act in 1970 and the Privacy act of 1974, which defined the rights of individual citizens and outlined the U.S. Government's responsibility for protecting the personal information it maintains (Davis, 2000).

Continued technological evolvements in the mid-to-late 1980s, including the personal computer, workstations, and communications networks, enabled even broader diffusion of database management, marketing, and telemarketing tools. Individuals and small organizations now had the computing capability to manipulate and store information that before required access to a mainframe. Further, new networking capabilities provided the ability to more easily distribute and share information with other organizations and individuals (Turner & Dasgupta, 2003). The Electronic Communications Privacy Act (ECP) of 1986 prohibited unauthorized interception and alteration of electronic communications and made it illegal for online services to disclose personal information without a warrant. The Computer Matching and Privacy Protection (CMPP) Act of 1988 regulated the use of computer matching of federal records subject to the Privacy Act except for legitimate statistical reason (Davis, 2000). A 1992 survey indicated that 76 percent of the public felt they had lost control over how information about them was circulated and used by business organizations (Louis, 1992).

Web User Privacy Concerns

Practically all nations are now monitoring their respective citizens' individual Internet usage, including:

- What they write in e-mail and to whom (the equivalent of opening the envelpoes of conventional private mail),
- What sites they browse on the Web (the equivalent of looking over shoulders at the book store), and often
- What they type on their "personal" computers—even if it is never sent over the Internet (the equivalent of standing behind us all the time, taking notes on our every act).

Unlike law enforcement investigations (as opposed to secret police monitoring), launched only after crimes have been committed, wholesale monitoring of Internet usage is done before any illegal act occurs (Caloyannides, 2003).

Continued advances in information technology in general, and the growth of Internetworking technologies specifically, further facilitate the collection, distribution, and use of personal information. Due to increasing Web users day by day people have also started raising concerns while doing online transactions over the Internet. A 1998 survey examining scenarios and privacy preferences suggests that Web users can be statistically clustered into three primary groups based on their attitudes and privacy (Ackerman, Cranor, & Reagle, 1999). Privacy fundamentalists (17 percent) are described as unwilling to provide any data to Web sites and are very concerned about any use of data. The pragmatic majority (56 percent) are concerned about data use but could be made comfortable by the presence of privacy protection measures such as laws and privacy policy statements, and the remaining respondents (27 percent) are categorized as marginally concerned (Turner & Dasgupta, 2003). Similar results from a separate study conducted in Germany in 2000 not only identify the privacy fundamentalists (30 percent) and the marginally concerned (24 percent), but also describe two distinct subgroups within the middle tier delineated as identity concerned (20 percent) and profiling averse (25 percent) (Grimm & Rossnagel, 2000).

The most pervasive individual Web privacy concerns stems from secondary use of information, defined as personal information collected for one purpose and used, subsequently, for a different purpose (Culnan, 1993). Studies suggests that (a) users are more willing to provide personal information when they are not identified, (b) some information is more sensitive than other, and (c) the most important factor is whether or not the information will be shared with other companies. Further, users overwhelmingly disliked unsolicited communications and any form of automatic data transfer. Most consumers want to be informed about what information is being collected from them, how the data will be used, and whether their information will only be used in an aggregate form. Users are less likely to perceive business practices as privacy invasive when they perceive that information is collected in the context of an existing relationship, is relevant to the transaction, will be used to draw reliable and valid inferences, and they have the ability to control its future use (Baker, 1999; Culnan, 1993).

Privacy Protection Laws

In many countries, governments have discussed and proposed laws to regulate privacy protection and mechanisms to punish people and organizations that break the rules. Until privacy laws are really enforced, however, companies will find few incentives to protect and respect user privacy, mainly because most users don't even realize that their privacy can be violated. A central problem is that behavior on the Web can't be controlled. To regulate the Web, governments would have to regulate code writing or how Web applications (browsers, Java, e-mail systems, and so on) function (Lessig, 1999). Also it is difficult to reach international consensus on Web privacy because the privacy concept is heavily dependent on widely variable cultural and political issues. Despite this, however, there is a set of common activities that are undoubtedly privacy invasion:

- Collecting and analyzing user data without the user's knowledge/consent or authorization,
- Employing user data in a way other than was authorized, and
- Disclosing or sending user data to others without the user's knowledge and authorization.

Even if international privacy laws existed, some countries and companies would still be likely to operate in an opprobrious way. Consequently, users can't rely on laws to protect their privacy. Mechanisms must exist to let users improve the protection of their data (Ishitani, 2003).

In 1991, the President of the Association for Computing Machinery (ACM) expressed support for fair information practices; a doctrine including the principles of notice, choice, access, and security; and urged observance by all organizations that collect personal information (White, 1991). Later on U.S. government asked the Commerce Department to work with the Federal Trade Commission (FTC) to encourage organizations to implement self-regulatory practices. An FTC report in 2000, however concluded that U.S. self-regulatory approaches were ineffective in safeguarding consumer information, marketing techniques employed to profile customers were increasingly intrusive, and congressional legislative action was warranted to protect consumer privacy online (Electronic Privacy Information Center, 2000). The self-regulatory approach adopted by the U.S. is in direct contrast with the government-mandated approach adopted by the European Union (EU). Under the EU's 1995, and subsequent 1997, Directive on Data Privacy, the burden is placed on companies and organizations—not individuals—to seek permission before using personal information for any purpose (Consumer International, 2003).

The EU member countries have agreed to stringent controls on personal information, much stronger than exists in the USA, which took effect on October 25, 1998. The EU is restricting the operation of American companies unless they fall in line with the EU guidelines and it is estimated that 90 percent of US companies have not addressed the EU directive. An example of one of the directives is that companies are required to inform customers when they plan to sell their personal information to other firms (Kruck, Gottovi, Moghadami, Broom, & Forcht, 2002).

In July 2000, however, the United States negotiated a safe harbor agreement with the EU commission, wherein U.S. companies can voluntarily self-certify to adhere to a set of privacy principles loosely based on the fair information practices developed by the commerce department and the EU Commission. The primary difference under safe harbor is the ability of U.S. companies to administer self-enforcement by the European Commissioner or other agencies for compliance with the explicit rules of the EU directive (Consumer International, 2003). Although the United States recently passed new online privacy legislation, including the Childerns Online Privacy Protection Act (COPPA), Provisions in the Gramm-Leach-Bliley Financial Modernization Act (GLB) and the Health Insurance Portability and Accountability Act (HIPAA), these laws are applicable to relatively narrow types of information and particular industry sectors (Turner & Dasgupta, 2003).

Privacy legislation came into existence in Australia in 1988. The Commonwealth Privacy Act 1988 laid down strict privacy safeguards which Commonwealth (federal) and ACT Government agencies must observe when collecting, storing, using, and disclosing personal information. This act also gave individuals access and correction rights in relation to their own personal information. Later on Australian Federal Parliament passed the Privacy Amendment (Private Sector) Act 2000 on December 6, 2000 to come into effect on December 21, 2001. This Act has empowered Australians for the first time; giving individuals the right to know what information private sector organizations hold about them and a right to correct that information if it is wrong (Moghe, 2003).

New Zeland's Privacy Act 1993 does not create a right of privacy nor is its recognition of privacy interests absolute (Slane, 2000). Its coverage includes both electronic and paper information. Any business based in New Zeland wishing to engage in electronic commerce with consumers must ensure its activities comply with the Privacy Act, to the extent that they involve personal information about their consumers. Personal includes any information about an identifiable living person, whether it is on a computer, in a paper file or in someone's head (Slane, 2000). The Privacy Act applies to the handling of all personal information collected or held by agencies, whether in the public or private sectors (Slane, 2000).

In New Zeland, consumers' privacy concerns can largely be met through business complying with the Privacy Act. To comply with information privacy principle 3 of section 6 of the Privacy Act 1993, New Zeland Web sites that collect personal information should include a privacy statement that sets out the purpose of the collection the uses and any disclosures that may be made of that information (Ministry of Economic Developement, 2000).

Privacy and Technology

The issue of who has control over personal data and how this data is used needs to be addressed at a global level in order for the Internet to develop into a trusted, widely acceptable international marketplace for the exchange of goods and services. The primary technology for collecting information on an individual's activities over the Internet has been the Web "Cookie." Cookies are digital information sent from a Web server and stored on the hard drive of an individual's computer by the browser software or network application. Cookies were designed to address the problem of statelessness inherent in the Hypertext Transfer Protocol (HTTP) (Kristol, 2002). Because a browser does not stay connected to a server, but instead makes a connection, sends its request, downloads the response, and makes a new connection to send another request, it severely limited the functionality of Web services and complicated application development. Web cookies provide a solution to this statelessness by allowing for continuity in the interaction between the browser and the Web server. The cookie has proven to be the most reliable, robust, and network friendly means to provide needed state functionality on the Web, although this functionality can also be provided by embedding state information in URLs, using hidden fields in HTML forms, or using the client's IP address (Kristol, 2002).

Web cookies can be classified into two general types: Session and Persistent (Berghel, 2001). The session cookies last only as long as the browser session with the server. However, persistent cookies remain stored on the hard drive of the client computer until they reach an expiration date or are deleted. Persistent cookies can be used to store information useful to both the user and the Web site, including account names, passwords, and past navigation streams. This cookie information is exchanged using the packet header and can be used by the Website to eliminate the need for users to log-in, set user preferences based on past behaviour, and to customize or personalize user experience (Harding, 2001). The persistent cookie also has more significant privacy implications because storage of navigational streams and log-in information could be used to monitor and track user browsing behaviour and linked to any other personal information provided. Persistent cookies can also be shared by a third party Web host and used to track activities at a particular Web-site or as a user moves from site to site (Turner & Dasgupta, 2003).

Web bugs are hidden images that can be covertly added to any Web page; e-mail, or Microsoft Word, Excel, or PowerPoint file and used to collect information about user bahaviour. Web bugs send messages back to a server indicating its location, including the IP address of the computer, the URL of the page, the time the Web page or document was viewed, the type of browser used, and the previously set cookie value. Web bugs can also be used to determine if and when a Web page, e-mail message, or document is opened, the IP address of the recipient, and how often and to whom information is forwarded and opened (Harding, 2001). Web bugs can also be used to associate a Web browser cookie to a particular e-mail address and read previously set cookie values. Thus, a source server with a very small or invisible window could be added to any Web site or Web-enabled file and used serendipitously for a variety of tracking, surveillance, and monitoring activities (Berghel, 2001). Monitoring browsing activities in and of itself is not considered by most Web users to be privacy invasive; however it is the ability to then link these activities back to an individual that has most consumers and privacy advocates alarmed (Turner & Dasgupta, 2003).

Registration and billing, and observation are two main ways for a company to gather personally identifying consumer information (Shapiro & Varian, 1999). A 1999 study found that more than half of surveyed Web sites were collecting personal identifying information and demographic information on users that connected to that site (Culnan, 1999).

Identifying information can also been obtained without permission by exploiting security holes in browsers, operating systems, or other software, including the creative use of ActiveX controls, Java, JavaScript, and VBScript code to retrieve information from the user's computer (McGraw & Morrisett, 2000). Sophisticated data mining tools that employ advanced statistical techniques allow organizations to perform analyses to uncover a great deal of information about Web site users, some of it considered personal and beyond what the user has knowingly agreed to provide (Mason, 2001). The high value of information has created great incentive for the information broker industry and made it increasingly difficult for users to control what, when, and how information about them is distributed and used.

Web Privacy Enhancing Technologies

One of the first technologies available for protecting privacy on the Internet was the anonymizer. Anonymizers provide the ability to sanitize packet headers passed from the client to the server. Early versions consisted of software that would act like a proxy server, intercepting all communication between the browser and the server and removing all information about the requester. Current versions use Secure Socket Layers (SSL) technology for sending URL requests, establishing an encrypted communications tunnel between the user and the anonymizer proxy, and routing traffic through a number of proxy servers (Electronic Privacy Information Center, 1999). This firewall- like technology disguises a user's IP address, similar to most Internet service providers, and supplies with dynamic IP addresses every time they log on. Software tools are also available that provide a pseudonym proxy for logging on the Web sites, giving users consistent access to registration based systems without revealing personal data (Gabber, 1999).

Web users can also install a filter, such as the one offered by Anonymizer. Filters are software programs that block cookies, banner advertisements and Web bugs. The disadvantage of filters is that they fail to consider consent; they block all cookies and thus users lose access to all personalized services, even those from the most trustworthy of sites. Also filters make privacy invasion difficult, but not impossible. A site can still identify users by IP address, interaction time, and geographical location, for example. Given this users might need additional levels of privacy protection (Ishitani, 2003). These tool provide a means to protect the network identity of the computer; however, there are also negative performance and reliability consequenses. In addition, some specialized proxy servers can be used to intercept and alter information between client and server (Berghel, 2002).

There are other technology-based solutions available for protecting privacy, including tools for filtering HTML allowing users to block certain URLs, anonymous re-mailers for sending and receiving e-mail messages, and software for managing Web cookies (Electronic Privacy Information Center, 1999). Cookie managers are used specifically to counter the placement of Web cookies on user hard drives. Most browsers have a parameter that can be set to either inform users when a site is attempting to install a cookie, allowing users the option to accept or decline it, or prevent any cookies from being installed. However common browser defaults are set to accept all cookies and most users are not aware or sophisiticated enough to change the browser defaults. Users also have the capability to go in and delete cookies from their browsers (Turner & Dasgupta, 2003). Another latest tool to protect privacy is Evidence Eraser—professional PC security software. It will destroy all evidence of the Internet activities stored deep in Windows' log files. Evidence Eraser exceeds Department of Defense specifications for PC data destruction. Their claim is that its ability to defeat even "forensic analysis" software used by many private investigators and law enforcement agencies. In addition, the user will reclaim disk space and increase PCs performance by permanently destroying cookies, cache files, temp files, browser history, temporary Internet files, and many more types of secret hidden data. Evidence Eraser will clean and compact your registry and also securely destroy the information contained in your index.dat file which is not accessible through Windows (Computer Privacy, 2003). Cookie Cutters and Anonymyzing Proxies are two popular independent privacy protection mechanisms. There are other software products and services that provide cookie management capability, allowing individuals to view, block, control, and remove existing cookies. Web bugs, however, are generally not affected by this so-called cookie crusher software technology (Berghel, 2001).

The Platform for Privacy Preferences (P3P)

Today, enormous amounts of information are being collected by many thousands of Web sites. While an effective technology, called SSL (Secure Socket Layer), exists for protecting the privacy of the transaction between a Browser and a Web Server, there is no protection once the information is on the Server and in the hands of the company or organization that "lured" you to them.

The 1998 World Wide Web Consortium (W3C)'s platform for privacy preferences (P3P) guidelines request developers of P3P agents to follow and support principles categorized into four groups: information privacy, choice and control, fairness and integrity, and security. These principles are also in accordance with the US principles of Fair Information Practices. In April 2002, the World Wide Web Consortium (W3C) developed its first release of a standard, the Platform for Privacy Preferences (P3P v.1)—a framework for Web privacy management. P3P offers a means for a Web site to provide server-side machine-readable privacy policies that Web browsers could use to automatically compare with the privacy preferences directed by the user (P3P 1.0, 2003). It provides a framework to describe categories of information and how that information can be used in standard computer readable format based on the extensible Markup Language (XML). P3P Web privacy framework includes following (Kolari, 2005):

- **Web Site Privacy Policy:** Web sites are required to publish their privacy policy in XML using the P3P policy vocabulary and store policy files in standard locations to facilitate user access.
- **User Privacy Preference Policy:** Users can specify their preferences in terms of a recommended policy language.
- **User Agent:** While accessing a Website, a P3P user agent (inbuilt into Web browser) will automatically retrieve the Website's P3P policy and compare it with user's privacy policy for conformance.

P3P has been touted as "privacy tool." In fact it is a tool that facilitates the transfer of information from your computer to Web sites. The system simply sets standards about transferring information and works with your browser. It works in the following way:

- Your personal information is stored in your browser in a standard format (name, address, credit card information, etc.)
- Web site privacy policies are translated into a standard format. This is done by answering a series of standard questions.
- The user sets their "preferences" in their browser. These preferences are based on answers to the standard set of questions used by the Web site. For example:
  - **Questions to Web Site:** Does Web site release personal information to third parties?
  - **Possible Answer:** Yes, NO, or Yes with specific permission from the user.
  - **User Preference:** If answer is "Yes" don't release information, If answer is "yes with specific permission" or "No" bring up a warning box.
- The privacy policy data is placed in a specific file at the Web site and the user's browser automatically downloads the privacy policy when the site is accessed.

- The privacy policy is then compared to the user preferences and decisions are made automatically to transfer information, not to transfer information, or to show a warning before the transfer. [Note: The initial version of P3P does not include the transfer of user information to the Web site but that is the eventual goal of the system].

P3P is actually a convenience tool for both consumers and marketers to facilitate shopping and other Internet commerce. Whether the system actually helps protect privacy depends on the specific way the questions are asked and the default settings it will have. Right now personal information is not transferred at all until a user enters it. With P3P data may be transferred automatically so there is no increase in the privacy level. The claims are that such a standard system will reduce the confusion seen now with ambiguous and non-standard privacy policies.

In order to implement P3P the software vendors will need to implement P3P into their software (browsers, program installation/registration software, etc.). The privacy policies will also have to be translated into answers to the standard set of questions and put into XML data format (P3P 1.0, 2006).

The Future of the P3P Standard Success

A study examining the privace practices of Web extensions found that privacy policy statements generally lack candor, provide loop-holes, use technical jargon and legalese, and are difficult for most users to use effectively (Martin, 2000). Additionaly, an organization can get the majority of users to accept its privacy policy by simply making it the default or the response that is provided if no user action is taken (Bellman, Johnson, & Lohse, 2001).

According to a critique of P3P it will be seen that P3P is dangerously myopic, and needs substantial enhancement. The five areas of critical need are:

1. More specificity in declaring the purpose behind taking information,

2. A means to establish a negotiated contract that goes beyond W3's APPEL (A P3P Preference Exchange Language),

3. A means in the law for policing the contracts obtained

4. A means for transitivity and universality of the protection on information, and

5. An IETF (Internet Engineering Task Force) definition that does not require the Web (specifically, the HTTP protocol) (Thibadeau Robert, 2003).

P3P works as a series of HTTP communications. The first is a Browser request to a Web Server for a file or an action. In this communication, the Browser says nothing about privacy to the Web Server. However, the Web Server responds to the Browser with whatever the Browser asked for, plus a special reference to a Privacy Policy Reference Page. The Browser or person operating it, can now determine what do with the Web Server's response based on the Privacy Policy Reference page provided by a second HTTP request. The Browser reads the Policy-Ref page and decides what to do. This Policy Ref page is in the language of XML. It has many very definite things it can say. A Privacy policy reference page is very special and can be used to determine whether the Browser should ever come back to that Web Server again, and whether information from a form on a Web page should be sent to that Web Server.

So in P3P, the Browser, at the very beginning, exposes itself to a minimum of two invasions of privacy. The first is the initial request to a Web Server page. The second is the request to the PolicyRef page specified in the first response by the Web Server (Thibadeau Robert, 2003).

P3P clearly provides a way to stipulate the purpose to which the user's information disclosure is put. This is highly commendable. Perhaps the choice of particular purposes is not so good.

According to the writers of P3P 1.0 it explicitly lacks the following desirable characteristics:

*   A mechanism to allow sites to offer a choice of P3P policies to visitors
*   A mechanism to allow visitors (through their user agents) to explicitly agree to a P3P policy
*   Mechanisms to allow for non-repudiation of agreements between visitors and Web sites
*   A mechanism to allow user agents to transfer user data to services

In effect, P3P 1.0 lacks the ability to negotiate with the Web Server on a contract, and to make a contract with the Web Server that could be legally binding. All of this is fundamental because the Web Server simply provides an ultimatum to the Browser. P3P also fails to provide a means for transitivity and universality of the protection of information. This is actually several things. The transitivity problem is how to protect your privacy after the information is handed to somebody else. If a violation of privacy is generally a misuse of information about you or information that you provide (e.g., a trade secret, a confidential comment to a Web master), then there must be a way in the privacy protocol to indicate that a privacy directive is essentially non-negotiable only back to the original owner, and this needs to be passed on to the next processor of the information (Thibadeau Robert, 2003).

But Finally P3P is taking us in the right direction to take care of Web privacy. It deserves to be supported and added to. P3P clearly represents a good start. People in all aspects of the Internet socio-economic-political system need to sit up and think this through for themselves.

The Present Scenario of P3P Implementation

According to Cranor, Byers, and Kormann (2003) only 53 of the top 556 Web sites were P3P-enabled (published valid P3P policies) as of May 2003. Ernst and Young (2004) P3P DashBoard report shows a very low increase in P3P adoption for the top 500 sites, from 16 percent (August 2002) to 23 percent (January 2004). Therefore, users seldom access Web sites with published P3P policy. This situation, together with P3P's limitation on the user side has resulted in low P3P adoption from users (Kolari, Ding, Shashidhara, Joshi, Finin, & Kagal 2005). Maintaining and building customer trust is an important criterion for the growth of e-commerce. A recent survey (DeVault, Roque, Rosenblum, & Valente, 2001) reports that 56 percent of online consumers believe that Websites do not adhere to their privacy policies and 90 percent of online consumers believe that independent verification is a sufficient measure for trusting a Web site. The P3P framework adopts a certificate based trust model. A P3P policy can estabish its trust by specifying its certifier, which is a trusted authority for accontability of P3P policy such as TRUSTe.com. However according to (Kolari et al., 2005) it does not incorporate trust sufficiently and have two main limitations. First, it is highly coupled to the presence of a certifier, whose adoption is low among Web sites. Second, in the absence of a privacy certifier the model makes a strong assumption that the presence of P3P policies is sufficient for building trust.Therefore, Kolari et al.(2005) further proposed the following two key enhancements of P3P as:

Enhancing P3P privacy preference language: A language is preferred with atleast having attributes like matching semantics, good to encode a wide range of user's preferences, extensible to constrain the behaviour of available privacy enforcement mechanisms.

Enhancing P3P Trust Model: Beside the certificate trust model, user should have more choices to establish trust in Web sites.

Conclusion

The privacy concerns are posing a barrier to the development of e-commerce. It is an issue that online business cannot afford to ignore because privacy concerns are hampering Internet business. Therefore, in spite of rapidly growing e-business, there are also indications that consumers are wary of participating in it because of concern about how their personal information is used in the online market place. Consumers have little privacy protection on the Internet. Privacy will have a widespread and deep influence on the economic vitality of cyberspace. Information is power, and privacy management is the control, and thereby the economic unleashing, of that power. P3P technology implementation is just the beginning of a long road ahead for all those involved in e-commerce and are concerned about privacy protection. Various privacy enhancing technologies and legislations promulgated by the Governments in different countries will also help to ensure Web privacy for secure e-commerce transactions. In this chapter we have tried to assess various technologies used by the organizations to monitor Web usage, legislations in some major countries and technologies available to protect the privacy. P3P implementation its and its future success potential have been discussed. Legislation, self-regulation, technical solutions and combination solutions are different ways that this can be implemented. Empirical evidence of application of privacy-enhancing technologies in organizations and for individual Web users in the future will strengthen research in this area.

Acknowledgment

We would like to thank the editor and referees for constructive comments and Elzie Cartwright, Communicative English Department of Atilim University, for nicely editing the manuscript.

References

Ackerman, M., Cranor, L., & Reagle, J. (1999). Privacy in e-commerce: Examining user scenarios and privacy preferences. *Proceedings of the ACM Conference on E-Commerce*, Denver, CO.

Adkinson, W.F., Eisenach, J.A., & Lenard, T.M., (2002). *Privacy online: A report on the information practices and policies of commercial Web sites*. Washington, DC: Progress & Freedom Foundation.

Anton, A.I., Earp, J.B., Potts, C., & Alspaugh, T.A. (2001, August 27-31). The role of policy and privacy values in requirement engineering. *Proceedings of the IEEE 5th International Symposium Requirements Engineering [RE'01]*, Toronto, ON, Canada (pp. 138-145).

Anton, A.I., Earp, J.B. & Reese, A. (2002, September 9-13). Analyzing Web site privacy requirements using a privacy goal taxonomy. *Proceedings of the 10th Anniversary IEEE Joint Requirements Engineering Conference (RE'02)*, Essen, Germany (pp. 23-31).

Baker, J. (1991). Personal information and privacy. In J. Warren, J. Thorwaldson, and B. Koball (Eds.), *Proceedings of the First Conference on Computers, Freedom, and Privacy* (pp. 42-45). IEEE Computer Society Press: Los Alamitos, CA.

Bakos, J., & Brynjolfsson, E. (1999). Bundling information goods: Pricing, profits, and efficiency. *Management Science, 45*(12), 1613-1630.

Baumer, D.B., Earp, J.B., & Poindexter, J.C. (2004). Internet privacy law: A comparison between the United States and the European Union. *Computer Security*, 23, 400-412.

Bellman, S., Johnson, E., & Lohse, G. (2001). To opt-in or opt-out? It depends on the question? *Communications of the ACM*, February, 25-27.

Bellotti, V. (1997). *Design for privacy in multimedia computing and communications environment in technology and privacy: The new landscape*. P.E. Agre & M. Rotenberg, Eds. Cambridge, MA: MIT Press, pp.63-98.

Berghel, H. (2001). Cyberprivacy in the new millenium. *IEEE Computer Magazine, 34*(1), 133-134.

Berghel, H. (2002). Hijacking the Web – Cookies revisited – Continuing the dialogue on personal security and underlying privacy issues. *Communications of the ACM*, April, 23-28.

Business Week-Harris Poll (2000). Results printed in *Business Week*, March 20.

Caloyannides, M. (2003). Society cannot function without privacy. *IEEE Security & Privacy, 1*(3), 84-86.

Chaum, D. (1997). David Chaum on electronic commerce: How much do you trust Big Brother. *IEEE Internet Computing*, November/December, 8-16.

Chung, W. & Paynter, J. (2002). Privacy issues on the Internet. *Proceedings of the 35th Hawaii Internaional Conference on System Sciences.*

Clarke, R. (1999). Internet privacy concerns confirm the case for intervention. *Communication of ACM*, (42), 60-67.

The Code of Fair Information Practices (1973). U.S. Department of Health, Education and Welfare, Secretary's Advisory Committee on Automated Personal Data Systems, Records, Computers, and the Rights of Citizens, VIII. Retrieved from http://www.epic.org/privacy/consumer/code_fair_info.html

Computer Privacy (2003). *Computer privacy: Evidence eraser*. Retrieved in 2003 from http://www.1-internet-eraser-pro-computer-privcay.com/evidence-eraser.html

Consumer International. (2001). Privacy@net: An international comparative study of consumer privacy on the Internet.

Cranor, L.F., Byers, S., & Kormann, D. (2003). *An analysis of p3p deployment on commercial, government, and children's Web sites as of May 2003*. Technical Report, AT&T Labs research.

Culnan, M. (1993, September). How did they get my name? An exploratory investigation of consumer attitudes toward secondary information use. *MIS Quarterly*, 341.

Culnan, M. (1999). Georgetown Internet privacy policy survey: Report to the Federal Trade Commission. Georgetown University, Washington, D.C. [Online] http://www.msb.edu./faculty/cunanm/GIPPS/mmexs

Davis, J. (2000). Protecting privacy in the cyber era. *IEEE Technology and Society Magazine,* Summer, 10-22.

DeVault, J.R., Roque, D., Rosenblum, J., & Valente, K. (2001). *Privacy promises are not enough*. Technical report, Ernst & Young.

Earp, J.B., Anton, A.I., Aiman-Smith, L., & Stufflebeam, W.H. (2005). *Examining Internet privacy policies within the context of user privacy values*, *52*(2) 227-237.

Electronic Privacy Information Center (1999). Surfer beware III: Privacy policies without privacy protection. Washington, DC, December, http://www.epic.org/reports/surfer-beware3.html

Ernst & Young (2004). *P3P dashboard report: Top 500 p3p dashboard.*

Federal Trade Commission. (1998). *Privacy online: A report to Congress*. Retrieved from http://www.ftc.gov/reports/privacy3/

Federal Trade Commission. (2000). *Privacy online: Fair information practices in the electronic marketplace, A Report to Congress.*

Gabber, E., Gibbons, P., Kristol, D., Mataias, Y., & Mayer, A. (1999). Consistent, yet anonymous access with LPWA. *Communications of the ACM,* 39-41.

Glaser, B.C. & Strauss, A.L. (1967). *The discovery of grounded theory.* Chicago, IL: Aldanine.

Grimm, R. & Rossnagel, A. (2000). Can P3P help to protect privacy worldwide? *ACM Mutimedia Workshop.*

Harding, W. (2001). Cookies and Web bugs: What they are and how they work together. *Information Systems Management, 18*(3), 17-25.

Ishitani, L., Almeida, V., Meira, W., Jr. (2003). Masks: Bringing anonymity and personalization together. *IEEE Security & Privacy, 1*(3).

Joss, M. (2001). Do you need a CPO? ComputerUser, Retrieved June 1, 2001, from http://www.computeruser.com/articles/2006.1.2.0601.01.html

Kolari, P., Ding, L., Shashidhara, G., Joshi, A., Finin, T., & Kagal, L. (2005). Enhancing Web privacy protection through decelarative policies. *Proceedings of the Sixth IEEE International Workshop on Policies for Distributed Systems and Networks (POLICY'05).*

Kristol, D. (2001). HTTP cookies: Standard, privacy and politics. *ACM Transactions on Internet Technology, 1*(2), 151-198.

Kruck, S.E., Gottovi, D., Moghadami, F., Broom, R., & Forcht, K.A. (2002). Protecting personal privacy on the Internet. *Information Management & Security, 10*(2).

Lessig, L. (1999). *Code and other laws of cyberspace.* Basic Books.

Louis, Harris and Associates, Inc. (1992). Harris-Equifax Consumer Privacy Survey Equifax Inc., Atlanta, GA.

Martin, D., Smith R., Brittain, M., Fetch, I., & Wu, H., (2000). The privacy practices of Web browser extensions. *Communications of the ACM,* February, 45-50.

Mason, R. (1986). Four ethical issues of the information age. *MIS Quarterly, 10,* 4-12.

Mason, R., Ang, S., & Mason, F. (2001). *Privacy in the age of the Internet.* In G. Dickson & G. DeSantis (Eds.), Information technology and the future enterprise: New models for managers. Upper Saddle River, NJ: Prentice-Hall.

McGraw, G. & Morrisett, G. (2000). Attacking malicious code: A Report to the Infosec Research Council. *IEEE Software,* September/October, 33-41.

Ministry of Economic Development (2000). New Zeland's Privacy Act and Electronic Commerce. Retrieved from http://www.privacy.org.nz/privacy/index.html

Moghe, V. (2003). Privacy management: A new era in the Australian Business Environment. *Information Management & Security*, *11*(2), 60.

Organization for Economic Cooperation and Development (OECD) (1980). OECD guidelines on the protection of privacy and transborder flows of personal data. [Online]. Retrieved from: http://www.oecd.org/EN/document/(),,EN-document-43-1-no-24-10255-4300.html

P3P 1.0 (2003). A new standard in online privacy. Retrieved from http://www.w3c.org/P3P/

Payton, F., (2001). Technologies that do steal! *Decision Line*, March, 13-14.

Platform for Privacy Preferences (P3P) (2006). http://www.privacy.net/p3p/

Raul, A.P. (2002). *Privacy and the digital state: Balancing public information and personal privacy.* Norwell, MA: Kluwer.

Rust, R., Kannan, P., & Peng, N. (2002). The customer economics of Internet privacy. *Journal of the Academy of Marketing Science*, *30*, 455-464.

Schoemann, F. (1984). Philosophical dimensions of privacy: An anthology. New York: Cambridge University Press.

Shapiro, C., & Varian, H. (1999). *Information rules: A strategic guide to the network economy.* Boston: Harvard Business School Press.

Slane, B. (2000). Killing the Goose? Information Privacy Issues on the Web. Retrieved from http://www.privacy.org.nz/media/Killgoos.html

Straub, D. & Collins, R. (1990). Key information liability issues facing managers: Software piracy, databases and individual rights to privacy. *MIS Quarterly*, June, 143-156.

Thibadeau, R. (2003). A critique of P3P: Privacy on the Web. Retrieved from http://dollar.ecom.cmu.edu/P3P critique/

Toscana, P. (2001). Taming the cyber frontier: Security is not enough! Retreived from http://www.untrust.com/news/taming-cyberspace.html

Turner, E.C., & Dasgupta, S. (2003). Privacy on the Web: An examination of user concerns, technology, and implications for business organizations and individuals. *Information System Management*, *20*(1), 8-18.

Warren, S., & Brandeis, L. (1980). The right of privacy. *Harvard Law Review*, *4*(5), 193-220.

Westin, A. (1967). *Privacy and freedom.* New York: Atheneum.

White, J. (1991). President's letter. *Communications of the ACM*, *34*(5), 15-16.

Section II

Privacy, Nations, and Laws

Chapter II

Is It Safe to Talk, Yet?
The Evolution of Electronic Privacy Law

John Thomas, Quinnipiac University School of Law, USA

Abstract

This chapter traces the development in the United States of legal protections of the right to privacy. It begins with the common law "right to be let alone" in the early 1900s and proceeds through the enactment of the U.S. Patriot Act in 2001 and the National Security Administration's warrantless wire tapping program revealed to the public in 2005. It concludes with a discussion of emerging electronic threats to the security of privacy of the public and concomitant challenges to lawmakers and law enforcers.

Introduction

The notion of a right to privacy first entered the legal lexicon in 1890 with the Harvard Law Review's publication of Samuel Warren's and Louis Brandeis' *The Right to Privacy* (1890). As the authors put it more than a century ago, law evolves in response both to perceived threats to the enjoyment of life and to social recognition of the value of that enjoyment:

That the individual shall have full protection in person and in property is a principle as old as the common law; but it has been found necessary from time to time to define anew the exact nature and extent of such protection. Political, social, and economic changes entail the recognition of new rights, and the common law, in its eternal youth, grows to meet the demands of society. (Warren & Brandeis, 1890, p. 195)

As a result, the eventual legal recognition of the right to privacy in "[t]houghts, emotions, and sensations" (Warren & Brandeis, 1890. p. 206) was inevitable:

The intense intellectual and emotional life, and the heightening of sensations which came with the advance of civilization, made it clear to man that only a part of the pain, pleasure, and profit of life lay in physical things. (Warren & Brandeis, 1890 p. 207)

Of course, recognized Warren and Brandeis, "[r]ecent inventions and business methods can create new needs for protection of what courts as early as 1834 called a right 'to be let alone'" (Warren & Brandeis, 1890. p. 208).

The passage of time has proven Warren and Brandeis prescient. Invention has driven both the need for privacy protection and the development of law to ensure that protection. From the telephone to the magnetic tape recorder, photography, the personal computer, wireless telephone, electronic payment systems, and the Internet, technology has created new challenges to our privacy and the law's ability to protect privacy. Indeed, security and privacy laws are the progeny of invention.

Origins of the "Right to Be Let Alone"

"The right to privacy" that Brandeis and Warren conjured derived from an earlier notion that Thomas McIntyre Cooley articulated in his *Treatise of the Law of Torts* (1879): "The right to one's person may be said to be a right of complete immunity: to be let alone" (Cooley, 1879, p. 29). Cooley, in turn, had found this right as a logical correlate to the right to own property. Property ownership entails the right to do with one's property what one wishes, limited only by the rights of other property owners to be free from interference caused by the actions of those on adjacent properties (Etzioni, 1999, p. 189). Linked together, these correlate rights produce a right to be let alone.

Warren and Brandeis argued for the recognition of a more generalized right. "[P]rivacy for thoughts, emotions, and sensations" (Warren & Brandeis, 1890, p. 206) should be protected by law "whether expressed in writing, or in conduct, in conversation, in attitudes, or in a facial expression." Moreover, this right should not exist just with respect to neighboring land owners, but "as against the world." (Warren & Brandeis, 1890. p. 213)

Warren and Brandeis did not live to see the courts of the United States embrace a right to privacy. That recognition came in the latter half of the 20th century. The United States Supreme Court first recognized the right of privacy from governmental intrusion in the context of contraceptive use in the 1965 decision of *Griswold v. Connecticut*, applied it to abortion in the 1973 decision of *Roe v. Wade*, and extended it to sexual relations in 2003 in *Lawrence v. Texas*.

This right to privacy is rooted in the Constitution, but not in any particular provision. Indeed, the phrase "right to privacy" does not appear in the Constitution. The Court located the right in the "penumbra" of explicitly recognized rights: the First Amendment's protection of speech and the freedom of association, the Third Amendment's prohibition against quartering soldiers in a house without the owner's consent, the Fourth Amendment's prohibition of unreasonable searches and seizures, the Fifth Amendment's prohibition against self incrimination, and the Ninth Amendment's pronouncement that the enumeration in the Constitution of specific rights shall not be construed to "deny or disparage" the existence of any other right.

The United States Constitution limits the government, not the individual. So, this newly recognized, if controversial, right only protects a person from governmental intrusion into his or her privacy. The vision of Warren and Brandeis, though, has also informed American tort law, which governs the rights of individuals with respect to the conduct of other individuals. In the late 19th century, some American courts began to recognize person's right to be free from the intrusion of other private citizens (Etzioni, 1999, p. 189). By the late 20th century, the American Law Institute crafted a "Restatement of Law" in an attempt to make this recognition universal in all United States courts. Largely successful in this endeavor, most courts now embrace Section 625A of the Second Restatement of Torts, which provides that "one who invades the right of privacy of another is subject to liability for the resulting harm to the interests of the other." The right is invaded by "unreasonable intrusion upon the seclusion of another" (Restatement (2nd) of Torts § 625A., 1977).

American law, then, beginning in the late 19th century, evolved to meet the social challenge of protecting an emerging right to privacy. A new challenge—electronic invention—would continue to provide further opportunity for legal evolution.

Early Legal Responses to Electronic Invention

Although mail and the telegraph presented some privacy challenges, the technological revolution that has challenged privacy law began in earnest with refinements in telephone technology in the 1920s. It was then that automated switching mechanisms eliminated operators from telephone calls and led telephone users to perceive their phone conversations as private (John, 1998, p. 206). That expectation led the Supreme Court in 1928 to consider whether wiretapping of telephone conversations amounted to a "search" subject to the unreasonable search and seizure prohibition contained in the Fourth Amendment. In *Olmstead v. United States*, Chief Justice Taft wrote, "The language of the amendment cannot be .... expanded to include telephone wires, reaching to the whole world from the defendant's house or office. The intervening wires are not part of his house or office, any more than are the highways along which they are stretched."

In dissent, Brandeis argued for a more flexible view of intrusion, essentially urging the Court to construe the law of privacy in a manner that would enable it to keep pace with the technology that threatened the "right to be let alone:"

Subtler and more far reaching means of invading privacy have become available to the government. Discovery and invention have made it possible for the government, by means far more effective than stretching upon the rack, to obtain disclosure in court of what is whispered in the closet.

Six years later, Congress embraced Brandeis's view and enacted section 605 of the Communications Act of 1934. The section provided, "[N]o person not being authorized by the sender shall intercept any communication and divulge or publish the existence, contents, substance, purport, effect, or meaning of such intercepted communications to any person." Despite its broad language, however, the statute had a limited scope: it applied only to federal, not state, officials.

The Communications Act of 1934 marked the entry of Congress into the privacy equation. The following years would witness a continued tussle between technology and law makers' attempts to safeguard or, in times of crisis, limit privacy in an ever-changing technological landscape.

A Survey of Pre-September 11, 2001 Technological and Privacy Law Developments

In the 1960s, war, politics, and technology coalesced to lead Congress to expand protection against intrusion into electronic privacy. Past abuses of wiretapping during the 1950s in conjunction with Joseph McCarthy's FBI-aided witch hunt of communists and law enforcement activities directed at civil rights and anti-Vietnam activists, galvanized Congress to enact the 1968 Wiretap Act. (Omnibus Crime and Control and Safe Streets Act of 1968, 18 U.S.C. §§ 2510–22.) The Act extended the protections of the 1934 Communications Act to state, as well as federal, officials. Most importantly, it extended the wiretapping prohibition to private individuals. Now, for the first time, telephone conversations were to "be let alone" not just from government intrusion, but from private intrusion.

While it may have been the telephone that shifted the privacy debate from the physical to the electronic, it was the advent of the computer that presented law and policy makers with their biggest challenge. First produced in 1946, by the early 1970s the computer's threat to personal privacy became apparent (HEW,1973, p. 29). One could glean not only communications from a computer, but financial and other highly sensitive personal information. In 1973, the U.S. Department of Health, Education, and Welfare issued what turned out to be a watershed publication: its report on "Records, Computers, and the Rights of Citizens" (HEW, 1973, p. 29). HEW observed the breadth of the computer's potential incursion into the lives of all citizens:

[A]*n individual must increasingly give information about himself to large and relatively faceless institutions, for handling and use by strangers—unknown, unseen, and, all too frequently, unresponsive. Sometimes the individual does not even know that an organization maintains record about him. Often he may not see it, much less contest its accuracy, control its dissemination, or challenge its use by others.* (HEW, 1973, p. 29)

Thus, HEW recommended, "Any organization creating, maintaining, using, or disseminating records of identifiable personal data must assure the reliability of the data for their intended use and must take reasonable precautions to prevent misuse of the data" (HEW, 1973, p. 42).

In response to HEW's report, Congress embarked on a now several decades old journey into the murky realm of e-privacy by enacting the Privacy act of 1974 (The Privacy Act of 1974, 5 U.S.C. §§ 552a, *et seq.*). Effective since September 27, 1975, the Act regulates the collection, maintenance, use, and dissemination of personal information. It applied only to the federal government and not to state and local authorities nor to individuals. In general, the act restricted disclosure of personally identifiable records maintained by agencies, granted individuals rights of access to agency records maintained on themselves and to seek amendment of those records, and established a code of "fair information practices" that created standards for collecting, maintaining, and disseminating records. The Act also restricted federal governmental use of social security numbers, but not private use. Consequently, today we find almost unfettered use of social security numbers by banking, lending, health care, and educational institutions.

Four years later, Congress addressed issues that the Privacy act did not. First, the Right to Financial Privacy Act of 1978 (12 U.S.C.§ 3401 *et seq*.) required that government officials use a warrant or subpoena to obtain financial information and that there be "reason to believe that the records sought are relevant to a legitimate law enforcement inquiry."

The second relevant piece of 1978 legislation has substantial reverberations in today's post-September 11 United States. The Foreign Intelligence Surveillance Act of 1978 (50 U.S.C. § 1801 *et seq*.) gives law enforcement officials greater leeway in accessing private information if the purpose of the investigation is to gather foreign intelligence. In other criminal investigational contexts, courts grant authority to gather information if there is probably cause to believe a crime is being or has been committed. Under FISA, however, law enforcement officials need only demonstrate that there is probable cause to believe that investigation's target is a "foreign power" or "an agent of a foreign power."

While FISA narrowed privacy rights, Congressional action in the following two decades broadened rights, often in response to court decisions that narrowed rights. For example, in 1980, Congress responded to the Supreme Court's opinion in *Zurcher v. Stanford Daily* by enacting the Privacy Protection Act of 1980 (42 U.S.C. §§ 2000aa *et seq*.,). In *Zurcher*, the Court held that journalists could not object to a search of a newspaper's premises for information (in this case, photographs of demonstrators) about other's criminal activities. With the Act, Congress extended special protection to journalists: "Notwithstanding any other law, it shall be unlawful for a government officer or employee, in connection with the investigation or prosecution of a criminal offense, to search for or seize any work product materials possessed by a person reasonably believed to have a purpose to disseminate to the public a newspaper, book, broadcast, or other similar form of public communication."

In the 1980s, Congress began to address specialized threats to electronic privacy. For example, the Cable Communication Policy Act of 1984 (42 U.S.C. § 551) prohibited cable companies from disclosing subscribers' viewing histories. The

Video Privacy Protection Act of 1988 (18 U.S.C. § 2710-11), enacted in response to reporters' attempts to discover the viewing habits of Supreme Court Justice nominee Robert Bork, codified a similar prohibition against disclosing video rental and purchase histories.

In the interim between the Cable and Video Acts, Congress turned its attention to more generalized concern about the newly recognized capabilities of computers. The Electronic Communications Privacy Act of 1986 (18 U.S.C. §§ 2510-22, 2701-11, 3121-27) regulated the "interception of communications" and access to stored communications. The Act defined electronic communications as, "any transfer of signs, signals, writing, images, sounds, data, or intelligence of any nature transmitted in whole or in part by a wire, radio, electromagnetic, photo electronic or photo optical system that affects interstate or foreign commerce."

In 1996, Congress turned its attention to the issue of electronic health information. The purpose of the Health Insurance Portability and Accountability Act (AHIPAA@) (42 U.S.C. §§ 1320d-8) was to "improve portability and continuity of health insurance coverage in the group and individual markets." Thus, it limited the ability of group health plans to disqualify applicants for pre-existing health conditions. Recognizing that the mandate would increase costs to insurers and providers, in an apparently misguided attempt to produce cost savings by other means, the legislation encouraged the use of electronic health records. That, in turn, led Congress to be concerned about the privacy of those e-health records. The regulatory provisions that accompany HIPAA mandate data care and security in the collection, storage, and sharing of "individually identifiable health information" and allow only the disclosure of the "minimum necessary" to effect treatment or payment.

The Congressional attempt at cost-savings proved misguided when health providers discovered the expense of complying with the privacy rules. Indeed, the Department of Health and Human Services that the first 10 years of implementation of the HIPAA privacy rules would cost 19 cents per health care visit, for a total of $16.6 billion (State Privacy, 2007).

For the first time, the citizenry discovered that privacy is not necessarily free.

In 1998, Congress continued with its topic-by-topic approach to privacy with the enactment of the Children's Online Privacy Protection Act. (15 U.S.C. §§ 6501-06) The Act defined a child as "an individual under the age of 13." It mandated that websites post privacy policies and obtain "parental consent for the collection, use, or disclosure of personal information from children."

Congress closed the 20th century with one more, specialized piece of privacy legislation. Or, perhaps, the Financial Modernization Act of 1999 (15 U.S.C. §§ 6801-09) is best characterized as an anti-privacy act, but only applicable in a very limited sphere. It allows branches or affiliates of a financial institution to share "nonpublic personal information

Post September 11, 2001 E-Privacy in the United States

As President George W. Bush's press secretary Ari Fleischer observed in January of 2003, on the eve of the Iraq invasion, "September 11th changed everything because it shows that we are indeed a vulnerable country" (White House, 2003). One component of the "everything" that changed was the value that the administration and lawmakers placed on privacy. The principal legislative reaction to the September 11 attack was the passage of the Uniting and Strengthening America by Providing Appropriate Tools Required to Intercept and Obstruct Terrorism, or USA PATRIOT Act. Passed by Congress on October 25, 2001 and signed into law by President Bush the next day, the Act's central provision is an expansion of governmental powers under the Foreign Intelligence Surveillance Act of 1978. Where FISA required a showing that the purpose of information gathering was to acquire information of a foreign government or its agents, the PATRIOT Act required a showing that foreign intelligence gathering is a "significant purpose" of the government's action. And, the Patriot Act enabled law enforcement personnel to obtain information on e-mail messages and "IP addresses" (18 U.S.C. § 3127(3)).

The Patriot Act's impact on privacy law was not merely definitional. It also was structural. FISA contained what became known as the "FISA Wall." The "wall," recognized by all branches of, prohibited the use in criminal prosecutions of evidence gathered in surveillance of foreign activity. The legal justification for the wall's existence lay in FISA's requirement that the primary purpose of activity that it authorizes be to obtain foreign intelligence information, and not to support criminal prosecutions.

Section 218 of the Patriot Act replaced "the purpose" with "a purpose" [50 U.S.C. §§ 1804(a)(7)(B) and 1823(a)(7)(B)]. It, thus, authorized law enforcement officials to use FISA information in criminal prosecutions so long as the surveillance was also premised on a non-prosecutorial purpose. After negotiations with Congress, the Bush Administration substituted "significant purpose" for "a purpose" in the Act's final draft.

Attorney General John Ashcroft subsequently issued regulations that effectively eliminated the wall. He authorized law enforcement officials to "have access to all information developed in" FISA investigations (Ashcroft, 2002). Initially ruled in violation of FISA, an appellate court upheld most provisions Attorney General Ashcroft's pronouncement (In re Sealed Case, 310 F.3d 717, 735 [FISA Ct. Rev. 2002]).

When the FISA wall came down, a dichotomy in privacy rights ascended. If the government does not suggest that a person is in any way connected to foreign intelligence, that person's privacy is relatively secure. But, if one of the purposes of the government's investigation is based on a suspicion that the investigation's target may provide a source of foreign intelligence, that person's privacy rights are much less secure.

In March 2007, the extent of the use of PATRIOT Act investigations and the paucity of legal, administrative, and practical limitations on those investigations became apparent. The FBI's Inspector General issued a report documenting that the FBI has issued 20,000 subpoenas annually of telephone, financial, and business records without prior courts approval. Yet, the report concluded, "the program lacks effective management, monitoring and reporting" (David Johnson & Eric Lipton, U.S. Report to Fault F.B.I. on Subpoenas, N.Y. Times, March 9, 2007). Indeed, the report concluded that nearly one fourth of the reviewed "information letters," as the subpoenas are known, involved violations of the applicable law (Solomon & Gellman, 2007).

What further complicates any attempt to describe federal privacy rights is that governing law may be beyond the reach of Congress or the courts. In 2005, the *New York Times* revealed that, shortly after September 11, 2001, President Bush had secretly authorized the National Security Administration to monitor international telephone calls and e-mail messages (Risen & Lichtbau, 2005). The President has premised the authority for the monitoring neither on Congressional legislation nor court decision, but on the inherent power of the commander in chief to protect the nation.

United States District Court Judge Anna Diggs Taylor rejected the administration's claim of executive authority to conduct the surveillance, asserting, "'There are no hereditary kings in America and no powers not created by the Constitution" (decision available at http://www.mied.uscourts.gov/eGov/taylorpdf/06%2010204.pdf). The Administration has appealed her decision.

The Other 50 Variables: State Privacy Laws

The vagaries of U.S. privacy law do not end with questions of interpretation of and authority for federal laws. Rather, the federal laws are but the starting point for analysis of privacy rights. Except when they are inconsistent and federal law, thus, preempts state law, federal law and the laws of the 50 states co-exist.

Certainly, federal law occupies the field of privacy's limits in international communications. But, states can, and do, regulate the privacy of arrest records, bank records, cable TV records, computer crime, credit reporting, government data banks, employment records, insurance records, mailing lists, medical records, school records, social security numbers, and tax records (Summary of state privacy laws, 2007).

The supremacy clause of the U.S. Constitution provides that federal laws trump conflicting state laws. At times, the applicable federal laws are explicit about their preemptive impact. For example, HIPAA provides that it is a floor for privacy protection of health information. States may provide greater protection (45 CFR Parts 160, 164).

The Patriot Act contains two explicit preemption provisions. Section 358 preempts conflicting state laws and requires consumer reporting agencies to disclose credit reports to federal investigators. Section 507 preempts conflicting state liability laws and requires educational institutions to turn over educational records.

In contexts where the preemption is not specific the central inquiry is whether one can comply with both the federal and state laws. If compliance with both is not possible, the federal law controls. Thus, confirming one's privacy rights and obligations is sometimes a difficult task.

Emerging Challenges

Litigation pending between the U.S. Department of Justice and the Google search engine company may be an indication that the Internet will be the venue for future skirmishes about electronic privacy rights (*Gonzalez v. Google*, 2006). In the lawsuit, the federal government is seeking information about potential violation the Child Online Protection Act. In an effort to use Google's data base to identify the law's violators, the Justice Department served a subpoena upon Google to turn over "a multi-stage random sample of one million URLs" and a computer file with "the text of each search string entered onto Google's search engine over a one-week period."

Google has responded, "Google users trust that when they enter a search query into a Google search box, not only will they receive back the most relevant results, but that Google will keep private whatever information users communicate absent a compelling reason" (Google response, 2006). The gravamen of Google's position brings us full circle in this chapter:

A real question exists as to whether the Government must follow the mandatory procedures of the Electronic Communications Privacy Act in seeking Google users' search queries. The privacy of Google users matters, and Google has promised to disclose information to the Government only as required by law. Google should not bear the burden of guessing what the law requires in regard to disclosure of search queries to the Government, or the risk of guessing wrong.

The questions of the future will be the same as the questions of the past. To what extent does technology affect our expectations of privacy? To what extent does the ability that technology gives others to see our private information empower them to see it? And, can pre-existing law be interpreted to fit new the new technological landscape, or must we continually craft new laws to accommodate a balance between expectations of privacy and the interest of the government and, sometimes, private individuals in discovering what the e-information contains?

Summary and Conclusion

So, one might ask, "What are my rights to electronic privacy in the United States?" The answer is, "it depends." And, it depends on a lot of variables. Are you currently in the U.S.? Are you communicating electronically with anyone outside of the U.S.? Do you reside in a state that protects your electronic privacy? Are you using the Internet? Have you visited a Web site that caters to children under the age of 13? Are you engaged in banking activity? Are you transmitting video or watching cable TV? Are your transmitting or receiving health information? And, maybe most importantly, regardless of the wishes of Congress or the courts, has the President of the United States authorized someone to view your private information?

The vision that this exercise produces is not atypical of the American legal landscape. The law is a quilt rendered patchwork by conflicting goals that sometimes seek protection of information and, at other times, seek and revelation of information. The patchwork is also informed by independent, and sometimes conflicting, sources for the laws' creations: courts and legislatures. And, those courts and legislatures exist in a republic at both the federal level. Finally, the political context, at times shaped by external sources of terrorism and at other times shaped by internal strife, pushes the law's evolution on a path that is anything buy linear.

So, what should the future hold? One might hope for a consistent, unified, over-arching, and adaptable body of law that can meet all of today's needs and most of the future's.

What will the future hold? In all likelihood, it will hold more of the same. Witness the newly-elected, Democratic Congress initiating legislation to reverse some of the Bush Administration's curbs on privacy. Will that trend hold after the 2008 election? Would another terrorist attack lead to measures similar to the Patriot act?

Warren and Brandeis accurately described existing law over 100 years ago: "Political, social, and economic changes entail the recognition of new rights, and the common law, in its eternal youth, grows to meet the demands of society" (Warren & Brandeis, 1890, p. 195). We can only hope that their vision holds for our future.

References

Etzioni, A. (1999). *The limits of privacy.* New York: Basic Books.

Gonzales v. Google, http://techlawadvisor.com/docs/gonzalez_google.html

Google's response: http://googleblog.blogspot.com/pdf/Google_Oppo_to_Motion.pdf

John, R. R. (1998). The politics of innovation. *DAEDALUS,* 4, 187-206.

Memorandum from John Ashcroft, Attorney General of the U.S. on Intelligence Sharing Procedures for Foreign Intelligence and Foreign Counterintelligence Investigations Conducted by the FBI to Director of the FBI, Assistant Attorney General for the Criminal Division, Counsel for Intelligence Policy, and U.S. Attorneys (March 6, 2002), http:// www.fas.org/irp/agency/doj/fisa/ag030602.html

Restatement (2nd) of Torts (1977) § 625A.

Risen, J. & Lichtbau, E. (2005). Bush lets U.S. spy on callers without courts. *New York Times*, December 16, p. A1.

U.S. Department of Health, Education, and Welfare, Records, Computers, and the Rights of Citizens: Report of the Secretary's Advisory Comm. on Automated Personal Data Systems 29 (1973).

Solomon, J. & Gellman, B. (2007). Frequent Errors in FBI's Secret Records Requests: Audit Finds Possible Rule Violations, *Washington Post*, March 9, p. A1.

State Privacy Report, http://www.cbs.state.or.us/ins/health_report/3253_health_report.pdf

Summary of state privacy laws available at http://www.epic.org/privacy/consumer/states.html

Warren, S. & Brandeis, L (1890). The Right to Privacy, *Harvard Law Review*, 4, 193-220.

White House, http://72.14.203.104/search?q=cache:3rnurnXOTV0J:www.white-house.gov/news/releases/2003/01/20030130-34.html+%22september+11th+changed+everything%22&hl=en&ct=clnk&cd=2&gl=us, 2003.

Chapter III

Assessing the Impact of Governmental Regulations on the IT Industry:
A Neo Institutional Theory Perspective

Sushma Mishra, Virginia Commonwealth University, USA

Amita Goyal Chin, Virginia Commonwealth University, USA

Abstract

Given the recent monumental events including the September 11th attack on the World Trade Center and the Pentagon as well as the Enron and MCI WorldCom debacles, people have witnessed, and more readily accepted, a significant increase in governmental authority, leading to a dramatic upsurge in the number of governmental regulations imposed on business organizations and society. Neo institutional theory suggests that such significant institutional forces may gravitate an otherwise highly disparate IT industry towards industry wide homogenization.

Introduction

IT infrastructure, processes, and security have been thrust to the forefront due to colossal catastrophes such as the September 11th attack on the World Trade Center and the Pentagon, illegal corporate activities, identity theft, and cyber crime. The plethora of governmental regulations that were successfully passed after these recent events hold business organizations unmistakably accountable, with serious consequences, including fines and imprisonment, for noncompliance. While such legislation may not directly be aimed at corporate IT, the omnipresence of information technology along with the indisputable gravity of these governmental regulations has forced most business organizations to revisit and subsequently revamp their IT infrastructure and processes in order to achieve legislative compliance.

The introduction of governmental regulations and the subsequent corporate restructuring may gravitate the IT industry toward a standardization and homogeneity which has traditionally been sorely lacking. Historically, the IT infrastructure within IT-oriented as well as non-IT-oriented organizations has been largely disparate. Perhaps this is a consequence of the unprecedented rapid advancement of the industry and the inability of the legal, social, and cultural forces to maintain pace. The industry as a whole has significantly suffered due to the lack of an orthodox organizational methodology and infrastructure.

Neo institutional theory (DiMaggio & Powell, 1983) provides a theoretical basis using which we are able to analyze and comprehend the behavior of particular organizations with respect to the industry of which they are a component. Today's IT-oriented organizations in particular are exposed to institutional forces, a prominent one of which is governmental regulations. Using the neo institutional theory perspective, we suggest that IT organizations, which traditionally are not standardized in structure, form, or method of operation will, in the face of social forces to which they are exposed, begin showing considerable similarity and standardization industry wide.

This chapter discusses some of the most significant of the governmental regulations recently mandated of the IT industry and their considerable impact and implications on information technology, both from a technical and managerial perspective. Employing neo institutional theory as the guiding framework for analysis, this paper suggests that the plethora of regulations being imposed on the IT industry are migrating organizations in the IT industry to conform and implement standardized processes and practices, resulting in the industry wide commoditization of IT.

The remainder of this chapter is organized as follows: we first present background discussion on neo institutional theory, including its basic tenets, followed by four major regulations currently influencing the IT industry and discusses some plausible impacts of these regulations on the information systems domain. Next, the neo institutional theory framework is used to develop a critical analysis to comprehend the impact of these regulations in accelerating organizational and institutional change in the IT industry. Finally, we draw conclusions and suggest some future research directions stemming from this work.

Background

Researchers (e.g., DiMaggio & Powell, 1983; Meyer & Rowan, 1977) of neo institutional theory focus primarily on the cause and implications of the observation that organizations in the same line of business, or industry, appear similar in their form and structure. According to neo institutional theory, organizational decision-making always occurs in the context of social political institutions. Meyer and Rowan (1977) claim that organizations do not rationally structure and organize their processes in response to environmental pressures; rather, they tend to respond in a similar manner to the same social forces to which they are exposed, thus developing similarity in both structure and form. This process of homogenization is called isomorphism (DiMaggio & Powell, 1983). "[I]isomorphism is a constraining process that forces one unit in a population to resemble other units that face the same set of environmental conditions" (Hawley, 1968 in DiMaggio & Powell, 1983, pp. 66).

Competitive isomorphism and institutional isomorphism are two kinds of isomorphic forces. Competitive isomorphism may be attributable to the various market forces acting on organizations. Institutional isomorphism on the other hand provides a basis for understanding the struggle amongst organizations for political power and legitimacy in society. Neo institutional theorists are more concerned about these latter kinds of forces.

Institutional isomorphism may be categorized in the following ways:

- **Coercive isomorphism:** Results from both the formal and informal pressure that is exerted upon a business enterprise from organizations upon which this business enterprise is dependent. Coercive isomorphism also refers to pressures from the society in which the business enterprise functions, particularly in the form of political expectations (e.g., governmental regulations). DiMaggio and Powell (1983) argue that the existence of a common legal environment does affect the behavior and structure of organizations, for it forces them to behave and operate in a manner that adapts to such legal requirements. Thus, the presence of overarching regulations tends to provide a common structure industry wide. As organizations grow in size and dominance in different areas of social life, coercive isomorphism reflects structures that are legitimated and institutionalized by government (Meyer & Rowan, 1977 in DiMaggio & Powell, 1983). This results in the homogenization of organizations in a given domain, reflecting conformity to wider institutions.

- **Mimetic isomorphism:** DiMaggio and Powell (1983) argue that not all intra-institutional isomorphism occurs as a result of coercive forces. Uncertainty in task as well as institutional environment promotes the imitation of actions amongst organizations. When their own goals are even somewhat ambiguous, organizations tend to model themselves after similar organizations within their own industry that they perceive to be more socially accepted and successful in economic terms, and that have successfully dealt with such uncertainties. Benchmarking or role modeling responses based on other organizations not only provides a concrete model for an organization to imitate but also provides a way to respond to uncertainty in seemingly a less risky way. Therefore, a level of homogeneity amongst organizations with similar uncertainties and business and institutional complexities results.

- **Normative isomorphism:** The origin of normative isomorphism lies in the concept of professionalization, which is defined as "the collective struggle of the members of an occupation to define the condition and methods of their work (DiMaggio & Powell, 1983, pp. 70)," so that there is a clear established cognitive base and legitimation for occupational autonomy. The established norms and behavior for a profession tend to shape all of the professionals entering that profession in a similar way, thus creating an isomorphic pattern amongst the professionals.

Two sources of normative isomorphism are generally identified: formal education and professional networks. In has been observed that "schools, colleges and universities are among society's major agents of socialization (Schein, 1968 in Siegel, Agarwal, & Rigsby, 1997)," providing legitimization in a cognitive base produced by university specialists. Professional and trade associations are also important vehicles for creating and enforcing normative rules and laws.

In any institutional system, the above factors are altogether present, interacting and promoting orderly behavior across an industry. However, the research in this area tends to emphasize one factor over another, depending on the problem that is being addressed and the particular perspective of the researcher(s). As Scott (2005) observes, "economists stress regulatory factors, political scientists and early sociologists [,stress] normative factors, while recent sociologists, anthropologists, and cognitive psychologists emphasize cultural-cognitive factors (p. 135)."

Neo institutional theory by no means suggests that organizations would not vary in their responses to institutional forces or would not attempt to shape such forces according to their own needs. Research in the healthcare industry has used the neo institutional framework extensively to study the impact of various regulations in shaping the management of hospitals. As Alexander and D'Aunno (2000) observed, "this interplay between broader context and interorganizational dynamics explains the variation in which corporatization expresses itself within the health care sector (p. 51)." Neo institutional theory argues that over a period of time, the presence of strong institutional forces homogenizes the overall response of the collection of organizations that operate within a similar industry.

Governmental Regulations

As enumerated in Appendix 1, the past decade has witnessed the injection of numerous governmental regulations into society. In this section we discuss the details of four such regulations—SOX, USA Patriot Act, HIPAA, and GLB. Discussion on additional regulations is left for future research.

Sarbanes-Oxley Act (SOX)

In the aftermath of the Enron and MCI WorldCom fiascos, the Sarbanes-Oxley Act (SOX), also known as the Public Company Accounting Reform and Investor Protection Act of 2002, was enacted in response to public anger with accounting fraud and corporate governance and reporting failures, and protects investors from fraudulent reporting by corporations (Moore 2005). SOX, applicable to public traded companies, mandates that companies employ stringent policies and procedures for reporting financial information accurately and in a timely manner.

SOX contains eleven titles, each of which contains multiple "Sections," which itemize the mandatory requirements (SEC, 2003). Several of these Sections have grave implications for key corporate executives, including the CEO, CFO, and CIO. Perhaps the most serious of the SOX Sections are Sections 302 and 906, which require signatures from the CEO and the CFO attesting that the information provided in the company's quarterly and annual reports is authentic and accurate (Volonino, Kermis, & Gessner, 2004). Furthermore, these key company executives bear the responsibility for any inaccurate representation of the reports, whether or not they possessed a priori knowledge of such errors. Section 906 holds CEOs, CFOs, and corporate directors both accountable and liable for the accuracy of financial disclosures. Unlike Section 302, Section 906 penalizes officers only if they knew of a possible problem or error when certifying a report (ITGI, 2004). Sections 103 and 802 specify audit record retention and security requirements (ITGI, 2004).

Section 401 requires the company to disclose not only balance sheet transactions, but also transactions not normally shown on the balance sheet. Additionally, all arrangements, obligations (including contingent obligations) and other relationships that might have a material current or future effect on the financial health of the company (ITGI, 2004) must be divulged. Section 401 restricts the use of pro forma information and directs companies to represent financial information in a manner consistent with generally accepted accounting principles (GAAP).

Section 404 requires that executives attest not only to the company's financial statements, but also to the control processes for the collection of the data supporting the financial statements (SEC, 2003; Gallagher, 2003). Section 409 requires real time disclosure of financial and operating events, requiring companies to disclose any events that may have material impacts on their financial condition or operations on a rapid and current basis (Volonino et al., 2004). Technological progress may soon define "rapid and current basis" to be within 48 hours following the occurrence of an event. Compliance with Sections 404 and 409 requires that each step in a business transaction—order, payment, storage of data, aggregation into financial reports,and so on—must be audited, verified, and monitored.

Section 802 requires the retention and protection of corporate records and audit documents and expressly includes e-records in the mandate (ITGI, 2004). This Section institutes criminal penalties for unauthorized document alteration or destruction.

Impact on the Information Systems Domain

It is both complex and expensive for organizations to comply with SOX. "In an annual survey of compliance, in IT by businesses, the estimated cost of compliance for year 2006 is more than $6.0 billionbillion, almost equal to the amount spent in 2005 which is $6.1 billion (Hagerty and Scott, 2005)." SOX significantly depletes available organizational resources (Bennett & Cancilla, 2005). SOX forces organizations to reevaluate IT governance practices (Fox, 2004), since both managerial and technical commitment is required to create the necessary organizational infrastructure necessary for compliance. Compliance requires internal control assessment measures in order to be prepared to cope with the demands of SOX, such as quarterly reporting, security policies, cost management, and external audits. Other issues that need considerable attention due to this legislation are: data management

(Volonino et al., 2004; Yugay& Klimchenko, 2004), which impacts data and systems security (Bertino, 1998); software development methodologies, which should now incorporate compliance issues as a component of the development lifecycle; and documentation and record keeping, which should now be strengthened to include versioning and audit ability (Peterson & Burns, 2005; Volonino et al., 2004).

Health Insurance Portability and Accountability Act (HIPAA) of 1996

HIPAA safeguards the privacy of medical records of patients by preventing unauthorized disclosure and improper use of patients' Protected Health Information (PHI) (CMMS, 2005). With a significant emphasis and monetary investment in the 1990s on the computerization of health services operations, the possibility of data manipulation and nonconsensual secondary use of personally identifiable records has tremendously increased (Baumer, 2000). HIPAA declares PHI "privileged," protecting individuals from losses resulting from the fabrication of their personal data. Businesses subjected to HIPAA are directed to protect the integrity, confidentiality, and availability of the electronic PHI they collect, maintain, use, and transmit.

Three major components of HIPAA are:

- **Privacy:** The privacy of individuals' health information in written, oral, and electronic form must be protected. Health information includes medical records, claims, and payment information, and almost all additional information related to patient health care.
- **Security:** Private information of individuals must be kept safe from damage of any kind. The purpose of this clause is to protect electronic patient information from alteration, destruction, loss, and accidental or intentional disclosure to unauthorized persons.
- **Transaction:** Various participants in the healthcare industries must effectively and electronically communicate patient information. Successfully meeting this requirement necessitates the privacy and security covenants also be met.

Impact on the Information Systems Domain

The cost of compliance with HIPAA to healthcare organizations, just for 2002, was $270 million (NetWorkWorld, 2003). This regulation has forced companies to revisit and reorganize their business processes. Compliance with HIPAA is not just a matter of technical products ensuring safe and secure data collection, transaction, and storage; rather, compliance is an issue of "organizational change management." It requires instituting new structures and patterns for health care companies to coordinate efficiently, trust other's intentions, and responsibly maintain and protect sensitive data (Huston, 2001). HIPAA compliance requires companies to constantly evaluate and test their internal controls over all business units and functional areas (Farris, 2004). Additionally, organizations must provide audit trails which are subject to external evaluation (Peterson & BurnsBurns, 2005), implement proper planning, institute privacy policies (Mercuri, 2004), and ensure controls in all data access points (Mercuri, 2004). Employing and adapting to technical solutions requires not only proper planning but also an overhaul in organizational processes. Data integrity (Mercuri, 2004), data security (Huston, 2001; Mitrano, 2003), transaction processing (Huston, 2001; Peterson & Burns, 2005), real time accessibility (Peterson & Burns, 2005), encryption and authentication techniques (Knorr, 2004), network communications (Huston, 2001), and disaster recovery techniques must all be investigated and modified in order to guarantee private patient data storage and interchange.

USA Patriot Act

As one response to the September 11, 2001 attack on the World Trade Center and the Pentagon, the Bush Administration proposed new legislation—the Uniting and Strengthening America by Providing Appropriate Tools Required to Intercept and Obstruct Terrorism Act, or the USA Patriot Act—just four daysafter the attacks (Swire, 2002). This act was primarily enacted to provide law enforcement agencies the tools necessary to investigate and apprehend those suspected of planning or executing terrorist acts.

The USA Patriot Act includes 10 major Titles (EPIC, 2001):

- Enhancing Domestic Security Against Terrorism (e.g., establishing agencies, availing military assistance, additional funding)
- Enhanced Surveillance Procedures
- International Money Laundering Abatement and Anti-Terrorist Financing Act of 2001 (e.g., deterring money laundering, enforcement of foreign judgments)
- Protecting the Border (e.g., controlling illegal entry, enhanced immigration provisions)

- Removing Obstacles to Investigating Terrorism
- Providing for Victims of Terrorism, Public Safety Officers, and Their Families
- Increased Information Sharing for Critical Infrastructure Protection (e.g., providing access to information conveniently for interrogation and detection purposes)
- Strengthening the Criminal Laws Against Terrorism (e.g., improving cybersecurity forensic capabilities, eliminating statute of limitation for terrorism offenses)
- Improved Intelligence (e.g., increased training and awareness of terrorism in government officials, foreign terrorist asset tracking center)
- Miscellaneous (e.g., review of the Department of Justice, feasibility study on use of biometric identifier scanning system, etc.)

The USA Patriot Act amends the following three previously passed regulations, resulting in increased governmental power and control:

- **Electric Communications Privacy Act (ECPA) of 1986:** ECPA defines rules and regulations for the protection of privacy of electronic communication. Under ECPA, the scope of electronic communication that could be made available was limited in order to protect the privacy rights of individuals. The USA Patriot Act expands what law enforcement agents may obtain from Internet Service Providers (ISPs). Without permission from the user, agents may acquire transactional data such as payment method, detailed session information, and IP addresses.
- **Foreign Intelligence Surveillance Act (FISA) of 1978:** FISA defines standards for wiretapping and the surveillance of electronic communication. Per the USA Patriot Act, ISPs are required to use additional devices for tracking inbound and outbound calls, and store data logs of these transactions.
- **Computer Fraud and Abuse Act (CFAA) of 1986:** CFAA defines rules and regulations for computer hacking and other unauthorized computer access resulting in intentional or unintentional damage. The USA Patriot Act extends the CFAA by blurring specific terminology and definitions such as that of "damage" or "intentional acts," empowering governmental authorities to more freely interpret semantics. It also provides guidelines for "protected" computers under CFAA.

Impact on the Information Systems Domain

The USA Patriot Act, focusing mainly on homeland security issues, is an umbrella act that has implications for a variety of industries including Telecommunications, Energy, Financial Services, and Water and Transportation. For example, banks must maintain financial transaction and account record keeping, scrutinize wire transfer activities, and establish due diligence policies, procedures, and controls to detect money-laundering activities. Security issues at the corporate, local, and national level is emphasized. Technical issues requiring evaluation for compliance with the USA Patriot Act include working with the surveillance devices for electronic communications like pen/trap technology and the storage of detailed data logs.

Managers must secure records and must be able to produce a variety of information upon request. Managerial concerns stemming from the USA Patriot Act include the cost of compliance with the law, and the successful interpretation of the stringent rules for ISPs. For example, ISPs must implement the infrastructural changes to accommodate extra storage space and technology, have real time retrieval of records, and be able to enforce strict security policies to protect important information.

Gramm-Leach Bliley

The Gramm-Leach-Bliley (GLB) Act, or the Financial Services Modernization Act of 1999, proposes regulations regarding the scope and interrelationships, particularly with respect to consumer privacy, of key financial industries—insurance, securities, and banking. (Prior to GLB enactment, the Glass-Steagall Act guided these industries.) Given the increased and tremendously heavy dependence on information technology to store, manipulate, and use data, maintaining the sanctity of consumer data and customer relationships has become of paramount importance. GLB requires that companies which engage in financial activity must respect the privacy of customer data and undertake such measures as are necessary to protect the data while in organizational care, custody, and control.

GLB authorizes eight federal agencies and all sstates to enforce three major rules regarding financial privacy, the safeguarding of personal information, and pretexting:

- **Financial Privacy:** The Privacy Rule requires that organizations that engage in financial activity provide customers copies of their privacy policy and explain their practices on sharing customer information.

- **Safeguarding of Personal Information:** The Safeguards Rule requires organizations protect the confidentiality and integrity of personal consumer information, and design, implement, and maintain the necessary security processes. This rule applies not only to the financial institutions which are primarily responsible for collecting this information from customers but also to all secondary users of this information, including credit rating agencies which receive this information from financial institutions.

- **Pretexting:** This provision of the GLB Act protects consumers from individuals and companies that obtain their personal financial information under false pretenses, a practice known as "pretexting."

Impact on the Information Systems Domain

GLB requires organizations to engage in financial activities such as preparing tax plans, providing customers the company privacy policy, and explaining corporate practices in sharing customer information (Berghel, 2005). The implications for information systems domain are manifold. Under GLB, compliance requires state-of-the-art expertise in hacking, malware, and social engineering (Berghel, 2005). This law has implications for upper management including the CIO, making him/her personally responsible for any oversight of compliance. Furthermore, under GLB, issues such as the absence of risk assessment, the absence of safeguards to control risks and failure, and the absence of service contracts for security standards would hold management accountable. That is, the CIO is required to be personally responsible for any compromise to the privacy of customer information. Under GLB, companies need to have expertise in dealing with hacking, malware, and social engineering. These are not skills over which the typical CIO has knowledge or mastery (Berghel, 2005). Therefore, a distribution of authority for administration and enforcement becomes necessary in order to comply with this law. With the GLB, organizational obligations to protect consumer privacy and the requirement to completely and accurately disclose the organization's policies become mandatory. GLB holds the CEO, the CIO, and the IT management responsible for safeguarding the public's interest.

Discussion: Institutional Perspective of the IT Phenomenon

Information Technology as an industry is immature, highly fragmented, and non-standardized. Most organizational tasks, ranging from the most simple to the highly complex, may be accomplished using a wide variety of solutions. Each organization chooses different solutions to solve the same tasks, oftentimes even developing hybrid solutions, all resulting in inconsistent and incompatible systems. This disparity is further heightened with the vastly varying methods of securing informational assets that are employed by organizations, the diverse systems development practices followed, the different underlying data models implemented in databases, and so on. Such behavior has rendered any collaboration efforts as arduous, often unachievable endeavors and resulted in an industry plagued with ad hoc, band-aid solutions to many common problems. Clearly, a necessity for the standardization of IT practices across the industry has emerged.

Neo institutional theorists have provided evidence that many modern organizational characteristics have their origins in public policy. The legal environment has become more pervasive, especially for the IT industry, with organizations facing ever increasing governmental intervention in the form of regulations. Edelman and Suchman (1997) describe the regulatory environment for organizations as a world where "law appears as a system of substantive edicts, invoking societal authority over various aspects of organizational life (p. 483)." The legal system, on behalf of society, takes the initiative to control organizational behavior. Some researchers, on the other hand argue that, regulatory environment often merely institutionalizes the indigenous practice of regulated population (Edelman & Suchman, 1997). These pressures from the institutional environment could lead to the standardization of operating procedures in order to gain legitimacy (Zucker, 1987). The regulatory forces are driving IT organizations towards a direction which ensures the standardization of processes, products and practices. In order to show conformity, IT organizations gradually can achieve similar standards across the industry, resulting in an unprecedented homogeneity of this industry.

In the research literature, the application of the neo institutional theory to the field of information technology has thus far been minimal. Research has largely been focused on the micro level analysis of inter-organizational conflicts within the IT industry. Neo institutional theory has been applied to IT at the micro level, that is, at the organizational level. Benders, Batenberg, and Blonk (2006), using the neo institutional theory framework, have argued that the use of ERP systems may lead to the standardization within and between organizations and that institutional pressures play a significant role in ERP adoption. They call it "technical isomorphism."

Adler (2005), studying the Software Engineering Institute's Capability Maturity Model (CMM®) for software development, uses institutional theory to focuses on the symbolic dimensions of the created object. He concludes that adherence to the CMM is a symbolic conformance to established standards.

Some recent research has concentrated on the institutional analysis of IT as an industry, and on the efforts of creating a standard development or implementation process for information technologies. King, Gurbaxani, Kraemer, McFarlan, Raman, and Yap (1994) argue that the lack of a coherent protocol for the creation of government policy for IT innovation signals a shortfall in the understanding of the vital role of government institutions in IT innovation. Governmental regulations in developing nations are geared towards the acceleration of IT innovation within their national boundaries. Robey and Holmstrom (2001) studied the implementation of governance support system in a government organization in Sweden. They analyzed the implications of the use of this technology at the organizational as well as the institutional level. They concluded that by focusing on both the organizational and institutional levels simultaneously, a comprehensive understanding of the global forces shaping the organizational and societal changes is achieved.

Jones, Orlikowski, and Munir (2004) argue that the broader institutional influences—such as political, industrial, economic, and global—that shape IT phenomenon have largely been ignored in IT research (p. 319). There is some awareness to have industry wide common benchmarks and practices that could lead to the standardization of the industry; however, this is primarily by practitioners rather than by academicians. The creation of maturity models (Fraser & Vaishnavi, 1997), governance standards such as the Control Objectives for Information and related Technology (COBIT), and the Committee of Sponsoring Organizations of the Treadway Commission (COSO), are examples of these endeavors (ISACA, 2004). But academic researchers are lagging behind in undertaking such institutional level research and creating a research agenda in this area.

From the Neo institutional theory perspective, the current state of the IT industry with increasing regulatory interventions is an unmistakable signal for organizations to become prepared to change their current IS practices. Institutional forces, such as regulations, are becoming stronger over time and are gradually standardizing the industry by compelling organizations to change in a uniform manner, and resulting in the commoditization of "IT" as a product. In the process of complying with new laws, IT organizations are streamlining their processes with better security measures, following standard development methodologies, adopting similar governance frameworks, welcoming audit practices, emphasizing internal controls, and are all migrating towards similar forms and similar structures.

Conclusion

The ubiquitous Internet has yielded a marketplace of global proportions. In juxtaposition with this atmosphere of global connectivity is the responsibility for information safety, security, privacy, and accuracy. Numerous governmental regulations have and are continuing to force organizations to revamp their IT infrastructures. IT has become a central organizational function and thus, governmental regulations often radically impact IT and business processes, particularly in terms of the cost of compliance, preparedness for external audit, organizational restructuring, sharing of data amongst enterprises, enhanced technical support and regular monitoring, and the assessment of business processes. Governmental regulations are usually proposed in reaction to growing public dissatisfaction and concerns (Milberg, Burke, Smith, & KallmanKallman, 1995). While they may be expensive and arduous to fulfill, these regulations present an opportunity for organizations to restructure and improve their information technology operations.

This chapter contributes theoretically to the existing body of IT research. The neo institutional theory is presented and applied for a unique institutional analysis of the IT industry. This work provides an analysis of the various implications of the many regulations recently imposed on the IT industry. Future research stemming from this work may include studying the impact of such standardization efforts at the institutional level of analysis. This work could also lead to research about organizational responses to such forces and its strategies to deal with such changes. Regulations are significantly altering and shaping current IT practices and processes and even further impacts of these laws on organizational structures and forms are inevitable. Empirical studies are required to measure the directions and intensity of resulting modifications.

References

Adler, P. S. (2005). The evolving object of software development. *Organization*, *12*(3), 401.

Baumer, D., Earp, J. B., & Payton, F. C. (2000). Privacy of medical records: IT iimplications of HIPAA. *Computers and Society*.

Benders, J., Batenberg, R., & Blonk, H. (2006). Sticking to standards:T Technical and other isomorphic pressures in deploying ERP-systems. *Information & Management, 43*(2), 124.

Bennet, V.,& Cancilla, B. (2005). IT responses to Sarbanes-Oxley. *IBM*. Retrieved on September 30, 2005 from http://www-128.ibm.com/developerworks/rational/library/sep05/cancilla-bennet/index.html

Bertino, E. (1998). Data Security. *Data & Knowledge Engineering, 25,* 199-216.

D'Aunno, T., Succi, M.& Alexander, J.A. (2000). The role of institutional and market forces in divergent organizational change. *Administrative Science Quarterly, 45,*679-703.

DiMaggio, P.J.& Powell, W.W. (1991). The iron cage revisited: Institutional isomorphism and collective rationality in organizational fields. In W. Powell & P. DiMaggio (Eds.), *The new institutionalism in organizational analysis* (pp. 63-82). The University of Chicago Press.

Edelman, L.B. & Suchman, M.C. (1997). The legal environments of organizations. *Annual Review of Sociology, 23,* 479-515.

Farris, G. (2004). Mitigating the oongoing Sarbanes-Oxley compliance process with technical enforcement of IT ccontrols. *DM Direct Newsletter*. DMReview.com.

Fox, C. (2004). Sarbanes-Oxley: Considerations for a fframework for IT financial reporting controls. *Information Systems Control Journal, 1*.

Fraser, M.D. & Vaishnavi, V.K. (1997). A former specifications maturity model. *Communications of the ACM, 40*(12), 95-103

Gallagher, S. (2003). Gotcha! Complying with financial regulations. *Baseline Magazine*. Retrieved on October 2, 2005 from http://www.baselinemag.com/article2/0,1397,1211224,00.asp

Hagerty, J. & Scott, F. (2005). SOX sspending for 2006 teto exceed $6B. AMR Research. Retrieved on November 29, 2005 from http://www.amrresearch.com/Content/View.asp?pmillid=18967

Huston, T. (2001). Security issues for implementation of e-medical records. *Communications of the ACM, 44*(9).

Information Systems Audit and Control Association (ISACA)(2004). *CISA Review Manual, 2004 Edition*. Rolling Meadows, IL: ISACA.

Information Technology Governance Institute. (2004). IT Control Objectives for Sarbanes-Oxley.

Jones, M., Orlikowski, W., & Munir, K. (2004). Structuration theory and information systems: A critical reappraisal.I In J. Mingers & L. Willcocks (Eds.) *Social theory and philosophy for information systems*. Chichester, UK: John Wiley & Sons, Ltd.

King, J.L., Gurbaxani, V., Kraemer, K.L., McFarlan, F.W., Raman, K.S., & Yap, C.S. (1994). Institutional factors in information technology innovation. *Information Systems Research, 5*(2), 139-169.

Klimchenko, V. (2004). SOX mandates focus on data quality and integration. DM Review, February.

Knorr, E. (2004). The bitter pill: Regulation has come to town, and IT will never be the same. *CIO Magazine*. Retrieved on September 20, 2005 from http://www.cio.com/archive/

Mercuri, R.T. (2004). The HIPAA-potamus in health care data security. *Communications of the ACM, 47*(7).

Meyer, J.W. & &Rowan, B. (1977). Institutionalized oorganizations: Formal structure as myth and ceremony. *American Journal of Sociology, 83*(2), 340-363.

Milberg, S.J., Burke, S.J., Smith, H.J.,& Kallman, A. (1995). Values, personal information privacy and regulatory approaches. *Communications of the ACM,38*(12).

Mitrano, T. (2003). Civil privacy and national security legislation: A three-dimensional view. *Educause R,Review,* November/December.

Moore, C. (2005). The growing trend of government involvement in IT ssecurity. *Proceedings from InfoSecCD Conference '04,* October.

NetWorkWorld. (2003). Retrieved on September 29, 2005 from http://www.networkworld.com/research/2003/0901regs.html?page=1

Peterson, Z.& Burns, R. (2005). Ext3cow: A time-shifting file system for regulatory compliance. *ACM Transactions on Storage, 1*(2), 190-212.

Robey, D., & Holmstrom, J. (2001). Transforming municipal governance in global context: A case study of the dialectics of social change. *Journal of Global Information Technology Management, 4*(4), 19.

Scott, W.R. (2005). *Organizations: Rational, natural and open systems* (5th Edition). Englewood Cliffs, N.J.: Prentice-Hall.

Siegel, P.H., Agarwal, S., & Rigsby, J.T. (1997). Organizational and professional socialization: Institutional isomorphism in an accounting context. *The Mid-Atlantic Journal of Business, 33*(1).

(SEC) U.S Securities and Exchange Commission. (2003).' Management's reports on internal control over financial reporting and certification of disclosure in exchange act periodic reports. Retrieved on September 30, 2005 from http://www.sec.gov/rules/final/33-8238.htm

Volonino, L., Kermis, G., & Gessner, G. (2004). Sarbanes-Oxley links IT to corporate compliance. *Proceedings of the Tenth Americas Conference on Information Systems*.

Yugay, I.& Klimchenko, V. (2004). SOX mandate focus on data quality and integration. *DM Review Magazine*. Retrieved on September 30, 2005 from http://www.dhttp://www.dmreview.com

Zucker, L.G. (1987). Institutional theories of organization. *Annual Review of Sociology, 13,* 443-464.

Appendix A: Major Regulations Effecting IT and the Year Passed (1995-2005)

Year	Major Regulation(s) Passed
1995	Disability Discrimination Act
	Information Technology Policy Act
	Paperwork Reduction Act
	Security and Classified Informtion Protection Act
1996	Economic Espionage Act (EEA)
	Economic Security Act
	Encrypted Communications Privacy Act
	*Health Insurance Portability and Accountability Act (HIPAA)
	Information Technology Management Reform Act
	Information Technology Reform Act
	National Information Infrastructure Protection Act
	Promotion of Commerce Online in the Digital Era (Pro-CODE) Act
	Telecommunications Act
1997	Communications Privacy and Consumer Empowerment Act
	Data Privacy Act
	Electronic Data Security Act
	Medical Information Privacy and Security Act (MIPSA)
	No Electronic Theft Act
	Secure Public Networks Act
	Security and Freedom through Encryption (SAFE) Act
	The Personal Information Privacy Act
1998	Data Protection Act
	Digital Millennium Copyright Act (DCMA)
	E-PRIVACY Act
	Government Paperwork Elimination Act
	Rehabilitation Act
1999	American Health Security Act
	American Inventors Protection Act
	Cyberspace Electronic Security Act
	Cyberspace Electronic Security Act (CESA)
	Digital Millennium Copyright Act
	Director of Central Intelligence Directive 6/3 (DCID)
	Government Information Security Act
	*Gramm-Leach-Bliley Act (GLBA) / Financial Services Modernization Act
	Promote Reliable On-Line Transactions to Encourage Commerce and Trade (PROTECT) Act

continued on following page

Appendix A: continued

Year	Major Regulation(s) Passed
2000	Children's Online Privacy Protection Act (COPPA)
	EU Safe Harbor Act
	Electronic Communications Act
	Freedom of Information Act
	Information Technology Act
	Internet Security Act
	Regulation of Investigatory Powers Act
	The Oceans Act
2001	Anti-terrorism, Crime and Security Act
	Cyber Security Information Act
	Government Information Security Reform Act (GISRA)
	*USA Patriot Act
	Visa Cardholder Information Security Program (CISP)
	Visa Integrity and Security Act
2002	Consumer Privacy Protection Act
	Cyber Security Information Act
	Cyberterrorism Preparedness Act
	E-Government Act
	Federal Information security Management Act (FISMA)
	Federal Privacy and Data Protection Policy Act
	Homeland Security Act
	Privacy Provisions of the E-Government Act
	Regulation of Investigatory Powers Act
	*Sarbanes-Oxley Act
	Technology, Education, and Copyright Harmonization Act (TEACH)
2003	California Online Privacy Protection Act
	Domestic Security Enhancement Act
	Government Paperwork Elimination Act
	Privacy and Electronic Communications Regulations
	Reporting Instructions for the E-Government Act
	Security Breach Information Act
	The Office of the Comptroller of the Currency Web-Linking Guidelines
2004	Environmental Information regulations
2005	Information Security Beach and Notification Act

Chapter IV

The Impact of the UK Human Rights Act 1998 on Privacy Protection in the Workplace

Bernd Carsten Stahl, De Montfort University, UK

Abstract

Privacy is one of the central issues in the information society. New technologies pose new threats to privacy but they may also facilitate new ways of protecting it. Due to the generally accepted importance of privacy, many countries now have explicit legislation to support privacy protection. At the same time there are philosophical debates about privacy, its definitions, meanings, and limitations. In this chapter I present the current state of legal protection of privacy in the United Kingdom. In doing so, I will argue that there are different philosophical concepts of privacy that underpin different pieces of legislation. I will explore what this may mean for the justification of privacy protection and speculate where the future development may be heading.

Introduction

Privacy is generally accepted as one of the main issues of computer and information ethics. New technologies raise a number of issues for privacy protection. Governments in many countries have recognised that this is a problem that their citizens are sensitive towards. Thus, there are laws and regulations that attempt to address the issue of privacy. Behind those laws, however, there are philosophical concepts of privacy that are not always easy to identify but that are important to recognise if one wants to understand how and why privacy is legally protected. This chapter will concentrate on the case of the UK and analyse the UK legislature's view of privacy. The main emphasis is on the question of employee privacy and how it is affected by different pieces of legislation.

The chapter will focus on the question whether the introduction of the European Convention on Human Rights (ECHR), which includes a right to privacy, heretofore unknown to English law, adds anything to employee privacy as delimited by the Data Protection Act 1998 (DPA) and the Regulation of Investigatory Powers Act 2000 (RIPA). There has been some speculation that says that privacy protection of employees was well established before the European Convention on Human Rights became British law through the Human Rights Act 1998 (HRA). The chapter will argue that such a view would be false because the HRA influences employer-employee relationship in a number of ways. The Article 8 provision of personal privacy is an important aspect of this. One could approach this question superficially by exploring how the HRA in general and Article 8 in particular have changed the nature of privacy protection in work relationships. However, this chapter will use a different strategy. It will concentrate on the very notion of privacy and explore the question whether there are different concepts of privacy underlying the Human Rights Act 1998 on the one hand and the Data Protection Act 1998 (DPA) or the Regulations of Investigatory Powers Act 2000 (RIPA) on the other hand.

In order to develop this argument, the chapter will begin with a brief review of the literature on privacy. It will then discuss the DPA and RIPA and how privacy is perceived and protected by both. In a subsequent step the chapter will discuss the nature of the impact of the ECHR on employment relationships and particularly on privacy considerations within those. The chapter will conclude by outlining the different implications of the respective notions of privacy and discussing possible reasons for the development of different concepts of privacy.

Privacy

There seems to be general agreement that privacy is important. There is much less agreement on why it is important or what it actually is (Weckert & Adeney, 1997). Gavison (1995) has identified several aspects of it. Privacy can be a situation, a right, a claim, a form of control, or a value. It relates to information, autonomy, identity, or access. Alternatively, it can be split into the aspects of confidentiality, anonymity, and data protection (Rotenberg, 1998).

Concerns of privacy can be followed back in time at least to the ancient Greeks (Arendt, 1958) but explicit legal recognition of the term in some jurisdictions did not come before the late 1800s (Sipior & Ward, 1995). The most widely spread definition was coined by Warren & Brandeis (1890, p. 205) who called privacy the "right to be let alone." This definition (often changed to the right to be "left" alone) is still used frequently today (Britz, 1999; Velasquez, 1998). This right to be left alone seems to be attractive and capture imaginations but it does not lend itself to clear legal (or moral) implementation.

In order to create more clarity, scholars have introduced different approaches to privacy. An important stream of the literature links privacy to control over information or control over access to information (Elgesem, 2001; Fleming, 2003; Tavani & Moor, 2001). A related approach is that of informational self-determination (Stalder, 2002). It defines privacy as the right to determine who accesses person-related data. This interpretation is widely spread in continental Europe but seems to have little resonance in the Anglo-American world. Another related approach is that of seeing privacy in terms of property. If person-related information can be treated as property, then privacy issues can be reduced to the more established (intellectual) property law (Spinello, 2000).

There is considerable disagreement on the degree to which privacy considerations vary between personal and employment situations. To some degree there are obvious differences as employers can and must invade their employee privacy in order to ensure that their work can be done. They may require sensitive information such as bank details to pay salaries or location data to ensure that employees undertake the tasks assigned to them. The below discussion will show, however, that this distinction between personal and employment life is difficult to sustain, which renders some monitoring practices problematic.

Privacy as an Intrinsic Value

There are further approaches to privacy that cannot be discussed in a short overview. What is important to briefly consider, however, is that there are a variety of reasons why it is valued. A basic distinction can be drawn between privacy as an intrinsic or instrumental value (Tavani, 2000). If privacy is an intrinsic value, then it requires no further external justification. On a very fundamental level one can see respect for privacy as an expression of respect for the other (Elgesiem, 1996; Introna, 2003), for an autonomous being. This would link with Continental European ethical theories in the tradition of Kant (1961) but also with 20th century existentialist ethics as developed mostly in France by thinkers from Sartre to Levinas. A related view of the intrinsic value of privacy stresses its importance for the development of a secure and reliable identity (Brown, 2000; Nye, 2002; Severson, 1997). It allows the individual to develop their autonomy, which is a necessary precondition for ethics in the Kantian deontological tradition (Brey, 2001; Spinello, 1997; van den Hoeven, 2001).

Privacy as an Instrumental Value

As an instrumental value, privacy has been described as important because a truly private space is necessary for mental health (Nissenbaum, 2001). It is required to trust others and, more generally, to develop good social relations (Gallivan. & Depledge, 2003; Johnson, 2001). A functioning society thus requires the provision of privacy for its members (Introna, 2000). Privacy is also closely related to power relationships. Surveillance, as one of the main organisational challenges to privacy, can be used to establish and strengthen power. This kind of thought is closely linked to Foucault's (1975) development of Bentham's Panopticon (Goold, 2003; Rule et al., 1995; Yoon, 1996).

Having now established that privacy is a value worth protecting, it is important to note at the same time that it is not an absolute value (Charlesworth, 2003). The simple thought experiment of a society with total protection of privacy shows that such a situation would lead to the collapse of rule and order. There must thus be limits to privacy. There are other considerations and values, which can override interests of privacy. One such set of values comes from employers. Employers have a variety of reasons for gathering data about their employees. These include the avoidance of "cyberslacking" (Siau et al., 2002, p. 75) and "cyberslouching" (Urbaczewski & Jessup, 2002, p. 80) and thus the increase of productivity. Data gathering, which is usually facilitated by the use of information and communication technology (ICT), also helps companies safeguard their property and it is also often described as an aspect of risk management. It helps organisations avoid risks of misuse of their equipment and of being held liable for misconduct of their employees.

Again, we cannot do justice to the variety of arguments raised in this respect. It is important in the context of this chapter, however, to raise these issues because they affect the standing and importance of privacy. We have now seen that privacy can be seen as an intrinsic value, which would render it similar to a human right. On the other hand, it can be seen as instrumental, and thus not worth defending for its own sake. Depending on which interpretation one prefers, the weighting of employee privacy interests against employers' commercial interests will come to different conclusions. The main argument of this chapter will be that the English tradition of privacy is based on the weaker instrumental view of privacy and thus facilitates abridgement of privacy. The contribution of Article 8 of the ECHR is then that it introduces a stronger (continental European) notion of privacy, which renders commercial interests less important. This starting point may need more elaboration than is possible here. Importantly, one can argue that even an instrumental view of employee privacy may require strong protection if the value it is meant to protect is of sufficient importance. This discussion would go beyond what can be achieved in this chapter. It should thus be made clear that the instrumental use which is of most importance for this argument is to be understood in the economic context. Or, to put it more bluntly, it is assumed that an instrumental view of privacy renders it easier to overwrite for economic purposes than an understanding of privacy as an intrinsic value. The coming sections will describe how such different understandings of the concept of privacy is reflected in current UK law by discussing the different ways in which privacy is protected through the DPA, RIPA, and the ECHR.

The Notion of Privacy in the Data Protection Act 1998 and Regulations of Investigatory Powers Act 2000

This section will briefly review the DPA and RIPA in order to deduce the underlying concept of privacy that informs both acts.

Privacy in the Data Protection Act 1998

The DPA was the UK's implementation of the European Directive 95/46/EC whose purpose was to create universal European standards for the collection, storage and processing of personal information. It limits the extent to which personal data can be gather and what can be done with it. Another important aspect is that it allows individuals to access and check information held about them. Data is defined in s 1(1) as information which is being processed automatically and is part of a filing system. The most important part of such data is data that is collected electronically.

The European Directive 95/46/EC aims to implement the OECD Fair Information Principles (Privacy Rights Clearinghouse, 2004). It therefore requires Member States in Article 6 to ensure that data is processed fairly and lawfully, that it is only used for the purpose it was collected for, that there is no excessive data collection, that the data is kept accurate, and that it is anonymised, where the identity of the individual is no longer needed. These fair information principles are incorporated into the DPA which provided the basis for the creation of the office of the Information Commissioner who oversees privacy issues. Individuals or organisations who want to collect personal information must register as data controllers and comply with the regulations of the act.

On the face of it, one could interpret the DPA as a strong means to ensure privacy. However, it is quite explicit about the need to consider employer interests in collecting data. To return to the above argument that there are the two views of privacy as an intrinsic or instrumental right, one can deduce from the practice of the information commissioner that it is seen as instrumental. While employers are forced to collect data only for relevant business purposes, there is no description of what would constitute a legitimate business interest (cf. Johnson, 2001). Such a conclusion is supported by Schedule 7 of the DPA which explicitly exempts employment-relevant data from some of the protection that personal information is generally afforded. This seems to suggest that employers' interests are not limited by a more fundamental right to privacy.

Privacy in the Regulations of Investigatory Powers Act 2000

Another important piece of legislation with regards to privacy in employment relationships is the RIPA. It goes beyond the DPA in that it applies to communication services that are not publicly available. It is the UK's implementation of the European Directive 97/46/EC. RIPA is important for this chapter because it affects employers' ability to interfere with communication. Originally aimed at telephone communication, it can arguably also be applied to email or other forms of electronic communication.

The RIPA states that it shall be an offence to intercept a communication transmission, even if it takes place on a private network. There are, however, exceptions (s 4), which render such interceptions lawful. These exceptions are elaborated in the Telecommunications (Lawful Business Practice) (Interception of Communications)

Regulations 2000. In s 3(1) some reasons for interception are named. They include quality control, national security, and crime prevention and detection. In practice this means that employers again have a right to breach the privacy of employees' electronic communication if they can establish a business interest for doing so. This arguably goes against the spirit of the Telecommunications Regulation 1999, which had the explicit aim of ensuring protection of fundamental rights and freedoms, and in particular the right to privacy, with respect to the processing of personal data in the telecommunications sector (Information Commissioner, 2005).

The implied understanding of privacy thus seems to be an instrumental one. Privacy of employees can be weighed against business interests of employers. A possible explanation of the apparently weak standing of privacy in DPA and RIPA and related regulations is that privacy is confined to the private sphere. By entering an employment relationship, employees lose any non-negotiable right to privacy. While the acts put the onus on employers to safeguard personal information insofar as they have no direct business case to use it, legitimate employer interests can override privacy concerns. Interestingly, a legitimate business interest is never defined.

Privacy in the Human Rights Act 1998

The HRA implements the European Convention of Human Rights as an integral aspect of British legislation. The HRA is mainly concerned with the relationship between citizens and state. An initial interpretation could therefore be that it does not affect private sector employment relationship. Such an interpretation would be misleading for a variety of reasons. The HRA can be applied directly by employees of public authorities because s 6(1) imposes a duty on public authorities to ensure they comply with the Convention. Employees in the private sector are supported in their privacy concerns because s 3a provides a general duty on British courts to interpret all legislation consistently with the convention. Finally, and most broadly, Article 1 (cf. Johnson, J, 2001) of The Convention requires states to secure Convention rights to everyone in their jurisdiction.

That means that Convention rights, when affected in employment relationships, can attain relevance in employment outside of public authorities. This is true for all human rights enumerated in the Convention, including the right to privacy as detailed in Article 8. Article 8 guarantees everyone the right to respect for his private and family life, his home and his correspondence. Section 2 details the limits to this right. The history of interpretation of Article 8 by the European Court of Human Rights has shown that the right to privacy is to be understood quite broadly. It relates to sexual identity, personal information, and phone calls from business premises.

HRA 1998 Case Law

An important case establishing the breadth of interpretation was *Halford v UK* (1997), where it was held that the interception of phone calls was a breach of privacy, even though the claimant was a member of the police and the calls were made from "business premises." This was upheld in *Valenzuela Contreras v Spain* (1999) where the court held that monitoring telephone conversations breached the right to respect for private life. Another implication of *Halford* was the support it lent to the contention that the state has an obligation to protect citizens' privacy. This was endorsed by *Douglas v Hello Ltd* (2001).

Arguably, the most important impact that the HRA has on privacy in employment is its influence on jurisprudence. Section 3 HRA requires courts to interpret all legislation in a manner compatible with HRA. This includes a different interpretation of reasonableness that employment tribunals need to apply. This means that employment tribunals will not draw a distinction between legislation governing public authorities and private individuals when considering issues of human rights, as established by *X v Y* (Employment: Sex Offender) [2004]. It also means that issues of fair trials (Article 6) can enter considerations of privacy. Evidence produced by covert means may not be admissible when it gathering it breached Article 8. Also, the HRA requires the interpretation of case law in a way compatible with Article 8, which may have further implications.

Despite the broad reach of Article 8, privacy is not considered an absolute right. It is therefore interesting to see how the European Court of Human Rights has weighed privacy considerations when compared with employers' interests. The question of the balance of rights is important if we are to understand the implied status of privacy. There are a number of cases which show that the Court uses a wide notion of privacy. In *Niemitz v Germany* (1992) it held that the search of a lawyer's office impinged the "private life" and "home" of the lawyer. The court established in *Botta v Italy* (1998) that "private life" included a person's physical and psychological integrity. Another landmark case showing the breadth of privacy when weighed against other considerations is the above mentioned *Halford*. *Kopp v Switzerland* (1999) furthermore shows that the Court goes so far as to question the application of valid national law when it can lead to breaches of Article 8.

There are also examples of case law where the Court held infringements of privacy as acceptable. Such infringements must conform with s 2 of Article 8 and with the principle of proportionality. In *MS v Sweden* (1999) the claimant complained about the fact that medical data had been provided to an employer which had subsequently led to the termination of her employment. The court held that there had been no violation of Article 8 because the interference had had a legitimate aim and was necessary in a democratic society. Another concern accepted by the court as over-riding privacy concerns is the prevention of crime. In *Friedl v Austria* (1996) the question was whether the state had the right to photograph members of a demonstration even though Friedl was not prosecuted. It was held that Article 8 was not violated because prevention of disorder and crime are legitimate aims of the state and necessary in a democratic society. A similar security-related judgement was made in *Leander v Sweden* (1987) where security concerns outweighed privacy. Leander was refused permanent employment on the basis of information held in a secret police file. And while his Article 8 rights were affected, this was deemed lawful because of security concerns.

HRA 1998 and other National Law

The HRA applies to all other legislation and its interpretation through the courts. That means that it also applies to the DPA and RIPA. It has established that considerations of proportionality, awareness and expectation of privacy play a role when the right to privacy of an employee is balanced with interests of an employer. The question of balancing competing rights and interests is thus a central issue of DPA, RIPA, and HRA. However, the above section should have shown that the implied concept of privacy is different in the HRA. It recognises the limited nature of the right to privacy but the limits are more explicit and narrower than the ones in DPA and RIPA. Most importantly, purely economic interests will find it more difficult to stand the test of proportionality than substantial considerations such as prevention of crime and security.

Conclusion

This chapter has put forward the argument that an important contribution of the HRA which goes beyond the DPA and the RIPA is its implied wider concept of privacy. If this is the case then it stands to reason that it will strongly influence the further development of British law. Since the HRA is somehow located on a "higher" level of law, it most likely will permeate its implications into the British legal system.

The reason why the DPA and RIPA are based on different concepts of privacy than the HRA is probably the different legal tradition they stem from. Even though both DPA and RIPA are English laws that embody European Directives, they are much more closely linked to the English legal system. Their drafting and subsequent interpretation is based o n the English liberal tradition with its strong emphasis on free trade and autonomy of the economic sphere. The Convention, on the other side, is strongly linked with the continental European legal tradition where privacy is a well established right. In Germany, for example, the right to informational self-determination has been established by the Constitutional Court to have constitutional standing, despite the fact that it is not explicitly named in the constitution (http://de.wikipedia.org/wiki/Informationelle_Selbstbestimmung). One can thus argue that this recognised right to privacy as an intrinsic value is finding its way into the British legal system via the HRA. Whether this is desired and acknowledged by the British legislature and executive is a different question. However, it seems to be a step in regulating the economic sphere by importing rights, such as privacy, which in the liberal tradition are confined to the privacy of home and family.

The chapter has undertaken a conceptual analysis investigating philosophical and jurisprudential issues. It is thus not aimed at managerial applicability. That does not mean, however, that it has no managerial relevance. If the trajectory described in this chapter continues, then it stands to reason that privacy as a human right will gain further recognition, which will affect organisational standards and procedures. Managers will simply have to take employee privacy rights more seriously and they will have to undertake a re-evaluation of the justification of any privacy infringements, for example by employee monitoring.

One even could go one step further than this. Privacy is only seen as one human right among many in the ECHR. An increased recognition of privacy by employers could be interpreted to mean that employee (human) rights need to be strengthened. There is thus scope for speculation that the growing importance of privacy rights may pave the way for a further humanisation and democratisation of employment. Privacy could thus be seen as one aspect of the work improvement activities that have long captured the imagination of many scholars, such as the socio-technical approach in the field of information technology or information systems (Mumford, 2003). Such thoughts are of course speculative and one needs to realise that there is also strong resistance to the very idea of the Human Rights Act in the UK. However, the example of privacy shows that political processes can promote employee rights and that an understanding of conceptual foundations is crucial for appreciating how such political processes can be turned into societal reality. Research such as the work presented in this chapter can then be perceived as a contribution to overcoming traditional views of employment as the "master servant relationship of the early twentieth century" (J. Johnson, 2001, p. 168) and replace it with a more measured and equitable relationship which the European Convention of Human Rights stands for.

References

Arendt, H. (1958). *The human condition*. 2nd edition Chicago: The University of Chicago Press.

Brey, P. (2001). Disclosive computer ethics. In R.A. Spinello & H.T. Tavani (Eds.), *Readings in Cyberethics*. Sudbury, MA Jones and Bartlett, pp. 51-62.

Britz, J.J. (1999). Ethical guidelines for meeting the challenges of the information age. In L.J. Pourciau (Ed.), *Ethics and electronic information in the 21st century*. West Lafayette, Indiana: Purdue University Press, pp. 9-28.

Brown, W.S. (2000). Ontological security, existential anxiety and workplace privacy. *Journal of Business Ethics, 23*, 61-65.

Charlesworth, A.J. (2003). Privacy, personal information and employment. *Surveillance & Society, 1*(2), 217-222.

Elgesem, D. (2001). The structure of rights in directive 95/46/EC on the protection of individuals with regard to the processing of personal data and the free movement of such data. In R.A. Spinello & H.T. Tavani (Eds.), *Readings in cyberethics*. Sudbury, MA: Jones and Bartlett, pp. 350-377.

Elgesiem, D. (1996). Privacy, respect for persons, and risk. In C. Ess (Ed.), *Philosophical perspectives on computer-mediated communication*. Albany, NY: State University of New York Press, pp. 45-66.

Fleming, S. T. (2003). Biometrics: Past, present, and future. In R. Azari (Ed.), *Current security management & ethical issues of information technology*. Hershey, PA: IRM Press, pp. 111-132.

Foucault, M. (1975). *Surveiller et punir: Naissance de la prison*. Paris: Gallimard.

Gallivan, M. J. & Depledge, G. (2003): Trust, control and the role of interorganizational systems in electronic partnerships. *Information Systems Journal*, (13), 159-190.

Gavison, R. (1995). Privacy and limits of law. In D.G. Johnson & H. Nissenbaum (Eds.), *Computers, ethics & social values*. Upper Saddle River, NJ: Prentice Hall, pp. 332-351.

Goold, B. J. (2003). Public area surveillance and police work: The impact of CCTV on police behaviour and autonomy. *Surveillance & Society, 1*(2), 191-203,

Hoffmann-Riem, W. (2001). Wider die Geistespolizei. *Die Zeit Nr. 50*, June 12, p. 13.

Information Commissioner (2005). Privacy and Communication. Retrieved on August 30, 2005 from http://www.informationcommissioner.gov.uk/eventual. aspx?id=35

Introna, L. (2000): Privacy and the computer - Why we need privacy in the information society. In R. M. Baird, R. Ramsower, & S. E. Rosenbaum (Eds.), *Cyberethics - Social and moral issues in the computer age*. New York: Prometheus Books, pp. 188-199.

Introna, L. (2003). Workplace surveillance "is" unethical and unfair. *Surveillance & Society, 1*(2), 210-216.

Johnson, D. G. (2001). *Computer ethics*. 3rd edition Upper Saddle River, NJ: Prentice Hall.

Johnson, J. (2001). The potential impact of the Human Rights Act 1998 on employment law. *Business Law Review, 22*(7), 164-168.

Kant, I. (1961). *Grundlegung zur Metaphysik der Sitten*. Stuttgart: Reclam.

Mumford, E. (2003). *Redesigning human systems*. Hershey, PA: Information Science Publishing.

Nissenbaum, H. (2001). Toward an approach to privacy in public: Challenges of information technology. In R. A. Spinello & H. T. Tavani (Eds.), *Readings in cyberethics*. Sudbury, MA: Jones and Bartlett, pp. 392-403.

Nye, D. (2002). The "privacy in employment" critique: A consideration of some of the arguments for "ethical" HRM professional practice. *Business Ethics: A European Review, 11*(3), 224-232.

Privacy Rights Clearinghouse (2004). A review of the fair information principles: The foundation of privacy public policy. Retrieved September 1, 2005 from http://www.privacyrights.org/ar/fairinfo.htm

Rotenberg, M. (1998). Communications privacy: Implications for network design. In R. N. Stichler, & R. Hauptman (Eds.), *Ethics, information and technology: Readings*. Jefferson, NC: MacFarland & Company, pp.152-168.

Rule, J. B., McAdam, D., Stearns, L., & Uglow, D. (1995). Preserving individual autonomy in a information-oriented society. In D. G. Johnson, & H. Nissenbaum (Eds.), *Computers, ethics & social values*. Upper Saddle River, NJ: Prentice Hall, pp. 314-332.

Severson, R. J. (1997). *The principles of information ethics*. Armonk, NY/London: M. E. Sharpe.

Siau, K., Fui-Hoon Nah, F., & Teng, L. (2002). Acceptable Internet use policy. *Communications of the ACM, 45*(1), 75-79.

Sipior, J. C. & Ward, B. T. (1995). The ethical and legal quandary of e-mail privacy. *Communications of the ACM, 38*(12), 48-54.

Spinello, R. (1997). *Case studies in information and computer ethics.* Upper Saddle River, NJ: Prentice Hall.

Spinello, R. (2000). *Cyberethics: Morality and law in cyberspace.* London: Jones and Bartlett.

Stalder, F. (2002). Privacy is not the antidote to surveillance. *Surveillance & Society, 1*(1), 120-124.

Tavani, H. (2000). Privacy and security. In D. Langford (Ed.), *Internet ethics.* London: McMillan, pp. 65-89.

Tavani, H. T. & Moor, J. T. (2001). Privacy protection, control of information, and privacy-enhancing technologies. In R. A. Spinello, & H. T. Tavani (Eds.), *Readings in cyberethics.* Sudbury, MA: Jones and Bartlett, pp. 378-391.

Urbaczewski, A. & Jessup, L. M. (2002). Does electronic monitoring of employee Internet usage work? *Communications of the ACM, 45*(1), pp. 80-83.

van den Hoeven, J. (2001). Privacy and the varieties of informational wrongdoing. In R. A. Spinello, & H. T. Tavani (Eds.), *Readings in cyberethics.* Sudbury, MA: Jones and Bartlett, pp. 430-442.

Velasquez, M. (1998). *Business ethics: Concepts and cases.* 4th edition. Upper Saddle River, NJ: Prentice Hall.

Warren, S. & Brandeis, L. (1890). The right of privacy. *Harvard Law Review, 4*(5), 193-220.

Weckert, J. & Adeney, D. (1997). *Computer and information ethics.* Westport, CT/London: Greenwood Press.

Yoon, S.-H. (1996). Power online: A post-structuralist perspective on computer-mediated communication. In C. Ess (Ed.), *Philosophical perspectives on computer-mediated communication.* Albany, NY: State University of New York Press, pp. 171-196.

Statutes (in Chronological Order)

Medical Records Act 1988

Directive 95/46/EC of the European Parliament and of the Council of October 24, 1995 on the protection of individuals with regard to the processing of personal data and on the free movement of such data

Directive 97/46/EC, concerning the processing of personal data and the protection of privacy in the telecommunications sector

Human Rights Act 1998

Data Protection Act 1998

Regulation of Investigatory Powers Act 2000

Telecommunications (Lawful Business Practice) (Interception of Communications) Regulations 2000

Cases

Botta v Italy (21439/93), (1998) 26 E.H.R.R. 241

Douglas v Hello Ltd [2001] QB 967

Friedl v Austria: (1996) 21 E.H.R.R. 83

Halford v United Kingdom (20605/92) [1997] I.R.L.R. 471 (1997) 24 E.H.R.R. 523

Kopp v Switzerland, (1999) 27 E.H.R.R. 91

Leander v. Sweden (1987) 9 E.H.R.R. 433 ECHR

MS v. Sweden (1999) 28 E.H.R.R. 313 ECHR

Niemitz v Germany (1992) 16 E.H.R.R. 97

Valenzuela Contreras v Spain, (1999) 28 E.H.R.R. 483; [1998] H.R.C.D. 744 (ECHR)

X v Y (Employment: Sex Offender) [2004] EWCA Civ 662 ; [2004] I.C.R. 1634

Section III

Privacy and Technology

Chapter V

Privacy Preserving Data Mining:
Taxonomy of Existing Techniques

Madhu V. Ahluwalia,
University of Maryland, Baltimore County (UMBC), USA

Aryya Gangopadhyay,
University of Maryland, Baltimore County (UMBC), USA

Abstract

This chapter gives a synopsis of the techniques that exist in the area of privacy preserving data mining. Privacy preserving data mining is important because there is a need to develop accurate data mining models without using confidential data items in individual records. In providing a neat categorization of the current algorithms that preserve privacy for major data mining tasks, the authors hope that students, teachers and researchers can gain an understanding of this vast area and apply the knowledge gained to find new ways of simultaneously preserving privacy and conducting mining.

Introduction

Data mining, also referred to as knowledge discovery in databases (KDD), has been embraced with much enthusiasm by researchers and market analysts due to its promise to reveal information useful for scientific and technical research, business intelligence, and decision-support. A multitude of tools and techniques to facilitate knowledge discovery have therefore been developed and used increasingly. In the post 9/11 era, interest in data mining techniques has escalated due to their usefulness in counter-terrorism activities. However, the revelation of private information that may occur with data mining is unconstitutional. Laws have been enforced to forbid the U.S. Department of Defense to conduct data mining unless deemed necessary for security purposes. It also is mandatory that all operations of U.S. government agencies involving data mining ensure individual privacy. This conflict has given birth to a novel research direction known as the privacy preserving data mining.

Privacy preserving data mining entails two notions: 1) extracting or mining knowledge from large amounts of data and 2) performing data mining in such a way that data privacy is not compromised. This is a daunting task in an information age where we generate data with every move that we make. One challenge is the ease with which unauthorized parties can deduce confidential information from released data sources. Also known as the inference problem, this difficulty is discussed at length by Samarati (2001) and Sweeney (2002). Another major challenge is nailing down the concept of privacy. Whose privacy ought to be protected, an organization's or an individual's (Clifton, Kantarcioglu, & Vaidya, 2002)? How do we measure privacy (Pinkas, 2002)? What kind of adversarial models do we deal with (Gangopadhyay & Ahluwalia, 2006; Pinkas, 2002)? In addition to these issues that complicate the development of models and algorithms to preserve privacy, there are other legal, commercial, governmental, philosophical, ethical, and personal perspectives that need to be incorporated into the definition of privacy. However, this makes it even more difficult to address privacy concerns and provide a universally satisfactory resolution to the problem. Finally, all privacy-enhancing technologies influence the outcome of data mining to some extent. Depending on the modifications made to the data or the accuracy of information obtained from subjects who are unwilling to divulge their personal data due to privacy concerns, knowledge discovery tools might taint the results so that they exhibit lower accuracy or, sometimes even worse, false knowledge. Therefore, it is necessary to strike a balance between the need to privatize data and to retain the meaningfulness of the data mining results.

As mentioned earlier, there is no dearth of tools and techniques to achieve the twin goals of sufficient privacy of input data and sufficient utility of mining results in the data mining community today. There is, however, a lack of literature that provides an overview of the many different models and algorithms used in privacy preserving data mining (PPDM). Summarizing and classifying the various PPDM techniques presents a clear picture of the work performed in this area. It also allows future work to be classified in the right category and bring order to this new research area (see Figure 1 for taxonomy of current PPDM techniques). The last review presented in this context proposed a classification hierarchy to analyze the research accomplished in PPDM (Verykios et al., 2004a). Since then, no work has been published that provides taxonomy of the existing PPDM research. We extend the work presented in Verykios et al. (2004a). This work classifies the approaches taken to conduct PPDM, based on five dimensions: data distribution, data modification, data mining algorithm, data or rule hiding and privacy preservation. Data distribution refers to situations where all data is either located at a single site or a logically related database is stored over two or more physically independent sites. Data modification simply means altering the original values of a database. By data algorithm, Verykios et al. (2004a) refer to the data mining task, for example, association rule, classification or clustering, for which data is modified. Data or rule hiding presents a choice to either hide raw data or aggregated data. Finally, privacy preservation refers to the technique used to preserve data privacy. Data privacy is preserved when data are selectively modified, that is, only sensitive or confidential data values are altered. Data should be selectively modified in order to preserve the utility of the modified data. If all data are modified, all meaningful information is lost. The techniques used to preserve the privacy of data are heuristic-based, cryptography-based and reconstruction-based. Heuristic-based techniques are used because modifying data selectively or hiding aggregated data or rules is a complex or an NP-Hard problem. Cryptography-based techniques have only been applied where data is distributed at multiple sites. Finally, reconstruction-based techniques reconstruct the original distribution of the data from randomly perturbed data. One of the drawbacks of classifying existing work on PPDM in the way proposed by Verykios et al. (2004a) is that no PPDM technique falls clearly under any one particular dimension. Generally, PPDM algorithms can be grouped under more than one dimension; for instance heuristic-based techniques have been applied both for data and rule hiding (Gangopadhyay & Ahluwalia, 2006; Saygin, Verykios, & Clifton, 2001) and there are PPDM algorithms that work both for centralized as well as distributed data scenarios (Mukherjee, Chen, & Gangopadhyay, 2006). Moreover, a reconstruction-based technique may well be a heuristic technique (Agrawal & Srikant, 2000). We provide a true classification hierarchy that clearly categorizes most existing techniques.

Our contribution is to organize the current PPDM related work into well-defined groups to facilitate conceptualizing this broad field. This chapter provides an outline of the different approaches that have been taken to conduct data mining securely.

The solutions or algorithms that have been developed to mine data securely depend on the data-mining task at hand. We outline PPDM solutions for major data mining tasks, such as classification, association and clustering to give the reader an idea of the type of solutions that have been developed to solve each of these problems. We do not attempt to present all currently existing PPDM algorithms. Instead, each algorithm presented introduces a new perspective on simultaneously preserving privacy and conducting useful mining. We believe that our work will provide a broad and a solid foundation for new researchers in the field of PPDM and give them a strong foothold to start their careers as PPDM researchers. We start with a look at the meaning of privacy from different perspectives, and then discuss the theoretical background and taxonomy of the current privacy preserving data mining techniques. Different classes of privacy preserving data mining solutions are outlined briefly. Contrasts, comparisons and examples are given where necessary. Finally, we present the course of future research in the area of privacy preserving data mining.

An Overview of Privacy

Typically, privacy is viewed in the context of individual data; Alice must not know that Bob's annual salary is x amount of dollars or that he owns a property in downtown Washington D.C. If Alice cannot trace the salary/property attribute values to Bob, Bob's privacy is protected. Here, privacy is seen as the ability to identify an individual. However, there is another view. This view applies to data mining in general. Here, the aim is to learn from a body of data. The adversary gets to know the overall patterns and trends from the data collection. Known as corporate privacy in contrast to individual privacy, an adversary must be prevented from breaching this privacy. Individual and corporate privacy issues are discussed in (Clifton et al., 2002).

In matters of privacy, the intent, behavior and the knowledge base of an adversary are crucial. Each one of these aspects is discussed below to present an overall idea of how it relates to privacy. Adversarial intent or motive has been considered in the context of secure multi-party computation (SMC) (Pinkas, 2002) and (Lindell & Pinkas, 2002), where data sources are distributed across several sites. Adversarial behavior is also discussed under SMC (Clifton et al., 2002). Adversarial knowledge base has been discussed in the context of association rule mining (Gangopadhyay & Ahluwalia, 2006).

Multi-party computation settings distinguish between a semi-honest and a malicious adversary. Honesty and deception show the intent of parties involved. Semi-honest adversaries are simply curious. They obey protocol specifications, however are keen on analyzing the results of mining in order to obtain additional information from the analysis. Malicious adversaries purposely deviate from the specification in order to gain additional information. In the data mining setting, malicious adversaries can define their input to be an empty database. The output obtained is, then, the result of running an algorithm against the other party's database alone. This is a gross violation of the other party's confidential data. But unfortunately, the research community that deals with SMC offers no solution to prevent such an attack. It just assumes that real-life adversaries are semi-honest and not malicious. Further, it also assumes that in real-life, the parties involved in SMC do not collude. Non-collusion reflects a party's behavior in that it refrains from combining its data with any other party to gain meaningful information from the combined data. Consequently, there are no solutions to preserve privacy in a multi-party computation environment where adversaries collude and/or are malicious.

The knowledge base of adversaries is targeted in the context of association rule mining (Gangopadhyay & Ahluwalia, 2006). We present adversaries with different levels of prior knowledge and discuss the likelihood with which these adversaries can determine the raw data from the privatized data. We are of the opinion that prior knowledge about the instances (rows) of a database is more damaging than prior knowledge about the dimensions (columns) of a database. We also offer a solution to handle adversaries with and without prior knowledge.

We have given our readers pointers to literature where technical issues related to privacy are a topic. We have mentioned that privacy has many meanings. Especially online privacy issues, which are important in the data-mining realm, are intrinsically complex because they represent an intersection of legal, commercial, governmental, ethical, personal, and global perspectives. Since privacy considerations involve technical and non-technical issues, we agree with Clifton et al. (2002) that solutions to achieving privacy must also be technical and non-technical. From a technical perspective privacy solutions should be feasible in terms of efficiency, security, and usability. The SMC discussion above suggests that technical solutions can be formulated without limitations in usability by making appropriate assumptions. Of consequence is whether the non-technical means are used prudently to realize these assumptions in the real world (Clifton et al., 2002).

Privacy Preserving Data Mining (PPDM): Background and Techniques

Privacy preserving data mining (PPDM) has been proposed as a solution to the problem of violating privacy while sharing data for knowledge extraction. It is a relatively new research direction with the objective of developing algorithms to modify the original data or mining techniques in such a way that the process of mining does not reveal private data and private knowledge, yet remains useful in that the original data distributions and correlations stay sufficiently intact.

For a substantial amount of research in the field of PPDM, the focus has been on the pool of data. Regardless of whether the data pool is mined or not, a data holder's first concern is protecting this data from public scrutiny. The data holder's objective may be anything from simply publishing the data to sharing it with fellow researchers or passing it to a data miner for analysis or computing a secure function of his input jointly with others. As a custodian of the data, the owner of the data must do something to the collection, if it must go public. In general, one assumes that techniques need to be developed because data changes hands. In specific, it is assumed that the development of techniques only makes sense for data that is distributed, because privacy loses its relevance when data is collected and mined at the same site (Vaidya, Clifton, & Zhu, 2006). While this is true, we consider the domain of privacy preserving data mining to also encompass centralized data scenarios, as data controlled by a single owner might need to change hands for the purpose of mining. Centralization and distribution of data impact privacy preserving data mining solutions. This is because some data mining tasks such as classification and association

Figure 1. Classification of the existing privacy preserving data mining techniques

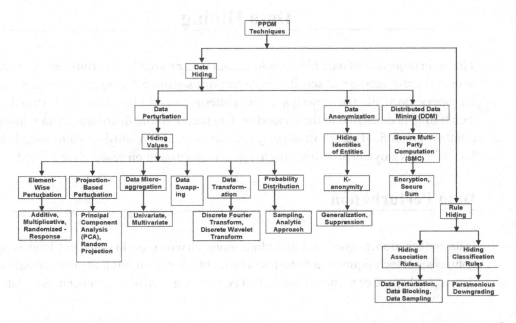

rules will give incorrect results, if the same data pool with different data distribution strategies were to be mined for good classifiers and robust association rules. Strictly defined, distributed data mining (DDM) is data mining where the data and mining are spread over many independent sites. Consider some vertically partitioned data, where attributes are dispersed over many sites. If we were to conduct association rule mining on such a data set, the correlations between attributes would not be captured as they would be captured from centralized data, and hence the association rules obtained would be distorted. So, different PPDM solutions have been developed based on whether the data is centralized or distributed. We will begin our journey across a multitude of techniques and methodologies with a classification of methods that have been adopted to secure data (see Figure 1).

The main work on privacy preserving data mining can be divided under two major categories: data hiding and rule hiding. While sensitive data is obfuscated in both categories, in the former original data patterns are disclosed whereas in the latter some original data patterns are hidden. The underlying data patterns are preserved in both instances. Data patterns are characteristics of data. These characteristics manifest themselves in different ways depending on the kind mining performed on the data; for instance in association rule mining, the underlying data patterns are the relationships among data items, in classification and cluster analysis, the properties of data that categorize data under one group or another are the data patterns. And in outlier analysis, rare events or noise in the data are considered data patterns.

Data Hiding

The main objective of data hiding is to design new protocols to perturb, anonymize or encrypt raw data so that sensitive data remains sensitive during and after the mining operation while the underlying data patterns can still be discovered. Broadly, data hiding is discussed in the context of data perturbation, distributed data mining (DDM), its sub-field secure multi-party computation (SMC), and data anonymization. We refer to Vaidya et al. (2006) for a detailed discussion on research in PPDM.

Data Perturbation

Data perturbation, a common data-hiding approach with roots in statistical databases, comprises of techniques that distort data element-wise, methods that project original data to a subspace or a smaller space, that is, reduce dimensions or attributes of data,

data microaggregation, data swapping, data transformation and probability distribution. The idea behind perturbing data is to solve data mining problems without access to actual data. Normally, original data distributions are reconstructed from known perturbing distributions to conduct mining. Data perturbation relies on the fact that users are not equally protective of all values in their records. Hence, while they may not mind giving true values of certain fields, they may agree to divulge some others only as modified values. Most data perturbation techniques have been applied to sensitive numerical attributes, although there are also examples of perturbing categorical and Boolean data in the literature.

Element-wise perturbation of numerical data, also known as random perturbation distorts sensitive attributes by adding or multiplying random noise directly to each value of the sensitive attribute. It is used to distort the most frequently encountered numerical or quantitative data type such as salary, age and account balances. **Additive perturbation** (AP) was first proposed by Agrawal and Srikant (2000). The technique involves using n independent and identically distributed sensitive random variables X_i, $i = 1, 2, ..., n$, each with the same distribution as the random variable X, and their n original data values $x_1, x_2, x_3, ..., x_n$. To hide these data values, n independent samples $y_1, y_2, y_3, ..., y_n$, are drawn from n independent random variables Y_i, $i = 1, 2, ..., n$, each with the same distribution as the random variable Y which has mean $\mu = 0$ and standard deviation σ. The owner of the data shares the perturbed values $x_1 + y_1, x_2 + y_2, x_3 + y_3, ..., x_n + y_n$ and the cumulative distribution function F_y for Y with the public. Agrawal and Srikant (2000) prove that it is possible to accurately estimate or reconstruct the distribution F_x of the original data X from the perturbed data. They provide this proof by using the reconstructed distributions to build decision tree classifiers and showing that the accuracy of these classifiers is comparable to the accuracy of classifiers built with the original data.

It may be noted that the exact distribution of X is impossible to reconstruct. In fact, the accuracy with which a data distribution can be estimated depends on the reconstruction algorithm, and one of the criticisms against Agrawal and Srikant's approach is that they ignore the convergence behavior of their proposed reconstruction algorithm. It is believed that a given reconstruction algorithm may not always converge, and even if it does, there is no guarantee that it provides a reasonable estimate of the original distribution. A reconstruction algorithm that not only converges, but also does so to the maximum likelihood estimate of the original distribution is proposed by Agrawal and Aggarwal (2001). It is known as the Expectation Maximization (EM) algorithm. For very large data sets, the EM algorithm reconstructs the distribution with little or almost no information loss.

Another objection raised against the method suggested by Agrawal and Srikant is that it does not account for the fact that knowing the original distribution can cause a breach of data privacy. Applying Agrawal and Srikant's technique to categorical data, Evfimevski, Srikant, Agrawal, and Gehrke (2002) simply replace each item in a transaction by a new item using probability p. They show that while it is feasible to recover association rules and preserve privacy of individual transactions using this approach, the discovered rules can be exploited to find whether an item was present or absent in the original transaction, which also constitutes a breach of data privacy. They, therefore, propose a technique, which in addition to replacing some items also inserts "false" items into a transaction such that one is as likely to see a "false" itemset as a "true" one.

Kargupta et al. (2003a, 2003b) question the use of additive perturbation and point out that random additive noise can be filtered out in many cases which is likely to compromise privacy. Therefore, any noise that is a function of the original values, such as noise that results from multiplication, is more likely to produce better results in terms of privacy protection. **Multiplicative perturbation (MP)** is performed either by multiplying a random number r_i with *mean* = 1 and small variance with each data element x_i (Muralidhar, Batrah, & Kirs, 1995) or by first taking a log of data elements, adding random noise, and then taking the antilog of the noise-added data (Kim & Winkler, 2003).

There are inherent differences in the additive and the multiplicative data perturbation approaches. While the results of AP are independent of the original data values, that is, the expected level of perturbation is the same regardless of whether the original data value is 10 or 100, MP results in values that are in proportion to the original values, that is, the distortion is less if the original value is 10 and more if it is 100. In general, the higher the variance of the perturbing variable, the higher the distortion and privacy.

While both additive and multiplicative perturbation techniques preserve data distributions, neither one of them preserves distances between data points. This means that they cannot be used for simple yet efficient and widely used Euclidean distance-based mining algorithms such as k-means clustering[1] and k-nearest neighbor classification[2]. Distance measures are commonly used for computing the dissimilarity of objects described by variables, that is, objects are clustered based on the distance between them. Adding or multiplying random noise to attributes or variables can remove clusters and neighbors (also defined by distance from the given object) where they do initially exist. Oliveira and Zaïane (2003a) and Chen and Liu (2005), therefore, discuss the use of random rotation for privacy preserving clustering and classification. A multiplicative perturbation technique that preserves distance on expectation and is also ideal for large-scale data mining is discussed in Liu et al. (2006a, 2006b). Element-wise random perturbation also does not fair well for association rule mining of numerical data, because association rules depend on individual data values and if these data values are perturbed element-wise, associations and correlations between them go hey wire. This is also pointed out by Wilson and Rosen (2003), who empirically prove that perturbation, regardless of whether it is additive or multiplicative alters the relationships between confidential and non-confidential attributes.

Element-wise perturbation of categorical data is used by Evfimevski et al. (2002) to conduct secure mining of association rules and by Du and Zahn (2003) to build decision-tree classifiers. The technique used is known as **Randomized Response** and is mainly suitable to perturb categorical data. It was first proposed by Warner (1965) to hide sensitive responses in an interview. The technique allows interviewees to furnish confidential information only in terms of a probability.

Projection-based perturbation involves the use of techniques such as Principal Component Analysis (PCA) and random projection to map the original data to a subspace in such a way that properties of the original space remain intact. PCA is a common technique for finding patterns, that is, highlighting similarities and differences in data of high dimension. To analyze a high dimensional data set, PCA simplifies it by reducing it to lower dimensions. Thus, if a data set consists of N tuples and K dimensions, PCA searches for k-dimensional orthogonal, that is, perpendicular vectors that can best be used to represent the data, where $k \leq K$. The orthogonal vectors are obtained by factoring a covariance matrix into eigenvalues and eigenvectors. The highest eigenvalue is the first principle component of the data set and the eigenvector associated with it accounts for the maximum variability in the data. Lowest eigenvalues and their corresponding eigenvectors may be ignored without much loss of information. PCA has been used as a data reconstruction technique in (Huang, Du, & Chen, 2005) and random projection is proposed by Liu et al. (2006b) to preserves both the correlations between attributes as well as the Euclidean distances between data vectors by multiplying the original data with a lower dimension random matrix. While PCA is unsuitable for large, high-dimensional data due to computational complexity of the order $O(K^2N) + O(K^3)$, random projection is not suitable for small data sets because of loss of orthogonality in data of small size. Additionally, the randomness associated with the performance of random projection is not practical in real world.

Data microaggregation is a widely used technique to hide sensitive microdata by aggregating records into groups and releasing the mean of the group to which the sensitive data belong, rather than the sensitive values themselves. In addition to the techniques mentioned here, all techniques listed under data transformation below are also examples of data microaggregation. Data microaggregation has been used to secure statistical databases in (Domingo-Ferrer & Mateo-Sanz, 2002; Hansen & Mukherjee, 2003). While Hansen and Mukherjee (2003) present an efficient polynomial algorithm to optimally aggregate and privatize a single attribute, Domingo-Ferrer and Mateo- Sanz (2002) consider a clustering technique to aggregate all attributes, in addition to univariate (single attribute) microaggregation. Multivariate (multiple attributes) microaggregation has also been proposed in the area of data mining by Aggarwal and Yu (2004) and lately by Li and Sarkar (2006). Aggarwal and Yu (2004) split the original data into clusters of predefined size. The mean, covariance and correlations of the original data are preserved in these clusters and are used to simulate replacement data, which is disseminated for mining purposes. Li and Sarkar (2006) propose a kd-tree based approach for PPDM. This method involves selecting a non-sensitive attribute with the largest variance from all given numeric attributes and using the median of the selected attribute to divide a given data set into two groups. Selecting an attribute with the largest variance to start the splitting process optimizes the process of partitioning. Splitting data at the median of the selected attribute ensures that within each subset, the numeric values of the attribute selected to split data are relatively close to each other. The splitting process continues on the partitioned sets until the leaf nodes contain the values for the sensitive attribute. Sensitive and homogeneous values at each leaf are then replaced by the average of all sensitive values at that leaf. Both of these multivariate microaggregation techniques have their limitations. Aggarwal and Yu's (2004) approach does not guarantee that only records closest in statistical characteristics comprise a group. The kd-tree based approach does not discuss why and how patterns are preserved.

Data swapping was first proposed by Dalenius and Reiss (1982). The idea behind swapping is to interchange values of specific records in such a way that the underlying statistics remains unchanged. This ensures that the data retains its utility for mining purposes even after the sensitive values are masked.

Data transformation techniques make use of mathematical approaches such as Fourier-related transforms and Discrete Wavelet Transform (DWT) to break a signal (or an original series) down into coefficients that retain most of the characteristics of the original series and those that do not. The former are called high-energy/low-frequency coefficients and the latter are known as low-energy/high-frequency coefficients. Most transformation techniques applied in the area of PPDM exploit this feature to preserve high-energy coefficients and thus preserve the original data patterns and discard low-energy coefficients, and thereby mask sensitive data values.

Mukherjee et al. (2006) recommend using Discrete Cosine Transform (DCT) to prepare data for Euclidean distance-based mining algorithms such as k-means clustering and k-nearest neighbor classification. The distance preserving property of the DCT is exploited. Some level of data privacy is also offered by manipulating the DCT coefficients, but a rigorous analysis of privacy is missing. Bapna and

Gangopadhyay (2006) test the performance of the Haar and the Daub-4 wavelet transforms in preserving privacy and maintaining the predictive accuracies of SVMs[3], Naive Bayesian and Adaptive Bayesian networks. Their experiments show that both transforms preserve the privacy for real valued data, in addition to preserving the classification patterns.

Preserving association patterns and privacy is the focus of yet another wavelet-based PPDM approach presented at the Secure Knowledge Management (SKM) workshop in 2006 (Gangopadhyay & Ahluwalia, 2006). Here, properties of wavelets preserve the underlying patterns of the original data in the privatized data shared for mining. A sort-, transform- and duplicate- operation of the data preprocessing phase also protects the privacy of the original data values either by changing the values or anonymizing them in the transformed data. Our approach of using only the row-orthonormal matrix reduces the row dimension of the data by a factor of two, compared to the approach of Liu et al. (2006a, 2006b), which reduces the attribute dimensions. Our methodology thus maintains the attribute semantics in the privatized dataset. The distribution of the privatized values has a mean that is identical to the mean of the distribution of the original values, but a standard deviation that is lower than the standard deviation of the original values due to the aggregation effect of wavelet transforms. The noise-reducing aggregation effect of wavelets is exploited to preserve the patterns. This is also an advantage over the random perturbation techniques discussed above, which distort the relationships between attributes. Apart from these advantages, the wavelet decomposition completes in a single iteration over the data set. It requires little storage for each sequence and linear time[4] in the length of the sequence. Wavelet transforms are therefore scalable in contrast to PCA, which is data-dependent. Any change in the data size affects the covariance between variables and hence the PCA calculations.

Probability distribution involves replacing the original data either by a sample from the same population and probability distribution as the original data (Liew, Choi, & Liew, 1985) or by its distribution (Lefons, Silvestri, & Tangorra, 1983). Liew et al. (1985) prove that privacy of a single sensitive numerical or categorical attribute can be protected by using the attribute's probability distribution to simulate new values and by substituting the original attribute values by new values. Lefons et al. (1983) propose an analytical approach for protecting multi-numerical sensitive attributes by substituting the original sensitive database by its probability distribution.

Distributed Data Mining (DDM)

Distributed data mining assumes multiple data sources in contrast to a single central data source that is typically taken for granted in KDD (Knowledge Discovery in Databases). However, collection of data in central warehouses to support data mining makes misuse easier. Therefore, it is imperative that PPDM techniques that operate over distributed data also be developed. This need is also justified in light of the fact that due to communication bottlenecks, existing algorithms for distributed data mining focus mainly on the problem of efficiently getting the mining results from different data sources rather than addressing data holders' privacy concerns.

A simple approach to data mining over distributed sources without sharing data is to run the data mining algorithms at each site independently and combine the results (Prodromidis, Chan, & Stolfo, 2000). However, undetected cross-site data correlations and diversity as well as data redundancy at different sites produce globally invalid results. Still, the fact that global mining models are built by exchanging only a small amount of information among participating sites makes DDM a logical choice for many distributed PPDM tasks. Vaidya and Clifton (2003) address distributed PPDM for k-means clustering, Kantarcıoglu and Vaidya (2003) for building a Naïve Bayes classifier, and Vaidya and Clifton (2002) for mining association rules.

Secure multi-party computation (SMC) considers the problem of two or more non-trusting parties who wish to jointly compute a common function of their local inputs without revealing their local private data. In the SMC context, a protocol guarantees privacy only if each of the participating parties learn nothing more from this exercise other than their own input and the output of the joint function. Yao (1982) gives an example of two millionaires who wish to know who is richer without inadvertently finding out any additional information about each other's wealth. Other examples include knowledge discovery among intelligent services of different countries and collaboration among corporations without revealing trade secrets (Kantarcioglu & Clifton, 2003). It should be noted that SMC is a special case of DDM.

Yao (1982) first investigated secure two-party computation and developed a provably secure solution. Goldreich (1998), then, extended this to multiparty computation and showed that computing a function privately is equivalent to computing it securely. The framework thus developed for secure multiparty computation eventually considered several different security models.

The main building block of secure computation is Oblivious Transfer[5]. Typically, encryption is used, but it is no way mandated, for example, the secure sum protocol uses no encryption, yet is secure from the SMC perspective. Several PPDM algorithms for distributed data have been developed using SMC protocols (Kantarcioglu & Vaiya, 2003; Prodromidis et al., 2000; Vaidya & Clifton, 2003).

Figure 2. De-identified health data

		Quasi-identifiers		Sensitive
	ZIP	Age	Native-Country	Ailment
1	20872	19	Saudi Arabia	Sleep disorder
2	20863	17	Canada	Sleep disorder
3	20864	18	United States	Substance Abuse
4	20874	18	United States	Substance Abuse
5	21240	36	India	Asthma
6	21250	37	China	Sleep disorder
7	21260	31	Russia	Substance Abuse
8	21275	32	Canada	Substance Abuse
9	20862	21	United States	Asthma
10	20868	28	Japan	Asthma
11	20873	27	Canada	Asthma
12	20879	29	Germany	Asthma

Data Anonymization

Data anonymization aims at preventing an adversary from mapping sensitive information to an individual with the help of information provided in attributes known as quasi-identifiers. In other words, anonymization prevents individual identifiability. Samarati and Sweeney (1998) introduced the k-anonymity model which allows hiding identities of entities whose sensitive data must stay private. As an example, consider a databases containing sensitive information on health and finances of various individuals. Such information is routinely made public by removing primary identifiers such as names and SSNs. However, by putting together some partial identifiers such as zip, gender, race, nationality, or native-country, snoopers can easily re-identify de-identified records. This happens because some other agency publishes data, which, although devoid of sensitive information, contains primary and partial identifiers. For instance, Bob's school publishes Bob's and his classmates' name, zip, age, native-country, and the different teams they all play baseball for, in a monthly sports magazine. There is nothing confidential about the teams Bob play for, but linking this information with a supposedly privatized table such as the one in Figure 2, it is easy to find out the ailment Bob has. This is because the concatenation of zip, age and native-country in the health data can be matched with the same in the sports data that announces his name. The k-anonymity model (Samarati & Sweeney, 1998) and (Sweeney, 2002) amends this violation of Bob's privacy.

Figure 3. Health data with k = 4

	Quasi-identifiers			Sensitive
	ZIP	Age	N-C	Ailment
1	208**	< 20	*	Sleep disorder
2	208**	< 20	*	Sleep disorder
3	208**	< 20	*	Substance Abuse
4	208**	< 20	*	Substance Abuse
5	212**	>= 30	*	Asthma
6	212**	>= 30	*	Sleep disorder
7	212**	>= 30	*	Substance Abuse
8	212**	>= 30	*	Substance Abuse
9	208**	2*	*	Asthma
10	208**	2*	*	Asthma
11	208**	2*	*	Asthma
12	208**	2*	*	Asthma

Figure 4. Health data with k = 4 and l = 3

	Quasi-identifiers			Sensitive
	ZIP	Age	N-C	Ailment
1	208**	<= 30	*	Sleep disorder
4	208**	<= 30	*	Substance Abuse
9	208**	<= 30	*	Asthma
10	208**	<= 30	*	Asthma
5	212**	> 30	*	Asthma
6	212**	> 30	*	Sleep disorder
7	212**	> 30	*	Substance Abuse
8	212**	> 30	*	Substance Abuse
2	208**	<= 30	*	Sleep disorder
3	208**	<= 30	*	Substance Abuse
11	208**	<= 30	*	Asthma
12	208**	<= 30	*	Asthma

Since quasi-identifiers link sensitive data to explicit identifiers, quasi-identifiers are generalized or suppressed in such a way that they become identical for k records, where $k > 1$. For any particular data hiding solution k is a constant. Generalization involves substituting some or all attribute values with a coarse value as shown in Figure 3. Here, among other generalizations, zip codes 20872, 20874, 20863 and 20864 of Figure 2 are generalized to 208** and age in the range 17-19 has a coarse value < 20. Suppression involves withdrawing all information, as shown for the attribute native-country in Figure 3, or suppressing a tuple completely. Hence, Figure 3 is a 4-anonymous version of Figure 2. It shows similar values of quasi-identifiers in 3 sets of 4 tuples. If any combination of quasi-identifiers in the 4-anonymized data shown in Figure 3 now maps to a record in the sports database, so do $k - 1$ (4-1) other records of Figure 3.

The k anonymization model is not full-proof. If an antagonistic teammate knows that Bob lives in the zip code 20862 and is a 21-year-old from the US, he concludes that Bob suffers from asthma. This is because the sensitive property, asthma is homogenous for all four records 9, 10, 11, 12. Alternatively, a malicious teammate may know that Bob's friend is a 19-year-old from Saudi Arabia, who currently lives in the zip code 20872. Based on the background knowledge that Saudi men abstain from drugs and alcohol, he concludes with near certainty that Bob's friend suffers from sleep disorder.

If, however, the values of the sensitive attributes are well represented in each group, the adversary will never know that Bob, a 21-year-old from the zip code 20862 has asthma (see Figure 4, rows 2, 3, 11, and 12). Likewise, even if he knows that Bob's friend is extremely unlikely to have an alcohol or a drug related problem, he is still unsure whether this friend has asthma or a sleep disorder. This solution is proposed by Machanavajjhala, Gehrke, Kifer, and Venkitasubramaniam (2006). It recommends l-diversity in addition to k anonymity to ensure that all tuples with similar values of quasi-identifiers have diverse values for their sensitive attributes. Figure 4 is a 3-diverse version of Figure 3 where k stands for anonymity in quasi-identifiers and l for diversity in sensitive attributes.

Many algorithms have been proposed to refine the k-anonymity framework. While some start from the original dataset and systematically generalize it into one that is k-anonymous (Hundpool & Willenborg, 1996) and (Sweeny, 1998), others start with a fully generalized data set and systematically specialize it into one that is minimally k-anonymous (Bayardo & Agrawal, 2005).

Generalization and suppression techniques affect the accuracy and completeness of data respectively. They are the costs incurred for privacy. Hence, the larger the value of k, the more private the data because the probability of correct inference due to linking cannot exceed $1/k$, however, at the same time the larger the loss of information. Therefore, optimal k-anonymity that generalizes and suppresses minimally to ensure anonymity is required (Meyerson & Williams, 2004). k-anonymization is optimum based on some quantifiable cost metric. Cost metrics measure information loss due to generalization and suppression. Some useful cost metrics are proposed by Bayardo and Agrawal (2005) and Iyengar (2002). In general, most algorithms developed to k-anonymize data sets run in polynomial or exponential time and do not provide any guarantees of optimality.

Rule Hiding

Privacy preserving data mining techniques discussed thus far obscure data items that are an input of data mining algorithms. There is, however, also a need to obscure the output of mining data when this output threatens to reveal sensitive data and/or sensitive knowledge. Functional dependencies between sensitive and non-sensitive data items, deductive rules, and an adversary's prior knowledge allow inferences that divulge sensitive data and/or knowledge from the results of mining. Rule hiding is the approach taken to sanitize data in such a way that some specific association, classification and clustering rules are hidden, but the underlying patterns can still be discovered. Since a considerable amount of work in the category of output privacy deals with preventing the disclosure of sensitive association rules, data altering techniques that hinder mining confidential attribute correlations are discussed next.

Association rule mining deals with the problem of selectively hiding sensitive associative rules while minimizing the impact on non-sensitive rules. The objective is to guarantee an appropriate balance between hiding restrictive patterns and disclosing non-restrictive ones, that is, between privacy and knowledge discovery. However, Atallah, Elmagarmid, Ibrahim, and Verykios (1999) formally prove that finding such an optimal solution for sensitive large item sets is NP-hard. Therefore, a number of heuristic approaches have been suggested in the literature to address optimal sanitization in the context of association rule mining. These approaches alter or sanitize the original data set using distortion, blocking, or sampling techniques.

An association rule is characterized by two measures, the support and the confidence. In general, algorithms for the discovery of association rules detect only rules whose support and confidence are higher than a minimum threshold value. Such rules are known as "significant rules." Therefore, one simple and effective way to hide some sensitive patterns is to modify a given database so that the support and confidence of a given set of sensitive rules mined from the database, decreases below the minimum support and confidence values. Most heuristic approaches aim at doing this. Although, it is not clear how one would know what these user-specified thresholds could be. The distortion approaches (Oliveira & Zaïane, 2003; Verykios et al., 2004b) introduce false values to the data sets to reduce the significance of a given set of rules. However, these false values reduce the trustworthiness and usefulness of the data sets as well. The blocking approach (Saygin et al., 2001) overcomes this problem by introducing unknown values to the data set, but does not minimize the information loss, nor does it prevent privacy breaches on the modified data set. Knowledge of the blocking approach applied allows an adversary to infer actual values of all unknown values and hence discover confidential association rules. The sampling approach (Clifton, 2000) releases only subsets of the source database to hide sensitive rules.

For classification rule hiding a technique known as parsimonious downgrading is discussed in Chang & Moskowitz (1998). This technique disallows building strong classifiers from the data that is downgraded, that is, trimmed of sensitive values.

In sum, this section gives an overview of the existing techniques to analyze large amounts of data without seeing confidential data and information. It notes that the main consideration in PPDM is hiding both sensitive data and sensitive knowledge.

Future Trends

Despite the emergence of an ever-increasing number of privacy-preserving data mining techniques, their application in the real world is virtually non-existent. Vaidya et al. (2006) suggest continued research in the area to address this problem. Specifically, they recommend putting together a toolkit that will enable solving data mining tasks that are inconceivable due to privacy concerns. We support such a project with enthusiasm; however we feel that most of the current methods in privacy preserving data mining are only applicable to instance-based learning methods such as k -nearest neighbor classification, naïve Bayesian classifier, and support vector machines that do not make the structures that are learned explicit. For a comprehensive guide to privacy preserving data mining tools and techniques, it is therefore necessary to focus on the creation of privacy preserving techniques that suit data mining tasks with explicit knowledge representation such as quantitative association rules, decision trees, and Bayesian networks. We have taken the first step in this direction in our work (Gangopadhyay & Ahluwalia, 2006) based on using wavelet transforms for privacy preserving association rule mining. Modification and extension of this work to build decision tree classifiers, Bayesian networks, and regression trees will provide a general wavelet-based framework to solve data mining tasks that produce explicit knowledge structures in their output. The development of a toolkit replete with privacy preserving approaches for data mining tasks with explicit as well as non-explicit knowledge structures will constitute a giant leap in raising the awareness, adoption and integration of the privacy preserving data mining technology with existing applications.

Another issue that deserves much attention is defining the concept of privacy. A central issue in privacy preserving data mining is privacy itself. Ironically, while a variety of privacy preserving data mining techniques have emerged in a matter of a few years, an in-depth analysis of privacy is lost in the mire of algorithm development. A rigorous analysis of privacy requires that frameworks supporting easier privacy proofs be developed. Such frameworks should consider the intent, behavior and prior knowledge of an adversary. Once again, we point to our work (Gangopadhyay & Ahluwalia, 2006) that considers privacy in the context of varying amount of prior knowledge of an adversary. Apart from these technically challenging issues, there are also non-technical issues involving legal, commercial, governmental, and ethical perspectives that need to be considered to strengthen the concept of privacy.

References

Aggarwal, C. C., & Yu, P. S. (2004). *A condensation approach to privacy preserving data mining*. Paper presented at the 9th International Conference on Extending Database Technology, pp. 183-199.

Aggarwal, G., Feder, T., Kenthapadi, K., Motwani, R., Panigrahy, R., Thomas, D., & Zhu, A. (2005). Anonymizing tables. In *Proceedings of the 10th International Conference on Database Theory* (ICDT 2005) (vol. 3363, pp. 246-258).

Aggarwal, G., Feder, T., Kenthapadi, K., Motwani, R., Panigrahy, R., Thomas, D., & Zhu, A. (2005b). Approximation Algorithms for k-Anonymity, *Journal of Privacy Technology*.

Agrawal, D., & Aggarwal, C. (2001). *On the design and quantification of privacy preserving data mining algorithms*. Paper presented at the 20th ACM SIG-MOD SIGACT-SIGART Symposium on Principles of Database Systems, pp. 247-255.

Agrawal, R., & Srikant, R. (2000). *Privacy preserving data mining*. Paper presented at the 2000 ACM SIGMOD Conference on Management of Data, pp. 439-450.

Atallah, M. J., Elmagarmid, A. K., Ibrahim, M., & Verykios, V. S. (1999). *Disclosure limitation of sensitive rules*. Paper presented at the IEEE Knowledge and Data Engineering Workshop, pp. 45-52.

Bapna, S., & Gangopadhyay, A. (2006). A wavelet-based approach to preserve privacy for classification mining. *Decision Sciences, 37*(4), 623-642.

Bayardo, R. J., & Agrawal, R. (2005). *Data privacy through optimal k-anonymization*. Paper presented at the ICDE, pp. 217-228.

Bingham, E.& Mannila, H. (2001). *Random projection in dimensionality reduction: applications to image and text data*. Paper presented at the 7th ACM SIGKDD International Conference on Knowledge Discovery and Data Mining, San Francisco, CA.

Chang, L. & Moskowitz, I. S. (1998). *Parsimonious Downgrading and Decision Tree Applied to Inference Problem*. Paper presented at the New Security Paradigms Workshop, Charlottsville, VA.

Chen, K., & Liu, L. (2005). *A Random Rotation Perturbation Approach to Privacy-Preserving Data Classification*. Paper presented at the IEEE Intl. Conf on Data Mining 2005, Houston, TX, pp. 589–592.

Clifton, C. (2000). Using sample size to limit exposure to data mining. *Journal of Computer Security, 8*(4), 281-307.

Clifton, C., Kantarcioglu, M. & Vaidya, J. (2002). *Defining privacy for data mining*. Paper presented at the Proceedings of the Next Generation Data Mining Workshop.

Dalenius, T., & Reiss, S. P. (1982). Data-swapping: A technique for disclosure control. *Journal of Statistical Planning and Inference, 6*, 73-85.

Domingo-Ferrer, J., & Mateo-Sanz, J. M. (2002). Practical data-oriented microaggregation for statistical disclosure control. *IEEE Transactions on Knowledge and Data Engineering, 14*(1), 189-201.

Du, W., & Zhan, Z. (2003). U*sing randomized response techniques for privacy preserving data mining*. Paper presented at the 9th ACM SIGKDD International Conference on Knowledge Discovery and Data Mining, pp. 505-510

Evfimevski, A., Srikant, R., Agrawal, R., & Gehrke, J. (July 2002). *Privacy preserving mining of association rules*. Paper presented at the 8th ACM SIGKDD International Conference on Knowledge Discovery and Data Mining (KDD'02), pp. 217-228.

Gangopadhyay, A. &. Ahluwalia, M. (2006). *Preserving privacy in mining association rules*. Paper presented at the The Second Secure Knowledge Management Workshop (SKM), Brooklyn, New York.

Goldreich, O. (1998). *Secure multi-party computation*. Unpublished manuscript, Department of computer science and applied mathematics, Weizmann Institute of Science, Rehovot, Israel.

Han, J. & Kamber. M. (2001). *Data mining: Concepts and techniques.* Morgan Kaufmann.

Hansen, S. L., & Mukherjee, S. (2003). A polynomial algorithm for optimal univariate microaggregation. *Knowledge and Data Engineering, IEEE Transactions on, 15*(4), 1043-1044.

Huang, Z., Du, W., & Chen, B. (2005). *Deriving private information from randomized data.* In Proceedings of the 2005 ACM SIGMOD international conference on management of data, pp. 37-48).

Hundpool, A. & W., L. (1996). *Mu-Argus and Tau Argus: Software for statisical disclosure control.* Third International Seminar on Statistical Confidentiality.

Iyengar, V. (2002). *Transforming data to satisfy privacy constraints.* Paper presented at the Proc. of the Eighth ACM SIGKDD Int'l Conf. on Knowledge Discovery and Data Mining, pp. 279 - 288.

Kantarcioglu, M., & Clifton, C. (2004). Privacy-preserving distributed mining of association rules on horizontally partitioned data. *IEEE Transactions on Knowledge and Data Engineering, 16*(9), 1026-1037.

Kantarcioglu, M. & Vaidya., J. (2003). *Privacy preserving naïve bayes classifier for horizontally partitioned data.* Paper presented at the IEEE ICDM Workshop on Privacy Preserving Data Mining,

Kargupta, H., Datta, S., Wang, Q., & Sivakumar, K. (2003a). *On the privacy preserving properties of random data perturbation techniques.* Paper presented at the ICDM.

Kargupta, H., Datta, S., Wang, Q., & Sivakumar, K. (2003b). Random data perturbation techniques and privacy preserving data mining. *Knowledge and Information Systems, 7*(4), 387-414.

Kim, J. J., & Winkler, W. E. (2003). *Multiplicative noise for masking continuous data* (No. #2003-01). Washington D.C.: Statistical Research Division, U.S. Bureau of the Census.

Lefons, E., Silvestri, A. & Tangorra, F. (1983). *An analytic approach to statistical databases.* Paper presented at the 9th International Conference on Very Large Data Bases, pp. 260-274.

Li, X. B., & Sarkar, S. (2006). A tree-based data perturbation approach for privacy-preserving data mining. *IEEE Transactions on Knowledge and Data Engineering, 18*(9), 1278-1283.

Liew, C. K., Choi, U. J., & Liew, C. J. (1985). A data distortion by probability distribution. *ACM Transactions on Database Systems* (TODS), *10*(3), 395-411.

Lindell, Y. & P., B. (2002). Privacy preserving data mining. *Journal of Cryptology*, *15*(3), 177-206.

Liu, K., Giannella, C. & Kargupta, H. (2006a). An attacker's view of distance preserving maps for privacy preserving data mining. In *Proceedings of the 10th European Conference on Principles and Practice of Knowledge Discovery in Databases* (PKDD'06).

Liu, K., Kargupta, H., & Ryan, J. (2006b). Random projection-based multiplicative data perturbation for privacy preserving distributed data mining. *IEEE Transactions on Knowledge and Data Engineering*, *18*(1), 92-106.

Machanavajjhala, A., Gehrke, J., Kifer, D., & Venkitasubramaniam, M. (2006). *l-diversity: Privacy beyond k-anonymity*. Paper presented at the 22nd IEEE International Conference on Data Engineering (ICDE 2006), p. 24.

Meyerson, A. &. Williams, R. (2003). *General k-anonymization is hard*. Carnegie Mellon School of Computer Science Tech Report.

Meyerson, A. & Williams, R. (2004). *On the complexity of optimal k-anonymity*. ACM PODS Conference.

Mukherjee, S., Chen, Z. & Gangopadhyay. A. (2006). A privacy preserving technique for Euclidean distance-based mining algorithms using Fourier-related transforms. *VLDB Journal*, *15*(4), 292-315.

Muralidhar, K., Batrah, D., & Kirs, P. J. (1995). Accessibility, security, and accuracy in statistical databases: The case for the multiplicative fixed data perturbation approach. *Management Science*, *41*(9), 1549-1564.

Oliveira, S. R. M., & Zaïane, O. R. (2003a). *Privacy preserving clustering by data transformation*. Paper presented at the 18th Brazilian Symposium on Databases, pp. 304–318.

Oliveira, S. R. M., & Zaïane, O. R. (2003b). *Protecting sensitive knowledge by data sanitization*. Paper presented at the proc. of the 3rd IEEE International Confernce on Data Mining, pp. 613-616.

Oliveira, S., & Zaiane, O. R. (2004). *Privacy-preserving clustering by object similarity-based representation and dimensionality reduction transformation*. Paper presented at the Workshop on Privacy and Security Aspects of Data Mining (PSDM'04).

Pinkas, B. (2002). Cryptographic techniques for privacy preserving data mining. *SIGKDD Explorations*, *4*(2), 12-19.

Prodromidis, A., Chan, P. & Stolfo, S. (2000). Advances in distributed and parallel knowledge discovery, In *Meta-learning in distributed data mining systems: Issues and approaches*. AAAI/MIT Press.

Samarati, P. (2001). Protecting respondents' identities in microdata release. *TKDE*, *13*(6), 1010-1027.

Samarati, P. & Sweeney, L. (1998). *Protecting privacy when disclosing information: k-Anonymity and its enforcement through generalization and suppression*, Proceedings of the IEEE Symposium on Research in Security and Privacy.

Saygin, Y., Verykios, V. S., & Clifton, C. (2001). Using unknowns to prevent discovery of association rules. *ACM SIGMOD Record*, *30*(4), 45-54.

Sweeney, L. (1998). Datafly: *A system for providing anonymity in medical data.* Database Security XI: Status and Prospects, 11th Int'l Conf. on Database Security, 356-381.

Sweeney, L. (2002a). Achieving k-anonymity privacy protection using generalization and suppression. *International Journal on Uncertainty, Fuzziness and Knowledge-based Systems*, *10*(5), 571-588.

Sweeney, L. (2002b). K-anonymity: A model for protecting privacy. *International Journal on Uncertainty, Fuzziness and Knowledge-based Systems*, *10*(5), 557-570.

Vaidya, J. S., & Clifton, C. (2002). Privacy preserving association rule mining in vertically partitioned data. Paper presented at the 8th ACM SIGKDD International *Conference on Knowledge Discovery and Data Mining*, pp. 639-644.

Vaidya, J. S. &. Clifton, C. (2003). *Privacy-preserving k-means clustering over vertically partitioned data.* Paper presented at the 9th ACM SIGKDD International Conference on Knowledge Discovery and Data Mining, pp. 206-215.

Vaidya, J., Clifton, C., & Zhu, Y. (2006). *Privacy preserving data mining.* New York, Springer.

Verykios, V. S., Bertino, E., Fovino, I. N., Provenza, L. P., Saygin, Y., & Theodoridis, Y. (2004a). State-of-the-art in privacy preserving data mining. *ACM SIGMOD Record*, *33*(1), 50-57.

Verykios, V. S., Elmagarmid, A. K., Elisa, B., Saygin, Y., & Elena, D. (2004b). Association rule hiding. *IEEE Transactions on Knowledge and Data Engineering*, *16*(4), 434-447.

Warner, S. (1965). Randomized response: A survey technique for eliminating evasive answer bias. *Journal of the American Statistical Association*, *60*(309), 63-69.

Wilson, R. L., & Rosen, P. A. (2003). Protecting data through 'perturbation' techniques: The impact on knowledge discovery in databases. *Journal of Database Management*, *14*(2), 14-26.

Witten, I.H. a & Frank, E. (2005). *Data mining: Practical machine learning tools and techniques*. 2nd ed. Morgan Kaufmann Publishers.

Yao, A. C. (1982). *Protocols for secure computation*. Paper presented at the IEEE Symposium on Foundations of Computer Science.

Yi, B. K., & Faloutsos, C. (2000). *Fast time sequence indexing for arbitrary lp norms*. Proceedings of 26th International Conference on Very Large Data Bases, pp. 385-394.

Endnotes

[1] k-means is a partitioning method to divide a set of n objects (records) into k clusters so that the resulting intra-cluster similarity is high but the inter-cluster similarity is low. Cluster similarity is measured based on the distance between the object and the mean value of the objects in a cluster. The objective is to minimize the squared error (Han & Kamber, 2001).

[2] k-nearest neighbor classifiers assign an unknown sample (record) to a class that is most common among its nearest neighbors. A "neighbor" is defined in terms of Euclidean distance (Han & Kamber, 2001).

[3]   Support vector machines (SVMs) are a set of related supervised learning methods that can perform binary classification (pattern recognition) and real valued function approximation (regression estimation) tasks. They belong to a family of generalized linear classifiers.

[4]   A discrete wavelet transform (DWT) halves the data at each iteration resulting in fast computational speed. The DWT algorithm has a complexity of $O(n)$ for an input vector of length n.

[5]   Oblivious transfer is a one of the most important protocol for secure computation. It is based on cryptography.

Chapter VI

Rational Concerns about Biometric Technology:
Security and Privacy

Yue Liu, University of Oslo, Norway

Abstract

The increasing use of biometric technology is often accompanied by grandiose claims about its ability to enhance security and the debate over the perceived threats that it poses to the notion of privacy. By focusing on the security and privacy concerns the biometric technology raises, this chapter gives critical analysis on the complexities involved through rational discussions, technology assessment and case examples. It clarifies the prevalent misconceptions concerning the biometric technology and finds that biometric technology alone can not provide an answer to security issues. The inherent nature of biometric technology provides enormous potential for undermining privacy. However, security and privacy are not necessarily two contradictory concepts where biometrics is concerned.

Introduction

Across the various contexts in which it is applied, **biometric technology** (hereinafter also termed "biometrics") raises multiple **rational** concerns. This chapter aims to give some idea of the complexities involved in biometric technology by focusing on the **security** and **privacy** concerns it raises. To what extent do and will biometrics affect privacy and security? Exactly what is the special nature of biometric data compared with other personal data? Is the increasing use of biometrics just a question of "balance" or "trade-off" between privacy and security? It is with these sorts of questions that this chapter is concerned. In tackling such questions, the chapter also aims to clarify some of the misconceptions that inform parts of the legal discourse around biometrics.

Background

Put simply, biometric technology involves the use of automated methods for verifying or recognizing the identity of a living person based on their physiological or behavioral characteristics.[1] Most people get to know about biometrics from what they observe in science-fiction movies like Spielberg's *Minority Report*, in which people are regularly subjected to eye scans for identification, control, and/or advertising purposes when they take public transport, enter office buildings, or simply walk in the street. Seductive claims also have been made about the ability of biometrics to defeat terrorism and organized crime. Biometrics figure increasingly as the centerpiece technology in implementing counterterrorist policy.

Much technology inspires not only hope but also fears, and development of innovative technology has almost always raised new legal concerns. This is certainly true in the case of biometric technology. Increasing use of biometrics has led to fears of an acceleration in the speed at which our society becomes a surveillance society with scant room for personal privacy and autonomy. Doubts also have been raised about the level of security that increased use of biometrics can actually deliver. It further is feared that the loss of privacy may lead in turn to a host of other problems, such as increasing social stigma, discrimination in employment, barriers to gaining health insurance and the like. With the growing use of biometrics, it is of paramount importance that discussions about the ethical, social, and legal implications of the technology take place. In such discussions so far, privacy and security concerns often have figured prominently[2]—and for good reason, as this chapter highlights.

To begin with, the chapter outlines the special nature of biometric technology and biometric data. It then discusses the relationship between biometric technology and privacy. Following on from this, the relationship between biometric technology and security is analyzed in the light of technology assessment and case examples. The final section presents conclusions.

Special Nature of Biometric Technology and Biometric Data

Generally speaking, biometric technology involves using part of the human body or behavior as mechanisms for human identification or authentication. Fingerprints, irises, faces, retinal images, veins, and voice patterns are all examples of actual or potential biometric identifiers. These data are collected by sensor devices, transformed into digital representations and then, via algorithms, the data become so-called biometric templates. These biometric templates are then stored somewhere for later matching against other collected data.[3]

As indicated above, the matching can be used for either authentication or identification purposes. Biometric authentication involves a "one-to-one" (1:1) search whereby a live biometric sample presented by a person is compared to a stored sample previously collected from that individual, and the match confirmed (Cavoukian et al., 2007, p.6) This sort of match answers the question, "is the person who they claim to be?" In this process, no searching or matching of a central database is necessary, though such a database can still be used, provided that some other identifiable data, such as a serial number, are used to "look up" an individual in the database. In contrast, biometric identification refers to the ability of a computer system to uniquely distinguish an individual from a larger set of individual biometric records on file (Cavoukian et al., 2007, p.6) This also is known as a "one-to–many" (1: N) search designed to determine identity based solely on biometric information. This sort of match intends to answer the question, "who is the person?" To support identification, a central database must be built containing a large set of individual biometric records. So theoretically a central database of biometric records could allow the system controller to find out who the person is provided the latter is already registered in the central database. During the matching process, the live biometric sample will be compared with all the registered biometric samples in the central database. Upon a successful match, the person's identity will be released from the central database.

The "Bio" Nature of Biometric Data and Biometric Technology

Compared with knowledge-based or token-based methods of authentication/identification, biometric technology is unique in the sense that it uses part of the human body or behavior as the basis of the authentication and/or identification method. What is the significance of the fact that a body-related characteristic is used as an identifier or verifier? To answer this question, we need to first investigate what biometric data are.

Genetic and Health Related Data

The raw information at the heart of biometrics is by its very nature personal. It is intimately connected to the individual concerned (the "information subject"). If one takes the most popularly used and known form of biometric information—fingerprints—as an example, it has been claimed that even a fingerprint too smudged for ordinary identification could provide forensic scientists with sufficient DNA[4] to construct a "DNA fingerprint,"[5] thus providing investigators with a powerful new tool in the search for evidence of crime. Moreover, there is a rather large body of work tracing the genetic history of population groups through the study of their fingerprint-pattern characteristics.[6] It also has been proven that there exists a mysterious linkage between certain fingerprints and certain birth defects and diseases (Woodward 1997b). From examining a person's retina or iris, a medical expert can determine that the person may be suffering from common afflictions like diabetes, arteriosclerosis and hypertension; further, unique diseases of the iris and the retina also can be detected.[7]

However, the informational status of the biometric templates that are generated and applied in identification/authentication systems is somewhat unclear. As indicated above, a biometric template is digitalized data of a person's physical or behavioral characteristics, not the raw information or image itself. The template is generated by application of a given algorithm. There is as yet no solid proof that the templates themselves actually contain medical information, though they are very likely to do so. A template is as unique as the raw biometric data from which it is generated. It is possible to reconstruct from a template the part of the raw biometric data that is used for creating the template.[8] Generally, templates will only contain information necessary for comparison. However, what is necessary for comparison is neither fixed nor predetermined. As the biometric template should retain the special features of the raw biometric data as identifier, it unavoidably becomes necessary to include some relatively unique and permanent features which are related to genetic information or health (Bromba, 2006). However, it is not certain if the information captured in the template would be sufficient for medical diagnostic purposes. Nonetheless, it is still reasonable to claim that there is generally a link between biometric information and genetic and/or health information. The latter has been widely recognized as sensitive information about individuals and, quite often, their relatives.

It has been claimed by one observer that "[b]iometrics is not a branch of medicine but rather a special form of mathematical and statistical science" (Ploeg,1999, p. 43). The same observer goes on to state that "we should perhaps not expect to be able to determine any intrinsic meaning of biometric data, or the biometric body in general, but investigate quite specifically what uses and practices biometrics will become part of" (Ploeg,1999, p. 43). According to another observer, "with almost all biometric devices, there is virtually no personal information contained therein. From my fingerprint, you can not tell my gender, you can not tell my height, my age, or my weight. There is far less personal information exposed by giving you my fingerprint than by showing you my driver's license" (Wayman, 1998, p. 11).

At first glance, these statements seem to make sense, but they are based on the assumption that technology will stop developing. It is true that there is presently no verified report about easy and fast disclosure of health information directly from biometric data; moreover, possible linkage between biometric data and health information is only reported in relation to certain kinds of biometric data. Yet as the technology develops, it is quite reasonable to predict that such disclosure and linkage may be possible in the future. The potential is clearly present. Hence, the long-term problem here is whether the data controller (i.e., the person/organization in possession of the biometric data) *will* make such linkages.

It could be countered that even if biometric data have the potential to disclose sensitive information, they are not designed to be used that way, so there is no need to worry. However, biometric features make it difficult to escape from situations of misuse in the hands of individuals or governments – with or without malicious intent. "Function creep" can occur; indeed, many privacy advocates contend that function creep is inevitable. For example, Simon Davies opines:

The history of identification systems throughout the world provides evidence of "function creep"—application to additional purposes not announced, or perhaps even intended, at the commencement of the scheme. [...] The existence of a relatively high-integrity scheme would create irresistible temptations to apply it widely, and inter-relate many hitherto separate collections of personal information (Davies, 1994, p. 44).

An additional purpose can be valuable or detrimental to society, but the point here is that the potential of biometric data cannot be restricted by the purposes for which they are/were originally used. There is no absolute guarantee that biometric data will not be used for revealing health information, though it would take a significant technological shift to go from current biometric systems to systems that reveal such information (Feldman, 2003, p. 667).

Relative Uniqueness, Universality, and Stability

The common idea that biometric technologies are capable of identifying individuals through one-to-many matching across large, shared databases is based on the belief that biometric identifiers are unique and universal. It has been established that each person is supposed to have unique fingerprints, irises, face, and DNA. For instance, fingerprints have been used in forensic research for many years as purportedly unique identifiers of criminals. However, some recent cases have revealed that identification by use of fingerprints has been overturned on appeal at court.[9] In fact, the "uniqueness" of a fingerprint in forensic science remains an *assumption* without watertight proof.[10] The belief that latent fingerprints can be matched to a single person is "the product of probabilistic intuitions widely shared among fingerprint examiners, not of scientific research. There is no justification based on conventional science, no theoretical model, statistics, or an empirical validation process" (Stoney, 1997, p. 72).

Nevertheless, it is worth pointing out that there is not yet any solid proof that this *assumption* is wrong either. Hence, it may be true that fingerprints *per se* are unique. Yet it does not necessarily follow that the latent fingerprint is unique too. Neither does it necessarily follow that the thumbprint template which simply extracted certain features of a raw thumbprint image can be as unique as its origin. The template may be based on a blurred, dirty, and/or incomplete image of the thumbprint which may affect the accuracy of the collected biometric information, making the biometric template's uniqueness more difficult to be guaranteed. Even DNA, which is widely recognized as the most accurate biometric identifier, is exposed to criticisms. While it is true that each individual (except identical twins) has a unique sequence of genes,[11] in the forensic DNA identification process, only a subset of a particular gene is used for identification. Hence, Professor Alec Jeffreys, a pioneer in developing modern DNA testing techniques, has pointed out that DNA testing is not an infallible proof of identity:

[m]odern commercial DNA profiling compares a number of genetic markers—often five or 10—to calculate a likelihood that the sample belongs to a given individual. Jeffreys estimates the probability of two individuals' DNA profiles matching in the most commonly used tests at between one in a billion or one in a trillion, "which sounds very good indeed until you start thinking about large DNA databases". In a database of 2.5 million people, a one-in-a-billion probability becomes a one-in-400 chance of at least one match. (Lawless, 2004)

It is not guaranteed either that the fuzzy biometric template which actually uses just part of the DNA sequence will be 100 percent unique. Thus, the "uniqueness" of biometric data is not absolute, it is *relative*. The biometric templates generated from them are even less unique due to their "fuzzy" nature. This also affects the stability of the biometric data.

The universality of biometrics also is relative. One problem with the widespread use of biometrics is that there are few biometrics—apart from DNA—that everyone has. Not everyone will have a particular biometric trait, or an individual's biometric trait may be significantly different from the "normal" expected trait. For example, some people may be missing fingerprints due to skin disease—a factor which may cause more problems when enrolling a large population into a fingerprint-based register. Discrimination concerns also may be raised in such a case. Therefore, a large-scale biometric scheme will usually need to utilise more than one biometric—for example, both fingerprint and face—to ensure that all people can be enrolled in it.

Unlike passwords or tokens, biometric identifiers are by their nature supposed to be stable over time; without such stability, their utility will be quite limited.[12] Fingerprints, irises, and DNA are widely recognized as stable biometrics, while faces, keystroke, and voice patterns give rise to more skepticism concerning their stability as people get older. However, the stability of even the former types of biometric data is not absolute. For instance, the image of a fingerprint pattern is "plastic" and does not remain as stable as is commonly imagined. Each time that you place your fingerprint on a finger-scanner, the pattern may appear to be the same from a short distance, but there are actually small differences in the pattern due to dryness, moisture, and elasticity conditions of the skin. Moreover, cuts and scratches can alter the pattern. It is thus likened somewhat to "fuzzy" decryption (Dorizzi, 2005). Iris, another popular biometric measurement, though has been regarded as highly accurate; the process unfortunately also suffers from difficulty in consistently obtaining a valid image. The iris often is occluded by eyelids and eye lashes. In addition, data collection also can be hindered by specular reflections in uncontrolled lighting situations (Retica Systems Inc., 2005). Similar problems also apply to other relatively stable biometric identifiers.

The Automatic Nature of Biometric Data and Biometric Technology

Using parts of the human body as a key clue to identity is not new. It is reported, for example, that in China in the 2nd century BC, thumbprints were put on clay seals used on important documents, while in 14th century Persia, various official government papers bore fingerprint impressions (Scottish Criminal Record Office, 2002). Nonetheless, biometrics is presently defined as involving automated techniques. The "automated" aspect is said to differentiate biometrics from the larger field of human identification science (Wayman, Jain, Maltoni, & Maio, 2004, p. 1). The biometric data are processed by computers and the "bio" information is put in digital form from the moment of its creation. Compared to visual comparison of signatures or photographs, biometric identification is ostensibly less fallible and potentially much faster, and because of its "automatic" nature, biometric technology is endowed with great potential.

Fuzzy Unicode of Individual

Biometric data have been compared with various other more traditional bio-centric forms of identification such as a photograph and thumbprint that use ink print.[13] It may appear that biometric data are not or at least less logically distinguishable from these images with regard to technical or moral values.[14] Yet is this true?

Unlike a primitive image from which one can dissociate oneself by various superficial means, the biometric data are regarded as more reliable and accurate, though it has been recognized that there is presently no perfectly accurate biometric technology.[15] The relatively stable biometric data are associated with relatively unique biometric features. As a fuzzy match is deployed during verification or identification, the main characteristics of certain biometric features are digitalized regardless of superficial changes.

For example, the hand geometry technology uses a 32,000-pixel CCD digital camera to record the three-dimensional shape of the hand from silhouetted images projected within the scanner. The scanner does not register surface details, such as fingerprints, lines, scars, dirt, or fingernails.[16] The scanner typically takes over 90 measurements of the length, width, thickness, and surface area of the hand and four fingers. Superficial changes that may affect correct identification are thus controlled for at the outset. In this sense, the biometric data are akin to a fuzzy unicode of each individual, by which the body becomes an object the identity of which is determined by mathematical means. Indeed, as it has been commented, "it is possible that the expanding technologies may eventually mean that the most important identity information may be that contained in a digital body" (Harte, 2004, p. 57). This unicode is deemed to be relatively accurate and reliable and controlled by data controllers. Since it is a digital representation of a human being, like all other computerized data, it is easily reproduced, transmitted, analyzed and re-used while the data subjects have little if any de-facto control over it, and little if any knowledge of it or of how it will affect them in the real world. As Feldman warns: "There is a danger that the more we focus on biological characteristics, the less we remember the intangible aspects of a person's character. As a result perhaps we should be wary of moving toward a society that constantly reduces us to our biological characteristics" (Feldman, 2003, p. 666).

Furthermore, the fuzzy nature of the Unicode differentiates it from other existing personal code such as personal numbers or passport codes, because it is regarded as relatively stable and permanent. Certainly, while personal numbers and passport codes are unique for each person, when compromised they are technically very easy to change and they have no "physical" linkage to a certain individual.

Possible Linking and Tracking

John D. Woodward has pointed out that "if facial recognition or other biometric databases become interlinked, then the threat to information privacy has the potential to increase significantly" (Woodward, 2001a, p. 7). Biometric identifiers provide the possibility of interlinking disparate databases in an automatic way, worldwide. This possibility depends, of course, to some extent on standardization. Currently, the interoperability of biometric identifiers is still weak,[17] but there is a trend towards increased interoperability. For instance, the International Civil Aviation Organization (ICAO) has recently adopted a global, harmonized standard for the integration of biometric identification information into passports and other machine-readable travel documents.[18] In addition, the US National Institute of Standards and Technology (NIST) has published a "Common Biometric Exchange File Format" (CBEFF) aimed at promoting interoperability of biometric-based application programs and systems developed by different vendors.[19]

Thus, the balkanization of biometric information is on its way to becoming a thing of the past and it can be reasonably expected that the linkage and tracking ability of biometrics will be developed and utilized to the full. It is not difficult to imagine a future situation in which an individual must use one particular standard biometric to pay tax, enter the workplace, go shopping, travel, and obtain medical service. Such use of a biometric "key" would open up for possible linkage of each of these records and transactions, allowing in turn government or business to compile a comprehensive profile of the individual's actions.

Biometric ID systems have the potential to locate and track people physically. Of course, tracking can be accomplished without biometrics. For example, RFID, personal numbers, passwords, and IP addresses can all be used as identifiers for tracking purposes. Initially, then, tracking potential seems not to be a special characteristic of biometric technology. Nevertheless, such technology does create a heightened level of concern here as it may facilitate surreptitious tracking.

Traditional authentication methods using, for example, passwords or tokens, rely on either something one knows or something one has, while RFID tags usually have to be on something one wears or carries. The collection of such information requires to some extent the data subjects to *do* something, but the biometric features of individuals are not secrets, and are something individuals inherently have. Certain biometric features like fingerprints and facial images can be collected without the cooperation of the data subjects. However, due to its inaccuracy, particularly in large-scale matching, much current biometric technology does not have the capacity to facilitate accurate large-scale tracking. Such tracking may be more feasible to realize sooner by using RFID technology. Nevertheless, the potential still exists for improvement of biometric technology to allow for its use in large-scale tracking in the future or to realize large-scale tracking with the help of RFID. We see an example of this mutuality in the recent development of biometrically enhanced passports that are fitted with RFID tags.

Privacy and Biometric Technology

In the international law of human rights "privacy" is clearly and unambiguously established as a fundamental right to be protected. Article 12 of the 1948 Universal Declaration of Human Rights (UDHR) and Article 17 of the 1966 International Covenant on Civil and Political Rights (ICCPR) both stipulate that "no one shall be subjected to arbitrary interference with his privacy, family, home, or correspondence, nor to attacks upon his honor and reputation." Article 8 of the 1950 European Convention on Human Rights and Fundamental Freedoms (ECHR) is to similar effect, stating that:

1. Everyone has the right to respect for his private and family life, his home and his correspondence.

2.   There shall be no interference by a public authority with the exercise of this right except such as is in accordance with the law and is necessary in a democratic society in the interests of national security, public safety or the economic well-being of the country, for the prevention of disorder or crime, for the protection of health or morals, or for the protection of the rights and freedoms of others.

The issue of privacy is central to concerns about biometric technology. To evaluate the various privacy concerns requires, in the first instance, an understanding of what privacy and privacy rights entail. Amongst the most influential explications of the privacy concept are the following:

- The right to be let alone (Warren & Brandeis, 1890-91).
- A state of limited accessibility: secrecy, solitude, and anonymity (Gavison, 1980, p. 428).
- An interest in control of information about oneself (Westin, 1967).

As the variation in these explications shows, privacy is a multifaceted concept that is difficult to define using one simple formulation. However, this difficulty should not imply that privacy concerns lack importance. As it has been pointed out, "in one sense, all human rights are aspects of the right to privacy" (Fernando, 1981, p. 184).

Engaging in extensive debate over the exact meaning of the privacy concept is unnecessary for the purpose of this paper. It suffices to note that there are two main groups of privacy-related interests that are directly pertinent when labelling the issues that have arisen in contemporary discussion about the ethical and legal implications of biometrics. The first group of interests falls under the rubric of "informational privacy" and concerns the control of personal information. These interests give rise to attempts to establish rules governing the collection and handling of personal data. Information privacy lies at the very heart of discussion over biometrics. The second interest group falls under the rubric of "physical privacy" and concerns protection from intrusive searches and seizures, particularly the protection of persons' physical selves against invasive procedures, such as drug testing and body-cavity searches (Fernando, 1981, p. 184). The widespread use of biometric technology may invade our physical privacy in several ways. Furthermore, it also is relevant to introduce the discussion of property rights in privacy, a discussion which concerns the appropriation and ownership of interests in human personality (Rothstein, 1997, p. 33). Property notions are not necessarily inherent in privacy interests but it could perhaps be useful for the law to use the doctrine of property to protect individuals' biometric information in the private sector—a possibility explored further on in this paper.

Information Privacy and Biometric Technology

Regardless of whether an individual voluntarily provides a biometric identifier or is forced to surrender it, they are giving up information about themselves (Woodward, 1997a). Once collected, the control over the biometric data shifts from the data subject to the organisation that has access to the data. As biometric data are intimately linked with individuals in a relatively unique way, the data are usually considered as "personal."[20] Information privacy is, therefore, the most significant concern about biometric technology. Losing control over personal data is the main challenge biometric technology poses to informational privacy, and such loss can occur in various ways.

Unnecessary Collection

A central principle of rules grounded in informational privacy is that the collection of personal information should be limited to those data that are necessary and relevant to a legitimate purpose (Bygrave, 2002, p. 59 et seq.). As mentioned previously, it is difficult to predict exactly what biometric technology may bring but it is clear that it has broad potential to provide an extremely convenient and cost effective way to gather and analyse biometric data. From such data, it is potentially possible to get health, racial and medical information about individuals which is not necessary for authentication or identification. This possibility also raises concerns about the possible disclosure and/or compromise of such information.

Another feature of biometric data is that they can identify people. However, when the purpose of collecting the biometric data is just for authentication, and there is little or no benefit in having stronger user identification, it is difficult to justify the collection of strong unique identifiers.

An interesting point of view concerning the health-related nature of biometric technology is that this technology benefits those who do not go to the doctor, and helps them to detect diseases earlier. (Young, 2001).This claim may make sense to some extent, but the problem here is that, unless the data subjects are clearly informed about this potential and consent to it, the technology effectively makes compulsory a kind of medical check-up, thus undermining individuals' privacy interests in relation to their own health information, including their interest in being able to choose not to know certain details of health status. Moreover, the data controllers here have ordinarily no legal right to collect and keep such health information. Neither do they ordinarily have the right to share the information with other interested organizations, such as insurance companies.

Unauthorised Collection

Biometric technology together with use of RFID augments the possibility of covertly collecting biometric information. Although only certain biometric patterns—for example, facial, voice, and/or gait—can be theoretically collected without the data subject's knowledge, with help of RFID-enhanced cards, which are now being widely used for storing biometric data,[21] all kinds of personal data (including biometric data) could be collected, tracked and profiled without the data subject's knowledge or consent.

In the US legal context, the criterion of "reasonable expectation of privacy" developed pursuant to the Fourth Amendment to the US Constitution,[22] has been invoked in commentary on the legality of the use of facial-recognition systems and other biometric technologies in public spaces. Here, our primary focus will be on facial-recognition technology, in part because it has great potential to be widely used for covert collection of biometric information. It is important to note, though, that the facial recognition technology currently used in practice has very high False Acceptance Rates (FAR) and False Rejection Rates (FRR) (UKPS, 2005, p.7). Concomitantly, that technology is presently not yet sophisticated enough to usefully undertake large-scale matching tasks, especially for the purpose of accurate identification in such settings as airports or subway stations. As it has been commented, "[t]he area where the technology has not yet matured is in the area of surveillance. Contrary to the portrayal of face recognition technology and popular culture, the technology cannot easily pick a face out of a crowd" (Kenyon, n.d.).

This notwithstanding, the legal commentator Susan McCoy has discussed some of the privacy implications of such technology when it is incorporated into video surveillance systems aimed at public places, and it is worth considering her views here. A point of departure of her discussion is the argument that people have a reduced expectation of privacy in public settings, and, additionally, that no individual can reasonably expect to maintain privacy in a public forum.[23] Based on an analysis of the US Supreme Court decisions in *Katz*[24] and *Kyllo*[25], McCoy goes on to list several reasons why facial-recognition technology of the above-mentioned kind does not violate privacy:[26]

1. Facial recognition is implemented in an open field; there cannot be a reasonable expectation of privacy in public places.

2. Video surveillance is not a search regulated by the Fourth Amendment because it is capturing exactly what the naked eye beholds. "What a person knowingly exposes to the public ... is not a subject of fourth Amendment protection."

3. Facial-recognition technology only identifies criminals who are filed in the system's databases and does not automatically store images of ordinary citizens who pass by its line of sight. Biometric technology was designed to locate and identify criminal not innocent people.

4. Facial-recognition technology does not violate privacy rights because it is merely making a procedure currently used by law enforcement more efficient; it employs the same procedures as fingerprinting. If fingerprinting does not violate the constitution, then neither should facial-recognition technology.

Each of these four arguments is very interesting. At the same time, they expose misunderstanding of the technologies concerned as well as a controversial understanding of the legal doctrine of "reasonable expectation of privacy." There is no simple answer as to whether facial recognition violates the right to privacy, as it can be applied in various ways, some of which are more privacy friendly (or privacy invasive) than others. However, it is generally the case that a covert facial-recognition system is inherently privacy invasive. Below I try to respond to McCoy's arguments one by one, in the order they are listed above.

Argument 1: Certainly, it is true that people generally have less reasonable expectations of privacy in public places. Yet, as also emphasised in leading case law, notions of privacy remain tied to the individual rather than certain categories of space.[29] Although the Court in the *Kyllo* decision invalidated the disputed search because it occurred in and around a residential home, it does not follow that there is no privacy or reasonable expectation of privacy in existence at other places; it only means that the protection of privacy in respect of those other places may be more controversial or difficult to uphold. Whether the use of facial-recognition systems or other biometric technology in public places violates privacy depends on specific applications.

Argument 2: McCoy seems to equate facial-recognition technology with video surveillance technology in general, at least in respect of the privacy interests at stake. It is important to remember, though, that the two technologies are not fully commensurate. Traditional standard video surveillance may not equal the facial-recognition technology we are talking about here. Traditional video surveillance, beginning with simple closed-circuit television monitoring (CCTV), is just a means of observing at a distance what happens or happened in a certain area. With the development of video cassette recorders, the observations were able to be preserved on tapes. Later, digital computer technology has come to be used for capturing, storing and analysing more detailed images. Only the latest generation of video surveillance tools includes automated facial recognition. The software for facial recognition captures an image of a person's face, generates a template of that image, then compares the template against other templates saved in a database. In so doing, the software makes it possible for law enforcement officials to proactively target and monitor persons of interest. Theoretically, the software can be used for both authentication (one-to-one) and identification (one-to-many) matches, but, in practice, it is usually used for screening (negative identification).[30] Generally, unless a special privacy-friendly system is applied, the templates stored in the database also are linked with other personal information.

In the facial-recognition scheme, people are checked against a database one by one; they are, as a point of departure, all under suspicion, and for no apparent reason. By contrast, in traditional standard video surveillance, people typically only are subjected to attention and identification when they actually commit some crime (or carry out other non-conformist actions). Criminals generally will not attract special attention under such systems if they do not do something overtly illegal. For example, video surveillance of a shop will usually not pick out a person unless they steal goods; otherwise they remain anonymous and are not checked against some database. Whether this kind of surveillance is problematic is outside the scope of this paper, but it is clear that the biometric facial-recognition system is more privacy invasive than traditional standard video surveillance.

McCoy claims that one knowingly exposes one's face to the public. This claim is true to some extent, yet it is arguably true also that facial-recognition technology greatly expands the exposure of one's face and enables access to considerably more information than would be available to the ordinary public view of a police officer; the technology reveals, in other words, more than just a face. And, generally, the data subjects will effectively have no right to refuse such scanning. Even if an individual expects to be watched by law enforcement officers, they do not generally expect to be automatically checked against a particular database and then monitored if a positive match is made. But this is what happens with facial-recognition systems: "To the extent that the database tracks the location of faces it successfully scans, it operates as a homing device on a person's movements" (Brogan, 2002).

In this context, it is pertinent to note the recent case of *Peck v. UK*,[31] decided by the European Court of Human Rights. The case dealt with a situation in which a man, Mr. Peck, was filmed by a CCTV camera installed by a municipal authority to oversee a railway station. Peck was filmed some distance from the station, without his knowledge. The CCTV footage of him was later disclosed to the mass media, again without his knowledge, and then televised. The Court held that both the initial CCTV recording of Mr. Peck and the subsequent disclosure to the mass media constituted an interference with his rights under Article 8 of the European Convention on Human Rights (ECHR), despite the fact that Mr. Peck was filmed when out in a public area. This aspect of the decision appears to widen the scope of what is regarded as private under ECHR Article 8. The Court suggests that a distinction can be drawn between different sets of public circumstances, partly on the basis of the extent to which the surveillance concerned is reasonably foreseeable on the part of the subject. As a result, public authorities—at least in Europe—cannot assume that filming of subjects in a public place will not under any circumstances engage privacy rights, even when simple CCTV is being used.

Argument 3: It may be argued that only an individual whose templates happen to match the saved data on a criminal is recorded and monitored. However, this also is another naïve misconception of the biometric technology. Facial recognition can be used both for authentication and identification, depending on the kind of application adopted. There are various ways the facial recognition system can be applied. For verification purposes, all individuals' facial images are collected. This is the case, for instance, with the US VISIT program: visitors' facial images are collected in advance, and saved in a huge database with their other personal data. The facial recognition can be used in various ways, and the level of privacy invasiveness depends on how it is applied. There is no absolute guarantee that innocent people's biometric templates will not be stored, or matched for verifying their identity and tracking their movements. McCoy's argument only makes some sense when facial recognition is only used for screening; however, even in this case there is high possibility of FAR when the current state of the technology is used in the public space, due to the poor quality of the technology. This means a lot of innocent people's personal information also will be generated even when facial recognition technology is not being misused.

Argument 4: It is claimed above that facial recognition technology is "merely making a procedure currently used by law enforcement more efficient" and the comparison is drawn to fingerprint matching in forensic science and the police officer standing in a crowd with a stack of mug shots, comparing them to people who walk past him. However, the efficiency increase actually changes the effect of the activity on privacy. In the traditional manual settings described above, whether this be fingerprint matching in the laboratory or police detection by the roadside, there is a certain delimited time, place, purpose, and reason for the checking process. The policeman stands at a certain place checking people pass by because it is a place where a certain criminal or criminals may appear, and it is only these persons who are the aim of the surveillance. The latent fingerprint is matched against the database of criminals because it is collected at a crime scene. However, the automated facial-recognition system has far more comprehensive surveillance capability: it may be operated at many places, around the clock, and for a broad range of purposes. While the present limitations of such systems mean that they tend currently not to be aimed at finding one or several particular criminals out of thousands of people passing by, they may be implemented with such goals in the future—thus making for an even more privacy-invasive society.

Unauthorised Use: Function Creep

The unauthorised use of biometric data is the greatest risk that biometric technology poses to informational privacy. Unlike other personal data, biometric data are special by their nature, which also determines the great potential of their various uses. It is not the intended use of biometric technology that is seen as problematic, but the other possible purposes it may be used for.

For example, fingerprints have been used in forensic identification. The collection of such information will facilitate police searches. By virtue of this, the database of biometric information could be used as a database of criminal records. Law enforcement authorities will be able to conduct surveillance on the general population without any evidence of wrongdoing.

Moreover, as a relatively unique identifier, biometric data not only enables individuals to be tracked, but creates the potential for the collection of individual's information into a comprehensive profile by linking the various databases together. The automatic nature of biometric identifiers makes it easy to copy and otherwise be shared among countless public and private sector databases. An article in a hotel trade publication points out that "with the use of this (biometric) technology a front desk clerk could know instantly at check-in that Mr. John Smith during his last stay purchases: three Cokes from the mini-bar, two martini's in the lounge, ate dinner at the hotel restaurant where he ordered the special and since his last visit has moved from Chicago to Atlanta" (Rinehart, 2001). The record of Mr Smith's alcohol consumption may be used by his insurance company who may be curious about Mr Smith's alcohol consumption and want to rank his risk of getting a heart or liver disease. Information in this profile may be used out of context to the detriment of the data subject, and unjust decisions about them would be made simply by automatically analysing this profile, which may contain incomplete or inaccurate data. And all this could be done without the consent or knowledge of the data subjects.

As indicated above, "function creep" is unavoidable (Davies, 1994). The widely-cited example on point is the US Social Security Number, which is used for a broad range of purposes.[32] It has been claimed that "any high-integrity identifier (like biometrics) represents a threat to civil liberties, because it represents the basis of a ubiquitous identification scheme, and such a scheme provides enormous power over the populace. All human behaviour would become transparent to the state, and the scope for non-conformism and dissent would be muted to the point envisaged by the anti-Utopian novelists" (Clarke, 1994, p. 34).

Loss of Anonymity

Anonymity has been frequently linked with autonomy; it is a key to people's sense of freedom. The ever-increasing quantity of personal data online makes it more and more convenient to track and profile individuals by government or private organizations. Consequently, anonymity may turn out to be the only tool available for ordinary people to defend themselves against being profiled. However, widespread use of biometric technology will substantially undermine people's ability to be anonymous. It has been argued, though, that it is possible to use biometric technology for anonymous authentication. (Grijpink, 2004; Impagliazzo & More 2002). Yet it also has been pointed out that if one really wants to be anonymous then biometric technology is not the appropriate technology of choice since biometrics, by nature, are generally inconsistent with anonymity.[33] Biometric systems are created to identify or authenticate people, and it will generally not be a large task to link, directly or indirectly, a biometric identifier to other personal data.

Woodward has argued that "to the extent there is less individual anonymity today than in decades or centuries past, biometrics is not to blame" (Woodward, 2001). He goes on to claim that while a biometric identifier is very accurate, "it is not the first nor is it the only identifier used to match or locate information about a person"(Woodward, 2001) Therefore, he concludes, "it is not obvious that more anonymity will be lost when biometrics is used" (Woodward, 2001). These arguments seem to make sense at first sight, as they use a fact as their premise, yet the conclusion drawn is misleading for the following two reasons:

First, the author underestimates the reach of biometric data. He uses "name," "social security numbers," and "account numbers" as examples of "other numerical identifiers" to compare with biometric data, and infers that since there were many other identifiers before biometrics, the latter should not be blamed for lack of anonymity. As discussed before, biometric data are special by their nature and by their usage potential. There is no existing identifier such as name or social security number that can be really equate with biometrics. Names can be changed, misspelled and numerous same names in the world can be found. A social security number is not universal at all; it is often restricted to a particular jurisdiction. As for account numbers, it is not usual to see people use these as authentication methods other than for obtaining financial service, and such numbers also can be changed and/or restricted to a certain location and time period. As a matter of fact, no existing identifier can expose so much about us as biometric data can, nor is there any other identifier that is *supposed to be* so universal, long-lasting,[34] and intimately linked to us as biometrics. To say that the use of biometrics will not cause more loss of anonymity is overly optimistic.

Second, Woodward infers that because biometrics are not the only identifiers that may erode anonymity, biometrics should not be blamed for such erosion. This is like saying that because A is not the only person that commits this crime, he should not be punished or stopped. Despite the fact that there exist many means to erode anonymity in the modern world, it still cannot be denied that biometric systems are detrimental to anonymity.

Physical Privacy and Biometric Technology

Physical privacy is the right to be free from unwanted, unreasonable intrusions into, or searches of, one's body. It is concerned with bodily integrity (and, indirectly, emotional integrity, together with human dignity). Issues revolving around physical privacy include schemes for compulsory immunisation, blood transfusion without consent, compulsory provision of samples of body fluids and body tissue, and compulsory sterilisation (Clarke, 2000). Physical privacy also is defined as freedom from contact or monitoring by others.[35] Physical privacy is not usually the focus of the discussion on biometric information, but it is difficult to delineate clearly and neatly the relationship between an individual's bodily integrity and bodily information, on which the demarcation between the rights to physical privacy and informational privacy is based. Determining exactly when bodily matter becomes data and information is challenging—as the case of DNA illustrates. In any case, it is important not to completely sever discussion about use of body data from use of the body; to do so ignores the close and constitutive link between these data and a person's identity as embodied person (Plogue, 2001).

The severity of breaches of bodily integrity in the context of biometrics may differ from other cases of physical invasion of bodily boundaries. Compared with many medical examinations, the collection of biometric information with current technology is significantly less "intrusive" even when it is compulsory.[36] Nonetheless, most capture of biometric data requires some infringement of the data subject's personal space. Iris and fingerprint scanning require close proximity of biometric sensors to the body part, such as eyes, hands, fingertips. The adoption of other types of biometric technology may incur use of relatively invasive processes, such as substance-abuse testing, body screening and genetic screening, and may therefore be regarded as intruding into persons' physical privacy, even if the collection of biometric data is unsuccessful for various reasons. In the context of law enforcement and forensic identification, it is quite clear that fingerprinting, DNA-testing, and various other forms of bodily searches raise issues concerned with physical privacy (Plogue, 2001).

Most countries have laws and rules related to such kinds of searches in order to protect the individual against abusive state exercise of power. It is noteworthy that in the US legal context, "searches" under the Fourth Amendment to the US Constitution may include the gathering of physiological information from individuals.[37] In most Western-European countries, there is usually a distinction between searches *on* the body—such as searching of clothes, skin, fingertips, face—and searches *in* the body (Plogue, 2001). The former type of search is usually more relevant for biometric schemes. However, when no actual touching is involved—the case with, for example, facial recognition or voice recording—it becomes quite hard to categorise the search as inside or outside of the body. Even when collecting DNA samples, the means can be quite inconspicuous—the case, for example, when obtaining a person's DNA from their lost hair. Although this kind of collection is physically non-invasive, it is still argued as involving a serious breach of integrity, particularly if such collection does not have a specific goal of finding evidence and the like related to a particular crime, but is only for generating identity information of an individual.[38]

In the discussions on the relation between biometrics and privacy, moral, and legal concerns about physical privacy usually take a backseat to concerns about informational privacy. The mere fact that an individual is subject to "intrusion" by biometric technology is not the focus of most legal and social commentators, because the harm of this "physical intrusion" is not regarded as strong as the consequence of losing control of one's biometric information. The criteria of purpose and subsequent use of the biometric data seem to be more and crucial for the discussion. Yet for some people with certain cultural or religious backgrounds, the mental harm of this physical intrusion may be quite serious.[39] It also bears emphasising that biometric systems and their application may engender new and more intensive forms of surveillance that impact negatively on one's physical privacy. This should be kept in mind as the gathering of biometric information (including DNA samples) becomes increasingly easy, routine, comprehensive, and inconspicuous.

Some authors consider as an invasion of physical privacy the possible harm to hygiene which could be caused by biometric technologies and the use of biometric sensors.[40] However, this view stretches the notion of privacy too far. Biometric technology may infringe an individual's right to full health, but hygienic problems do not directly violate the right to privacy as such. Biometric technology may cause violation to physical privacy when it consists of unreasonably intrusive collection of biometric data, even if no actual physical harm is suffered by the data subject.

Property Rights: A Worthwhile Protection Measure?

One consequence of the development of information technology is debate over the extent to which existing legal concepts are adequate to capture the numerous ways in which computer data are subject to misuse. In particular, the question has been raised as to whether ascribing property rights to information might provide effective means of controlling such misuse.[41] The idea of ownership in information—especially personal information—is quite controversial. Wacks has stated, for example, that "there is no compelling case for applying the concept of property to 'personal information'…adequate legal means already exist without the need to manufacture new property rights" (Wacks, 1989, p. 49). In my view, the right to privacy is not based directly on a property right.[42] Moreover, I am mindful of the possibility that applying property rights to personal data creates conceptual confusion.[43] Nevertheless, it is worth considering whether property rights may strengthen the legal protection of personal information and bring about a more efficient allocation of such protection, particularly against the background of enormous growth in the commercial exploitation of personal data. Flaherty writes pointedly: "Although I have a congenital dislike for the notion that one should be allowed to sell one's privacy to the highest bidder, almost everything else is for sale in our capitalistic societies. In this case, in fact, we have been giving away our personal, private information for free, because we are not smart enough to insist on payments for its use at the outset" (Flaherty, 1999, pp. 19-38).

Ken Laudon and others have argued that the creation of a delimited property right over commercial exploitation of personal information has great promise as a tool for protecting personal data.[44] The essential principle they envisage would be that no information could be legally sold or traded for any commercial purpose without express permission from the person concerned. Data subjects would be entitled to gain benefits akin to royalties from the trading of their personal information. In the absence of clearly expressed wishes, the default condition would be "no release." Establishing a normative system of this kind would—at least in theory—enhance the protection of data subjects' privacy.

Hence, it might be beneficial to recognize a property right in relation to commercial exploitation of biometric data. Being intimately linked to an individual and helping to make them special and unique, such data ought arguably to belong to the individual from whom they are ultimately derived. The discourse of property rights, particularly during the 19th century, has been a liberal discourse focusing on individual freedoms and rights. The category of "property" has marked the boundary of the public /private dichotomy (Vandervelde, 1980). There also have been suggestions that genetic information should be shared as a form of "familial" property amongst family members who have a legitimate common interest in the information[45] (Wersz et al. eds, 1995).

An important catalyst for debate over the proprietary aspects of body-related information was the decision of the Californian Supreme Court in *Moore*.[46] The court refrained from extending property rights to individuals over their own body parts, stating that to do so would have too broad of a social impact and that such an extension must be carried out by legislation. At the same time, the court seemingly felt at ease when affirming the defendant's property rights over the cell line derived from Moore's tissues, asserting that this cell line was manufacture created from the labour of the researchers.

The court's decision is controversial and has attracted much criticism. Kahn suggests that the court privileged science and the market at the expense of the individual (Kahn, 2000). He believes that by focusing on the appropriation of identity, it may be easier to secure rights over biological materials for individuals and groups. Kahn takes as a point of departure for his argument the fact that there has been some recognition in the American legal system of a property right inhering in certain characteristics of an individual such as their name and likeness.[47] Here I quote Kahn at length to make his point clear:

Granting legal recognition to the constitutive element of identity is a logical corollary of recognizing its outward manifestation in names or images. Indeed projections of one's identity serve in turn to reconstitute and maintain it as it grows and evolves. The jurisprudence of identity does not construct identity as a static, fixed object but rather as an organic, complex and evolving manifestation of the self that changes over time and across context. Protecting projection of identity, therefore, also involves protecting the ongoing constitution of the self. The appellate Court in Moore simply makes this relationship more explicit. By focusing on DNA, the court emphasized the value of relations and objects that constitute the self. (Kahn, 2000, pp. 938-939)

This discourse is particularly relevant to biometric information. Although biometric information is not exactly the same as DNA or body tissue, it is closely linked with these. Moreover, unlike the DNA and body tissue which is usually not taken as representations of an individual's identity in the social context, biometric information may construct people's identity in the same way as people's name and image. Biometric information receives wide social recognition as a representation of identity. Hence, such information could reasonably be argued as belonging to the individual it is meant to represent.

In the biometric context, the property right in privacy is frequently raised in connection with the biometric data stored in databases or smart cards. Whether biometric data per se or certain kinds of biometric data should be regarded as genetic information or genetically-related information is still debatable. Nevertheless, the introduction of a property right in privacy could at least provide an effective means of privacy protection when biometric data are concerned. The right to property in privacy is based on a moral value of privacy, but it also entails the legal power to possess, use, transmit, exchange or alienate objects. Because the property right is a negative right, which requires other people to refrain from interfering with an owner's possessing, using and handling the things that are owned, without the owner's consent, it can create a solid legal basis for the data subject to restrict others from infringing their control over their biometric data. If unauthorised use of biometric data occurred, data subjects would arguably have a stronger legal basis for requiring increased damages payment. The right would not necessarily stop data controllers from collecting or reusing biometric data, but would compel them to pay compensation to data subjects for making commercial or non-commercial use of the data. This recognition can bolster individuals' right to own or at least control in a meaningful way, biometric information stemming from them. It may concomitantly help generate a new balance of power between individuals and the organisations that exploit biometric data.

Security and Biometric Technology

Biometric technology frequently has been linked with security goals. For example, it is extolled as the most secure and convenient form of authentication because biometrics "cannot be borrowed, stolen, forgotten or forged" (Subcomm, 2001, p. 42). There also has been discussion about the balance between security and privacy, including biometrics' inroads on civil liberties in the name of public safety. Yet, as pointed out by Clement, the so-called "trading off" between privacy and security is an inappropriate way of looking at the issue—"a distraction that prematurely concedes and obscures a dangerous presumption" (Clement, Guerra, Johnson, & Walder, 2002, p.195). The strong conviction in the efficacy of technology may really be a romanticized illusion. Human beings have an almost blind faith in all things scientific (Clement et al., 2002, p.195), and biometrics is certainly cloaked in a "scientific" mantle.

Technology Limitations

The fuzzy nature of biometrics poses novel challenges and can create new security holes. Unlike passwords or plain text, each time a biometric is measured the observation might differ. In the case of fingerprint matching, for example, the reading might change because of elastic deformations in the skin when placed on the sensor, or because of dust particles, oil, and so on. Moreover the devices that are in use—cameras, sensors, and so on—are, like human eyes and feelings, imperfect; they will not always be able to distinguish subtle differences between people.

As Wilson shows, biometric authentication entails a long chain of processing steps, all of which are imperfect (Wilson, 2005, p. 14). The imperfection is caused by various factors, and is at the same time unavoidable as the body parts measured can never be exactly the same each time. A biometric device has to be able to tolerate to some extent the variations of the input; inevitably this means the system may make mistakes. Consequently, accuracy of a biometric system cannot be measured exactly. The system accuracy is commonly assessed in terms of the system's tendency to generate a False Acceptance Rate (FAR), which is equivalent to a False Match Rate (FMR) or False Rejection Rate (FRR), which is equivalent to a False Non Match Rate (FNMR). These error rates are often just estimated for the portion of user population that is not subject to exception handling[48]. FAR and FRR vary inversely, so for one technology under fixed operation conditions, lowering one error rate will necessarily raise the other.

Different types of biometric devices have widely differing FRR and FAR, partly according to the parameters of the specific application. Where a device serves a small population, a higher FRR may not make much difference. In larger populations or with frequent use of the device, a high FRR can affect enough people to make the system impractical.

As intimated above, no biometric technique is completely accurate. Facial recognition, the primary biometric selected by ICAO in 2002, has actually a very low accuracy percentage in uncontrolled lighting situations, and the false positive rate (FPR) is unknown in large-scale applications.[49] In the real world, to accurately identify suspects under uncontrolled situations out of a large group will arguably be very difficult, and the system also will be affected by such things as age and glasses. Even iris recognition, which has been widely accepted as based on a relatively very accurate biometric, is still not sufficiently accurate for common deployment.[50] Most biometric technology has not yet been proved to be successful under large-scale applications. A report released by the European Commission in March 2005 warned that, on the technological side, there is currently a lack of independent empirical data. (European Commission's Joint Research Centre, 2006). Bruce Schneier, a specialist on security issues, observes that even with a 99.9 percent accuracy rate, the result would be frequent false positives, perhaps in the number of hundreds or thousands, at sites where there were large numbers of individuals, such as at airports. In the end, guards would come to disregard all hits, rendering the system useless (Schneier, 2003, p. 189). However, it has been argued that biometric technology can at least be more accurate than human beings in checking identity.[51] Unfortunately, no solid evidence has yet been established to prove this claim. Even if it is true, it does not necessarily follow that biometric technology can perform its task satisfactorily in light of the considerable money and effort it costs, nor that it can be an adequate substitute for traditional authentication methods. As Dr. Ted Dunstone has emphasised, it is just an alternative and a convenient one.[52]

Professor Andela Sasse, a biometrics expert, recently advised UK parliamentarians that biometric technologies were "a lot less mature" than manufacturers made out.[53] Biometric technology is based on the assumption that human pattern recognition, finger prints, irises and faces will stay the same over time, which is not true. Moreover, "even if the underlying biological traits of interest are truly unique, it does not follow that our machinery will be able to measure them faithfully." (Wilson, 2005, p. 4). The *relatively* unique and stable nature of biometric data causes a lot of technical problems for the accuracy of biometric technology.

There are other practical problems with biometric technology too. In Germany, where the e-passport scheme has been started, complaints have arisen about various aspects from price to privacy concerns, as well as technique difficulties. Teeth and smiles can confuse the facial recognition system, and the distance between the chin and forehead on the photo must be not less than 32 mm but not more than 36mm. It is not easy for people to abide by all these specifications. (Laitner & Williamson, 2005, p. 8).Furthermore, there can be at least the perception of discrimination against certain group of people who are unable to use the biometric system for reasons of ethnicity, physical disability, medical conditions etc.

Biometric technology has been long recognized as a useful weapon to combat fraud. However, the computer systems that are used to process biometrics are exposed to the same kind of manipulation as other computers. People can access, erase, or alter what is stored there. "In the end, security depends upon people...but the weak link is the systems, procedures, and people who implement them" (Norman,2003). In addition, there are reports of cases in which the system can be fooled without difficulties. For instance, studies have shown that thin fingerprint-pads adhered to fingers have managed to fool scanners (Higgins, 2003). Just recently, a German computer security consultant has shown that he can clone the electronic passports that the United States and other countries are beginning to distribute (Zetter, 2006). More sophisticated methods of biometrics fraud also may appear with the development of technologies. It goes without saying that to steal or reproduce a fingerprint is still more difficult than stealing a key or a smart card, but we have to be clear that it is not always necessary to steal the real finger or iris to compromise the system.

Misconceptions of Biometric Technology

The technology limitation of biometric technology, however, is not a complete indictment of the technology. The more serious problem is the misconception about the security level that biometric technology can guarantee for us.

The difficulty of challenging a false biometric match is particular troubling in situations that involve government agencies or criminal investigations. For example, over-reliance on digital images of fingerprints led the FBI to wrongly suspect an Oregon lawyer of involvement in the 2004 Madrid train bombings (Leyden, 2004). In that case, the suspect was lucky enough to be released when the Spanish investigators matched the fingerprints to an Algerian, forcing the FBI to admit it was wrong. However, in cases where no other match is found, and there exist a false match and an overconfidence in the technology, innocent people could remain in jail.

Another extreme is that "the reliance on such flawed security measures might ultimately compromise security further by reducing vigilance and paying less heed to other warning signs" (Roy, 2005). The Ressam case reflects that it was purely human skill that prevented a terrorist attack.[54] When Ressam attempted to enter the USA, he had an authentic Canadian passport issued under a false identity. The computer system cleared him by his ID, but custom agents felt he was suspicious because he was sweating, fidgety, and avoided eye contact. Hence, the most relevant question we need to point out here is that the ability to accurately identify an individual does not mean that we really know what the individual would do, unless he is already in our suspect list, and we identify him from the database. As for numerous potential terrorists with clean backgrounds and authentic ID, biometric identification can do nothing. The ability of finding out "who you are" does not mean that we necessarily know what an individual had committed and what he might commit. It has been shown that even with biometric technology at hand, the terrorists behind the 9/11 attacks would not have been stopped (Turley, 2000).

Security Problems Posed by Biometric Technology

As we can see from above discussions, biometric technology is far from mature as it is portrayed to be. In practice, it will inevitably commit various errors. These errors are likely to be compounded by the frequent absence of "fall-backs" in the event of identity theft (Wilson, 2005, p. 18). No security system is perfect, and a truly secure system always contains a well-functioning fall-back measure when critical breach happens. Generally, once a biometric is compromised, it is compromised forever. In the event of biometric identity theft, there would appear to be no alternative but to withdraw the user from the system.

It has been reported, though, that some research has shown it is possible to transform a biometric iris template so that it assumes a new format that is unique to a particular application. Thus, a template generated in a format corresponding to a particular application A could not be misappropriated and used to authenticate a user for application B.[55] In addition, there also are reports about research on cancellable biometrics.[56] Instead of enrolling with your true finger (or other biometric), the fingerprint is intentionally distorted in a repeatable manner and this new print is used. If, for some reason, your original fingerprint is stolen, an essentially "new" fingerprint can be issued by simply changing the parameters of the distortion process. This technology may enhance the security level of biometric technology, but several problems still remain:

- It might not protect against replay attack, if the attacker has copied the user's actual biometric character (by, e.g., photographing the iris).[57]

- In the first method of using different formats in extracting the iris template, it may mean some information is thrown away. If each template from the one character is different, then each template has fewer bits of entropy that it would have if it were only one. That is, each template is "fuzzy" and this has to erode the accuracy, leading to higher false match rates.[58] Generally accuracy and whole image are required for biometric identification.[59]

- These methods are still very much at experimental level, and are not ready for commercial deployment for the next several years.[60]

- It is not known for sure how much correlation there is between one template and another. If an attacker can get hold of a template (and/or the original biometric character) they may be able to predict what the next generated template will look like.[61]

Besides these problems, it is clear from many existing biometric applications and biometrics advocates that building up a centralised personal database with links to identification and verification systems is supposed to be a fundamental part of the whole biometric system. This also creates a great "honey net" for crackers. The implementation of a centralised system would require widespread access from various remote locations. This may generate significant numbers of failures and make the system prone to be cracked by "physically accessing one of the sites, by finding some communication-based vulnerability, or by bribing or corrupting someone with access to the system" (Kent, 2006).Through this access, identity theft or alteration of data could be achieved without many difficulties. Moreover, with such a complex centralised "security" system, a failure at one location is likely to cause cascading effects throughout the whole system. Such kinds of failures can be achieved either through a physical attack on the infrastructure or a cyber-attack.[62] It has been noted that especially in the absence of costly dedicated networks, an Internet-based system would "inevitably be the target of malicious attacks as well as subject to unintentional or incidental damage".[63] In other words, the so-called "security" system would actually generate less security and more vulnerability.

Will it then be more secure to store the biometric templates in a portable device? It has been argued that the best method to avoid central storage and to be both secure and privacy friendly, is to store the biometric information on a portable device, such as a mouse, mobile, laptop computer, or smart card. However, this solution has been criticized as "a worrying gimmick, closely equivalent to writing the PIN on the back of your credit card" (Wilson & Prints, 2004). A majority of commercial fingerprint detectors can be fooled by replica prints. So if you lose your phone or smart card a clever thief will find your biometric security information very conveniently left behind all over the keypad (Wilson & Prints, 2004) A robust liveness detection system is needed to combat such fraud, yet in commercial practice, it remains uncommon in fingerprinting systems (Wilson, 2005, p. 12–20).

Another major security concern is that biometric technology adds a new dimension to identity theft (Clarke, 2001). For instance, when a national ID card with bio-metric identifier is used, the weaknesses of a card system may increase the risk of identity theft. Criminals and others could masquerade as someone else at the point when the card is issued--this could become a very effective form of identity theft (Neill, 2005). A widely used biometric identifier at various occasions may actually facilitate easier identity theft at one place. Once this happens, it will be extremely difficult to issue another biometric identifier or prove it actually happens. Although some people argue that biometric technology will be a good solution for combating identity theft, biometric identifiers will not solve the problem of identity theft facing the elderly community. Biometric systems in use now are successful because the number of people enrolled is limited. When the system fails, human administrators are available to assist in the authentication process. Creating an automated system on a national scale is beyond the capability of any of the existing technologies. Simply by merging the existing systems into a single central database would cause the reliability of those systems to be lost. Further, biometric databases would be subject to new forms of abuse which may be more difficult to correct and will pose significant consequences for individuals whose biometric identifier is compromised (Rotenberg, 2002).

Future Trends and Conclusion

The challenge of confronting any radically developing technology is that it must be approached with a broad understanding of the practical and technological realities and limitations. As we embrace the biometric technology, however, we have to pause to consider some of the implications of its widespread implementations, especially its potential risks to privacy. Biometric information is a special category of personal information which is intimately linked to our physical body, while having the potential to become a relatively unique and stable digital representation of each individual in the computer world. Our right to informational privacy and physical privacy may all be at risk with unlimited use of such technology. Ascribing property rights to biometric information may alleviate this risk somewhat but is regarded by many as a relatively controversial move.

Biometrics' current state of effectiveness still leaves much to be desired. The quality and accuracy level of biometric technology as it now stands do not actually offer the gains in security as demonstrated by many vendors or advocators. Having addressed some of the misconceptions around the technology, it is perhaps worth noting that biometric technology alone can not provide an answer to security issues. The inherent nature of biometric technology provides enormous potential for undermining privacy, despite the fact that, as it stands now, such technology does not offer all the matching, tracking and linking possibilities that are commonly envisaged. The inaccuracies and the security risks posed by biometric technology have, rather ironically, added more security problems, something not generally known. As mentioned previously, biometric technology for the near future at least is more likely to function as a convenient alternative or supplement to traditional authentication methods than as a security enhancement tool.

The key issue regarding biometric technology is not choosing between security and privacy. If we allow ourselves to see through tunnel vision and balance solely the enhancement of security against the sacrifice of privacy, then the trade-offs are easily cast in doubts. The present developing biometric technology does not actually offer the gains in security as expected, in spite of the invasion of privacy that occurs when it is implemented. If biometric technology is going to be adopted without strict restrictions, then it casts into doubt the very value of liberty and privacy it is designed to protect. Even if the creation of a surveillance society may insulate us to some extent from some types of security threats, it may very well swap one inequality for another, and in the process, raise more problems than it solves.

Nonetheless, it also is true that a lot depends on the details surrounding the various biometric technologies and their related applications. Biometric technology may evolve to be more privacy friendly and security enhancing than it is now. It is important to recognise that privacy and security are not necessarily two contradictory concepts where biometrics is concerned. The means and application of biometric technology are the key issues here. They need to be further studied by technical experts as well as law and policy makers.

References

Agre, P. E. (2003). Your face is not a bar code: Arguments against automatic face recognition in public places. Retrieved February 15, 2007 from http://polaris. gseis.ucla.edu/pagre/bar-code.html

Alterman, A. (2003). A piece of yourself: Ethical issues in biometric identification. *Ethics and Information Technology, 5*, 139-150.

Amnesty International Canada (2001). *Protecting human rights and providing security.* AI comments with respect to Bill C-36, Ottawa.

Ashbourn, J. (2006). *The societal implications of the wide scale introduction of biometrics and identity management.* Background paper for the Euroscience Open Forum ESOF 2006 in Munich. Retrieved February 20, 2007, from http://www.statewatch.org/news/2006/jul/biometrics-and-identity-management.pdf, p.16

Bates, B. (1991). *A guide to physical examination and history taking* (5th ed.). Hagerstown: Lippincott Williams & Wilkins.

Berman, J. & Mulligan, D. (1999). Privacy in the digital age. *Nova Law Review, 23*(2), 551–582.

Braithwaite, M., Seelen, U. C. V., Cambier, J., Daugman, J., Glass, R., Moore, R., & Scott, I. (2002). *Application-specific biometric templates.* IEEE Workshop on Automatic Identification Advanced Technologies, Tarrytown, NY, March

14–15. Retrieved February 1, 2007, from www.cis.upenn.edu/~cahn/publications/autoid02.pdf

Brogan, J. D. (2002). Facing the music: The dubious constitutionality of facial recognition technology. *Hasting Communications & Entertainment Law Journal, 25*, 65–81.

Bromba, M. (2006). On the reconstruction of biometric raw data from template data. Retrieved February 1, 2007, from http://www.bromba.com/knowhow/temppriv.htm

Bygrave, L. A. (2002). *Data protection law: Approaching its rationale, logic and limits*. The Hague: Kluwer Law International.

Castle, M. N. (1998). *Hearing on biometrics and the future of money.* Committee on Banking and Financial Services, Washington, D.C., May 20.

Cavoukian, A. (1998). *Privacy and biometrics: An oxymoron or time to take a 2nd look.* Information and Privacy Commissioner, Ontario; Address given by Ann Cavoukian to the Computers, Freedom and Privacy 98 Conference in Austin, Texas, February. Retrieved August 7, 2005, from http://www.ipc.on.ca

Cavoukian, A. (2003). *National security in a post 9/11 world: The rise of surveillance...the Demise of Privacy?* Retrieved February 1, 2007, from http://www.ipc.on.ca/images/Resources/up-nat_sec.pdf

Cavoukian, A. (2004). Tag, you're it: Privacy implications of radio frequency identification (RFID) technology. Retrieved February 1, 2007, from http://www.ipc.on.ca/images/Resources/up-rfid.pdf

Cavoukian et al. (2007). *Biometric encryption: A positive-sum technology that achieves strong authentication, security and privacy*. Retrieved January 30, 2008, from http://www.ipc.on.ca/images/Resources/up-1bio_encryp.pdf

Center for DNA Fingerprint Diagnostics. (2006). DNA fingerprinting. Retrieved February 1, 2007, from http://www.cdfd.org.in/dfpser.html

Charatan, F. B. (1996). New Jersey passes genetic privacy bill. *British Medical Journal, 313*, 71.

Clarke, R. (1994). Human identification in information systems: Management challenges and public policy issues. *Information Technology & People, 7*(4), 6–37.

Clarke, R. (2000). Beyond the OECD guidelines: Privacy protection for the 21st century. Retrieved February 1, 2007, from http://www.anu.edu.au/people/Roger.Clarke/DV/PP21C.html#Priv

Clarke, R. (2001). Biometrics and privacy. Retrieved September 6, 2006, from http://www.anu.edu.au/people/Roger.Clarke/DV/Biometrics.html

Clement A., Guerra, R., Johnson, J., & Walder, F. (2002). National identification schemes (NIDS): A remedy against terrorist attack? In K. Brunnstein & J. Berleus (Eds.), *Proceedings of the sixth conference on human choice and computers: Issues of choice and quality of life in the information society* (pp. 195–205). Boston: Kluwer.

Cockfield, A. J. (2003). Who watches the watchers? A law and technology perspective on government and private sector surveillance. *Queen's Law Journal, 29*, 2.

Cole, S. (2000). Myth of fingerprints: A forensic science stands trial. *Lingua Franca, 10*(8), 54–62.

Cowley, S. (2005). IBM works toward replaceable biometrics. Retrieved September 5, 2006 from http://www.csoonline.com.au/index.php/id;260154133;fp;8;fpid;8

Dangelo, K.B. (1989). How much of you do you really own - A property right in identity. *Cleveland State Law Review, 37.*

Davies, S. (1994). Touching big brother: How biometric technology will fuse flesh and machine. *Information Technology & People, 7*(4), 38–47.

Department of communications and department of Justice (1992). *Privacy & computers.* Ottawa: Information Canada, pp.13-14.

Dorizzi, B. (2005). *Biometrics at the frontiers: Assessing the impact on society. Technical impact of biometrics.* Background paper for the Institute of Prospective Technological Studies, DG JRC – Sevilla, European Commission. Retrieved February 1, 2007, from http://cybersecurity.jrc.es/docs/LIBE%20Biometrics%20March%2005/TechnologicalImplications_Dorizzi.pdf

Electronic Privacy Information Center (EPIC) & Privacy International (PI). (2005). *Privacy and human rights: An international survey of privacy laws and developments.* Washington, D.C.: EPIC/PI.

European Commission's Joint Research Centre (JRC) (2006). Biometrics at the Frontiers: Assessing the Impact on Society. Retrieved February 1, 2007, from ftp://ftp.jrc.es/pub/EURdoc/eur21585en.pdf

Ezovski, G. M. (2005). Biometric passports: Policy for international and domestic deployment. *Journal of Engineering and Public Policy, 9.* Retrieved February 1, 2007, from http://www.wise-intern.org/journal/2005/Ezovski.pdf

Feldman, R. (2003). Considerations on the emerging implementation of biometric technology. *Hastings Communications & Entertainment Law Journal, 25*, 653–682.

Fernando, V. (1981). Legal personality, privacy and the family. In Henkin, L. (Ed.), *The international bill of rights* (pp. 184–208). New York: Columbia University Press.

findBIOMETRICS.com (n.d.). Hand geometry – Now and in the future. Retrieved February 1, 2007, from http://www.findbiometrics.com/Pages/hand_finger%20articles/hand_2.html

Flaherty, D. H. (1999). Visions of privacy: Past, present and future. In C. Bennett & R. Grant (Eds.), *Visions of privacy: Policy choices for a digital age* (pp. 21–39). Toronto: University Of Toronto Press.

Gavison, R. (1980). Privacy and the limits of law. *Yale Law Journal, 89*, 421–471.

Gomm, K. (2005, October 21). U.K. passport agency: "Iris recognition needs work." *ZDNet Asia*. Retrieved July 12, 2006, from http://www.zdnetasia.com/news/security/0,39044215,39283306,00.htm

Grijpink, J. (2004). Two barriers to realizing the benefits of biometrics. Retrieved September 3, 2006, from http://www.cs.uu.nl/people/grijpink/docs/

Hammond, G.R.(1981). Quantum physics econometric models and property rights to information. *McGill Law Journal, 27*, 47.

Harte, A. (2004). Privacy and identity in a changing world. *Australasian Psychiatry, 12*(1), 55–57.

Have, H.A.M.J. & Welie, J.V.M. (eds) (1998). *Ownership of the human body. philosophical considerations on the use of the human body and its parts in healthcare,* Dordrecht: Kluwer Academic Publishers.

Hert, P. D. (2005). *Biometrics: Legal issues and implications.* Background paper for the Institute of Prospective Technological Studies, DG JRC – Sevilla, European Commission. Retrieved January 3, 2007, from http://www.statewatch.org/news/2005/apr/jrc-biometrics-paul-de-hert.pdf

Higgins, P. T. (2003). Fingerprint and hand geometry. In J. K. Brownlow (Ed.), *Biometrics* (pp. 25–41). McGraw-Hill.

Holladay, A. (2002). Do identical twins have identical DNA? Retrieved February 1, 2007, from http://www.wonderquest.com/twins-dna.htm

International Biometric Group (n.d.). How do identification and verification differ? Retrieved February 11, 2006, from http://www.biometricgroup.com/reports/public/reports/identification_verification.html

IBG (2002). The BioPrivacy application impact framework 2002. Retrieved February 2006 from http://www.bioprivacy.org/

ICAO. (2004). Biometrics deployment of machine-readable travel documents: Technical Report, Version 2.0. Retrieved February 1, 2007, from http://www.icao.int/mrtd/download/documents/Biometrics%20deployment%20of%20Machine%20Readable%20Travel%20Documents%202004.pdf

Impagliazzo, R. & More, S. M. (2002). Anonymous credentials with biometrically-enforced non-transferability. Retrieved September 3, 2006, from http://portal.acm.org/ft_gateway.cfm?id=1005150&type=pdf&coll=&dl=ACM&CFID=15151515&CFTOKEN=6184618

Inness, J. C. (1992). *Privacy, intimacy and isolation*. Oxford, New York: Oxford University Press.

Jian, A. K., Ross, A., Uludag, U. (2005). Biometric template security: Challenges and solutions. Retrieved June 5, 2006, from http://www.ee.bilkent.edu.tr/~signal/defevent/papers/cr1805.pdf

Kahn, J. (2000).Biotechnology and the legal constitution of the self: Managing identity in science, the market and the society. *Hastings Law Journal, 51,* 909-952.

Kent, S. T. (2006). IDs – not that easy: Questions about national wide identity system. Retrieved February 1, 2007, from http://www7.nationalacademies.org/ocga/testimony/IDs_Not_That_Easy.asp

Kenyon, L. D. (n.d.). Five years later ... Airport video technologies evolve in wake of 9/11. Retrieved September 4, 2006, from http://governmentvideo.com/articles/publish/article_962.shtml

Keogh, E. (2001). An overview of the science of fingerprints. *Anil Aggrawal's Internet Journal of Forensic Medicine and Toxicology, 2*(1). Retrieved January 4, 2007, from http://www.geradts.com/anil/ij/vol_002_no_001/papers/paper005.html

Laitner, S. & Williamson, H. (2005, November 9). E-passport is no laughing matter. *Financial Times*. Retrieved February 1, 2007 from http://www.ft.com/cms/s/d51ee8d0-50c6-11da-bbd7-0000779e2340.html

Laudon, K.(1996).Markets and privacy. *Communications of the ACM, 39,*(9), 92-104.

Lawless, J. (2004). Fingerprint privacy concerns. *CBS News*. Retrieved September 4, 2006, from http://www.cbsnews.com/stories/2004/09/08/tech/main641998.shtml

Leyden, J. (2004, May 26). FBI apology for Madrid bomb fingerprint fiasco. *The Register*. Retrieved August 10, 2006, from http://www.theregister.co.uk/2004/05/26/fbi_madrid_blunder/

Lin M. (1996). Conferring a federal property right in genetic material: Stepping into the future with the Genetic Privacy Act. *American Journal of Law and Medicine, 22*, 109–134.

McCoy, S. (2002). Comment: O' big brother where art thou? The constitutional use of facial-recognition technology. *John Marshall Journal of Computer & Information Law, XX*(3), 471–485.

Moo-Young, R. (2001). Eyeing the future: Surviving the criticisms of biometric authentication. *North Carolina Banking Institute, 5*(Spring), 421–435.

National Institute of Standards and Technology. (2001). Common biometric exchange file format (CBEFF) (NISTIR 6529). Retrieved June 3, 2006, from http://www. itl.nist.gov/div895/isis/bc/cbeff/CBEFF010301web.PDF

National Science and Technology Council (NSTC) (2006). *Privacy & Biometrics: Building a Conceptual Foundation.* Committee report, 48.

Norman, D. (2003). Don Norman's jnd.org: Recommended readings. Retrieved February 1, 2007, from http://www.jnd.org/recommended_readings.html (reviewing Bruce Schneier, *Secrets & lies: Digital security in a networked world*).

O'Connor, S. M. (2002). Biometrics and identification after 9/11. *Bender's Immigration Bulletin, 7*, 150.

O'Neill, R. (2005, August 2). IDologists. *Sydney Morning Herald.* Retrieved February 1, 2007, from http://www.smh.com.au/news/next/idologists/2005/08/01/1122748570079.html?oneclick=true

Ploeg, I. (1999). Written on the body: Biometrics and identity. *Computers and Society*, March, 37–44.

Ploeg, I. (2001), Biometrics and the body as information: Normative issues of the socio-technical coding of the body. Retrieved August 11, 2006 from https://www.bmg.eur.nl/smw/publications/vdp_02.pdf

Prins, J.E.E. (1998). Making our body identify for us: Legal implications of biometric technologies, *Computer Law & Security Report, 14*(3), 159–167.

Reichman, N. (1987) Computer matching: toward computerized systems of regulations, *Law and Policy*, October, 404.

Retica Systems Inc. (2005). Eye biometrics. Retrieved September 6, 2006, from http://www.retica.com/site/biometrics/index.html

Ricketson, S. (1977). Confidential information ever property: a new proprietary interest, *II Melbourne University Law Review, 223;*

Rinehart, G. (2001). Biometric payment: The new age of currency. *Hospitality Upgrade Magazine*, Spring. Retrieved December 1, 2006, from http://www.hotel-online.com/News/PressReleases2000_1st/Mar00_BiometricCurrency.html

Rotenberg, M. A. (2002). Joint hearing on identity theft involving elderly victims before the special committee on aging. Retrieved September 7, 2006, from http://www.epic.org/privacy/biometrics/testimony_071802.html

Rothstein, M. A. (Ed.). (1997). *Genetic secrets: Protection of privacy and confidentiality in the genetic era*. Yale: Yale University Press.

Roy, B. (2005). A case against biometric national identification systems (NIDS): "Trading-off" privacy without getting security. *Windsor Review of Legal and Social Issues, 45*(March), 59–61.

Rule, J. & Hunter L. (1999). In C.J Bennet & R. Grant (Eds.), Property rights in personal data, visions of privacy: Policy choices for the digital age, pp. 174-175. University of Toronto Press.

Scanlon, T. (1975). Thomson on privacy. Philosophy & Public Affairs, 4, 315–322.

Schneier, B. (2000). Secrets and lies: Digital security in a networked world. New York: John Wiley & Sons.

Schneier, B. (2003). Beyond fear: Thinking sensibly about security in an uncertain world. New York: Copernicus Books.

Scottish Criminal Record Office. (2002). History of fingerprints – A timeline. Retrieved June 21, 2006, from http://www.scro.police.uk/fingerprint_history.htm

Stoney, D. A. (1997). Fingerprint identification: Scientific status. In D. L. Faigman, D. H. Kaye, M. J. Saks, & J. Sanders (Eds.). Modern scientific evidence: The law and science of expert testimony, pp. 368–399. St Paul, MN: West Publishing.

Stuckey, J.E. (1981). The equitable action for breach of confidence: is information ever property? *Sydney Law Review, 9*, 402.

Thomson, J. J. (1975). The right to privacy. *Philosophy and Public Affairs, 4*, 295–314.

Thornburg, R.H. (2002). Comment, face recognition technology: The potential Orwellian implications and constitutionality of current uses under the fourth amendment. *John Marshall Journal of Computer & Information Law*, 20, 321–323.

Tomko, G. (1998). *Biometrics as a privacy-enhancing technology: Friend or foe of privacy?* Privacy Laws & Business 9th Privacy Commissioners'/ Data Protection Authorities' Workshop. Retrieved February 2, 2005 from http://www.dss.state.ct.us/digital/tomko.htm

Turley, J. (2000, January 9). National ID: Beware what you wish for. *Los Angeles Times*. p. B.13.

UK Passport Service (2005). Biometrics Enrolment Trial, Management Summary, p. 8.

UKPS (2005). *UKPS Biometrics Enrollment Trial*. Retrieved March 18, 2007, from http://www.passport.gov.uk/downloads/UKPSBiometrics_Enrolment_Trial_Report.pdf

US Fed News Service (2006). Australia: Smartcard for surveillance, Including US State News, Washington, D.C. June 5, 2006.

Vandervelde, K. (1980). The new property of the nineteenth century: The development of the modern concept of property. *Buffalo Law Review, 29*, 325–367.

Warren, S. & Brandeis, L. (1890-91). The right of privacy. *Harvard Law Review, 4*, 193–220.

Watson, J. D. (2004). *DNA: The secret of life*. New York: Knopf.

Wayman, J. L. (1998). *Biometric Identification and the Financial Services Industry*, p.265.

Wayman, J. L. (1998, May). *Biometrics in Human Services, 2*(2).

Wayman, J. L. (2000a). A definition of "biometrics". In J. L. Wayman (Ed.). *National Biometric Test Centre Collected Works 1997-2000* (pp. 21–23). San Jose State University. Retrieved February 1, 2007, from http://www.engr.sjsu.edu/biometrics/nbtccw.pdf

Wayman, J. L. (2000b). When bad science leads to good law: The disturbing irony of the *Daubert* hearing in the case of *U.S. v. Byron C. Mitchell*. Retrieved February 1, 2007 from http://www.engr.sjsu.edu/biometrics/publications_daubert.html

Wayman, J., Jain, A., Maltoni, D., & Maio, D. (2004). *Biometric systems: Technology, design and performance evaluation*. London: Springer.

Wersz, D., C., et al. (eds.). (1995). *Guidelines on ethical issues in medical genetics and the provision of genetic services*. Geneva, WHO, at 7.2.2.

Westin, A. F. (1970). *Privacy and freedom*. New York: Atheneum.

Wilson, S. (2005). Lockstep submission to senate privacy inquiry. Retrieved August 26, 2006, from http://www.aph.gov.au/senate/committee/legcon_ctte/privacy/submissions/sub11.pdf (pp.12–20)

Wilson, S. & Prints, T. (2004, August 14). *New Scientist*. Retrieved August 13, 2006, from http://www.newscientist.com/aricle.ns?id=mg18324604.200

Woodward, J. D. (1997a). Biometrics: Identifying law & policy concerns. Retrieved June 12, 2006, from http://www.cse.msu.edu/~cse891/Sect601/textbook/19.pdf

Woodward J. D. (1997b). Biometrics: Privacy's foe or privacy's friend? *Proceedings of the Institute of Electrical and Electronics Engineers, 85*(9), 1480–1492.

Woodward, J. D. (2001a). *Super bowl surveillance: Facing up to biometrics*, Rand Issue Paper 209. Retrieved February 1, 2007, from http://www.rand.org/pubs/issue_papers/2005/IP209.pdf

Woodward, J. D., (2001b). *Army biometric applications: Identifying and addressing socio-cultural concerns*, RAND Corporation.

Zetter, K. (2006, August 3). Hackers clone e-passports, *Wired*. Retrieved February 1, 2007, from http://www.wired.com/news/technology/0,71521-0.html?tw=rss.technology

Endnotes

[1]   See further, e.g., Wayman (2000a).

[2]   See, e.g., Cavoukian (2003); Woodward (1997a).

[3]   For more detailed explanation of biometric technology, see, e.g., Wayman et al. (2004).

[4]   DNA (deoxyribonucleic acid) contains the genetic specifications for the biological development of all cellular forms of life. DNA is a long polymer of nucleotides and encodes the sequence of the amino acid residues in proteins using the genetic code, a triplet code of nucleotides. See, e.g., Watson (2004).

[5]   DNA fingerprinting is a technique by which an individual can be identified at molecular level from certain repeating sequences in the DNA present on different chromosomes. These genetic markers are known to vary from individual to individual (except in the case of identical twins). See further Center for DNA Fingerprint Diagnostics (2006), DNA fingerprinting, retrieved June 15, 2006, from http://www.cdfd.org.in/dfpser.html.

[6]   See Keogh (2001) and references cited therein.

[7]   Cf. Bates (1991).

[8]   See, e.g., Jian, Ross, Uludag (2005); Bromba (2006).

[9]   See, e.g., Cole (2000).

[10]   See, e.g., Cole (2000).

[11]   See, e.g., *Holladay (2002)*.

12   See, e.g., Schneier (2000, pp. 141–145).

13   See, e.g., *Messing v. the Bank of American* 143 Md. App.1792 A.2d 312 (2002).

14   See, e.g., Schneier (2000).

15   For more explanation see, Wayman et al. (2004).

16   See, e.g., findBIOMETRICS.com (n.d).

17   According to the author's interview with Prof. Roger Clarke, Xamax Consultancy Pty. Ltd., Canberra, August 5, 2006.

18   The 188 Contracting States that adhere to ICAO are obligated to issue only ICAO-standard Machine-Readable Passports (MRPs) by April 1, 2010. See ICAO (2004).

19   National Institute of Standards and Technology (2001).

20   See, e.g., Hert (2005).

21   See further Cavoukian (2004).

22   The seminal judgment being that of Justice Harlan in *United States v. Katz*, 389 U.S. 347 (1967).

23   See, e.g., McCoy (2002) and references cited therein.

24   *United States v. Katz*, 389 U.S. 347 (1967).

25   *Kyllo v. United States*, 533 U.S. 27, 33 (2001).

26   McCoy (2002).

27   See *Kyllo*, 533 U.S. 27, 33 (2001).

28   See *Katz*, 389 U.S. 347, 351.

29   See, e.g., *Kyllo*, 533 U.S. 27, 32–33. See also the decision of the European Court of Human Rights in *Peck v. UK*, Application 44647/98, decision of May 15, 2001. The latter judgment is elaborated on further below.

30   See further, e.g., Bolle et al. (2003, p. 26). Screening establishes that a person is not on some watch list of "interesting" people.

31   *Peck v. UK*, Application No.44647/98, decision of May 15, 2001.

32   See further Woodward (1997, p. 1486) and references cited therein.

33   Personal interview by author with Dr. Ted Dunstone, Chair of the Biometrics Institute in Australia, Sydney, August 14, 2006. See also Crompton (2002).

34   Due to the limitation of the biometric technology, no biometric today provides lasting signatures on electronic transactions, though it is supposed to be. We will return to this in section 4 about security and biometrics.

35   See, e.g., *Griswold v. Connecticut*, 381 U.S. 479, 494 (1965).

36   To the author's knowledge, there are no documented cases of biometrics actu-
     ally causing direct physical harm to a person.

37   *Smith v. U.S.*, 324 F.2d 879 (1964).

38   See generally Have & Welie (1998).

39   See, e.g., Woodward (1997, p. 1488) and references cited therein.

40   See further Woodward (2001b).

41   See, e.g., Hammond (1981.p.47);Ricketson (1977, p. 223); Stuckey (1981,
     p.402)

42   See too, e.g., Inness (1992, pp. 28–39); Scanlon (1975, pp. 315–322).

43   See too. e.g., Wacks (1989. p. 48)

44   See further Laudon (1996, pp. 92–104); Rule & Hunter (1999, pp. 174–
     175).

45   Wersz *et al.* (eds.). (1995).

46   *Moore v. Regents of the University of California*, 51 Cal.3d 120 (1990).

47   See, e.g., *Roberson v .Rochester Folding Box Company,* 171 N.Y. 538, 64
     N.E. 442 (1902); *Brown Chemical Co.v. Meter*, 139 U.S. 540 (1891); *Minton
     v. Smith*, 276III. App. 128 (1034).

48   Any biometric system will need an "exception handling" procedure that involves a
     manual matching process. See, e.g., Bolle et al. (2003, p. 9).

49   See, e.g., Ezovski (2005).

50   See further Gomm (2005, October 21).

51   Interview by author with Dr. Ted Dunstone, Chair of the Biometrics Institute
     in Australia, Sydney, August 14, 2006.

52   Interview with Dr. Ted Dunstone, Chair of the Biometric Institute in Australia,
     Sydney, August 14, 2006.

53   U.S. Federal News Service (2006).

54   See further Schneier (2000, p. 58).

55   See further Braithwaite, Seelen, Cambier, Daugman, Glass, Moore, & Scott
     (2002).

56   See further Cowley (2005).

57   E-mail correspondence from Mr. Stephen Wilson, Chairman of Lockstep
     Consulting (www.lockstep.com.au), September 7, 2006, on file with author.

58   Id.

[59]   E-mail correspondence from Prof. Roger Clarke, Xamax Consultancy Pty. Ltd., Canberra, September 7, 2006, on file with author.

[60]   E-mail correspondence from Mr. Stephen Wilson, September 7, 2006; E-mail correspondence from Dr. Ted Dunstone, September 8, 2006, on file with author.

[61]   E-mail correspondence from Mr. Stephen Wilson, September 7, 2006.

[62]   Id.

[63]   Id.

Chapter VII

Business Cases for Privacy-Enhancing Technologies

Roger Clarke, Xamax Consultancy Pty Ltd, Australia;
University of New South Wales, Australia;
Australian National University, Australia;
and University of Hong Kong, Hong Kong

Abstract

Many categories of e-business continue to under-achieve. Their full value cannot be unlocked while key parties distrust the technology or other parties, particularly the scheme's sponsors. Meanwhile, the explosion in privacy-intrusive technologies has resulted in privacy threats looming ever larger as a key impediment to adoption. Technology can be applied in privacy-enhancing ways, variously to counter invasive technologies, to enable untraceable anonymity, and to offer strong, but more qualified pseudonymity. After their first decade, it is clear that privacy-enhancing technologies (PETs) are technically effective, but that their adoption lags far behind their potential. As a result, they have not delivered the antidote to distrust in e-business. If individuals are not spontaneously adopting PETs, then the opportunity exists for corporations and government agencies to harness PETs as a core element of their privacy strategies. The financial investment required is not all that large. On the other hand, it is challenging to attract the attention of executives to an initiative of this nature, and then to adapt corporate culture to ensure that the strategy is successfully carried through. This chapter examines PETs, their application to business needs, and the preparation of a business case for investment in PETs.

Introduction

A substantial technical literature exists that describes privacy-enhancing technologies (PETs). On the other hand, there is a very limited literature on why organisations should encourage the adoption of PETs, invest in their development, and provide channels for their dissemination. The purpose of this chapter is to present a framework within which organisations can develop a business case for PETs.

The chapter commences by considering contexts in which trust and distrust of organisations by individuals are important factors in the achievement of organisational objectives. An examination is then undertaken of how an organisation's privacy strategy can make significant contributions to overcoming distrust and achieving trust. The role of information technology is then considered, including both privacy-invasive technologies ("the PITs"), and those that protect and enhance privacy. A taxonomy of PETs is presented, which distinguishes among mere pseudo-PETs, PETs that are designed as countermeasures against specific PITs, tools for uncrackable anonymity ("savage PETs"), and "gentle PETs" that seek a balance between nymity and accountability. Opportunities for organisations to incorporate PET-related initiatives within their privacy strategies are examined, and the development of business cases is placed within a broader theory of cost-benefit-risk analysis.

Trust and Distrust

This chapter is concerned with how organisations construct business cases for the application of technology in order to preserve privacy. The need for this arises in circumstances in which firstly either trust is lacking or distrust inhibits adoption, and secondly effective privacy protections can be a significant factor in overcoming the trust gap.

Trust is confident reliance by one party about the behaviour of other parties (Clarke, 2002). It originates in social settings. Many of the elements evident in social settings are difficult for organisations to replicate in merely economic contexts. Hence a great deal of what organisations call trust is merely what a party has to depend on when no other form of risk amelioration strategy is available to them.

If trust can be achieved, then it may become a positive driver of behaviour. A more common pattern, however, is for distrust to exist. This represents an impediment to fulfilment of the organisation's objectives, because it undermines the positive impacts of other drivers such as cost reductions and convenience.

During their headlong rush onto the Internet during the last decade, many organisations have overlooked the importance of human values to the parties that they deal with. Both consumers and small businesspeople feel powerless when they deal with larger organisations. They would like to have "friends in high places" who can help them when they encounter difficulties. They also fear the consolidation of power that they see going on around them, as governments integrate vast data collections, corporations merge and enter into strategic alliances, and "public-private partnerships" blur organisational boundaries across sectors. As a result, distrust is more commonly encountered than trust.

One context within which trust is critical is the relationship between employers on the one hand, and employees and contractors on the other. In some countries, particularly the USA, employers have been intruding into their employees' data, into their behaviour—not only in the workplace but also beyond it—and even into their employees' bodies in the form of substance-abuse testing, and even the insertion of identity chips. Such measures substitute a power-relationship for loyalty, with the result that employees become exactly what the employer treats them as—sullen opponents who are likely to disclose company secrets and even to commit sabotage. The negative impact on corporate morale and performance is even more marked in the case of staff members on whose creativity the organisation depends for innovation, because a climate of surveillance and distrust chills behaviour and stultifies creative thought and action (Clarke, 2006a).

Other contexts in which trust is critical are external to the organisation: the various aspects of e-business, particularly business-to-consumer (B2C) e-commerce, but also e-government (government-to-citizen—G2C), and even business-to-business (B2B) e-commerce if there is considerable disparity between the parties' size and hence market power.

The adoption of e-business depends on the parties perceiving benefits in adoption that are sufficient to overcome the disbenefits. The costs involved include the effort of turning one's attention to a new way of doing things, understanding it, acquiring and installing relevant software, and learning how to use it. But widespread cynicism exists about the reasons why e-business is being introduced. There are well-founded fears that large organisations will seek opportunities to reduce their level of service, and to transfer costs and effort to the other party—particularly where that other party is less powerful, such as a consumer/citizen, or a small business enterprise.

Organisations do indeed apply e-business to achieve those essentially negative purposes, but they have more constructive aims as well, including:

* effectiveness in achieving organisational objectives;

- efficiency, in the sense of low resource consumption in relation to the value of the outcomes—including cost-reduction as well as cost-transfer;
- flexibility over the short term; and
- adaptability over the medium-term.

Achieving progress in the application of electronic tools is important to many organisations. One of the greatest impediments to the adoption of the various categories of e-business has been lack of trust in other parties or the technologies involved. Credible privacy protections are a key factor in ameliorating the poor relationships that derive from distrust.

Privacy Strategy

The activities of large organisations do not naturally protect the privacy of employees, nor of customers and suppliers. On the contrary, the increase in the scale of corporations and government agencies through the 20th century, the greater social distance between institution and individual, the greater dependence on data instead of human relationships, and the de-humanising nature of computer-based systems, have together resulted in large organisations both being perceived to be, and being, seriously threatening to privacy.

If organisations are to avoid distrust arising from their privacy-invasive behaviour, and particularly if they wish to use their behaviour in relation to people as a means of inculcating trust, then they need to adopt a strategic approach to privacy. This section introduces privacy strategy and outlines key techniques.

Concepts

Organisations are ill-advised to consider privacy, or indeed any other potentially significant social factor, in isolation. Rather, privacy should be considered within the context of the organisation's mission and corporate strategy. Because the primary dimension of privacy is that relating to personal data, strategic information systems theory provides an appropriate basis for analysis (Clarke, 1994a).

Fundamentally, people want some space around themselves. Privacy is most usefully understood as the interest that individuals have in sustaining a "personal space," free from interference by other people and organisations (Clarke 2006a).

People do not identify with "privacy in the abstract," so the full power of public opinion is seldom brought to bear. One result of this has been that American legislators have been able to ignore public concerns and instead satisfy their donors by sustaining the myth that "self-regulation" is good enough. The substantial protections embodied in the OECD Guidelines (OECD 1980) and the EU Directive (EU 1995 and its several successors) have been reduced to a limited and entirely inadequate sub-set referred to as the "safe harbor" provisions (FTC 2000, DOC 2000).

The flaw in this approach is that people identify very strongly with "privacy in the particular." The statute books of the U.S. and its states are flooded with over 700 laws, most of them knee-jerk responses to privacy problems that exploded into the public eye (Rotenberg, 2004; Smith, 2002). Even countries that have broad information privacy protections are beset by these flurries from time to time. Public concern about privacy invasions continues to grow, as organisations harness technology and its applications with ever more enthusiasm. Demands for personal data are teaching people to be obstructionist. When dealing with organisations, it is best for them to obfuscate and lie in order to protect their private space. As irresponsible applications of technology continue to explode, and continue to be subject to inadequate protections and even less adequate regulation, these flurries are occurring more frequently (Clarke, 2006b).

Given this pervasive distrust, organisations that are dependent on reasonable behaviour by the individuals they deal with need to implement a privacy strategy, in order to dissociate themselves from the mainstream of privacy-invasive corporations and government agencies. The foundations of privacy strategy were laid out in Clarke (1996), and expanded and updated in Clarke (2006c). The principles are:

- Appreciate privacy's significance;
- Understand your clients' needs;
- Generate positive attitudes to your organisation by meeting those needs;
- Revisit your process designs;
- Treat customers as system-participants;
- Differentiate your organisation.

Key elements of a process to develop a privacy strategy are:

- A proactive stance;
- An express strategy;
- An articulated plan;

- Resourcing; and
- Monitoring of performance against the plan.

Privacy-Sensitive Business Processes

A minimalist privacy plan involves a privacy policy statement that goes beyond the limited assurances dictated by the law. People appreciate clear, direct statements that are not qualified by large volumes of bureaucratic, lawyer-dictated expressions. Guidance is provided in Clarke (2005).

Real credibility, however, depends on more than mere statements. There is a need for organisations' undertakings to be backed up by indemnities in the event that the organisation breaches them. Complaints-handling processes are needed, to provide unhappy clients with an avenue to seek redress. Constructive responses to complaints are essential. Indeed, these are stipulated by industry standards relating to complaints-handling (ISO 10002 2004). A self-confident organisation goes further, and explains the laws that regulate the organisation, links to the sources of the law, and provides contact-points for relevant regulators.

To underpin privacy statements and indemnities, an organisation needs to ensure that its business processes are privacy-sensitive. This is a non-trivial task. Firstly, it is necessary for all business processes to be reviewed against a comprehensive set of privacy requirements. Secondly, it requires that privacy impact assessments (PIAs) be undertaken for each new project that is undertaken that involves impositions on individuals or the use of personal data. A PIA is a process whereby the potential privacy impacts and implications of proposals are surfaced and examined (Clarke, 1998a).

Together, these measures can enable an organisation to at least reduce distrust by individuals, and, if well conceived and executed, can deliver the organisation a reputation among its employees and clientele that encourages appropriate behaviour, and even provides it with competitive advantage.

Technology's Role

The remainder of this chapter looks beyond the base level of privacy-sensitive business processes, and focusses on the role of organisations' use of technology in order to reduce the distrust held by the organisation's employees and e-business partners, or even enhance the degree of trust.

Information technologies have largely had a deleterious impact on privacy. Those that have a particularly negative impact, such as visual and data surveillance, person location and tracking, and applications of RFID tags beyond the retail shelf, are usefully referred to as "privacy-invasive technologies" ("the PITs"). The first sub-section below addresses the PITs.

A further and more constructive way of treating privacy as a strategic variable is to apply technology in order to actively assist in the protection of people's privacy, hence "privacy-enhancing technologies" or "PETs."

The history of the PETs is commonly traced back to applications of cryptography by David Chaum (1981, 1985, 1992). The term "privacy-enhanced mail" (PEM) was used at least as early as the mid-1980s, in the RFC series 989 (February 1987), 1040 (January 1988), and 1113-1115 (August 1989), which defined a "Privacy Enhancement for Internet Electronic Mail." PEM proposed the use of cryptography to protect the content of email from being accessed by anyone other than the intended recipient. The more general term "privacy enhancing technology" (at that stage without the acronym) has been traced by EPIC's Marc Rotenberg to CPSR (1991).

The first use of the acronym to refer to a defined category of technologies appears to have been by John Borking of the Dutch Data Protection Authority in 1994. A report was published as ICPR (1995) (see also Borking, 2003; Borking & Raab, 2001; Burkert, 1997; Goldberg, Wagner, & Brewer, 1997). Annual PET Workshops have been held since 2000, with significant contributions from computer scientists in Germany and Canada as well as the USA. These diverge somewhat in their interpretation of PETs from that of the Data Protection Commissioners of The Netherlands, Ontario, and Germany, in particular in that they focus strongly on nymity.

A wide variety of tools exist (EPIC 1996-). More are being devised. It is useful to distinguish several broad categories. Some are used as countermeasures against PITs. Others provide users with anonymity on the Internet. Because anonymity is, by definition, unbreakable, there is an inevitable conflict with accountability. For this reason, tools for anonymity are referred to here as "savage PETs." An alternative is to promote tools that provide pseudonymity. This must be breakable in order to enable the investigation of suspected criminal behaviour; but it must be breakable only with sufficient difficulty, in order to attract people to use it and to overcome distrust. This group of tools is referred to in this chapter as "gentle PETs." Finally, some measures have been referred to by their proponents as PETs, but deliver little of substance, and are accordingly referred to in this chapter as "pseudo-PETs." Each of these categories of technology is addressed below.

The PITs

There are many applications of technology whose primary function is to gather data, collate data, apply data, or otherwise assist in the surveillance of people and their behaviour. A useful collective term is "privacy-intrusive technologies," or "the PITs." Among the host of examples are data-trail generation and intensification through the denial of anonymity (e.g., identified phones, stored-value cards, and intelligent transportation systems), data warehousing and data mining, video-surveillance, stored biometrics, and imposed biometrics (Clarke, 2001a, 2001d).

A current concern is the various categories of "spyware" (Stafford & Urbaczewski, 2004). This is being applied by corporations to assist in the protection of their copyright interests, gather personal data about customers and project high-value advertising at consumers, and by fraudsters to capture authentication data such as passwords. The cumulative impact of PITs on consumers and citizens is heightened distrust of both large organisations and information technology.

One aspect of an organisation's privacy strategy is the examination of the technologies the organisation uses in order to appreciate the extent to which they are privacy-intrusive, and the extent to which that privacy-intrusiveness may militate against achievement of the organisation's objectives.

Pseudo-PETs

There have been attempts to take advantage of the PET movement by applying the label to techniques that provide only nominal protection. The most apparent of these is so-called "privacy seals," such as TRUSTe, Better Business Bureau, and WebTrust. They are mere undertakings that have no enforcement mechanism, and are just "meta-brands"—images devised in order to provide an impression of protection (Clarke, 2001c).

Another "pseudo-PET" is Platform for Privacy Preferences (P3P-W3C 1998-). P3P was originally envisaged as a means whereby web-sites could declare their privacy undertakings, and web-browsers could compare the undertakings with the browser-user's requirements, and block access, or limit the transmission of personal data accordingly. But P3P was implemented server-side only, with the result that it contributes very little to privacy protection (Clarke, 1998a, 1998c, 2001b; EPIC 2000).

Counter-PITs

Many PETs assist people to defeat or neutralise privacy-invasive technologies and hence are usefully referred to as "Counter-PITs." Examples include SSL/TLS for channel encryption, spam-filters, cookie-managers, password managers, personal firewalls, virus protection software, and spyware-sweepers.

Although many protections are already productised, opportunities remain for organisations to contribute. For example, there is a need for services that display to the browser-user information about the owner of an IP-address before connecting to it, and for the monitoring of inbound traffic for patterns consistent with malware and hacking, and outbound traffic for spyware-related transmissions (DCITA 2005).

Savage PETs

For many people, that first category of PETs is unsatisfactory because they still permit organisations to accumulate personal data into dossiers and profiles. A much more aggressive approach is available. One class of PETs sets out to deny identity and to provide untraceable **anonymity**. Examples include genuinely anonymous ("Mixmaster") remailers and Web surfing schemes, and genuinely anonymous e-payment mechanisms. (The inclusion of "genuinely" is necessary, because some remailers and payment mechanisms have been incorrectly described as "anonymous," even though they are actually traceable).

Such techniques exist, and will always exist, nomatter what countermeasures are developed. Major literature in this area includes Chaum (1981, 1985, 1992); Onion (1996); Syverson, Goldschlag, and Reed (1997); Clarke (2002); and Dingledine, Mathewson, and Syverson (2004). See also Freehaven (2000). For a critical review of policy aspects, see Froomkin (1995).

Gentle PETs

Where they are successful, "Savage PETs" work against accountability, because they reduce the chances of retribution being wrought against people who use them to assist in achieving evil ends. It would be highly beneficial if a balance could be found between anonymity on the one hand, and accountability on the other.

The means of achieving this is through "protected pseudonymity." It is the most technically challenging, and at this stage the least developed of the categories. The essential requirement of a gentle PET is that very substantial protections are provided for individuals' identities, but in such a manner that those protections can be breached when particular conditions are fulfilled.

Underlying this approach is a fundamental principle of human freedom that appears not yet to have achieved mainstream understanding: people have multiple identities, and to achieve privacy-protection those identities must be sustained. This favours single-purpose identifiers and militates against multi-purpose identifiers (Clarke, 1994b, 1999).

The protections against breach of protected psuedonymity must be trustworthy, and must comprise an inter-locking network of legal, organisational and technical features. If the power to override the protections is in the hands of a person or organisation that flouts the conditions, then pseudonymity's value as a privacy protection collapses. Unfortunately, governments throughout history have shown themselves to be untrustworthy when their interests are too seriously threatened; and corporations are dedicated to shareholder value alone, and will only comply with the conditions when they are subject to sufficiently powerful preventative mechanisms and sanctions. The legal authority to breach pseudonymity must therefore be in the hands of an independent judiciary, and the case for breach must be demonstrated to the court.

A range of technical protections is needed. The creation and controlled use of identities needs to be facilitated. The traffic generated using protected pseudonyms needs to be guarded against traceability, because that would enable inference of an association between a person and the identity. In addition, there must be technical support for procedures to disclose the person's identity, which must involve the participation of multiple parties, which in turn must be achieved through the presentation of reliable evidence (Goldberg, 2000).

These features are unlikely to be satisfied accidentally, but must be achieved through careful design. For example, the original "anonymous remailer", anon. penet.fi (1993-96), was merely pseudonymous because it maintained a cross-reference between the incoming (identified) message and the outgoing ("anonymised") message, and the cross-reference was accessible to anyone who gained access to the device—including Finnish police, who do not have to rely on judicial instruments as authority for access, because they have the power to issue search warrants themselves (Wikipedia, 2002).

The notion of "identity management" has been prominent. The mainstream approaches, those of Microsoft Passport, and of the misleadingly named "Liberty Alliance," are in fact privacy-invasive technologies, because they "provide" identities to individuals, and their fundamental purpose is to facilitate sharing of personal data among organisations. Microsoft's "Identity Metasystem" (Microsoft, 2006),

Figure 1. A classification scheme for business case techniques

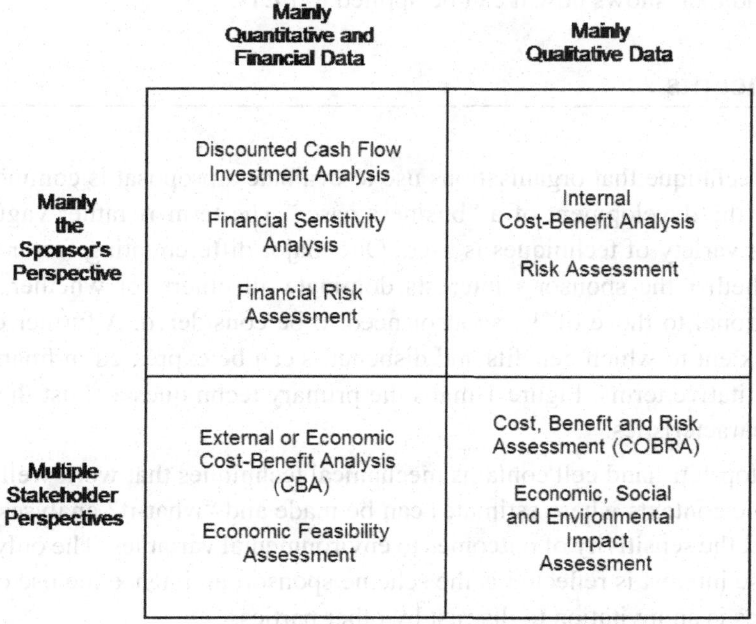

	Mainly Quantitative and Financial Data	Mainly Qualitative Data
Mainly the Sponsor's Perspective	Discounted Cash Flow Investment Analysis Financial Sensitivity Analysis Financial Risk Assessment	Internal Cost-Benefit Analysis Risk Assessment
Multiple Stakeholder Perspectives	External or Economic Cost-Benefit Analysis (CBA) Economic Feasibility Assessment	Cost, Benefit and Risk Assessment (COBRA) Economic, Social and Environmental Impact Assessment

based on Cameron (2005), is more sophisticated, but also fails to support protected pseudonymity.

The need is for "demand-side" identity management tools that are PETs rather than PITs (Clarke, 2004; Clauß, Pfitzmann, Hansen, & Van Herreweghen, 2002). Organisations need to utilise multiple means to protect their interests, rather than imposing unjustifiable demands for strong authentication of the identity of the individuals that they deal with—because that approach is inherently privacy-invasive, and generates distrust.

Business Cases for PETs

An organisation that is distrusted by staff or customers because of privacy concerns needs to consider using PETs as a means of addressing the problem. This section examines how organisations can evaluate the scope for PETs to contribute to their privacy strategy, and hence to their business strategy as a whole. There appear to be very few references to this topic in the literature, but see MIKR (2004, pp. 38-45).

The first sub-section clarifies the much-abused concept of "a business case." The second then shows how it can be applied to PETs.

Concepts

The technique that organisations use to evaluate a proposal is commonly referred to as the development of a "business case." The term is rather vague, however, and a variety of techniques is used. One major differentiating factor among them is whether the sponsor's interests dominate all others, or whether perspectives additional to those of the sponsor need to be considered. A further distinction is the extent to which benefits and disbenefits can be expressed in financial or other quantitative terms. Figure 1 maps the primary techniques against those two pairs of characteristics.

The top-left-hand cell contains mechanical techniques that work well in relatively simple contexts where estimates can be made and "what-if" analyses can be used to test the sensitivity of outcomes to environmental variables. The only stakeholder whose interest is reflected is the scheme sponsor; and hence the use of these techniques is an invitation to distrust by other parties.

The bottom-left-hand cell is relevant to projects in which the interests of multiple parties need to be appreciated, and where necessary traded off. But the distrust impediment can seldom be reduced to the quantitative form that these techniques demand.

The techniques in the top-right-hand cell are applicable to a corporation that is operating relatively independently of other parties but cannot express all factors in neat, quantitative terms. Even in the public sector, it is sometimes feasible for an agency to prepare a business case as though it were an independent organisation (e.g., when evaluating a contract with a photocopier supplier, or for the licensing of an electronic document management system). Internal Cost-Benefit Analysis involves assessments of benefits and disbenefits to the organisation, wherever practicable using financial or at least quantitative measures, but where necessary represented by qualitative data (Clarke, 1994; Clarke & Stevens, 1997). Risk Assessment adopts a disciplined approach to considering key environmental factors, and the impact of potentially seriously disadvantageous scenarios. Once again, however, only the interests of the scheme sponsor are relevant, and the perspectives of other parties are actively excluded.

More complex projects require the more sophisticated (and challenging) techniques in the bottom-right quadrant of Exhibit 1. For example, a government agency cannot afford to consider only the organisation's own interests. It must at least consider the needs of its Minister, and there are usually other agencies with interests in the matter as well.

Outside the public sector, it is increasingly common for organisations to work together rather than independently. In some cases this takes the form of tight strategic partnerships, and in others looser value-adding chains. In yet others, "public-private partnerships" inter-twine the interests of corporations and government agencies. At the very least, most organisations work within infrastructure common to all participants in the relevant industry sector, or within collaborative arrangements negotiated through one or more industry associations. Such projects therefore depend on "win-win" solutions, and the business case must reflect the perspectives of the multiple stakeholders.

Some of the biggest challenges arise where there is significant disparity in size and market power among the participants, especially where the success of the undertaking is dependent upon the participation of many small business enterprises. Appropriate approaches for such circumstances are discussed in Cameron and Clarke (1996) and Cameron (2005).

The discussion in this sub-section has to this point assumed that all participants are organisations. There are many projects, however, in which the interests of individuals need to be considered, because their non-participation, non-adoption, or outright opposition, may undermine the project and deny return on investment. Clarke (1992) drew to attention the then-emergent concept of "extra-organisational systems" such as ATM and EFTPOS networks, and the need to ensure that consumers' interests are reflected in the system design, by engaging with consumers and their representatives and advocates. Engagement requires information dissemination, consultation, and the use of participative design techniques. The rapid emergence of the open, public Internet in the years immediately following the publication of that paper enabled an explosion of such extra-organisational systems.

Yet corporations have seldom considered their customers as stakeholders, and even government agencies frequently leave them aside from business case evaluations. Organisations that want to avoid the distrust impediment need to apply the business case techniques in the bottom-right-hand corner of Exhibit 1, in order to reflect the perspectives of all of the important stakeholders, including human users and other individuals affected by the scheme. Impact and risk assessment activities need to encompass at least privacy, but the scope may need to extend to broader social and economic aspects such as accessibility, accidental discrimination against minorities, and the need for workplace re-training.

Application

This chapter's focus is the use of PETs as an adjunct to corporate privacy strategy. The application of PETs needs to be evaluated and a business case developed. Because of the multi-stakeholder context, and the difficulties of quantifying many of the benefits and costs, the relevant business case techniques are those in the bottom-right-hand quadrant of Figure 1.

This sub-section applies to PETs the business case concepts discussed above. It firstly identifies various ways in which an organisation might seek to use PETs as a means of overcoming distrust by its staff or by relevant segments of the public, particularly its customers or prospects. It then considers the kinds of benefits that may be able to be achieved, the costs and other disbenefits that may be incurred in the process, and the risks involved. Finally, approaches to reaching a conclusion about the proposal are examined.

Ways to Work with PETs

There are various ways in which organisations can utilise PETs in their privacy strategy. They include the following:

- fund research into or the development of PETs:
  o   by the organisation itself;
  o   by others;
- provide or support awareness, education and training in relation to the development, deployment, installation and/or use of PETs;
- support open source licensing of PET software, in order to enhance its availability, and to increase confidence in its integrity;
- promote the use of PETs;
- design and adapt the organisation's e-business services in order to ensure that they work with PETs and do not work against them;
- support the distribution of PETs;
- actively distribute PETs to employees and/or customers.

Benefits

Incorporating PETs into an organisation's privacy strategy provides tangible evidence of its intentions. Such actions are likely to be rated more highly than the mere assurances set out in privacy policy statements, at least by some target segments, and by representatives of and advocates for consumers.

Areas in which benefits can be sought include the following:

- if the target-market includes segments that are particularly sensitive to privacy concerns, they can be attracted by the organisation's strong privacy orientation, as evidenced by its commitment to PETs;
- a similar impact may be achieved if the target-market involves client segments that value ethical behaviour and the provision of choice (whether or not those individuals are themselves privacy-sensitive);
- a strong privacy image may be compatible with the organisation's brand and reputation and hence enhance its effectiveness and value. This depends, of course, on some means whereby the measures relating to PETs influence corporate image;
- marketing and/or brand-projection effects may enable enhanced market-share, and consequent increased transaction revenue or reduced customer acquisition costs; or it may encourage greater participation (e.g. in voluntary statistical surveys by a government service) or more honest information provision (to corporations and government agencies alike);
- greater adoption arising from a PET-related initiative may result in enhanced service delivery to clients.

Because PET-related projects signal the organisation's willingness to address negative perceptions of its activities, and involve the engagement of stakeholders, benefits may arise from the mere act of conducting business case analysis, even if the eventual decision is to not proceed with the initiative.

Costs and Other Disbenefits

There are costs involved in such measures. It is unlikely that the financial costs would be high relative to the scale of any reasonably large organisation's budget. On the other hand, an initiative of this kind inevitably involves considerable executive and managerial effort, and adaptation of business processes, and, perhaps more challengingly, adaptation of organisational culture.

To have the desired effect, the initiative needs to be integrated into the organisation's marketing communications mechanisms, in order to convey the message to the targeted market-segments. Moreover, the preparation of a business case using a method with necessarily broad scope is itself potentially expensive.

Risks

Many benefits and disbenefits are inevitable or at least highly likely. But some further impacts may or may not arise, depending on various environmental factors.

One potential is that a project of this nature, and deep analysis of it, may be divisive among the participants, because their perspectives may be distinctly different. Another possibility is that the intentions may be seen as inappropriate, perhaps by the media, or by a regulator, or by a competitor or industry association. A further concern is the possibility of failure or non-adoption, which could result in disappointment and loss of morale.

Factors that embody significant risk need to be the subject of a management strategy.

The Net Effect

Each organisation, in its own context, needs to evaluate the net effect of the benefits and disbenefits, moderated by the risks. There are many circumstances in which project sponsors can extract sufficient benefit from a PET-related initiative to make it well worth the effort, investment and management of the risks. And even where the net effect of an initiative is not attractive, the effort invested in preparing a business case can pay dividends, by pointing the project team towards a variant in the approach that will overcome the primary disbenefit or risk.

Even if the costs appear high, investment in PETs may well be justified as a strategic measure, rather than one that needs to be formally justified by means of discounted cash flows. This is because it is of the nature of infrastructure, or an enabler. One strategic opportunity is differentiation leading to competitive advantage, particularly first-mover advantage—such as market-share gains through the attraction of users dissatisfied with other suppliers. Another is where a PET initiative has the capacity to unblock adoption processes, such that e-business initiatives that would otherwise stall can instead flourish.

Conclusion

Organisations need to appreciate that the achievement of their objectives may be seriously hindered by distrust of e-business and of the organisations that provide e-business services. Organisations need to adopt a positive approach to the privacy of the parties that they deal with, and to conceive, articulate and implement a privacy strategy.

For some corporations and government agencies, simple approaches based on privacy impact assessment and privacy-sensitive business practices may suffice. For others, however, avoiding distrust and instead inculcating trust demands more substantial initiatives. Initiatives in relation to PETs can make important contributions towards their overall privacy strategies.

As with any other project, a business case is needed. Care is necessary in selecting the appropriate approach to adopt, because the perspectives of other key stakeholders have to be reflected, particularly the parties whose participation is crucial. This chapter has provided an overview of the rationale and the process involved, together with indicators of benefits, disbenefits and risks.

Using the guidance in this chapter, an organisation can evaluate the potentials that PETs offer to staff, or to key customer segments, and build the business case.

Acknowledgment

This chapter was stimulated by an invitation from Mike Gurski, Director of the Privacy Centre of Excellence of Bell Information & Communications Technology Solutions in Toronto, and Caspar Bowden, Chief Privacy Advisor EMEA, Microsoft, of London and Toulouse. A preliminary version was presented at the Executive Session of PETS 2005—5th Workshop on Privacy-Enhancing Technologies, June 2, 2005, Cavtat, Croatia.

References

Except where otherwise noted, URLs were checked in January 2007.

Borking, J.J. (2003). *The status of privacy enhancing technologies, Certification and security in e-services: From e-government to e-business.* Kluwer.

Borking, J.J. & Raab, C. (2001). Laws, PETS and other technologies for privacy protection. *Journal of Information, Law and Technology, 1*(February).

Burkert, H. (1997). Privacy-enhancing technologies: Typology, critique, vision. In P.E. Agre & M. Rotenberg (Eds.), *Technology and privacy: The new landscape.* MIT Press.

Cameron, J. (2005). Ten concepts for an e-business collaborative project management framework. *Proceedings of the 18th Bled eConference,* Bled, Slovenia, June.

Cameron, K. (2005). The laws of identity. Microsoft, May. Retrieved from http://msdn2.microsoft.com/en-us/library/ms996456.aspx

Chaum, D. (1981). Untraceable electronic mail, return addresses, and digital pseudonyms. Communications of the ACM, 4(2). Retrieved from http://world.std.com/~franl/crypto/chaum-acm-1981.html

Chaum, D. (1985). Security without identification: Transaction systems to make big brother obsolete. *Communications of the ACM, 28*(10). Retrieved from http://www.chaum.com/articles/Security_Wthout_Identification.htm

Chaum, D. (1992), Achieving electronic privacy. *Sci. Am.*, 96-101. Retrieved from http://www.chaum.com/articles/Achieving_Electronic_Privacy.htm

Clarke, I., Miller, S.G., Hong, T.W., Sandberg, O. & Wiley, B. (2002). Protecting free expression online with Freenet. *IEEE Internet Computing* (January-February). Retrived from http://freenetproject.org/papers/freenet-ieee.pdf

Clarke, R. (1988). Information technology and dataveillance. *Communications of the ACM, 31*(5). Retrieved from http://www.anu.edu.au/people/Roger.Clarke/DV/CACM88.html

Clarke, R. (1992). Extra-organisational systems: A challenge to the software engineering paradigm. *Proceedings of the IFIP World Congress*, Madrid, September. Retrieved from http://www.anu.edu.au/people/Roger.Clarke/SOS/PaperExtraOrgSys.html

Clarke, R. (1994a). The path of development of strategic information systems theory. Xamax Consultancy Pty Ltd, July 1994, at http://www.anu.edu.au/people/Roger.Clarke/SOS/StratISTh.html

Clarke, R. (1994b). Human identification in information systems: Management challenges and public policy issues. *Information Technology & People, 7*(4), 6-37. Retrieved from http://www.anu.edu.au/people/Roger.Clarke/DV/HumanID.html

Clarke, R. (1996). Privacy, dataveillance, organisational strategy. *Proceedings of the I.S. Audit & Control Association Conference (EDPAC '96)*, Perth, May 28, 1996. Retrieved from http://www.anu.edu.au/people/Roger.Clarke/DV/PStrat.html

Clarke, R. (1998a). Privacy impact assessment guidelines. Xamax Consultancy Pty Ltd, February 1998. Retrieved from http://www.xamax.com.au/DV/PIA.html

Clarke, R. (1998b). Platform for privacy preferences: An overview. *Privacy Law & Policy Reporter,* 5(2), 35-39. Retrieved from http://www.anu.edu.au/people/Roger.Clarke/DV/P3POview.html

Clarke, R. (1998c). Platform for privacy preferences: A critique. *Privacy Law & Policy Reporter, 5*(3), 46-48. Retrieved from http://www.anu.edu.au/people/Roger.Clarke/DV/P3PCrit.html

Clarke, R. (1999). Identified, anonymous and pseudonymous transactions: The spectrum of choice. In S. Fischer-Hübner, G. Quirchmayr, & L. Yngström (Eds.), *User identification & privacy protection: Applications in public administration & electronic commerce.* Kista, Schweden, IFIP WG 8.5 and WS 9.6, June 1999. Retrieved from http://www.anu.edu.au/people/Roger.Clarke/DV/UIPP99.html

Clarke, R. (2001a). Introducing PITs and PETs: Technologies affecting privacy. *Privacy Law & Policy Reporter, 7*(9), 181-183, 188. Retrieved from http://www.anu.edu.au/people/Roger.Clarke/DV/PITsPETs.html

Clarke, R. (2001b). P3P re-visited. *Privacy Law & Policy Reporter, 7*(10). Retrieved from http://www.anu.edu.au/people/Roger.Clarke/DV/P3PRev.html

Clarke, R. (2001c). Meta-Brands. *Privacy Law & Policy Reporter, 7*(11). Retrieved from http://www.anu.edu.au/people/Roger.Clarke/DV/MetaBrands.html

Clarke, R. (2001d). Person-location and person-tracking: Technologies, risks and policy implications. *Information Technology & People, 14*(2), 206-231. Retrieved from http://www.anu.edu.au/people/Roger.Clarke/DV/PLT.html

Clarke, R. (2002). Trust in the context of e-business. *Internet Law Bulletin, 4*(5), 56-59. Retrieved from http://www.anu.edu.au/people/Roger.Clarke/EC/Trust.html

Clarke, R. (2004). *Identity management: The Technologies Their Business Value Their Problems Their Prospects.* Xamax Consultancy Pty Ltd, March, Retrieved from http://www.xamax.com.au/EC/IdMngt.html

Clarke, R. (2005). Privacy statement template. Xamax Consultancy Pty Ltd, December. Retrieved from at http://www.anu.edu.au/people/Roger.Clarke/DV/PST.html

Clarke, R. (2006a). What's Privacy? Xamax Consultancy Pty Ltd, July 2006. Retrieved from http://www.anu.edu.au/people/Roger.Clarke/DV/Privacy.html

Clarke, R. (2006b). Vignettes of corporate privacy disasters. Xamax Consultancy Pty Ltd, September 2006. Retrieved from http://www.anu.edu.au/people/Roger.Clarke/DV/PrivCorp-0609.html

Clarke, R. (2006c). Make privacy a strategic factor - The why and the how. *Cutter IT Journal, 19*(11), 26-31. Retrieved from http://www.anu.edu.au/people/Roger.Clarke/DV/APBD-0609.html

Clauß, S., Pfitzmann, A., Hansen, M. & Van Herreweghen, E. (2002). Privacy-enhancing identity management . *IPTS Report,* Issue 67 (September). Retrieved from http://www.jrc.es/home/report/english/articles/vol67/IPT2E676.htm

CPSR (1991). CPSR co-sponsors meeting on encryption, privacy and communications. *CPSR News Volume, 9*(2). Archived at http://web.archive.org/web/20040705115955/http://www.cpsr.org/publications/newsletters/issues/1991/WinSpr1991/crypt.html

DCITA (2005). Taking care of spyware. DCITA, September 2005. Retrieved from http://www.dcita.gov.au/search/click.cgi?url=http://www.dcita.gov.au/__data/assets/pdf_file/30866/Taking_Care_of_Spyware.pdf&rank=2&collection=search

Dingeldine, R., Mathewson, N. & Syverson, P. (2004). Tor: The second-generation onion router. *Proceedings of the 13th USENIX Security Symposium*, August. Retrieved from http://tor.freehaven.net/cvs/doc/design-paper/tor-design.html

DOC (2000). Safe Harbor overview. U.S. Department of Commerce. Retrieved from http://www.export.gov/safeharbor/sh_overview.html

EPIC (1996-). EPIC online guide to practical privacy tools. Retrieved from http://www.epic.org/privacy/tools.html

EPIC (2000). Pretty poor privacy: An assessment of P3P and Internet Privacy. Electronic Privacy Information Center and Junkbusters, June. Retrieved from http://www.epic.org/Reports/prettypoorprivacy.html

EU (1995). Directive 95/46/EC of the European Parliament and of the Council of 24 October 1995 on the protection of individuals with regard to the processing of personal data and on the free movement of such data. European Union, October 24. Retrieved from http://ec.europa.eu/justice_home/fsj/privacy/docs/95-46-ce/dir1995-46_part1_en.pdf

Freehaven (2000-). Anonymity bibliography. Retrieved from http://freehaven.net/anonbib/

Froomkin, A.M. (1995). Anonymity and its enmities. J. Online L., http://www.law.cornell.edu/jol/froomkin.htm, 1995, at http://www.wm.edu/law/publications/jol/95_96/froomkin.html

FTC (2000). Privacy online: Fair information practices in the electronic marketplace: A Federal Trade Commission report to Congress. Federal Trade Commission, May. Retrieved from http://www.ftc.gov/reports/privacy2000/privacy2000.pdf

Goldberg, I. (2000). *A pseudonymous communications infrastructure for the Internet.* PhD thesis, UC Berkeley, December. Retrieved from http://www.isaac.cs.berkeley.edu/~iang/thesis-final.pdf

Goldberg, I., Wagner, D., & Brewer, E. (1997). Privacy-enhancing technologies for the Internet. *Proceedings of the 42nd IEEE Spring COMPCON*, February.

IPCR (1995). Privacy-enhancing technologies: The path to anonymity. *Information and Privacy Commissioner* (Ontario, Canada) and *Registratiekamer* (The Netherlands), 2 vols., August. Retrieved from http://www.ipc.on.ca/web%5Fsite. eng/matters/sum%5Fpap/papers/anon%2De.htm

ISO 10002 (2004). Quality management -- Customer satisfaction -- Guidelines for complaints handling in organizations. International Standards Organisation. Retrieved from http://www.iso.org/iso/en/CatalogueDetailPage.CatalogueDe tail?CSNUMBER=35539&ICS1=3&ICS2=120&ICS3=10

Microsoft (2006). The identity metasystem: Towards a privacy-compliant solution to the challenges of digital identity. Microsoft, October. Retrieved from http:// www.identityblog.com/wp-content/resources/Identity_Metasystem_EU_Privacy.pdf

MIKR (2004). Privacy-enhancing technologies: White paper for decision-makers. Dutch Ministry of the Interior and Kingdom Relations, December. Retrieved from http://www.dutchdpa.nl/downloads_overig/PET_whitebook.pdf

Onion (1996-). Onion-Router.net. Retrieved from http://www.onion-router.net/Publications.html

OECD (1980). OECD guidelines on the protection of privacy and transborder flows of personal data. Organisation for Economic Co-operation and Development, Paris. Retrieved from http://www.oecd.org/document/18/0,2340,en_2649_201185_1815186_1_1_1_1,00.html

PET Workshops (2000-). Workshops on privacy enhancing technologies. Retrieved from http://petworkshop.org/

Rotenberg, M. (2004). *The privacy law sourcebook: 2001.* Electronic Privacy Information Center. Retrieved from http://www.epic.org/bookstore/pls2004/

Smith, R.E. (2002). Compilation of state and federal privacy laws. *Privacy Journal,* with a 2006 Supplement. Retrieved from http://www.privacyjournal. net/work1.htm

Stafford, T.F. & Urbaczewski, A. (2004). Spyware: The ghost in the machine. *Commun. Association for Information Systems, 14,* 291-306. Retrieved from http://web.njit.edu/~bieber/CIS677F04/stafford-spyware-cais2004.pdf

Syverson, P., Goldschlag, D., & Reed, M. (1997). Anonymous connections and onion routing. *Proceedings of the 18th Symposium on Security and Privacy,* Oakland. Retrieved from http://www.onion-router.net/Publications/SSP-1997.pdf

W3C (1998-). Platform for privacy preferences. World Wide Web Consortium, Retrieved from http://www.w3.org/P3P/

Wikipedia (2002-). Penet remailer. Retrieved from http://en.wikipedia.org/wiki/Penet_remailer

Section IV

Privacy and Organizations

Chapter VIII

Privacy through Security:
Policy and Practice in a
Small-Medium Enterprise

Ian Allison, The Robert Gordon University, UK

Craig Strangwick, ABC Awards Ltd, UK

Abstract

The chapter discusses how one small business planned for, and implemented, the security of its data in a new enterprise-wide system. The company's data was perceived as sensitive, and any breach of privacy as commercially critical. From this perspective, the chapter outlines the organizational and technical facets of the policies and practices evidenced. Lessons for other businesses can be drawn from the case by recognizing the need for investments to be made that will address threats in business critical areas. By highlighting the need for organizations to understand the nature of the risk and the probability of an event occurring, the security approaches highlight the need to address both the threats and actions in the event of an incident to reduce the risk to privacy.

Introduction

Privacy often is discussed in the literature as an ethical issue, whereby members of society are perceived to have a right to privacy and that right is considered to be eroded through the application of information technology. The Internet and supporting architectures are considered to make privacy more vulnerable because behaviour can be monitored, personal data can be commodified and exchanged, and data can be combined from different sources to enable analysis of individuals' records (e.g. Spinello, 2006; Tavani, 2004). The invasion of privacy is seen to occur through the access to, and control of, personal information.

Consequently, debates in the literature focus on what we understand privacy to be, the degree to which privacy can be taken as a right, to what degree privacy should be protected and how computer technology affects privacy. In other words, the morality of individual, organizational, and societal actions is evaluated. What is ignored in these debates is the business implication of privacy and how this shapes information security activity within organizations.

Security research, on the other hand, focuses on the threat of attack by hackers or malware, and the tools and technical solutions available to address these threats. The need to develop secure architectures or build applications that avoid security pitfalls, whilst important, mostly does not address the way in which such decisions affect privacy.

This chapter, therefore, seeks to straddle these two fields to show how organizations need to take privacy into account as a business issue in order that this shapes information security policies and practice. To achieve this we draw on the experiences of one small-medium enterprise (SME). The formal definition of SMEs varies from country to country, but for the purposes of this chapter we have defined SMEs as employing less than 500 people. This definition does not mean that the lessons are not applicable to larger organizations but that the focus of the study, and data drawn from previous studies, matches this definition.

The remainder of this chapter begins by outlining why privacy is a business issue, recognising the financial and legal imperatives organizations face. Current security policies and practices in SMEs worldwide are then reviewed highlighting the weaknesses currently evident in the way that SMEs approach their information security.

The focus of the chapter is a case study based on ABC Awards Ltd, a small UK-based assessment body who offers vocational qualifications through a variety of learning centres. The study relates to their development of an enterprise-wide information system and underpinning infrastructure. Policy and practice were developed to support the business security needs in line with the legal and commercial need for protection of privacy of personal data. The analysis is structured to focus on people and organizational issues, and on technical issues, to show the inter-relationship between these aspects of information security management.

Privacy as a Business Issue

The violation of privacy through computer technology is often related to acts of snooping on individuals. Edgar (2003) gives examples of how computers have been used to identify potential prospective sales targets, verify the status of debtors' bank accounts, and find out about the activities of customers. These examples show how organizations are seen to invade privacy in order to make business decisions based upon private data. Moor (2004) therefore calls for increased legal protection so as to reduce excess harm and risk to the individual at the expense of the organization.

Organizations are already under a clear legal obligation, at least in some countries, to protect private data and to use it only in accordance within defined guidelines. Laws on data protection have developed since the 1970s. France (2004) noted the way that the European Directive (95/46/EC) in 1995 produced harmonisation of these laws across Europe. The resulting laws supported the free flow of data between businesses in different parts of the continent as the Directive provided a standard level of protection. However, she also highlights that it was not the moral but the trade imperatives that led to the development of the initial UK Data Protection Act (1984). Previous parliamentary investigations had been less than convinced by the ethical cause.

The current UK Data Protection Act (1998) is built upon eight principles that constrain the way that data is collected, processed, and stored. For example, organizations have to ensure the data is accurate, held only as long as necessary, not excessive, and secured.

Elsewhere though, such as Australia, small businesses are exempt from privacy legislation. The US, too, has minimal legal protection for private data, with small business required to offer little security of data, and some make a profit from selling on that data. As a result some argue this leaves them "woefully behind" Europe (Tavani, 2004, p. 146). The US Government appears to side with business interests, who fear the cost of implementing data protection legislation would undermine economic efficiency. Tavani (2004) argues that this is alarmist and there is minimal overhead as most US organizations operating in Europe have done so without profits suffering.

Indeed, on the contrary, it could be argued not paying appropriate attention to privacy could be a detriment to business profits. As Holmes (2006, p. 2) puts it, "carefully thought-out privacy controls make good business sense" as it has a considerable impact on sales. He shows how getting this right has been beneficial at Bell Canada. Microsoft also has recognised that it needs to ensure privacy as part of its products and services (Fleischer & Cooper, 2006). In areas related to Internet activity, Microsoft's policies and practices have been overhauled to ensure compliance with the EU privacy rules. Fleischer and Cooper (2006) conclude by highlighting the importance of privacy for the business and the need to involve key stakeholders in decisions about privacy policy.

There are though many examples of organizations who have suffered loss of profits as a result of under-mining customer privacy; the "size of the monetary penalty should fool no one" (Holmes, 2006, p. 1). Nissenbaum (2004) gives the example of Lotus Marketplace, a software package that brought together publicly available information about individuals in one system. The package was due to be launched by Lotus and Equifax in the early 1990s. They did not anticipate the level of public complaint: 30000 letters of protest were received. The package was withdrawn from the market. Cartmanager, an online shopping cart software provider, broke its own privacy policy by selling customer data thereby infuriating both online users and the merchants who had incorporated the software on their Web sites; their reputation was damaged for some time (Holmes, 2006). Similarly, one of the UK's largest banks, HSBC, found itself on the front page of national newspapers in August 2006 because of a security loophole putting customer data at risk via its Internet banking systems requiring its CEO to write a strong rebuttal highlighting the potential impact of the article on its business (Guardian, 2006).

As a consequence, organizations need to focus on ensuring customer trust. "Trust means stakeholders feel safe in the hands of these enterprises and are confident in the secure delivery of their products and services along with protection of their private information" (Reece, 2007, p. 1). Reece (2007) goes on to argue that trust must be earned through excellence of operations and leading edge information protection. Good information protection requires organizations to recognise the value of the information and develop policies accordingly. Good privacy polices should not be seen as a dam but as a finely tuned control valve allowing business to continue effectively whilst maintaining the integrity and security of personally valued data (Holmes, 2006).

The financial implications of a lack of trust are significant. For instance, e-commerce usage has stalled because of a lack of trust (Holmes, 2006). Internet users place great value on security measures that make identity theft less likely (Poindexter, Earp, & Baumer, 2006). At The Woolwich, a UK bank, security was seen as a critical element in their adoption of e-banking following the embarrassment suffered by their parent bank where security breaches led to huge media coverage (Shah & Siddiqui, 2006). Low information security effectiveness could have wide-spread implications for competitive advantage: "the enormity of potential losses arising from IS security abuses should motivate them to raise their deterrent efforts so as to enhance there IS security effectiveness" (Kankanhalli, Teo, Tan, & Wei, 2003, p. 152).

So in summary, if a business was to inadvertently release private data then the damage to the reputation and trust in the market that would have an immediate, and at least proportionate, impact on the business's finance. Even ignoring the possibility of litigation, the loss of custom could be substantial. This risk is all the more likely where trust is a paramount element of the service provided, such as in financial or other personal service organizations. Organizations are aware of these risks to their business: it is already seen as a major constraint on the growth of e-business. On this basis then, security of systems should be considered from a customer privacy perspective, as well as ensuring business processing can be maintained.

Security Policy and Practice in SMEs

The growth of e-business has increased the criticality of any security incidents, mounting risks to privacy through new forms of attack, and the legal implications of breaches. Large organizations therefore have become far more aware of the need to take action to address the security risks arising from using information systems, resulting in a drop in the number of incidents (DTI, 2006). Previous studies, however, (e.g., Kankanhalli et al., 2003) have shown that small businesses are less likely to address this issue and are ignorant of the technologies available. Such organizations have become more vulnerable therefore to the threats relating to their information systems and have seen a rise in incidents.

Equally, the security of business transactions and personal data is not simply dependent upon the security of the network. From a survey of SMEs in Hong Kong, Chung and Tang (1999) conclude security management is an important success factor for the adoption of information systems in SMEs. So as new customer-based information systems are designed, developed, procured and deployed the privacy related security issues of the information system need careful consideration.

With the increasing use of the Internet and mobile technologies by smaller organizations, enabling them to be more flexible and diverse in their operations, the threats are broadening. Effective security management is therefore essential for all organizations in this increasingly interoperable world in order to ensure that the information remains confidential, available and retains integrity. Yet, Chang and Ho (2006) found the smaller business is likely to be less effective in the application of critical factors outlined in the security management standard ISO17799 with smaller organizations resisting making investments in this area. Here then we will review the extent of the issue.

Gupta and Hammond (2005) undertook a survey of SMEs in the USA. Their findings provides an insight into current information security practice within small businesses based on questionnaires drawn from organizations across a variety of sectors, including services, construction, utilities and finance. Keller, Powell, Horstmann, Predmore, and Crawford (2005), similarly, interviewed 18 system administrators in small businesses to evaluate systems security practice. Their findings provide a more personalized view from network professionals working in small organizations. There is a natural difference between these findings resulting from the variation in the type of samples: network specialists will be intrinsically more knowledgeable than the average SME manager. Below, these data sets are used to evaluate SMEs' security management policies and their use of security technologies.

Security Management Policies

Table 1 summarises level of adoption of security management policies by small businesses. The levels of planning and policy definition are low in comparison to larger organizations. Only 41 percent of small businesses have written a security policy that will protect customer privacy (Gupta & Hammond, 2005) in comparison to 76 percent of large organizations (Fulford & Doherty, 2003). The reasons for this difference relate to expertise, resources, and an understanding of the risk.

Table 1. Policies and procedures currently in place (adapted from Gupta and Hammond, 2005)

Document	% of respondents
Data recovery procedures	47
Computer use and misuse policy	43
Information security policy	41
Information security procedures	33
Business continuity plan	24
Data destruction procedures	21

SMEs lack the skills, knowledge and experience that would give the understanding and necessary motivation to develop comprehensive security policies (Gupta & Hammond, 2005). With little perception of the risks, managers focus their attention to other business priorities. It is difficult to overcome the lack of knowledge as small businesses often do not have the financial resource to hire consultants to address the skills gap.

The result of these resource constraints is more evident in some areas of security policy than others. Some types of planning activities such as data destruction procedures and business continuity planning are particularly low. However, privacy is especially vulnerable if obsolete data is not destroyed effectively or during a crisis situation, where it may be deemed a lower priority than recovering the systems.

Security professionals are more aware of these needs; Keller et al. (2005) found 50 percent of the companies interviewed had an emergency action plan and a further third had begun to develop one. However, they too found the quality of the plan was variable as the plans ranged from simple back up procedures to a full disaster recovery plan including copies of working machines at another site. With the emphasis being placed on the policies and procedures for security rather than on handling the situation in the event of an incident, unforeseen problems related to the loss or inadvertent disclosure of private data could easily occur in the moment of crisis.

Security Technologies

Whilst power surge protectors and back up systems were the most used technologies (Table 2), small organizations are generally most concerned about viruses (Gupta & Hammond, 2005). So the majority seek to protect themselves through anti-virus

Table 2. Security technologies in use (adapted from Gupta & Hammond, 2005)

Technology	% of respondents
Power surge protectors	79
Data back up systems	65
Anti-virus	57
Firewalls	43
Redundant systems	35
Intrusion detection system	25
Security evaluation systems	9

software. Keller et al. (2005) found that the systems administrators were less concerned about virus attacks, with only about a quarter of their interviewees believing that viruses were a major threat. This lower concern may be because they had taken action to militate against such problems by implementing an anti-virus tool and appropriate management policies. All the systems administrators had implemented some form of firewall, two thirds of which were a hardware solution.

Employees often are considered to be a major threat, either due to malicious attack or unintentional action. Trim (2005) highlights that hacking by internal staff is a growing problem, with a suggested figure of one third of hacking incidents resulting from internal activity. Privacy of data should not though be thought of in relation to security from external attack, but by ensuring integrity of data from all forms of unauthorised access and corruption (Spinello, 2000). So, integrity of the data requires that those who have a right to access the data can do when they need it, so as to be able to process business or make appropriate decisions based on that data, for instance.

Privacy of personal data can be put at risk by poor practice or premeditated action by employees. Gupta and Hammond's (2005) respondents, however, considered insider access abuse was of least concern. Whether this is because of the higher level of trust resulting from a perceived employee commitment or due to the ignorance of the business managers is difficult to say. What is evident is that, in contrast, the system administrators regarded internal personnel as the primary threat (56 percent of respondents) (Keller et al., 2005).

So, in summary, SMEs have tended to adopt off-the-shelf security technologies in the expectation that these will suffice in the protection of their business data and therefore the privacy of their client base. This ignorance leaves them vulnerable to the release of private information through either malicious attack or poor management practice. The business implications are similarly significant whatever causes the breach of privacy and client trust.

Small businesses therefore need to reevaluate their policies and procedures, and change their security technology, to be more effective in dealing with actual security concerns (Gupta & Hammond, 2005). The absence of such policies makes organizations more vulnerable to internal or external attack, and therefore a breach of privacy.

Small businesses should take better preventative measures so that the information remains confidential, available and retains integrity. The remainder of the chapter outlines how one small business set about changing the security culture to protect its business and the privacy of its clients, highlighting the lessons that other organizations might draw from this case.

Case Study

Company Background: ABC Awards

ABC Awards is a national awarding body, accredited by the Qualifications and Curriculum Authority (QCA) to develop and offer vocational qualifications eligible for public funding. ABC was formed through a consortium of four regional awarding bodies by pooling their existing qualifications and resources in order to compete with larger companies such as Edexcel, and City and Guilds. ABC is a non-for-profit company and although it receives no public funding most of its customers are publicly funded.

ABC award qualifications across a number of fields, such as in skill-based trades like welding, hobbies such as flower arranging and art, or general life skills such as foreign languages. The development of qualifications includes liaising with subject specialists, training providers, and sector skills councils and employers to determine programmes of study that meet the UK skills needs and then writing specifications for units and qualifications. The business currently has over 500 qualifications, and at any one time up to 200 under development, reflecting the pace of change in the UK skills market.

Accredited qualifications are offered to over 1,400 colleges, universities and private training providers. The services to customers include administering the whole process from registrations to certification as well as quality assuring the delivery of learning, the provision of tutor support and specifications for coursework and exams, external assessment and moderation of candidates work and certificate production. Data sharing services also are provided to the various government departments as a condition of national accreditation status.

Within ABC, the organization records 500,000 enrolments per annum to their qualifications from candidates at the various centres of study. The required confidentiality of the data is high as the database contains sensitive personal data related to the studies (covered under the UK Data Protection Act) and company financial data related to payments for the assessments. The privacy issues relate to physical representations of the data (e.g., candidate transcripts, certificates) as well as the electronic, and with the distributed nature of the business the issues relate to securing the data in all potential locations. Privacy of candidate data was acknowledged as a strategic priority given that a small lapse could result in significant loss of business in a saturated market, where reputation is a vital component for qualification providers competing fiercely to win and retain market share.

As a non-for-profit entity with the stated objectives of contributing to the UK education system, ABC is actively involved in many partnerships including the development of new national diplomas, and various Government collaboration projects involved in reducing bureaucracy and duplication across the education sector. ABC also has in the past entered into partnerships with related private sector service providers such as authors of study guides and learning resources that can accompany its qualifications when being sold to colleges.

The four regions each have their own offices and local area network. Each regional body runs as a separate business in addition to the ABC activities. ABC operates as a stand-alone commercial entity. It is therefore necessary to maintain legally separated networks whilst providing the necessary inter-connectivity for the personnel.

The business employs approximately 50 staff members located across the four regional offices. Functions include business development, marketing, ICT systems, finance and administration, with approximately half of staff involved in administration and customer support. In addition the business has over 700 contractors involved in development and delivery. Roles include consultants, lead examiners, script markers, question authors, and visiting moderators. A small number of personnel work from home or travel extensively so need remote access.

Systems

ABC has an internal development function that recently replaced the individual legacy systems of the four member organizations. In response to the strategic need to create an enterprise-wide awards management system, a project was established to create a new software and hardware architecture, supported by appropriate information management practices. The company has deployed a wide area network capable of supporting the short term and high priority business processing requirement. The network connects the four offices to servers located in Nottingham which hosts the company's bespoke Awards Management System (AMS) used for transaction processing and document production.

Table 3. Principles adopted to ensure security of data

	Security Management Policy Development	Security Practice
Organizational Issues	Manage risks	End user education
	Total cost of ownership	Least privilege access
Technical Issues	Develop security policies	Defence in depth
	Use of external resources	Monitoring of systems

The company also has recently introduced an e-commerce Web site that takes registrations data from colleges and integrates with the AMS. ABC recently outsourced its email and collaboration systems with an externally hosted Microsoft Exchange Server.

The current systems development strategy is based on further extending the services to customers with more features available online and a staged move towards e-assessment and support for e-learning including real-time online invoicing, on-screen results entry, support for electronic portfolios and e-moderation and on-screen testing.

This chapter does not detail all of this work, but focuses on the way that privacy issues shaped the approach to security, and how security was designed into each area of the system. Our policy throughout was to ensure privacy of data by ensuring the system and organization were secure from accidental, deliberate and opportunistic attack. The security policy was based on the international information security standard for best practice (ISO17799). The practices were relevant to ABC partner companies, and capable of being implemented by most SMEs.

The approach taken can be categorised into issues focused on addressing people and organizational aspects of ensuring security, and the technical underpinning to support those needs. The following sections are organized on this basis highlighting how for each aspect the policies were formed and put into practice. Table 3 outlines the principles adopted and discussed below.

It will be shown that organizations need to understand the real risks and build security management policies on them; evaluate technological solutions and external hosting decisions on the total cost of ownership; build systems with defence in depth where the first line of defence is users who are aware of the issues; and to minimise the chance of unauthorised access by defaulting to a policy of least privilege access and monitoring the network to maintain confidence to ensure the security policy is working.

Organizational Issues: Policy and Practice

Manage Business and Security Risks

Undertaking e-business is a considerable risk: interruption of financial transactions, revealing sensitive data or intellectual property to competitors, or logistics information can be used to disrupt normal distribution operations (Shih & Wen, 2005).

Organizations need to invest in information security measures to ensure security incidents do not undermine the advantages that the technology brings, especially across e-business operations. The threat of security breaches hinder the expansion in e-business (Fulford & Doherty, 2003). New technologies increase this concern; wireless communications and mobile devices are now integral elements of the supply chain. The benefits of such technologies also are their biggest vulnerabilities: network exposure and rogue access can be achieved without need for physical access to the network infrastructure (Shih & Wen, 2005).

So, the information security professional should always assume that the systems will at some time be compromised and therefore plan appropriate defences and recovery strategies. Their key task is how to avoid, mitigate, and manage the risks that this places on the business. So, security managers need to be risk aware. Kankanhalli et al. (2003), however, found that SMEs applied fewer security deterrents than larger organizations. Yet, where greater deterrents and preventative measures were applied by organizations then greater information security effectiveness resulted. To judge the survivability of an organization's systems it is necessary to judge the level of disruption caused to essential services as a result of any incident (Redman, Warren, & Hutchinson, 2005). For system survivability it is necessary to ensure protection against threats and quick response to the effects when one occurs.

Early in the requirements engineering phase of the project, information privacy was considered as a key requirement for the system and a risk analysis was conducted in line with the recommendations of ISO17799 to determine the high priority risks that needed to be considered. Prior to this project, as with many small businesses, risk analysis was not a mature, evolving process within the business but more of an ad-hoc tool used after the event or a paper based exercise used to satisfy regulators or requirements for a continuous improvement program.

Risk analysis began by clearly understanding what information security means, ISO7799 defines information security as the preservation of information confidentially, integrity and availability. The high level system and user requirements were then considered against these categories to determine security requirements for the new system.

It is important in such analysis to ensure the risks are based on actual, rather than perceived, threats. So, previous incidents that had occurred across the business's systems over recent years were analysed before considering the planned systems and any additional risks that would result from the implementation. Previously, the perceived risk to confidentiality had been focused on unauthorized access and theft of data, and loss of data and systems through virus infection. These are not to be dismissed, but the historical analysis showed that most incidents had concerned information integrity and availability. Also upon resolution of information availability problems, an information integrity problem was common and related to the loss of availability.

Incidents affecting information integrity included corrupt database files and documents through unplanned outages and failure of UPS, data processing errors through lack of training and incorrect software functions. There had been no reports of unauthorized access or theft of data and incidents of infection by virus were minor and resolved easily by updating virus definitions and removing the virus before any real damage had been done. However, the business was aware that this risk to personal data could not be ignored as it moved towards an integrated e-business solution that would enable transactions to be processed across the regions and eventually direct by assessment centres.

Total Cost of Ownership

SMEs do not have a culture of security management and have tended to resist the need to invest in information security technologies and practices (Giannacopoulos, 2002). Indeed, Gupta and Hammond (2005) found that a variety of international surveys highlighted that nearly half of organizations stated budget considerations as the reason for poor security procedures and implementation. However, this culture is slowly changing as managers realize that even the smallest business is becoming prone to attack (Giannacopoulos, 2002).

Even where organizations are willing to invest in physical security devices such as firewalls, many small companies struggle to appreciate the return on investment for an integrated security policy. The reason for this in part is due to marketing within the IT security industry, with vendors marketing products as a single solution to security, but products can only be as good as the configurations and the configurations only as good as the policies they implement.

One way to overcome this perception is by moving to a financial model that uses total cost of ownership (TCO), or life-time cost, as the basis for making judgments. Many small businesses are not familiar with the concept of TCO and frequently make decisions based on the purchase price alone or purchase price plus some well understood maintenance costs. The broader organizational costs, such as inability to process business, loss of client trust, loss of data integrity or confidentiality, should be part of the costing model. Security threats might devastate an organization's financial position with single incidents often costing more than £30,000 (approximately US $60000) and occasionally as much as £500,000 (US $1m) (Shih & Wen, 2005). Only by being aware of these costs will managers recognize the potential savings of their investment in an overall security infrastructure. So as well as using these broad outline costs, security managers need to estimate the cost of impact on their own enterprise and in the event of an incident calculate the actual cost as a way of evidencing the value of preventative measures.

By understanding how well the security supports the overall business objectives or the risk involved in each solution then management are able to make more informed decisions. Also, due to the high degree of coupling involved in networks and software layers there are many other costs to be considered even when simply adding a firewall. These include the cost of impact on existing systems and any reconfiguration that may need to be done, impact on future upgrades to the network, increased use of network resources, bandwidth and power, more points of failure in the network, additional insurance.

One example of the use of total cost of ownership at ABC was in the selection of firewalls. Identifying the overall cost and benefits of the various options meant assessing different combinations of firewalls. Issues considered in the decision included the level of capability of particular technologies; how selection of vendors could improve the bundled costing; whether the technology would require consultancy support due to the level of complexity; and the long-term availability support and trouble shooting. So, in terms of the costs, it was the whole solution, not just parts, that was measured, so taking into account support factors, staff costs, dependency and impact (e.g., implications for other new purchases), ongoing monitoring and support, and the risk of downtime or breach of confidentiality.

Least Privilege Access

Many security incidents are caused by user error when the user has inappropriate access to systems. In SMEs, there generally is poor user account management, for example, active user accounts for staff that have left, unrestricted remote access and local user accounts. These vulnerabilities provide easy targets for hacking or malware intrusion to go un-noticed. Policies were created whereby members of the consortium agreed to ensure that a named member of staff was accountable for account creation and deletion.

While least privilege access is an ideal to aim for, implementing it in an SME is usually very difficult as default access is usually the norm. Previously at ABC all users could do anything. In order to move from one extreme to the other, new systems being deployed can begin to follow a methodology whereby all users begin with very limited access whilst learning and training and then progress through security levels in a structured manner. Access privileges were changed in the design of the network and the enterprise-wide awards management application. For example, application permission rules were defined based on roles such as a "centre administrator" and granting of the permissions to individuals is administered by authorized users. The advantage of this approach is that it protects staff from mistakes and unintended privacy infringement.

For the design of the application detailed task analysis during the requirements stage enabled permissions to be defined clearly prior to implementation. For each type of record being stored by the system the four basic operations (create, read, update, delete) were used to define the permissions on each area. As part of the solution, ABC recognized and considered the trade-off between the need to make the system secure but not at the expense of making the roles of the employees so difficult that they could not operate effectively.

End User Education

Earlier we noted that employees are a significant risk to the security of the business. End users pose a threat to a company both through intended and unintended actions. In addition to deliberate attack, end users also provide a risk through their actions and ignorance. It therefore is logical to assume this would be addressed through employee training and awareness. However, Keller et al. (2005) note that surveys show that training and awareness were the lowest on the list of priorities for companies. Users, though, also are your best ally in detecting problems and are therefore the first layer in the defence. They can spot problems early. To enable employees to assist in the defence of the network, managers need to share more information relating to attacks, malware, and other vulnerabilities.

A survey by Ernst and Young in 2001 (cited in Fulford & Doherty, 2003, p. 107), however, found that the dissemination of organizational security policies and knowledge to employees is a low priority. The reason for this lack of dissemination is a lack of trust in the employees. Managers perceive that there is a risk from malicious employees as well as the possibility of anyone being approached and coerced by outside agencies. Also, "managers are reluctant to share or divulge sensitive and in many cases confidential data and information. This is because unnecessary leaks can result in inappropriate publicity for the organization that has been targeted by hackers or organized crime syndicates" (Trim, 2005, p. 494).

The development of usage policies is essential to both educate staff and protect the employer. However, policies are insufficient as a vehicle for education. Direct communication of defined policies and practices to all employees is necessary to ensure they become more knowledgeable about the risks involved.

The approach used at ABC was three-fold. Firstly the organization sought to raise awareness and understanding of the issues. It then provided alternative methods that could be used to achieve the same business goals. Finally, it re-configured systems and changed some policies to make it less likely that the practice would continue.

One example issue was Internet usage. Activities such as the receipt of e-mail and downloading materials from the Internet had become a major risk. These were addressed through security policies and technology, but making users aware of the risks was essential. User training began with awareness of the issues including information on high and low probability and high and low impact Internet threats. The concept of trusted and non-trusted sources was discussed, as well as high level principles of packet filtering, firewalls, and malicious code. Next users were trained on the safe use of the Internet and e-mail, for example the opening of attachments that are not from trusted sources, browsing safe and restricted sites, and managing their own security settings after making informed decisions about the threats. Permissions were then changed on the network with administration rights being removed to reduce the potential for intrusion by spyware in the event of an intrusion occurring.

In summary the organizational issues are:

- Ensuring that risk management is core to the ongoing privacy of client data. Risk management should be based on actual rather then perceived risks, therefore historical analysis of incidents should be monitored. At ABC this identified the need to focus on data integrity and availability as well as unauthorized access.
- Security selection and justification should be based on the total cost of ownership that models in the potential cost of loss of client data privacy or integrity.
- Ensure personnel access and education policies focus on the business implications of the erosion of privacy and therefore trust. In an SME end user staff can be a vital part of the security of the system as well as a potential risk.

Technical Issues: Policy and Practice

Security Policies

As discussed above, the literature shows that small businesses are less likely to have security policies than larger businesses, and where policies do exist the quality of those policies varies significantly. Fulford and Doherty (2003, p.106) recognize that effective information security management is "predicated on the formulation, dissemination and operation of an information security policy." They report that whilst the importance of security policies is well understood, many surveys show that there is a low level of uptake and the policies that do exist are often inadequate. Many smaller organizations focus on the technical solutions, but Trim (2005) shows that policy and technological solutions go hand-in-hand.

Changes in technological solutions should be based upon a security policy. Without a policy, security practices will be undertaken without any clear strategy, purpose or common understanding. So important is this area of management that there is now an international standard (ISO 17799) that states the principal tenants of information security management policies, such as ensuring that the policy is aligned to business objectives.

In line with the section above, a starting point to developing policy is to start with risk assessment; specifically identifying those risks and likely causes that could compromise the information systems availability, confidentiality or integrity. One survey found that organizations ranked this as the second most important factor affecting the success of information security policy, after management commitment (Fulford & Doherty, 2003).

In an SME the risk management activity also can be used to address some of the other key factors related to understanding security requirements and communicating the policy to employees. By involving the organization's management team in developing the risk assessment they are made aware of how the business objectives and priorities are related to security.

The process of developing a security policy is an educational experience for a small business, and will bring a higher level of awareness and understanding; these are

Table 4. Policies developed at ABC

Policies Developed at ABC Awards
Organizational security policy: business priorities and responsibilities; the ABC infrastructure including all significant hardware and networks from an ABC user workstation to the ABC servers and backup device; the system users and types of services that each requires; the different services and protocols that need to be supported by the systems and infrastructure.
Access and permissions: the authentication and access controls required.
Service level agreements: systems availability and response times; agreed minimum standards at each regional office in order to connect to the systems.
End user policy: use and misuse rules
Archiving: destruction of obsolete and retention of historical data
Data recovery: data Back up and recovery; business continuity plans and decision protocols in the event of incidents; testing procedure
Monitoring: policy for checking for activity and utilization on network and servers.

essential if the business requires the higher level skills in application that are needed to implement security measures. Implementing any security measures without an underlying policy will lead to problems in both understanding and configuration.

Policies are not fixed and should be revisited as part of the regular review and control process. Each policy should state what the review cycle is and the responsibilities for undertaking that review. The reviews at ABC are informed by current experience, business changes or future plans, and new technologies or known good practice.

External Resources

As we recognised earlier, small businesses can lack the knowledge and skills to ensure the security of their systems. There are, though, many sources of assistance available for small businesses. Some of this may come at a cost, if it is necessary to engage consultants with specific knowledge of products and systems. ABC, though, took advice from many free or relatively cheap sources by attending relevant conferences and workshops, working with a local university, and discussing options with vendors in pre-sales activity. Knowledge was developed by discussing concepts, technologies and policy decisions.

When developing procurement strategies it is important to understand the location of value in different types of products and services. For a large company the location of value in a service might be the economy of scale it provides for cost reduction whilst for a smaller company it may be the ease of implementation.

External hosting of business applications in state of the art data centres is becoming popular for companies without existing skills to manage servers and firewalls and can be cost effective when the total cost is considered. Alternatively, in-house management can be more cost effective for bespoke requirements if existing skills are available and the scalability is not too large. Both approaches can be used by selecting the functions to outsource.

For the SME, hosting e-mail and Web site services internally are sometimes considered as a low cost option but this is based on several incorrect assumptions and lack of understanding of the TCO. There sometimes is a desire to increase utilization of existing investments in servers and this drives the decision to host on existing equipment. Many SMEs assume that if they have purchased a server and it has spare disk space then hosting e-mail services on it is beneficial as it makes use of spare capacity and reduces costs. The problem is that this approach reduces the redundancy in the server and increases the risks.

Defence in Depth

Security is an ongoing and normal concern when offices use interconnected IT systems. SMEs should define their boundaries and ensure the security on that perimeter because vulnerability at one office is capable of being exploited to allow unauthorized access to another office. Often organizations have inadequate firewall management and any physical security measures are often circumvented to suit the business and staff.

At ABC, the first objective was the deployment of an Intranet capable of supporting the short term and high priority business processing requirements for employees at each regional office. ABC used Virtual Private Network (VPN) connections between the offices. So it was decided that all communications taking place over public infrastructure (Internet) should be encrypted between the two network perimeters using industry strength IPSec. For a site to site connection this was done between the host firewall/VPN appliance and the client sites firewall. In this case the users

Figure 1. Defence in depth: Network security

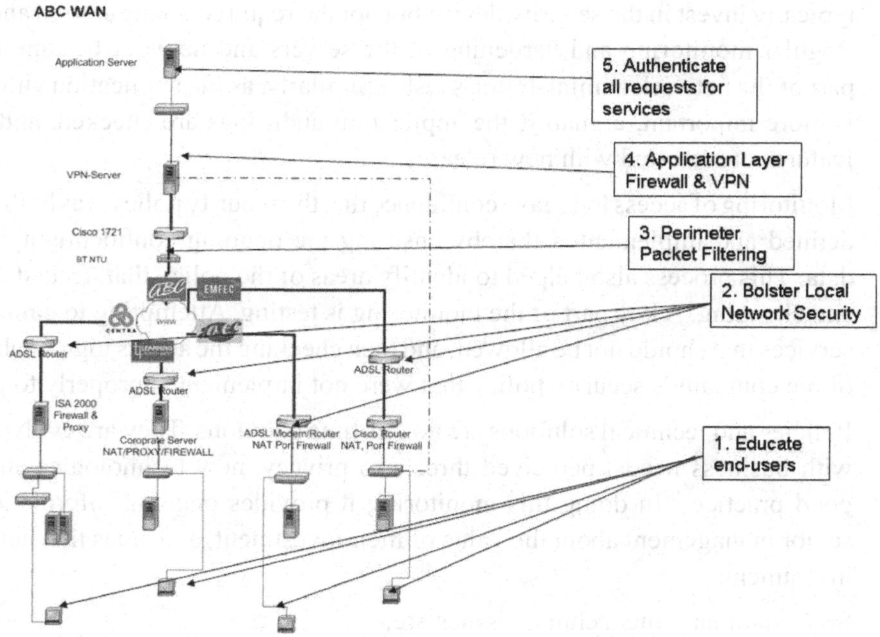

are known and can be validated. The defence of the network was designed so that it was protected at different levels, as shown in Figure 1.

Due to the costs of wide area network infrastructure, users at the remote offices needed to access the system by routing requests over the public, un-trusted Internet. The systems also needed to send potentially confidential information back to users over the same un-trusted Internet. This was protected using current industry standard tunnelling and encryption protocols.

The ABC firewall was implemented in two levels, the first level for packet level inspection and the second level for application level inspection. A global access schedule was implemented on the packet level firewall so that all traffic is blocked during specific times. The ABC application level firewall was capable user level account management, thus only allowing access for authorised users. Additionally, the application server was designed to perform user level authentication. The authentication was performed transparently to avoid the user having to re-enter their username and password.

Monitoring of Systems

Misconfiguration of security devices is common in SME's due to the skills needed to translate a written security policy into a set of unambiguous firewall rules. SMEs typically invest in the security device but not the required configuration and testing. Regular monitoring and hardening of the servers and network became a normal part of the network administrator's tasks. Similarly, as the application vulnerability is more important, arguably, the application audit logs are checked, and security features are retested with new releases.

Monitoring of access logs gave confidence that the security policy was both correctly defined and implemented thereby ensuring the ongoing confidentiality of client data. This process also helped to identify areas of the policy that needed clarifying and changing. A key part of the monitoring is testing. Attempting to gain access to services that should not be allowed, and then checking the access logs, enabled areas of the company's security policy that were not implemented properly to be found.

Policies and technical solutions are not all-time solutions. They are evolving in line with business needs, perceived threats to privacy, new technologies and known good practice. In doing this monitoring it provides ongoing information to the senior management about the value of their investment, and areas that need further investment.

So in summary, the technical issues are:

- Development of a security policy that can be used to support the technological decisions so that client confidentiality, data integrity, and system availability are maintained.
- Use of appropriate external resources to help improve business resilience against the threat of a breach of privacy.
- Design the systems so that they are secured at the boundaries and at different levels thereby reducing the business vulnerability to a loss of client trust.
- Monitor the system for potential breaches of confidentiality and adjust the policies and technical solutions accordingly.

Conclusion

Whilst privacy legal obligations vary from country to country, organizations have a financial, as well as moral, motive to minimize the chance of an inadvertent release of private data. This case is a contrast to practice in many SMEs that leave many risks unmanaged and bring little benefit other than protection from well understood and low probability risks. A key lesson from this case is that privacy needs to be understood from a business perspective: a breach of client confidentiality can have a significant impact on the reputation and therefore the income of an organization. Dealing with information security as a core business issue provides greater confidence that data privacy will be maintained.

Client information security needs to be at the forefront of the design of the architecture and the applications. Too often security is considered as an add-on feature after the initial developments, and therefore it is difficult to achieve. As was shown here, security management for SMEs is required from the early stages of systems development through risk assessment and then designing solutions that can evolve over time. Focusing on it from the beginning meant the purchase and development decisions were informed by surfacing the organizational risks and priorities, as well as the technical or functional requirements, thus providing the agility to respond to business level decisions without compromising the security.

In the assessment of risk, information security managers should plan for a breach of the system not just try to minimise the threat. The risks can inform the development of a range of policies, which should be evolving documents that reflect the ongoing nature of the business and the risks it faces. Policies and business priorities should shape the selection of security solutions and decisions on external hosting, but a final solution will encompass a mixture of technologies that needs to be evaluated by looking at the total cost of ownership.

Defence in depth gives the SME the ability to implement a comprehensive security policy within a constrained budget by defining multiple areas to focus efforts. Additional benefits are that the organization can use the approach to start a process of continuous improvement. The first line of defence is a knowledgeable user. User training is a vital element of the implementation process, as a change of culture is often required in small businesses.

Further work is required at three levels to build on this case study. In the company there is need to assess the impact of the approach adopted over time to ensure the business benefits were as anticipated. In the industry, we need to recognise the way that privacy issues are potentially business critical, and apply the lessons from this case elsewhere to test if the concepts are transferable. Finally, researchers should pay more attention to information security in SMEs as these are potentially the weakest link in the e-business supply chain. In particular, further codification of knowledge from other examples of good practice should be developed that are useful for other businesses, and in due course seek a common body of knowledge for information security in SMEs.

References

Chang, S.E. & Ho, C.B. (2006). Organizational factors to the effectiveness of implementing information security management. *Industrial Management and Data Systems, 106*(3), 345-361.

Chung, C-W & Tang, M-ML (1999). Computer based information systems (CBIS) adoption in small businesses: Hong Kong experience and success factors. *Journal of Global Information Technology Management, 2*(2), 5-22.

Department of Trade and Industry (DTI) (2006). *Information Security Breaches Survey*. Retrieved on May 17, 2006 from www.dti.gov.uk/sectors/infosec/index.html

Edgar, S.L. (2003). *Morality and machines (2nd Ed)*. Sudbury, MA: Jones and Bartlett Publishers.

Fleischer, P. & Cooper, D. (2006). EU Data privacy in practice – Microsoft's approach to compliance. *Computer Law and Security, 22*(1), 57-67.

France, E. (2004). Data protection in a changing world. In T.W. Bynum & S. Rogerson (Eds.), *Computer ethics and professional responsibility*, pp. 263-273. Malden, MA: Blackwell Publishing.

Fulford, H. & Doherty, N. F. (2003). The application of information security policies in large UK-based organizations: An exploratory investigation. *Information Management & Computer Security, 11*(3), 106-114.

Giannacopoulos, P. (2002). Why IT security matters for small and medium sized businesses. *New England Printer and Publisher, 65*(3), 30-32.

Guardian Newspaper (2006). Security flaw leaves 3m HSBC online accounts open to fraud., August 10. Retrieved from http://business.guardian.co.uk/story/0,,1841853,00.html

Gupta, A. & Hammond, R. (2005). Information systems security issues and decisions for small businesses: an empirical examination. *Information Management & Computer Security, 13*(4), 297-310.

Holmes, A. (2006). The profits in customer privacy, *CIO*, March 15. Retrieved in May 2007 from http://www.cio.com/article/19070/The_Profits_in_Customer_Privacy

Kankanhalli, A. Teo, HH., Tan, B.C.Y, & Wei, K.K. (2003). An integrative study of information systems security effectiveness. *International Journal of Information Management, 23*, 139-154.

Keller, S., Powell, A., Horstmann, B., Predmore, C., & Crawford, M. (2005). Information security threats and practices in small businesses. *Information Systems Management*, Spring, 7-19.

Moor, J.H. (2004). Towards a theory of privacy in the information age. In T.W. Bynum & S. Rogerson (Eds.), *Computer ethics and professional responsibility*, pp. 249-262. Malden, MA: Blackwell Publishing.

Nissenbaum, H. (2004). Toward an approach to privacy in public: Challenges of information technology. In R.A. Spinello & H.T. Tavani (Eds.), *Readings in cyberethics (2nd Ed)*, pp. 450-461. Sudbury, MA: Jones and Bartlett Publishers.

Poindexter, J., Earp, J., & Baumer, D. (2006). An experimental economics approach toward quantifying online privacy choices. *Information Systems Frontiers, 8*(5), 363-374.

Reece, J.C. (2007). Forget about security and privacy: Focus on trust. *CIO*, May 23. Retrieved in May 2007 from http://www.cio.com/article/112051/Forget_About_Security_and_Privacy_Focus_on_Trust

Shah, M.H. & Siddiqui, F.A. (2006). Organisational critical success factors in adoption of e-banking at the Woolwich bank. *International Journal of Information Management, 26*, 442-456.

Spinello, R. A. (2000). Information integrity. In D. Langford (Ed.), *Internet ethics*, pp. 158-180. London, UK: Macmillan Publishers

Spinello, R. A. (2006). *Cyberethics: Morality and law in cyberspace (3rd Ed.)*. Sudbury, MA: Jones and Bartlett Publishers.

Tavani, H.T. (2004). *Ethics and technology: Ethical issues in an age of information and communication technology.* Hoboken, NJ: Wiley.

Trim, P.R. J. (2005). Managing computer security issues: Preventing and limiting future threats and disasters. *Disaster Prevention and Management, 14*(4), 493-505.

Chapter IX

Privacy and Security:
Where do they fit into the Enterprise Architecture Framework?

Richard V. McCarthy, Quinnipiac University, USA

Martin Grossman, Bridgewater State College, USA

Abstract

Enterprise Architecture is a relatively new concept that has been adopted by large organizations for legal, economic, and strategic reasons. It has become a critical component of an overall IT governance program to provide structure and documentation to describe the business processes, information flows, technical infrastructure, and organizational management of an information technology organization. Many different enterprise architecture frameworks have emerged over the past 10 years. Two of the most widely used enterprise architecture frameworks (the Zachman Framework and the Federal Enterprise Architecture Framework) are described and their ability to meet the security and privacy needs of an organization is discussed.

Introduction

Change is constant; for many organizations it has become the business norm. Companies seek to reinvent themselves or must prove that they can adapt to remain competitive. The ability to react quickly is a critical component of many companies' business strategy. As a result, the need for organizations' information technology to be defined in a standardized structure has become increasingly critical. Over the past 10 years there has been a greater emphasis on standardization of information technology services to enable organizations to better manage their technology resources as well as their portfolio of requests for changes of those IT resources. Numerous **enterprise architecture frameworks** have been developed to help organizations document, describe, and manage their information technology environment and their relationship to the business that it supports. Several of these have been consolidated and have emerged as the *frameworks of choice* amongst many organizations.

Information technology governance has heightened the growing need to ensure that technology resources are secure and to adequately protect the privacy of the vast amounts of information that they contain. Two of the most widely used enterprise architecture frameworks are critically analyzed to examine the strength of their security framework. The **Zachman framework** and the **Federal Architecture Framework** are evaluated to analyze the extent to which they provide a framework to satisfy the privacy and security needs of an organization.

Numerous other frameworks exist. Some are highly specialized and others are designed to be adapted by the organization that is using them. Some, such as the Department of Defense Architecture Framework (DoDAF) specifically identify privacy and security guidelines and standards that must be adhered to.

This chapter begins by providing a definition of enterprise architecture. It then describes the Zachman and Federal Enterprise Architecture Frameworks. These were chosen because they are two of the most widely adopted enterprise architecture frameworks and because they have a sharp contrast in their approach. The chapter then concludes with a critical analysis of how well each framework meets the privacy and security needs of their users.

Enterprise Architecture

Bernard (2004) defines enterprise architecture as a management program and a documentation method that is combined to perform an actionable and coordinated view of the enterprise strategy, business processes, and resource utilization and information flow.

Schekkerman (2005, p. 13) defines enterprise architecture as "a complete expression of the enterprise; a master plan which 'acts as a collaboration force' between aspects of business planning such as goals, visions, strategies and governance principles, aspects of business operations such as business terms, organization structures, processes and data, aspects of automation such as information systems and databases; and the enabling technological infrastructure of the business such as computers, operating systems and networks."

Rico (2006, p. 1) defines enterprise architecture as "a comprehensive framework or taxonomy of systems analysis models for aligning organizational strategy with information technology. Strategies are plans to satisfy organizational goals and objectives by competing, based upon size, cost, variety, speed, quality, uniqueness, or innovation. Information technology refers to the computers, software and networks used for safely storing, processing, retrieving, and transmitting data and information. There is an expectation that organizations can satisfy their goals and objectives by aligning their strategy with their information technology. Enterprise architecture consists of defining an organization's (a) scope, (b) business model, (c) system model, (d) technology model, and (e) components."

The Federal Enterprise Architecture Framework (FEAF) (CIO Council, 2001) describes enterprise architecture as "a strategic information asset base, which defines the mission, the information necessary to perform the mission and the technologies necessary to perform the mission, and the transitional processes for implementing new technologies in response to the changing mission needs. Enterprise architecture includes the baseline architecture, target architecture, and a sequencing plan."

While enterprise architecture has been defined in many different ways each definition incorporates several common characteristics: they are holistic in scope, they include an integrated view of information technology processes, and they provide a description of the current technological environment, the desired technological state that an organization seeks to achieve and a plan to get from the current state to the desired state.

Enterprise architecture provides a view of the organization from four perspectives: (1) business, (2) technological, (3) information and (4) application. The business perspective outlines the key business functions, defining what is done, by whom, and where within the organization the process takes place. The technological perspective describes the current information technology architecture and the desired technological architecture. Technological architectures vary by organization. A well defined enterprise architecture takes into account the varied needs caused by different environments. The information perspective provides a description of the current information architecture, the future needs and a map to achieve those needs. The application perspective provides a view to move the organizations current systems applications to their desired state. For example, El Sawy, Malhotra, Gosain, and Young (1999) point out that enterprise architecture is an integral part of competing in an electronic economy.

Schekkerman (2005) surveyed 79 companies that are interested in enterprise architecture. Several reasons for the use of enterprise architecture frameworks were identified, each of which suggests that the overarching rationale for enterprise architecture implementation is the support of strategic information technology issues and decision making within an organization. Specific reasons for enterprise architecture use included using it as a road map for change, utilizing it to help manage the IT portfolio or support budget prioritization, helping support mergers and acquisitions, delivering new insights into the business, and supporting decision making.

Enterprise Architecture Framework Core Components

Enterprise architecture frameworks have five core components that must be supported. These include:

1. **Alignment:** Providing a framework to improve alignment of business and information technology objectives. This also should serve as a communication tool to assist in aligning business and information technology objectives.
2. **Integration:** Establishing an infrastructure that enables business rules to be consistently applied across the organization, documents data flows, uses, and interfaces.
3. **Value Creation:** The economic value of information technology is better measured in an environment where there is a higher potential for reusable hardware and software assets.
4. **Change Management:** Establishing a consistent infrastructure and formalizing the management of the infrastructure and information assets better enables an organization-wide change management process to be established to handle information technology changes.
5. **Compliance:** Enterprise architecture provides the artifacts necessary to ensure legal and regulatory compliance for the technical infrastructure and environment.

These critical elements are accomplished by looking at how information technology supports an organization from four principle perspectives:

1. **Business Architecture:** This is a result of defining the information technologies and strategies required to support the strategic goals and objectives of an organization. This generally assumes that the critical business processes within an organization are well defined and well understood.

2. **Information Architecture:** The information architecture identifies the business information required to support both the current and future business architecture. A key component of enterprise architecture is to define the current and future state of an information technology organization so that plans can be developed to bridge that gap.

3. **Application Architecture:** This identifies the application infrastructure required to support the strategic goals and objectives of the organization. It supports the efficient use of organization resources to support those goals and objectives. It provides a description of the interactions and interdependencies of the suite of organizational systems

4. **Technical Architecture:** This identifies the current technical infrastructure as well as the target platform needed to support the target business architecture (Shupe & Behling, 2006).

Weill and Ross (2005) demonstrated that enterprise architecture is a critical component of an IT governance program and that effective governance aligns IT investments with business priorities. In a survey of 300 companies worldwide they concluded that a correlation between superior governance and superior financial results was achieved when the enterprise architecture was one of the critical strategic drivers in place within an information technology organization.

Enterprise architecture is comprehensive in scope. To effectively meet the needs of an organization it must also provide a framework that ensures that the security and privacy needs are included to secure organizational assets.

Security and Enterprise Architecture Frameworks

Security infrastructure has become a critical component of the enterprise architecture of an organization. Organizations much secure their information from numerous internal and external threats.

Shupe and Behling (2006) identify information security elements to include:

1. Security policies that identify what areas employees should avoid or consider dangerous in the use of the organizations information technology. It must be updated regularly.

2. Firewalls to control legitimate and illegitimate access to the technical infra-structure of an organization.
3. Authentication is needed to provide a balance between the strong password protection policies and reasonable system access.
4. Encryption is required to secure the information infrastructure of an organiza-tion. Information assets have become a target security threat
5. Patching and change management is essential to enable the technical infra-structure to remain current with all available hardware and software intrusion prevention capabilities.
6. Intrusion detection and network monitoring is vital to ensure that ongoing monitoring takes places to vigorous safeguard the organizational technical infrastructure against continuous security threats.

Zachman Framework

The most widely used of the formal enterprise architecture framework models is the Zachman Framework. Developed in 1987, it defines a logical construct to control

Figure 1. The Zachman Enterprise Architecture Framework

The Zachman Framework	Data (What)	Function (How)	Network (Where)	People (Who)	Time (When)	Motivation (Why)
Scope (Planner)	Define What is Important to the Organization	Identify Key Business Processes	List Locations Where the Business Operates	Identify Organizations Important to the Business	List Key Business Events	Define Strategies and Goals
Enterprise Model (Owner)	Semantic Model	Business Process Model	Business Logistics Model	Workflow Model	Master Schedule	Business Plan
System Model (Logical Designer)	Logical Model (E/R D)	Application Architecture	System Architecture	Human-Computer Interface	Processing Schedule	Business Rule Model
Technological Model (Builder)	Physical Data Model	System Design	Technology Architecture	Presentation Architecture	Control Structure	Business Rule Design
Detailed Representations (Sub-Contractor)	Data Definition	Program	Network Architecture	Security Architecture	Timing Definition	Rule Strategy
Functioning Enterprise	Enterprise Data Model	Application Program Library	Physical Network	Comprehensive Business Organization	Business Schedule	Comprehensive Business Strategy

Figure 2. Privacy and security components of the Zachman Enterprise Architecture Framework

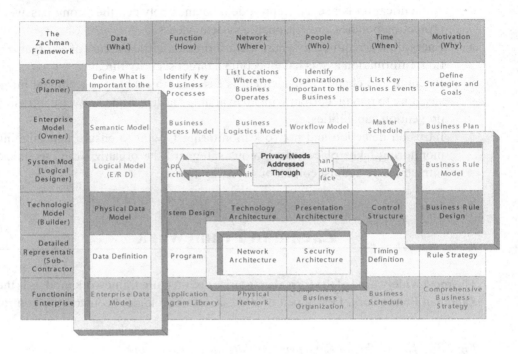

The Zachman Framework	Data (What)	Function (How)	Network (Where)	People (Who)	Time (When)	Motivation (Why)
Scope (Planner)	Define What is Important to the	Identify Key Business Processes	List Locations Where the Business Operates	Identify Organizations Important to the Business	List Key Business Events	Define Strategies and Goals
Enterprise Model (Owner)	Semantic Model	Business Process Model	Business Logistics Model	Workflow Model	Master Schedule	Business Plan
System Model (Logical Designer)	Logical Model (E/R D)	App... Archi...	...ys... Unit...	...an-...bute...face	...ng ...e	Business Rule Model
Technologic Model (Builder)	Physical Data Model	...stem Design	Technology Architecture	Presentation Architecture	Control Structure	Business Rule Design
Detailed Representation (Sub-Contractor)	Data Definition	Program	Network Architecture	Security Architecture	Timing Definition	Rule Strategy
Functioning Enterprise	Enterprise Data Model	Application Program Library	Physical Network	Business Organization	Business Schedule	Comprehensive Business Strategy

Privacy Needs Addressed Through

the interfaces and components of an information systems environment and provides a standardized method for considering all aspects of an information technology infrastructure. The framework utilizes a series of cells to describe the information, business and technical flows. These are organized by data, function, network, people, time and motivation that are principally driven by the business requirements of an organization. The framework successfully combines people, data and technology to show a comprehensive view of the inter-relationships within an information technology organization. It is principally driven by business requirements and although some standardized documentation is prescribed (e.g., data dictionary), it does not contain the formalized documentation structure of the Federal Enterprise Architecture Framework or the Department of Defense Architecture Framework models. It does however; present a formal picture of an entire enterprise from the perspectives of owner, designer and builder. This permits analysis of the information technology environment on the basis of WHO, WHAT, WHEN, and WHERE information is used (see Figure 1) (Zachman, 1987). Neaga and Harding (2005) have further described the Zachman Framework as a conceptual methodology that

describes how all specific architectures could be integrated into a single comprehensive enterprise architecture.

The Zachman Framework is a very detailed and visual description of the functional,
physical and personnel aspects of an enterprise. The framework consists of a matrix
that provides a visual representation that includes the perspective of developers
and end users.

More recently, the Open Group has also developed another flexible enterprise architecture framework (TOGAF) to provide organizations with a blueprint for control
of their IT resources.

The Zachman Framework describes an information architecture model that begins
by developing a semantic model of the information needs of an organization (see
Figure 2.0). It further prescribes the process that is to be used to transform data
needs into secure information assets. This consists of ensuring that access requirements are documented and described during the transformation process from logical
design to physical design. Also, business rule definition should clearly define any
restrictions upon access and use of information.

Privacy needs are addressed indirectly through the logical definition of information
needs. As information requirements are defined it is the responsibility of the designer
to ensure that through the definition of business rules, the privacy needs of an organization are met. The privacy needs begin first by defining the business processes
and uses of information within an organization; then the business process is further
defined to specifically identify how those needs are to be met. It is the responsibility
of the designer to ensure that privacy needs are considered; the framework does
not provide explicit guidelines to identify what should be considered or how they
are to be implemented.

Unlike privacy needs, security needs are specifically addressed by the Zachman
framework. At the detailed representation step, the framework addresses both the
technical security needs and the need to incorporate strong procedures within an
organization to ensure that security policies are upheld.

Public Sector Enterprise Architecture

In 1996 the Clingler-Cohen Act directed each branch of the U.S. Federal Government
to develop and maintain an enterprise architecture framework for its information
technology assets to maximize the benefits of these assets for the future. As a result
of this act, the CIO Council created the Federal Enterprise Architecture Framework

(FEAF). The purpose of the Framework is to provide a means to coordinate and control high priority inter-agency information technology issues in a controllable manner by permitting them to be built upon a common business platform. The FEAF was developed and subsequently expanded upon from the five-layer National Institute of Standards and Technology (NIST) framework. The NIST Framework consists of interconnected layers:

1. Business Architecture
2. Information Architecture
3. Information Systems Architecture
4. Data Architecture
5. Delivery Systems Architecture, supported by Hardware, Software, and Communications

In 2005, The Federal Enterprise Architecture Program Management Office adopted three core principles to guide its strategic direction. These principles include:

1. The FEAF is most useful when it is business driven; this includes sources such as presidential directives and agency strategic objectives.
2. Adoption of the FEAF will be achieved by proactive collaboration across agencies.
3. The government information technology resources will be improved and be more efficiently utilized by the adoption of the Federal Enterprise Architecture (CIO Council, 2005).

The CIO Council (1999, p.4) envisions that it "will serve as a reference point to facilitate the efficient and effective coordination of common business processes, information flows, systems, and investments among federal agencies and other governmental entities. In time, government business processes and systems will operate seamlessly in an enterprise architecture that provides models and standards that identify and define the information services used throughout the government." (p. 4)

The FEAF provides a means to link federal agencies' architecture activities for the purpose of developing interoperability standards to more effectively share information resources.

According to the CIO Council (1999), FEAF was developed to:

- Organize Federal information on a Federal-wide scale
- Promote information sharing among Federal organizations
- Help Federal organizations develop their architectures
- Help Federal organizations quickly develop their IT investment processes
- Serve customer needs better, faster and cost effectively

Eight components were analyzed to develop the first level of the FEAF. They consist of:

1. **Architecture drivers:** Business drivers that consist of administrative initiatives or legislative requirements. Design drivers including new or enhanced hardware or software.
2. **Strategic direction:** Consisting of the goals and vision of the organization to set the vision for the new target architecture.
3. **Current architecture:** Defines the enterprise architecture as it currently exists.
4. **Target architecture:** Defines the enterprise architecture that should be built to support the business processes that are part of the strategic IT direction.
5. **Transitional processes:** Provides support for the migration from the current architecture to the target architecture.
6. **Architectural segments:** This represents focused subsets of the entire enterprise architecture that represent a portion of the target architecture.
7. **Architectural models:** Define the business and design models that support the enterprise architecture.
8. **Standards:** Defines the best practices and methods for achieving the target architecture.

Level II of the FEAF provides greater detail for how the design and architecture components are related together in a push/pull relationship. The business pushes the design (consisting of data, architecture, standards, and technology) which in turn pulls the business by achieving new levels of service delivery (CIO Council, 1999). Level III of the Federal Enterprise Architecture Framework refines the level of detail further by providing three design architecture views (data, applications, and technology). Level IV of the Federal Enterprise Architecture Framework identifies the specific models that define the three architecture views and the models that describe the business design. These models are used to provide a baseline for the current architecture and support the development of plans to move to the target Federal Architecture. This level also defines the enterprise architectures plan.

Table 1. Federal Enterprise Architecture Framework architecture matrix

	Data Architecture	Applications Architecture	Technology Architecture
Planner Perspective	List of Business Objects	List of Business Processes	List of Business Locations
Owner Perspective	Semantic Model	Business Process Model	Business Logistics System
Designer Perspective	Logical Data Model	Application Architecture	System Geographic Deployment Architecture
Builder Perspective	Physical Data Model	Systems Design	Technology Architecture
Subcontractor Perspective	Data Dictionary	Programs	Network Architecture

Federal Enterprise Architecture Framework

The vision of the Federal Enterprise Architecture program, as defined by the Federal CIO Council is to "develop, maintain, and facilitate the implementation of the top-level enterprise architecture for the Federal Enterprise. This architecture will serve as a reference point to facilitate the efficient and effective coordination of common business process, information flows, systems and investments among Federal Agencies. In time, Government business processes and systems will operate seamlessly in an enterprise architecture that provides models and standards that identify and define the information services used throughout the Government" (CIO Council, 1999).

The FEAF consists of five reference models. These include the performance reference model, the business reference model, the service component reference model, the technical reference model, and the data reference model.

The performance reference model permits agencies to better manage IT investments by providing metrics that are incorporated into the enterprise architecture. This is accomplished by providing a common language that describes the measures and outputs used to achieve program and agency objectives. This enables cross agency comparison of measures and can be used to facilitate more efficient cross-agency resource allocation. The performance reference model has three primary objectives:

1. Improve strategic and operational decision-making by enhancing performance information.
2. Create a "clear line of sight" of inputs to outputs to better understand the contribution of each input.
3. Identify boundary spanning performance improvement opportunities (CIO Council, 2005).

The business reference model provides a mechanism to enable a functional view of business processes rather than their historical organizational view. The purpose is to encourage greater cross agency collaboration and sharing of resources.

The service component reference model seeks to provide a classification of service components across functional organizations to better enable cross sharing of resources and to reduce redundant services. It is intended to be both horizontal and vertical in its scope supporting both inter and intra agency resource sharing.

The technical reference model establishes the technical standards required to enable the delivery of service components. It provides the architectural basis for object reuse across agencies, thus helping to achieve economies of scale and cost savings through object reuse.

The data reference model promotes enterprise wide data standards by standardizing data context, data identification and data use. It is intended to promote improved data sharing capabilities across agencies by providing an enterprise wide information platform. This is an evolving process and the current data reference model is being updated (CIO Council, 2005).

The FEAF establishes four views of information technology architecture that utilize the first three columns of the Zachman Framework and the Spewak EA Planning Methodology (also referred to as E2AF) (CIO Council, 2001). The architecture includes business, data, applications and technology domains that serve as a reference point to guide the efficient flow of information, common business processes and technology across federal agencies of the U.S. government. Documentation standards have been developed for each systems domain within the architecture framework (see Table 1) that addresses four perspectives (also consistent with the Zachman Framework). These provide a standardized approach to documenting and describing the business, information, and technical flows of the complete application portfolio.

The Federal Enterprise Architecture Security and Privacy Profile, a scalable subsection of the Federal Enterprise Architecture Framework (version 2) supports the framework by:

1. Promoting an understanding of an organizations security and privacy requirements, the risks the organization faces and its capability to meet those requirements

2. Helping to select the best solutions for meeting requirements and improving current processes.

3. Providing a structure to enable agencies to select security solutions that are linked to meeting the enterprise needs (FEA Security and Privacy Profile, 2006).

The framework seeks to achieve a balance between the need for effective data management (recognizing the increasingly sensitive nature of data that it collects about individuals), the need to maintain a secure environment and the need to achieve business objectives (Hite, 2004).

Privacy and Security in the Federal Model

The FEAF is a prescriptive model that provides a detailed description for many of the components needed for an information technology organization to define and manage its technical and application infrastructure. The Federal model is intended to provide a single methodology for all branches of the U.S. federal government to utilize to meet all of their information technology needs, to standards those supports and to maximize their potential for reusable object development. The Federal model does not specifically dictate the format and content of the security and privacy procedures, rules or management guidelines needed to effectively administer them within an information systems application. It is assumed that privacy and security needs will be addressed during other components of the design process; but standards are lacking.

The Federal Enterprise Architecture Security and Privacy Profile provides a three stage process for the establishment of security requirements. The first stage, Identification, outlines how an organizations needs and capabilities fit into its respective agency within the federal government. Stage two, Analysis, introduces the idea of capital planning by supporting an organization leveraging currently deployed agency solutions to meet organizational objectives. The third stage, Selection provides an enterprise approach to ensure that security and privacy features are coordinated and budgeted across the entire organization. The three stage approach seeks to capture system security-level activities and use them to support enterprise wide security decisions.

The Privacy Act of 1974 is the foundational legislation that defines the privacy framework that the federal government of the United States must adhere to. Additional guidance describing the privacy of information about individuals is described in the E-Government Act of 2002. As a result of these acts (and other OMB guiding requirements), the Federal Security and Privacy Profile outlines 17 privacy control families that each agency must adhere to. Collectively, these describe in detail the notice, collection, acceptable use and rights and responsibilities for the management of personal data that each agency collects and maintains. Detail guidelines are included in the FEAF framework to ensure that each agency protects the privacy rights of individuals (FEA Security and Privacy Profile, 2006).

Conclusion

Enterprise architecture frameworks have become an integral part of an organization's information technology planning process. Numerous frameworks have emerged, each of which attempt to provide a definitive approach to assessing the current technology of an organization, its desired goals and the plan to achieve those goals. Enterprise architecture frameworks are comprehensive in scope and include all aspects of information technology. However, there are significant differences in the enterprise architecture frameworks that exist today. Additionally, these frameworks should be considered as an evolving process, with no framework that is completely comprehensive in its scope.

Differences exist in the frameworks in how they address the privacy and security needs of an organization. The Federal Enterprise Architecture Framework, which is utilized by all branches of the U.S. federal government that are not part of the Department of Defense, does not specifically address how privacy and security goals should be achieved. There is a gap in the framework that should be addressed in subsequent updates to ensure that these critical issues are consistently addressed by federal agencies and not left to the design considerations of each individual agency. This will support the goals of improving integration and data sharing.

The Zachman framework is the oldest and best known of the enterprise architecture frameworks. Originally designed as a mainframe enterprise architecture it has been extended to address all technology infrastructures. The Zachman framework specifically addresses security needs of an organization and prescribes a method for defining what should be included as well as how security should be managed within an information technology organization. The Zachman framework, like the Federal Enterprise Architecture Framework, is deficient in its treatment of support to address the privacy concerns of most organizations. The framework needs to be updated to specifically provide provisions for an organization to define and implement their privacy needs in a consistent manner across an organization.

References

Bernard, S. (2004). *An introduction to enterprise architecture.* Bloomington, IN: AuthorHouse.

Burk, R. (2005). *Enabling citizen-centered electronic government: 2005-2006 FEA PMO action plan.* White paper, Office of E-Government and Technology.

CIO Council (1999, September). *Federal enterprise architecture framework, Version 1.1,* White paper.

CIO Council, (2001, February). *A practical guide to federal enterprise architecture, Version 1.0.* Federal Chief Information Officers Council.

CIO Council (2005). *FY07 budget formulation FEA consolidated reference model.* White paper.

El Sawy, O., Malhotra, A., Gosain, S., & Young, K. (1999). IT Intensive value innovation in the electronic economy: Insights from Marshall Industries. *MIS Quarterly, 23*(3), 305-335.

Federal Enterprise Architecture Security and Privacy Profile, Version 2.0. White paper published by the CIO Council of the U.S. government.

Hite, R. (2004). *The federal enterprise architecture and agencies architectures are still maturing.* White paper, GAO.

Lankhorst, M. (2004). Enterprise architecture modeling- The issue of integration. *Advanced Engineering Informatics, 18,* 205-216.

McCarthy, R. & Barrett, D. (2005). The impact of the Sarbanes-Oxley Act on information technology: Two perspectives. *Proceedings of the International Association of Computer Information Systems Pacific conference,* Taipei, Taiwan, May 19-21, 437-442.

Neaga, E. & Harding, J. (2005, March). An enterprise modeling and integration framework based on knowledge discovery and data mining. *International Journal of Production Research, 43*(6), 1089-1108.

Richardson, G., Jackson, B., & Dickson, G. (1990). A principles-based enterprise architecture: Lessons from Texaco and Star Enterprise. *MIS Quarterly, 14*(4), 385-403.

Rico, D. (2006). A framework for measuring ROI of enterprise architecture. *Journal of Organizational and End-User Computing, 18*(2), 1-12.

Schekkerman, J. (2004). *How to survive in the jungle of Enterprise Architecture Frameworks.* Victoria, BC: Trafford.

Schekkerman, J. (2005), *Trends in Enterprise Architecture.* White paper, Institute for Enterprise Architecture Development.

Shupe, C. & Behling, R. (2006). Developing and implementing a strategy for technology development. *Information Management Journal, 40*(4), 52-57.

Weill, P. & Ross, J. (2005). A matrixed approach to designing IT governance. *MIT Sloan Management Review, 46*(2), 26-34.

Zachman, J.A., (1987). A framework for information systems architecture. *IBM Systems Journal, 26*(3) 276-292.

Chapter X

Information Systems Security:
A Survey of Canadian Executives

Frederick Ip, Queen's University, Canada

Yolande E. Chan, Queen's University, Canada

Abstract

This study assists organizations and researchers in examining investments in IS security. A questionnaire was developed and administered to managers in Canadian financial firms and educational organizations. The survey examined security threats and the countermeasures adopted by organizations to prevent and respond to security breaches. Data gathered were used to investigate the relationships between investment in security, perceived security, and organizational performance.

Introduction

Motivation for studying information security practices of organizations has come in part from the vast amount of concern, evidenced by media attention, on the topic of information security post-911. In the US Federal Bureau of Investigation and

Computer Security Institute's joint 2004 CSI/FBI Computer Crime and Security Survey, an estimated $141 million in losses from cyberspace breaches was reported by respondents (Gordon, Lawrence, Loeb, Lucyshyn, & Richardson, 2004). In addition, there have been highly publicized security breaches at data miners such as Lexus-Nexus and ChoicePoint (Saporito, 2005).

A December 29, 2005 *Security Focus* article states, "computer users and network administrators likely feel less safe after 2005. High-profile leaks of financial data left more than 50 million accounts containing credit card information and, in some cases, confidential details at risk" (Lemos). Hulme (2005) reports that "data breaches have been announced by some of the country's well-known banks, entertainment companies, telecommunications providers and universities. And this proves that such breaches can occur at even the most security conscious and diligent companies" (p. 34).

Estimates of the numbers of customers affected by breaches continue to be staggering. Culnan states in *The Cutter Benchmark Review* (2006), the "new [United States] laws requiring firms to notify customers in the event of a security breach resulted in reports of over 130 breaches affecting more than 55 million Americans" (Culnan, p. 6).

This study focuses on the security processes and resources used by organizations, the nature of security breaches faced, and employee perceptions of information security. First, related literature is presented. This is followed by a discussion of the research model and of research instruments developed to measure the constructs in the model. Next, a survey is described. We close by presenting key findings and recommendations.

Literature Review

This section provides an overview of the importance of security to the stewardship of information and knowledge in organizations. Using the Resource-Based View of the firm (RBV), the information resource and information-based competition are described.

Information and Knowledge

A distinction is often drawn in the literature between data, information and knowledge (Alavi & Leidner, 2001). Knowledge exists in people's minds. However, knowledge may also be embedded in artifacts such as organizational structure, processes, and technology that exist outside of people's minds (Grover & Davenport, 2001). For purposes of this research, the following definitions are used: *data* are raw numbers and facts, *information* is data that has been processed, and *knowledge* is authenticated information that enables action (Alavi & Leidner, 2001). This distinction may be extended to organizational repositories as well, yielding the terms databases, information bases and knowledge bases. In this chapter, the term knowledge bases is used loosely to refer to all three types of repositories.

Resource Based View of the Firm

According to the Resourced-Based View of the Firm (RBV), an organization may enjoy sustainable competitive advantage through the possession of key resources (Barney, 1991; Dierickx & Cool, 1989; Wade & Hulland, 2004). A resource is defined as "... all assets, capabilities, organizational processes, firm attributes, information, knowledge, etc. controlled by a firm to conceive of and implement strategies that improve its efficiency and effectiveness" (Barney, 1991, pg. 101). A resource is a source of sustainable competitive advantage if it satisfies the criteria of being *valuable, rare, inimitable*, and *non-substitutable* (Barney, 1991; Wade & Hulland, 2004). *Value* is the resource's ability to enable the firm to conceive and execute strategies; *rarity* is the heterogeneous distribution of the resource among the firm and its competitors; *inimitability* is the characteristic that the resource cannot be copied; and *non-substitutability* is the characteristic that the resource cannot be replaced by a similar resource (Barney, 1991).

Knowledge may be viewed as a resource. It is valuable in that it allows the organization to increase its ability to innovate, take advantage of its absorptive capacity, and recognize and respond to threats. Knowledge that is unevenly distributed may be rare. However, many entities may simultaneously use articulated knowledge; owners cannot exclude others from using the resource (Nelson & Romer, 1996). This property threatens the information-based resource's rarity and the advantage conferred by it. Organizations can prolong their competitive advantage by rendering the information resource private and immobile through practices that enhance secrecy and security (Mata, Fuerst, & Barney, 1995; Nelson & Romer, 1996).

In this study, we examine the extent to which managerial perceptions of the value of knowledge influence their willingness to invest in securing knowledge bases, and the outcomes of these security investments.

Information Security

The RBV literature recognizes that for organizations to extract competitive advantage from their information-based resources, they need to secure them. Researchers have examined other complementary motivations for securing information and described countermeasures to address threats to security.

Complementary drivers of information security include the desire to avoid potential liabilities arising from abuse of information systems, as well as customer demands for secure systems that protect their privacy. Straub and Collins (1991) identified software piracy, and violations of privacy and intellectual property rights as potential liabilities. Khoo and Zhou (2004) argued that for users to be willing to complete electronic transactions, the confidentiality and integrity of these transactions need to be protected. Dutta and Roy (2003) designed a simulation model of the drivers of information security and the impact of customer perception of risks on customer confidence. The perceived susceptibility of information systems to these liabilities and other threats is sometimes used as an indicator of security. Underlining the need for management attention, Goodhue and Straub (1991) described the construct of perceived adequacy of security measures. They related this construct to executives' perceived risk, security awareness and organizational actions.

Liabilities arise as a consequence of the failure to protect information from security threats. A threat "… is a circumstance that has the potential to cause harm or loss to computing resources…" (Wilson, Turban, & Zviran, 1992, pg. 107). These threats may be classified by their source, perpetrator, intent and consequences (Loch et al, 1992). Threats may originate from sources internal to the organization or external to the organization. The perpetrator may be human or computer programs. The threat may be intentional; however, unintended or accidental harm may also be sustained. Harm may take the form of disclosure of the information to unauthorized entities, destruction of information, modification of information or denying legitimate users access to the information resource.

Countermeasures are organizational responses to threats. Straub and Welke (1998) developed a framework for countermeasures called the countermeasures matrix. They identified four basic functions of countermeasures: to deter threats before they occur or are undertaken; to detect threats that are occurring; to prevent threats from causing harm or becoming actual breaches; and to remedy the effects of realized threats. They offered an approach for systematically selecting countermeasures based on threats identified (Straub & Welke, 1998). Countermeasures are one component of a complete information security system.

An information security system can be seen as part of a larger knowledge management system (Gallupe, 2001; Gold, Malhotra, & Segars, 2001). Providing security is one aspect of an organization's stewardship of its information resource. The responsibilities of this stewardship include the acquisition and/or generation, storage, security and on-going maintenance of the resource (Gallupe, 2001).

In practice as well as in research, it has become increasingly apparent that information security is not just a technological issue. It must be studied and addressed in the broader context of IT systems, and the formal and informal systems of organizations (Dhillon & Backhouse, 1996). Dhillon and Backhouse (2000) wrote that policies and rules are insufficient, that organizations must create "RITE" cultures that foster *responsibility* through knowledge and compliance with rules and roles; personal *integrity* and trustworthiness as a prerequisite of joining the organization; *trust* in employees to behave properly; and *ethicality*.

A complete information security system is a combination of governance policies, operational processes and technical artifacts. Governance includes practices and policies such as Acceptable Use Policies (AUP) and Codes of Ethics that set out the expectations of behaviour (Volonino & Robinson, 2004) and reduce personal denial of responsibility (Harrington, 1996). Operational processes include, for example, organization checks and balances and auditing (Volonino & Robinson, 2004), while technical artifacts include, for example, infrastructure and network security, cryptography, and intrusion detection (Panko, 2004). The British Standards for information security, BS 7799, is a commonly accepted practitioner standard. It addresses processes such as controlling logical and physical access to information resources, assessing and accepting risks, operational procedures, security maintenance procedures, incident responses, disaster recovery, and security reviews and audits (Li, King, Ross, & Staples, 2000).

Information security effectiveness: Providing information security is characterized by some as an exercise in risk management. It is necessary to determine how much risk exposure the organization is willing to bear, and weigh this against the costs of maintaining that level of security (Wilson et al., 1992). Thus, effectiveness should be a comparison of actual results against expected results. However, this is challenging as it is difficult to detect security breaches and to assess damage resulting from breaches (Wilson et al., 1992). Sometimes a surrogate measure used is perceived security effectiveness; however this is not ideal as perception may not necessarily coincide with reality (Goodhue & Straub, 1991). This is especially true when organizations are not always protecting their own information resources; impacts may not be restricted to just the organization and may be far reaching. The effectiveness of a security system is its ability to ensure the *confidentiality, integrity* and *availability* of information and resources, thus protecting the value of the information (Loch, Carr, & Warkentin, 1992).

Confidentiality is the keeping of secrets. Confidentiality is distinct from privacy in that confidentiality is concerned with the secrecy of information kept in trust, whereas privacy is the right to control the uses of one's own information (Greenaway, Cunningham, & Chan, 2002; Landwehr, 2001). A business protects the privacy of its clients by keeping their information confidential. Confidentiality is jeopardized by the threat of unauthorized disclosure.

Integrity involves ensuring that information is accurate. It is important not only because decisions need to be made by the organization based on the information but also because if inaccurate information is made publicly available, the firm may be held liable. Threats to integrity come in the form of modification or destruction of information.

Availability requires ensuring that information resources are accessible when they are needed. Availability is important because disruption of service may interrupt the operations of an organization. Threats to availability include denial of service attacks and viruses.

Intellectual Capital

The impact of security breaches may extend beyond financial costs to the organization. A breach may cause a business partner or customer to incur risk or tangible losses. The costs incurred by partners may cause partners to be wary of the organization in future interactions (Haahti, 2003; McGrath & Sparks, 2005). The breach may therefore negatively affect the organization's social capital.

Intellectual capital has many facets (Bontis, 1998). Allee (2000) documented six types of intellectual capital: Business relationships, human competence, internal structures, social citizenship, corporate identity, and environmental health. Knight (1999) described intellectual capital more simply as being composed of human, structural and external capital. Two types of intellectual capital focused on in this research are customer capital (in Knight's classification, a type of external capital) and human capital (internal capital).

Customer capital. Customer capital refers to the opinions, knowledge and values collectively held about the organization by its customers. It includes brand recognition and goodwill (Allee, 2000; Crowe, 1997; Knight, 1999). It may be measured by market share, customer retention, per-customer profitability, customer satisfaction, repeat orders, duration of customer relationships, and product and service quality (Buren, 1999; Crowe, 1997; Wang & Chang, 2005).

Human capital refers to the individual capabilities, knowledge, skills, experiences and problem-solving abilities that reside in people in the organization (Allee, 2000;

Figure 1. Research model

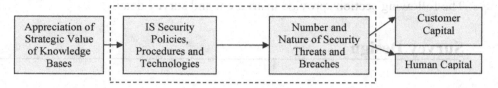

Knight, 1999). Measurements of human capital include the level of education, number of employee ideas adopted, turnover rate of employees and the use of knowledge management technologies (Knight, 1999; Wang & Chang, 2005).

Research Model and Questions

We arrive therefore at the following research questions:

R1: To what extent do organizations view their data, information and knowledge bases as strategic resources?

R2: How does this influence the range of policies, procedures and technologies that organizations implement to secure these resources?

R3: What economic and social consequences are associated with the organization's security practices?

The research model is depicted in Figure 1. It posits relationships among the following constructs: the organization's appreciation of the strategic value of its knowledge bases, the information systems security resources, the number and nature of security breaches experienced, and the organization's customer capital and human capital. It is recognized that time lags are involved as we move from left to right across the model. That is, an appreciation of the value of knowledge bases will not immediately be reflected in increased investments in security resources, and so on. However, we anticipate that over time, we will see the relationships outlined in Figure 1.

In summary, we expect that the more organizations value their knowledge bases, the greater will be their efforts to protect their knowledge bases, and the more secure their systems will be. We anticipate that the implementation of a comprehensive security system will create greater awareness and detection of security threats, but fewer actual security breaches. We expect that the greater the protection of customer and employee personal information, the less likely will we see erosion of customer capital and human capital.

In order to test our model, we developed instruments to measure the main constructs. The following sections provide instrument and survey details.

Survey Design

Instrumentation: Two questionnaires were developed—one to be addressed by the CEO/senior management and a second to be answered by the CIO/IS management. Existing instruments were used whenever possible, and pre-tested and refined for use in the current research. Appendix I presents the final versions of the instruments. Each organization was asked to ensure that both questionnaires were completed and returned (or the organization's data would not be examined). Participating organizations received a copy of the study's final report.

The Appreciation of the Strategic Value of Knowledge Bases construct was operationalized using the Resource-Based View's criteria for competitive advantage. Items were created to measure the dimensions of value, rarity, inimitability, and non-substitutability. A manipulation check was also included that attempted to directly measure the perception of the knowledge bases as strategic tools. Questions were directed to the CEO or an appropriate senior manager.

A CIO questionnaire to assess the IS Security Policies, Procedures and Technologies construct examined governance and policies, security assessment, security assurance, data confidentiality, availability, integrity, and security countermeasures. Respondents were also asked to rank several information security threats, and report on the number of breaches and the nature of those breaches. In addition, the Senior Management questionnaire examined Perceived Security using items provided by Goodhue and Straub (1991).

Questions in the Senior Management instrument also examined the organizations' perceptions and attitudes towards Customer Capital and Human Capital. These items were constructed using research by Allee (2000) and Knight (1999). Several items explored issues such as turnover and human resource budget allocations.

Validation: The survey items were first sent to industry representatives for their comments. Three rounds of instrument item/card sorting were also undertaken to further improve the face validity of the instruments. The participants of the card sorting exercises were professors and graduate students in Information Systems, Organizational Behaviour, and other business disciplines. This pre-test activity continued until the instruments were performing well. See Appendix II.

Analysis: The data gathered from the survey was analyzed using SPSS, a statistical analysis package, and PLS-graph, a partial least squares analysis tool (Chin, 1998). As some of the constructs in the research model were multi-dimensional, each dimension was modeled independently as suggested by Hulland (1999).

The majority of the constructs were modeled as "reflective," with items measuring the underlying latent variables. However, Number of Security Breaches, Human Capital and Customer Capital were modeled as "formative" constructs as their indicators did not reflect the constructs but were measures that together made up the constructs, and did not necessarily closely co-relate (Hoyle, 1999). For items that were scored on a five-point scale, responses were coded from 1, "strongly agree," to 5, "strongly disagree." For items that were scored on a three-point scale, responses were coded such that "none" was 1, "few" was 2, and "many" was 3. See Appendix I for more information.

Sample

The participants of the survey were organizations in the Financial and Educational industries in Canada. These industries were considered to be information and knowledge intensive. Target organizations (with > 100 employees) within these industry classifications were identified and contacted using Dunn and Bradstreet Business Directory information.

Survey Administration

Executives were initially contacted by mail and provided with two means of participating: 1) to return, via mail, the hardcopy surveys in the postage-paid envelopes provided, or 2) to participate online through a Web site maintained by the researchers. This Web site contained an equivalent soft version of the hardcopy questionnaires. That is, the hardcopy and online questionnaires had the same wording. Definitions for technical terms were provided in both media.

Two separate hardcopy questionnaires were sent to each firm—one for the CEO and another for the CIO. Separate Internet (URL) addresses for the corresponding questions were also provided. Each CEO and CIO was provided with a unique participant code so that corresponding CEO and CIO responses could be identified, matched and analyzed[2].

Results

Respondents: Responses were coded as received by mail or received through the Web site. Between Web respondents and mail respondents, at the 0.01 level of

Table 1. Construct reliabilities

Construct	Dimension	α
Security Effectiveness	Perceived Effective	0.869
Comprehensiveness of Security Measures	Governance policies	0.835
	Governance responsibilities for security	0.679
	Assessment	0.849
	Assurance	0.904
	Countermeasures	0.874
Perceived Security Effectiveness	Confidentiality	0.683
	Integrity	0.822
	Availability	0.745

significance, no significant difference was discovered between the rate or content of responses.

Using the date of the response, the respondents for each survey were divided into three equal groups. An analysis of variance (ANOVA) test was then used on each item to compare the two extreme groups, the earliest respondents and the latest respondents. At the 0.01 level of significance, one item was found to be significantly different among the CIO responses. It was found that the later the response, the more likely the respondent would agree with the statement: "*Each department or business unit is responsible for the security of its information assets.*" There was some ambiguity as to why the decentralization of responsibility was related to a slower survey response. Perhaps in decentralized organizations, information needed to respond to the survey was less readily available or difficult to collect; and more time was taken to get the survey to the appropriate person to respond. Consequently, it is possible that some non-respondents found it too difficult to identify the appropriate person to respond to the survey or too difficult to get the information to respond to the survey.

Response Rate: The CEO survey received 39 complete responses while the CIO survey had 34 complete responses. Twenty-two organizations responded fully to both surveys. This resulted in an overall response rate of 4 percent. A large number of organizations informed the authors that they were declining to participate in the study because of the sensitivity of the issues (security threats and breaches) being discussed. Most organizations contacted simply did not respond. Phone conversations with industry representatives suggested that organizations were not prepared to divulge security breach statistics and/or their security practices even to representatives of a trusted university. Because PLS is regression-based and has very modest data requirements, we were able to successfully complete several analyses. PLS requires only that there be at least five cases for each predictor in each regression that is run (Chan, 1992). By conducting simple bivariate analyses, we were able to obtain sufficient analytical power.

Reliabilities of constructs: Table 1 presents the Cronbach's alpha for each reflective construct's dimensions.

*Table 2. Comparison of means for policies, centralization of responsibilities, processes and expenditures (grouped by whether or not regular security audits are undertaken), *p<0.1,**p<0.05*

Does your organization regularly conduct information security audits?		Mean	Std. Deviation	Significance of difference
What is the security expenditure as a percentage of the IT budget?	No	0.041	0.03	0.053*
	Yes	0.121	0.114	
There are disaster recovery plans to address circumstances that severely negatively impact or stop the operations of the organization.	No	0.85	0.66	0.001**
	Yes	0.311	0.92	
All knowledge bases have an individual who is accountable for their security.	No	0.542	1.127	0.049**
	Yes	-0.203	0.893	
Assessment Processes				
Assessing information security is a requirement of all projects.	No	0.62	1.157	0.015**
	Yes	-0.284	0.828	
When assessing security risks, we classify them by the level of potential severity.	No	0.553	1.077	0.044**
	Yes	-0.207	0.912	
When assessing security risks, we classify them by their likelihood of occurrence.	No	0.536	1.153	0.051*
	Yes	-0.202	0.883	
Assurance Processes				
Security requirements for all information assets are frequently renewed.	No	0.536	0.793	0.042**
	Yes	-0.234	1.024	
We continually update our list of new information security threats.	No	0.561	0.908	0.03**
	Yes	-0.253	0.97	
We constantly explore methods to improve our information security systems.	No	0.56	0.973	0.037**
	Yes	-0.228	0.957	
We frequently ask for information about potential weaknesses and vulnerabilities of our security systems.	No	0.663	0.82	0.005**
	Yes	-0.334	0.909	
We perform statistical analysis of security incident data.	No	0.734	0.724	0.004**
	Yes	0.329	0.956	

Statistical Analyses

To examine the predictive validity of the instruments, the research model was examined using the data gathered. As mentioned above, for sufficient power in PLS, the number of cases examined must be equal to, or be greater than, five times the number of predictors in the most complex regression (Chan, 1992). It has been suggested that the number of cases should be eight to 10 times the number of predictors in the regression (Chin, 1998). For analyses where the statistical power was likely to be insufficient, model tests using PLS were not conducted. Simpler tests (t-tests, etc.) were employed instead. Below we highlight key findings.

Importance of Regular Security Audits

A comparison of the means of different items found that organizations that performed regular security audits differed from those that did not on a variety of measures (see

Table 3. Comparison of means grouped by whether or not regular security audits are performed. Items are from integrity, availability and countermeasures, *p<0.1, **p<0.05

Does your organization regularly conduct information security audits?		Mean	Standard Deviation	Significance of difference
Integrity				
We have processes that prevent the input of "bad" data.	No	0.598	1.35	0.017**
	Yes	-0.285	0.702	
We have software tools that prevent the input of "bad" data.	No	0.798	1.188	0.001**
	Yes	-0.352	0.683	
Availability				
We classify our information assets by the desired level of availability.	No	0.536	0.843	0.039**
	Yes	-0.242	1.003	
We provide systems support to ensure high levels of information resource availability.	No	0.723	1.298	0.005**
	Yes	-0.314	0.696	
Countermeasures				
We have software tools to predict security incidents before they occur.	No	0.44	0.949	0.08*
	Yes	-0.22	0.979	
We have organizational processes to prevent security incidents before they occur.	No	0.488	0.841	0.056*
	Yes	-0.232	1.01	
We have software tools to respond to security incidents.	No	0.537	1.081	0.048**
	Yes	-0.213	0.919	
We have organizational processes to detect external threats.	No	0.602	1.133	0.026**
	Yes	-0.233	0.868	
We have software tools to detect external threats.	No	0.53	1.088	0.049**
	Yes	-0.216	0.918	

Table 2). It was found that such organizations, on average, allocated more of the IT budget to security. These organizations also had significantly more disaster recovery plans, and were more likely to have individuals accountable for the security of knowledge bases. They were more likely to assess information security as a requirement for projects, and during such assessments, participants were more likely to classify risks by the level of severity as well as the likelihood of occurrence. Participants that had regular audits were more likely to have security assurance processes in place. Assessment seemed to go hand in hand with auditing. Furthermore, the assessment and audit processes likely gave rise to, or were the result of, the appointment of individuals who were accountable for securing knowledge bases. The data suggested that organizations that have audited processes to assess risk frequently also have disaster recovery plans to further manage and mitigate that risk.

Participant organizations that regularly conducted security audits were also found to more likely have processes and tools to ensure the integrity of the data in their knowledge bases, and the availability of their information resource. In terms of countermeasures, respondents that audited their security systems were also found to be more likely to have processes and tools to detect external threats, prevent security incidents and respond to security incidents. Table 3 presents the results in more detail.

Table 4. Comparison of means grouped by whether or not regular security audits are performed. Items are from security incidents, customer capital and human capital, $*p<0.1$, $**p<0.05$

Does your organization regularly conduct information security audits?		Mean	Standard Deviation	Significance of difference
Security Incidents				
Approximately what percentage of security incidents affected the confidentiality of data by disclosing it to unauthorized persons?	No	0.005	0.016	0.099*
	Yes	0.18	0.323	
Approximately what percentage of security incidents affected the availability of resources?	No	0.511	0.499	0.091*
	Yes	0.221	0.379	
Customer Capital				
We invest a great deal of resources in building our customer capital.	No	0.531	0.985	0.042**
	Yes	-0.283	0.79	
Human Capital				
What percentages of all employees have post-secondary education?	No	0.771	0.258	0.046**
	Yes	0.484	0.305	

Table 5. Correlation between different types of security incidents, *p<0.1, **p<0.05

		1	2	3	4	5	6	7
1	For approximately what percentage of security incidents were the source internal to the organization?	1						
2	For approximately what percentage of security incidents were the perpetrators non-human? (e.g., viruses, software bugs)	-0.290	1					
3	For approximately what percentage of security incidents was the motivation intentional (not accidental)?	0.016	0.016	1				
4	Approximately what percentage of security incidents affected the confidentiality of data by disclosing it to unauthorized persons?	0.252	-0.441**	-0.299	1			
5	Approximately what percentage of security incidents affected the integrity of data by destroying it?	0.277	0.122	-0.105	0.006	1		
6	Approximately what percentage of security incidents affected the integrity of data by modifying it?	-0.038	0.194	0.197	-0.125	0.531**	1	
7	Approximately what percentage of security incidents affected the availability of resources?	-0.327*	0.611**	0.087	-0.293	-0.119	-0.091	1

Table 6. Relationships between security measures and perceived security, *p<0.1, ** p<0.05

Path			R-square	Coefficient	t-Statistic	Support Received for Proposition
Centralization of Responsibility	→	Perceived Security	0.074	-0.272	0.55	Not supported
Policies	→	Perceived Security	0.080	-0.283	0.667	Not supported
Assurance	→	Perceived Security	0.154	0.392	1.636	Modest support
Assessment	→	Perceived Security	0.169	0.411	2.285**	Strong support
Countermeasures	→	Perceived Security	0.233	0.483	2.519**	Strong support

Table 7. Comparison of industry means for information security practices and perceived security, *p<0.1, **p<0.05

	Industry	Mean	Std. Deviation	Significance of difference
Spam	Education	-.287	.878	0.089*
	Financial	.271	.998	
Denial of Service	Education	-.354	.751	0.037**
	Financial	.334	1.08	
Theft of equipment	Education	-.323	.52	0.059*
	Financial	.305	1.218	
There are organizational policies for the protection of information.	Education	-.463	.989	0.005**
	Financial	.437	.777	
There are organizational guidelines outlining how to protect information.	Education	-.291	1.049	0.095*
	Financial	.275	.895	
There are disaster recovery plans to address circumstances that severely negatively impact or stop the operations of the organization.	Education	-.629	.87	0.00007**
	Financial	.594	.721	
All knowledge bases have an individual who is accountable for their security.	Education	.438	1.042	0.01**
	Financial	-.413	.778	
Security requirements for all information assets are frequently renewed.	Education	.361	1.014	0.036**
	Financial	-.341	.882	
We continually update our list of new information security threats.	Education	.309	1.033	0.076*
	Financial	.2914535	.9	
We frequently ask for information about potential weaknesses and vulnerabilities of our security systems.	Education	.3269924	1.01	0.059*
	Financial	.3088262	.913	
We provide systems support to ensure high levels of information resource availability.	Education	.3126561	1.185	0.072*
	Financial	.2952863	.699	
Approximately what percentage of security incidents affected the confidentiality of data by disclosing it to unauthorized persons?	Education	.00667	.018	0.029**
	Financial	.24333	.398	
Approximately what percentage of security incidents affected the availability of resources?	Education	.48067	.481	0.095*
	Financial	.20667	.381	
Percentage of security budget spent on disaster recovery	Education	.04115	.06	0.01**
	Financial	.18615	.179	
Does your organization regularly conduct information security audits? (Yes = 1, No = 0)	Education	.47	.514	0.002**
	Financial	.94	.243	

It appeared that whether or not audits were performed might also be linked to the types of security incidents participant organizations faced (see Table 4). Compared with their counterparts, organizations that regularly performed audits recognized a greater proportion of incidents that affected the confidentiality of data as well as a smaller proportion of incidents that affected the availability of their resources. One explanation is that the audits picked up more incidents that could affect confidentiality; thus organizations that did not perform audits underestimated the actual proportion of incidents of unauthorized disclosure. Secondly, since the audit process was possibly linked to greater efforts to ensure availability (see Table 4), the reduction in the proportion of incidents affecting availability might have been a reflection of the success of these efforts.

The use of security audits appeared to be related to customer capital and human capital. The data indicated that organizations that performed audits perceived that they invested a great deal in building their customer capital. This was consistent with the research model's premise that organizations that invest in their security systems value their customers' well-being and accumulate customer capital. Regarding human capital, it was found that organizations in the study that invested heavily in auditing processes had a lower proportion of employees with post-secondary education. This suggested that organizations hiring employees with reduced skills and education required stronger management controls.

Nature of Security Threats

Correlations between different types of incidents were also examined (Table 5). Generally, denial of service incidents were seen to originate from outside the organization. Incidents that affected data integrity through modification and incidents involving data destruction were significantly linked. While incidents involving non-human perpetrators (e.g., viruses and software bugs) were positively correlated with incidents that affected availability, they were negatively correlated with incidents that disclosed information. This suggested that threats such as viruses were not perceived as being related to information theft. This misperception should be a management concern because malware such as key loggers, spyware and Trojan horses *does* have the ability to steal information.

Support for the Research Model

Although limited analyses could be conducted using partial least squares analysis, the relationships among the IS Security Policies, the Procedures and Technologies construct and the Perceived Security[3] construct were examined using paired dimensions. Table 6 presents the results of the PLS analysis and results of the bootstrap procedure for each path.

The analysis provided support for a subset of the research model. The implementation of countermeasures, assurance processes and assessment processes appeared to contribute to greater perceived security. Of note was the fact that policies and centralization of responsibility appeared to be negatively (although not significantly) related to perceived security. A possible explanation for this relationship was that policies and centralization by themselves did not secure knowledge bases. Policies deterred some human threats and centralization set up a reporting structure and chain of responsibility; however, they would appear to have had no direct effect on the perception of knowledge base security.

The data indicated that organizations perceived their knowledge bases to be more secure when they had processes to assess risks, countermeasures to address threats and assurance processes to assure their security system was in working order. Therefore, for organizations to feel secure, the study suggests that they need more than policies and guidelines. They need to implement countermeasures and processes to assess risks and periodically verify that security mechanisms are being correctly utilized.

Industry Differences

As the survey was undertaken in two different industries, Finance and Education, industry-specific findings were also explored (see Table 7). Organizations in the two industries appeared to differ in their perceptions of key threats. Participants from Education tended to rank the threats of spam, denial of service attacks and malware as more important than Finance industry participants. A very significant difference was detected in denial of service attacks. These threats are usually launched using automated software and result in denying access to resources. This concern with availability was reflected in educational participants' lower confidence in the system support received and their perception of a greater proportion of incidents that affected the availability of their information resources. Financial organizations, on the other hand, appeared concerned about a greater proportion of incidents affecting the confidentiality of information.

Financial organization participants appeared to have in place more security policies, guidelines and disaster recovery planning. They also appeared to have more individuals accountable for the security of each information resource. In addition, the data indicated that their processes for assuring the security of their information systems differed from those in educational organizations in the following respects: they more frequently renewed their security requirements, updated their lists of threats, and gathered information about potential weaknesses and vulnerabilities. Moreover, financial organizations also allocated a greater degree of their security budget to disaster recovery and appeared to more regularly conduct security audits, with the cycles between each review tending to be shorter than the cycles for educational organizations. The longest cycle for financial participants was two years, while the maximum for educational participants was five years. These differences in security processes and policies no doubt helped to explain the differences in the perceived security of their computer resources.

Management Implications

Organizations face a variety of security threats. This study investigated the extent to which organizations view their knowledge bases as strategic resources and invest in protecting these resources. The study also examined employee and customer capital outcomes.

The survey data gathered suggested that financial organizations were perhaps more acutely aware than educational organizations of the strategic importance of their information systems and were investing more heavily in securing these resources. Financial institutions were found to be more likely to conduct security audits and were thus able to detect and address a wider range of threats. While educational participants viewed the threat of denial of service attacks as more important, financial organizations had a greater focus on the confidentiality of their information.

Data from the survey also indicated that while a range of security practices existed, they had differing effects on the perception of knowledge base security. Security assessment processes and countermeasures contributed most to the perception of knowledge base security. This suggests that not all security investments have the same human capital effect.

The data also suggested that security threats were grouped primarily in the minds of IT managers by the means by which they compromise computer systems (e.g., threats to the modification or destruction of data) and less in terms of their user consequences (e.g., spam which may affect resource availability or phishing which may affect confidentiality). This suggests that there could be greater client/user focus in security planning.

It was discovered that the (de)centralization of security responsibilities was linked to the nature and severity of the perceived security threats. Organizations that had separate, centralized security departments perceived a greater threat of sabotage.

They reported facing a greater proportion of incidents in which data had the potential of being destroyed. It was unclear whether these dedicated departments were formed in response to these incidents of sabotage or if they were simply better able to detect them.

Organizations that had more individuals responsible for the security of knowledge bases more regularly performed security audits and gave more attention to disaster recovery planning. These organizations also were more likely to have processes to assess risks, and countermeasures to detect and respond to threats. These organizations appeared to have a lower proportion of incidents that affected information resource availability. They also perceived that they were investing a great deal in building their customer capital.

In this way, partial support for the research model was provided by the survey data gathered. An appreciation of the importance of knowledge bases was linked with greater investment in security policies, procedures and technologies. This in turn influenced the number and nature of security threats and breaches. Organizations that perceived that they were making these security investments also believed that they had good customer and employee relations.

Research Implications

Limitations

This study, while helpful, had several limitations. The most serious was the relatively low statistical power because of the limited data that could be gathered from organizations on their information security practices. However, the data gathered permitted the testing and validation of the instruments and several of the bivariate relationships in the research model.

A second limitation of this research, also related to the sensitivity of the (data security) issue being investigated, was the difficulty experienced in accurately measuring some of the constructs. For example, despite pre-testing, the data gathered on the Number and Nature of Security Threats and Breaches did not demonstrate adequate variation. Of the 33 respondents providing data for the item asking about the number of past breaches encountered, almost all chose the response "0 to 10 breaches," avoiding higher response categories. As a consequence, surrogate/replacement measures had to be used in the data analyses. Particularly sensitive measures like this will need to be revised further before being used in other studies.

Recommendations for Future Research

Information security processes, breaches and impacts are difficult to accurately study. We recommend that future researchers establish in-depth relationships with organizations (e.g., via case studies and longitudinal research) before seeking to gather sensitive data. A survey approach is likely to provide accurate information that is aggregated (i.e., non-threatening to the organization). We recommend more small-scale, in-depth studies.

We would suggest also that the constructs and relationships outside the dotted box in the research model (see Figure 1) be investigated in greater detail in future studies. We gathered limited data on these constructs (the strategic value of knowledge bases, customer capital and human capital) and were only able to demonstrate weak empirical support for the proposed relationships. We would hope to see these sections of the research model tested in greater detail in future investigations. We would also encourage others to take advantage of the research tools or instruments we have developed. See Appendix I.

There are two constructs that we particularly recommend for future investigation. The first is Security Awareness. This construct, applied to an organization, refers not only to the security expertise and knowledge of the Information Security group, but to that of the organization as a whole. We invite researchers to examine its antecedents and outcomes. The second related construct is Security Culture. This addresses the breadth and depth of the security awareness and behaviors of the organization.

Security threats and breaches in contemporary organizations continue to evolve and intensify. Information security research has its challenges but remains vitally important to today's managers tasked with protecting and realizing value from the organization's knowledge bases.

References

Alavi, M., & Leidner, D. E. (2001). Review: Knowledge management and knowledge management systems: Conceptual foundations and research issues. *MIS Quarterly, 25*(1), 107-125.

Allee, V. (2000). The value evolution: Addressing larger implications of an intellectual capital and intangibles perspective. *Journal of Intellectual Capital, 1*(1), 17-32.

Barney, J. (1991). Firm resources and sustained competitive advantage. *Journal of Management, 17*(1), 99-120.

Bontis, N. (1998). Intellectual capital: An exploratory study that develops measures and models. *Management Decision, 36*(2), 63.

Chan, Y. E. (1992). *Business strategy, information systems strategy, and strategic fit: Measurement and performance impacts.* Ph.D. thesis, University of Western Ontario, Canada.

Chin, W. W. (1998). Issues and opinion on structural equation modeling. *MIS Quarterly, 22*(1), vii-xvi.

Crowe, M. (1997). Intellectual capital for the perplexed. *Harvard Management Update.* Boston: Harvard Buisness School.

Culnan, M. (2006). Privacy in search of governance. In: Doing privacy right: Using data and preserving trust. *Cutter Benchmark Review, 6*(1), 5-11.

Dhillon, G., & Backhouse, J. (1996). Risks in the use of information technology within organizations. *International Journal of Information Management, 16*(1), 65-74.

Dhillon, G., & Backhouse, J. (2000). Information system security management in the new millennium. *Communications of the ACM, 43*(7), 125-128.

Dierickx, I. & Cool, K. (1989). Asset stock accumulation and sustainability of competitive advantage. *Management Science, 35*(12), 1504-1511.

Dutta, A. & Roy, R. (2003). The dynamics of organizational information security. *Twenty-Fourth International Conference on Information Systems*, 921-927.

Gallupe, B. (2001). Knowledge management systems: Surveying the landscape. *International Journal of Management Reviews, 3*(1), 61-77.

Gold, A. H., Malhotra, A., & Segars, A. (2001). Knowledge management: An organizational capabilities perspective. *Journal of Management Information Systems, 18*(1), 185-214.

Goodhue, D. L & Straub, D. (1991). Security concerns of system users: A study of perceptions of system adequacy. *Information and Management*, (20), 13-27.

Gordon, L. A, Loeb, M. P., Lucyshyn, W., & Richardson, R. (2004). 2004 CSI/FBI computer crime and security survey, Retrieved December 3, 2004, from http://www.gocsi.com

Greenaway, K. E., Cunningham, P. H., & Chan, Y. E. (2002). Privacy orientation: A competing values explanation of why organizations vary in their treatment of customer information. 2002 AMA Marketing and Public Policy conference.

Grover, V. & Davenport, T. H. (2001). General perspectives on knowledge management: Fostering a research agenda. Journal of Management Information Systems,18(1), 5-21.

Haahti, A. (2003). Theory of relationship cultivation: A point of view to design of experience. *Journal of Business and Management, 9*(33), 303-322.

Harrington, S. J. (1996). The effects of codes of ethics and personal denial of responsibility on computer abuse judgements and intentions. *MIS Quarterly, 20*(3), 257-278.

Hoyle, R. H. (Ed.). (1999). *Statistical strategies for small sample research.* Thousand Oaks, CA: Sage.

Hulland, J. (1999). Use of partial least squares (PLS) in strategic management research: A review of four recent studies. *Strategic Management Journal, 20*(2), 195 -204.

Hulme, G.V. (2005). Data breaches: Turn back the tide—An information-security best practices primer to minimize the risks posed to business and consumer information. *Business Credit, 107*(9), 34-38.

Khoo, K. & Zhou, L. (2004). Managing Web services security. *Proceedings of the Americas Conference on Information Systems,* 4464 -4570.

Knight, D. J. (1999). Performance measures: For increasing intellectual capital. *Strategy & Leadership, 27*(2), 22 -27.

Landwehr, C. E. (2001). Computer security. *International Journal of Information Security, 1*(1), 3-13.

Lemos, R. (2005). Data security moves front and center in 2005. Security Focus, http://www.security focus.com/news/11366. From *Institute for the Study of Privacy Clips,* December 29, 2005.

Li, H., King, G., Ross, M., & Staples, G. (2000). BS7799: A suitable model for information security management. *Proceedings of the Americas Conference on Information Systems,* 205-211.

Loch, K. D, Carr, H. H., & Warkentin, M. E. (1992). Threats to information systems: Today's reality, yesterday's understanding. *MIS Quarterly, 16*(2), 173-186.

Mata, F. J., Fuerst, W. L., & Barney, J. B. (1995). Information technology and sustained competitive advantage: A resource-based analysis, *MIS Quarterly, 19*(4), 487-505.

McGrath, R., *Jr.* & *Sparks,* W. L. (2005). The importance of building social capital. *Quality Progress, 38*(2), 45-50.

Moore, G. & Benbasat I. (1991). Development of an instrument to measure the perceptions of adopting an information technology innovation. *Information Systems Research, 2*(3), 192-222.

Nelson, R. R. & Romer, P. M. (1996). Science, economic growth, and public policy. *Challenge, 39*(2), 9-21.

Saporito, B. (n.d.). Are your secrets safe? Retrieved March 4, 2005, from http://www.time.com/time/magazine/article/0,9171,1032374,00.html

Straub, D. W, Jr. & Collins, R. W. (1990). Key information liability issues facing managers: Software piracy, proprietary databases, and individual rights to privacy. *MIS Quarterly, 14*(2), 143-156.

Straub, D. W. & Welke, R. J. (1998). Coping with systems risk: Security planning models for management decision making. *MIS Quarterly*, *22*(4), 441-469.

Volonino, L. & Robinson, S. R. (2004). *Principles and practice of information security: Protecting computers from hackers and lawyers*. Upper Saddle River, NJ: Pearson.

Wade, M. & Hulland, J. (2004). Review: The resource-based view and information systems research: Review, extensions and suggestions for future research. *MIS Quarterly*, *28*(1), 107-142.

Wang, W. -Y. & Chang, C..(2005). Intellectual capital and performance in causal models: Evidence from the information technology industry in Taiwan. *Journal of Intellectual Capital*, *6*(2), 222 -236.

Wilson, J., Turban, E., & Zviran, M. (1992). Information system security: A managerial perspective. *International Journal of Information Management*, *12*(22), 105-119.

Appendix A: CEO and CIO Surveys: Questionnaire Items by Construct

CEO Survey

Strategic Value of Knowledge Bases

Value	Strongly Agree (1)	(2)	(3)	(4)	Strongly Disagree (5)
Our knowledge bases help us operate more efficiently.	1	2	3	4	5
Our knowledge bases help us in identifying market opportunities.	1	2	3	4	5
Our knowledge bases help us to create product/service innovations.	1	2	3	4	5
Our knowledge bases contribute to generating new business.	1	2	3	4	5
Our knowledge bases generate new business insights.	1	2	3	4	5
Our knowledge bases enable us to react quickly to competitive changes.	1	2	3	4	5

Rarity	Strongly Agree (1)	(2)	(3)	(4)	Strongly Disagree (5)
Our knowledge bases are unique.	1	2	3	4	5
Our knowledge bases contain information our competitors do not have.	1	2	3	4	5
Few of our competitors have knowledge bases such as ours.	1	2	3	4	5
Our knowledge bases contain rare information and knowledge.	1	2	3	4	5

Inimitability	Strongly Agree (1)	(2)	(3)	(4)	Strongly Disagree (5)
Our knowledge bases can be easily imitated by our competitors.*	1	2	3	4	5
It would take substantial time to recreate our knowledge bases.	1	2	3	4	5

It would take substantial monetary investment to recreate our knowledge bases.	1	2	3	4	5
Our knowledge bases are irreplaceable.	1	2	3	4	5
Our knowledge bases are more valuable to us than to our competitors or business partners.	1	2	3	4	5
Our knowledge bases are tightly integrated into our business processes.	1	2	3	4	5

Non-Substitutability	Strongly Agree (1)	(2)	(3)	(4)	Strongly Disagree (5)
There is no substitute for our knowledge bases.	1	2	3	4	5
Our knowledge bases are critical to our business operations. We cannot operate without them.	1	2	3	4	5
There are other methods to accomplish what we use our knowledge bases for.*	1	2	3	4	5
The value of our knowledge bases can be eroded by our competitors.*	1	2	3	4	5

Perceived as strategic tools	Strongly Agree (1)	(2)	(3)	(4)	Strongly Disagree (5)
Our knowledge bases are a competitive tool.	1	2	3	4	5
Our knowledge bases do not provide us with a competitive edge.*	1	2	3	4	5
We compete using our knowledge bases.	1	2	3	4	5
Our knowledge bases are a strategic necessity.	1	2	3	4	5

Perceived Security	Strongly Agree (1)	(2)	(3)	(4)	Strongly Disagree (5)
For our type of organization, our information security practices are very effective.	1	2	3	4	5
Information in our knowledge bases is very well protected.	1	2	3	4	5

Our computer resources are very well secured.	1	2	3	4	5
Our computer resources are frequently *unavailable.**	1	2	3	4	5
Our information systems are frequently *compromised* by security breaches.*	1	2	3	4	5

*reverse coded

Customer Capital

Percentage Ratings	%
Approximately what percentage of organizational revenue is the Customer Services Department's budget?	
Approximately what percentage of organizational revenue is the Marketing Department's budget?	
Approximately what percentage of revenue is spent on acquiring external customer databases?	
Approximately what percentage of customers are repeat customers?	
What is the approximate customer growth rate?	
What is the annual customer turnover rate? $$\text{Customer turnover} = \frac{\text{Number of customers that left}}{\text{Average number of customers}} \times 100$$	

Customer Capital	Strongly Agree (1)	(2)	(3)	(4)	Strongly Disagree (5)
We invest a great deal of resources in building our customer capital.	1	2	3	4	5
Our customers are very loyal.	1	2	3	4	5
The opinions held by our *customers* about our organization give us a competitive advantage.	1	2	3	4	5
The opinions held by our *suppliers* about our organization give us a competitive advantage.	1	2	3	4	5
The opinions held by our *distributors* about our organization give us a competitive advantage.	1	2	3	4	5
The opinions held by our *business partners* about our organization give us a competitive advantage.	1	2	3	4	5

The opinions held by our *community* about our organization give us a competitive advantage.	1	2	3	4	5
Customer capital is very important to our organization.	1	2	3	4	5

Human Capital

Percentage Ratings			%
As an approximate percentage of the entire firm, how many new employees join the firm annually?			
What is the average annual employee turnover rate of the organization? $\text{Employee turnover} = \dfrac{\text{Number of employees that left}}{\text{Average number of employees}} \times 100$			
What percentages of all employees have post-secondary education?			
As a percentage of revenue, what is the annual investment in employee training?			
What percentage of employees have been with the organization for:	<1 year		
	1-5 years		
	5+ years		

Human Capital	Strongly Agree (1)	(2)	(3)	(4)	Strongly Disagree (5)
Employees have made few valuable business suggestions in the past year.*	1	2	3	4	5
Employee suggestions are frequently adopted by the organization.	1	2	3	4	5
Employee suggestions are a valuable source of innovation for our organization.	1	2	3	4	5
Employee capital is very important to our organization.	1	2	3	4	5

Which of the following knowledge management technologies or practices are in place in your organization? Please check all that apply.	X
Communities of practice -a community of people that work together to solve problems of a common topic, or of a specific technical background.	
Company "yellow pages" -a directory of employees listing their expertise as well as their contact information.	

Employee mentoring -programs that allow experienced knowledgeable employees to teach and provide guidance to less experienced employees.	
Formal training courses -courses for providing employees with new skills and knowledge.	
Knowledge base of experiences - databases that contain documentation on knowledge acquired by the organization through past experiences. Examples may be case studies or solutions to problems.	

CIO Survey

Governance and Policies	None	Few	Many
There are organizational policies for the protection of information.	None	Few	Many
There are standard procedures for responding to security incidents.	None	Few	Many
There are organizational guidelines outlining how to protect information.	None	Few	Many
There are disaster recovery plans to address circumstances that severely negatively impact or stop the operations of the organization.	None	Few	Many

Centralization of Responsibility	Strongly Agree (1)	(2)	(3)	(4)	Strongly Disagree (5)
All knowledge bases have an individual who is accountable for their security.	1	2	3	4	5
Each department or business unit is responsible for the security of its information assets.	1	2	3	4	5
Information security is solely the responsibility of the IT department.*	1	2	3	4	5
Information security is solely the responsibility of the security department.*	1	2	3	4	5

Assessment	Strongly Agree (1)	(2)	(3)	(4)	Strongly Disagree (5)
Assessing information security is a requirement of all projects.	1	2	3	4	5
We consider cancelling projects that pose significant information security risks.	1	2	3	4	5
We have processes that identify security risk levels for our information assets.	1	2	3	4	5
We consider information security risks before approving projects.	1	2	3	4	5

	Strongly Agree (1)	(2)	(3)	(4)	Strongly Disagree (5)
When assessing security risks, we classify them by the level of potential severity.	1	2	3	4	5
When assessing security risks, we classify them by their likelihood of occurrence.	1	2	3	4	5

Assurance	Strongly Agree (1)	(2)	(3)	(4)	Strongly Disagree (5)
Security requirements for all information assets are frequently renewed.	1	2	3	4	5
We continually update our list of new information security threats.	1	2	3	4	5
We constantly explore methods to improve our information security systems.	1	2	3	4	5
We frequently ask for information about potential weaknesses and vulnerabilities of our security systems.	1	2	3	4	5
We perform statistical analysis of security incident data.	1	2	3	4	5

Confidentiality	Strongly Agree (1)	(2)	(3)	(4)	Strongly Disagree (5)
Sensitive data is protected from those who should not have access to it.	1	2	3	4	5
Information in our knowledge bases is adequately physically protected from unauthorized access.	1	2	3	4	5
Personal data is always stored separately from other data.	1	2	3	4	5
Sensitive information is disseminated only on a "need to know" basis.	1	2	3	4	5
Personal information is protected from disclosure by employees of the organization to unauthorized persons.	1	2	3	4	5

Integrity	Strongly Agree (1)	(2)	(3)	(4)	Strongly Disagree (5)
We have many processes that verify the integrity of our information.	1	2	3	4	5
Information assets are classified by levels of desired integrity.	1	2	3	4	5
We have processes that prevent the input of "bad" data.	1	2	3	4	5
We have software tools that prevent the input of "bad" data.	1	2	3	4	5

Data is safeguarded from unauthorized changes or use.	1	2	3	4	5

Availability	Strongly Agree (1)	(2)	(3)	(4)	Strongly Disagree (5)
We have extensive back-up systems that ensure the availability of our information assets.	1	2	3	4	5
We classify our information assets by the desired level of availability.	1	2	3	4	5
We provide systems support to ensure high levels of information resource availability.	1	2	3	4	5

Countermeasures	Strongly Agree (1)	(2)	(3)	(4)	Strongly Disagree (5)
We have organizational processes to predict security incidents before they occur.	1	2	3	4	5
We have software tools to predict security incidents before they occur.	1	2	3	4	5
We have organizational processes to prevent security incidents before they occur.	1	2	3	4	5
We have software tools to prevent security incidents before they occur.	1	2	3	4	5
We have organizational processes to respond to security incidents.	1	2	3	4	5
We have software tools to respond to security incidents.	1	2	3	4	5
We have organizational processes to detect external threats.	1	2	3	4	5
We have software tools to detect external threats.	1	2	3	4	5
We have organizational processes to detect internal threats.	1	2	3	4	5
We have software tools to detect internal threats.	1	2	3	4	5

Rank	*Threats* Please rank the following threats in terms of their importance to your organization (where 1 = most important, 12 = least important):
	Software piracy -the illegal copying or use of licensed software.
	Identity theft -illegally using another individual's personal identifying information for the purposes of gain.
	Spam -jargon for unsolicited, unwanted email or electronic junk mail.

	Denial of service -an action or series of actions designed to make unavailable an information resource unavailable for its intended purpose.
	Phishing -jargon for a form of fraud where a target is persuaded to reveal personal information from an e-mail masquerading to originate from a legitimate source.
	Theft of equipment.
	Theft of proprietary information.
	Sabotage.
	Social engineering -an attempt to gain access to sensitive information or facilities through the use of deception. Ex. an individual may look to have their arms full of documents and ask other, legitimate persons, to open the door to an area of restricted access.
	Unauthorized access by employees.
	Unauthorized access by outsiders.
	Malware, viruses -malicious software or code written with the purpose to cause harm to computer systems.

Breaches	Number of Breaches		
	0 -10	10 -50	50+
Approximately how many information security breaches occurred in the past year in your organization?	0 -10	10 -50	50+
Approximately how many security breaches of the past year had the potential for theft of confidential, personal information?	0 -10	10 -50	50+

Percentage Ratings	%
For approximately what percentage of security incidents were the source internal to the organization?	
For approximately what percentage of security incidents were the perpetrators non-human (ex. viruses, software bugs)?	
For approximately what percentage of security incidents was the motivation intentional (not accidental)?	
Approximately what percentage of security incidents affected the confidentiality of data by disclosing it to unauthorized persons?	
Approximately what percentage of security incidents affected the integrity of data by destroying it?	
Approximately what percentage of security incidents affected the integrity of data by modifying it?	
Approximately what percentage of security incidents affected the availability of resources?	

*reverse coded

Background Questions

Do you have a security department that is separate from your IT department?	Yes	No
What is the IT budget as a percentage of organization revenue? (For the purposes of this survey, please include purchase, maintenance, development, and implementation as well as training costs.)		Dollars ($)
What is the security expenditure as a percentage of the IT budget? (For the purposes of this survey, please include firewalls, training, awareness campaigns, assessment, audits and disaster recovery)		Dollars ($)

Approximately what percentage of your security budget is spent on:	Personnel		%
	Security awareness		%
	System audits		%
	Disaster Recovery		%
	Training		%
	Emerging Technologies		%
	System Maintenance		%
	Other (Specify):		%

Does your organization regularly conduct information security audits?	Yes	No
How many months are the cycles between each information security review?		Months

Human Capital

Percentage Ratings	%
As an approximate percentage of the IT department, how many new IT employees join the department annually?	
As an approximate percentage of the Security department, how many new security employees join the department annually?	
What is the average annual employee turnover rate of the IT Department?	
What is the average annual employee turnover rate of information security personnel? $Employee\ turnover = \dfrac{Number\ of\ employees\ that\ left}{Average\ number\ of\ employees} \times 100$	

What percentages of all IT employees have post-secondary education?		
What percentages of all security employees have post-secondary education?		
As a percentage of the IT budget, what is the annual investment spent on IT employee training?		
As a percentage of the security budget, what is the annual investment spent on security employee training?		
What percentage of IT employees have been with the organization for:	< 1 year	
	1 -5 years	
	5+ years	
What percentage of security employees have been with the organization for:	< 1 year	
	1 -5 years	
	5+ years	

Appendix B: Instrument Refinement

Card Sorting Exercise

To assess and improve face validity of the questionnaires, the individual questions or items were sorted and grouped (Moore and Benbasat 1991). In this procedure, the questions were printed on 3"x5" index cards with one item per card. On the back, the cards were numbered from 1 to 115. These cards were then presented as a deck to the card sorter.

Card Sorters

The card sorters were professors, MSc students, PhD students and research assistants from the disciplines of Information Systems, Organizational Behaviour and Marketing. Each sorter was given an hour to sort the items first into five main groups and then into subgroups. An instruction sheet identified the five main constructs and provided a list of definitions for terms. In the first two rounds, the sorters were not given labels for the groupings, while in the last round the sorter was given the labels for the sub-groupings as well. (A copy of the instructions is provided below.)

In the first round of sorting, there were three sorters, two PhD Information Systems students and an MSc Organizational Behaviour student. In the second round of sorting, there was one Information Systems professor, an Information Systems doctoral candidate and a Marketing master's candidate. The third and final round was aimed at readability. So an Information Systems research assistant performed the sort.

Analysis Procedures

For analysis, each response was entered into a spreadsheet, and the items were coded into the constructs that they were designed to be related to. For each participant, responses were then coded into main groups as well as subgroups. Their responses' main groupings were checked against the intended constructs for agreement as well as for agreement with the other card sorter's groupings. Items that were not correctly sorted into their intended main construct were flagged.

For each construct, the sub-groupings were analyzed as well. Items that were designed to measure the same dimensions of a construct were checked to see if they were grouped together. Items that were not sorted into the correct subgroups were also flagged for review.

Results

In the first round, with three sorters, there were 26 items flagged and reworded. In the second round, with three sorters, fourteen items were identified and reworded. In the final round, two items were identified and reworded. The results are presented in the following table.

Sorting round	Sorter	Number of incorrectly sorted items	Number of items reworded
	1	10	
1	2	18	26
	3	2	
	1	10	
2	2	12	14
	3	11	
3	1	2	2

Questionnaire Item Sorting Instructions

There is a set of 115 cards in front of you. On each of the cards there is written a question regarding one of the following concepts:

- Appreciation of the strategic value of knowledge bases: the degree to which organizations believe that their knowledge bases are of strategic value.
- Security resources: The policies, strategies, countermeasures and technologies that organizations have to secure their knowledge bases.
- Number and nature of security breaches: The variety and number of breaches of the organization's security system.
- Customer capital: The data, opinions, and values collectively held about an organization by customers, suppliers, market association and trade groups and government policy makers. The items in this survey will explore the effects of this as well as actions the organization may take to manage this.
- Human capital: individual capabilities, knowledge, skills, experience and problem-solving abilities that reside in people in the firm. This survey will look at what organizations may do to manage the human capital of employees as well as the effects of that capital.

Please sort the cards into the five categories. These groups do *not* have equal number of cards. The cards in each category should be related to each other as well as reflect the category definition. Some of the questions may have similar wording; please try to group them based on the underlying concept they are addressing.

After sorting into the five categories, please go through each pile and group the cards into as many logical sub-groupings as you would like. Once again, these sub-groupings do not need to be equal in number and different categories may have different numbers of subgroups.

Please keep the following in mind:

- you are free the change the grouping of the cards as you go through the exercise
- take your time
- after completing the sorting, please go through each pile to confirm that you are satisfied with the sort
- you may re-sort as many times as you like
- please refer to the definitions provided if you have questions

This is not a test! The purpose of this sorting exercise is to determine if the questions are related to the five categories as originally determined when the questionnaire was first drafted.

Thank you for your help with this research project.

Endnotes

[1] The authors acknowledge research assistance provided by Catherine Shea and thank the Social Sciences and Humanities Research Council of Canada and the Ontario Research Network for Electronic Commerce for funding provided.

[2] As it turned out, 56% of the CIO participants made use of the Web site and 44% of the CEO participants used the Web site to respond.

[3] The data gathered on the number of security breaches did not show adequate variation, so the Perceived Security construct was used as a proxy measure in the research model (see Figure 1) for the Number and Nature of Security Threats and Breaches.

Section V

Security and Privacy: Emerging Issues

Chapter XI

Emerging Technologies, Emerging Privacy Issues

Sue Conger, University of Dallas, USA

Abstract

With each new technology, new ethical issues emerge that threaten both individual and household privacy. This chapter investigates issues relating to three emerging technologies—RFID chips, GPS, and smart motes—and the current and future impacts these technologies will have on society. The outcome will be issues for social discussion and resolution in the coming decades relating to use of these technologies.

Background

New data losses of millions of individuals' personal information occur almost daily (Albrecht, 2002; Clarke, 1999; CNet, 2006). As losses amass, the realization grows that personal information privacy (PIP) is no longer managed by either individuals or the companies that collect the data. Research to date proposes that PIP is the

Table 1.

pri·va·cy (http://www,dictionary.com based on *Random House Unabridged Dictionary, 2006*	1.	the state of being private; retirement or seclusion.
	2.	The state of being free from intrusion or disturbance in one's private life or affairs: *the right to privacy.*
	3.	SECRECY.
	4.	*Archaic.* a private place.
pri·va·cy *The American Heritage® Dictionary of the English Language, Fourth Edition Copyright © 2000*	1. a.	The quality or condition of being secluded from the presence or view of others.
	b.	The state of being free from unsanctioned intrusion: *a person's right to privacy.*
	2.	The state of being concealed; secrecy.
pri·va·cy *WordNet® 2.1, © 2005 Princeton University*	1.	The quality of being secluded from the presence or view of others
	2.	The condition of being concealed or hidden

responsibility of individuals' forging contracts with corporations for protection of their data (Smith, 2004), that it is the responsibility of government to protect the individual from corporate abuses (OECD, 2000, 2003, 2006; Swire, 1997), or the responsibility of corporations to manage internal use (Cheung et al., 2005; Culnan, 1993; Culnan & Armstrong, 1999; Smith et al. 1996). These views are all corporate-centric but threats have expanded beyond the corporation to its data-sharing partners, resulting in data aggregation and sales that are largely unregulated and uncontrolled (Conger, 2006; Conger et al., 2005).

Dictionary.com has several definitions of privacy as shown in Table 1.

These definitions leave one with a clear expectation that individuals control their own physical visibility to the world. The legal definition further includes privacy in "personal matters."

Privacy can be thought of from several points of view (cf., OECD 1998; Smith 2004). On the one hand, the question is how the individual's inherent *right* to privacy can be protected, for example, by legislation. On the other hand, the individual has a *contractual* right of privacy, to control interactions with the world, including the release of private information such as address and social security number.

Figure 1. Information privacy model (Conger, et al., 2005)

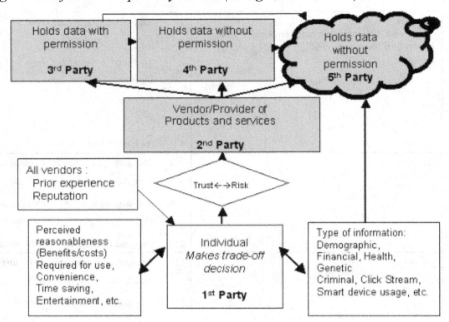

In the past, privacy concerns were limited to protecting one's credit card, home, or mailbox from theft. Privacy research in the past focused on collection, unauthorized secondary use, ownership, accuracy, and access (Conger & Loch, 1995; Culnan, 1993; Culnan & Armstrong, 1999; Loch & Conger, 1996; Smith et al., 1996). Most research never stated what data was collected, or described a limited domain of data relating to a given transaction and demographics that oversimplifies breadth of data that might be collected (cf. Chen & Barnes, 2007; Cheung et al., 2005; Cheung & Lee, 2004/2005; Culnan and Armstrong, 1999; Doolin et al., 2005; Drennan et al., 2006).

Now, users of the Internet, worry that "personally revealing information about them is automatically generated, collected, stored, interconnected and put to a variety of uses." (OECD 1998, p. 11). To accommodate the changes enabled by Internet technologies, a more complete view of the current state of PIP in business to consumer (B2C) transactions (see Figure 1) describes how an individual, the 1st party, comes to transact with a company, the 2nd party vendor/provider (Cheung, 2005, Conger et al., 2006).

Each unshaded box in Figure 1 and the arrows depicting the relationships between them represent areas in which significant research has already been conducted and incorporates the bodies of work summarized in Culnan and Armstrong (1999) and

Cheung et al. (2005). Part of the individual's decision includes what data to provide to the 2nd party based on the expected life and use of that data, perceived reasonableness of the data collected, expected benefits, and expectations of corporate use of the collected data (Conger et al., 2005).

A decision to transact is based on an idiosyncratic evaluation of risk versus reward versus trust (Chen & Barnes, 2007; Dinev & Hart, 2006; Gallivan & Depledge, 2003; Geffen et al., 2003; Malhotra et al., 2004). Violate, or appear to violate, any of the decision factors and transactions will not be enacted (Gaudin, 2007; Gauzente, 2004; Holes, 2006; McKnight et al., 2004; Mutz, 2005; Wang et al., 1998).

The shaded boxes and arrows depicting their interrelationships represent areas in which little or no research has been published. After a transaction is complete, the information is shared with any number of legal data-sharing entities, the 3rd-party data user who is a known external data-sharing partner, for example, a credit reporting company such as Experian who shares data with 2nd-party permission. Companies, such as Experian, generate their revenues by matching consumer information to transaction information, profiling consumers, and reselling the expanded information. The Experians of the world are not necessarily the problem unless their use or access to data violates their legal and contractual agreements. The greater vulnerabilities arise from Experian's data sharing partners, the 4th parties.

Third-party organizations resell or provide their information through legal requests to 4th-party organizations. Problems arise when 4th-party partners use data without 1st-party and/or 2nd-party permission. Such partnerships might be governmental pre-emption of data (ACLU, 2003; Ahrens, 2006; Cauley, 2006; DARPA, 2002; Myers et al., 2005; Seffers, 2000; Stanley & Steinhart, 2003; Waller, 2002), data aggregators, or legitimate data-sharing partners of the 3rd-party who violate the terms of their agreements. There is no actual way for, for instance Experian, to ensure proper use since compliance is self-reported. Further, government cooption of data has come under increasing scrutiny as violating constitutional rights to privacy provisions (Zeller, 2005). The U.S. is not alone in co-opting Internet search and other records about its citizens. Canadian authorities have had a legal right to "e-mail, Internet activity, and other electronic records" since 2004 (Smith, 2004). China uses Yahoo Internet e-mail data as the basis for jailing dissidents (Goodman, 2005).

Other 4th party organizations are non-government companies that, unknown to the user, install malware, spyware, or other technically legal software on Internet user machines. In one study, Google found about 10 percent of Web pages, out of 4.5 million Web pages, were found to have spyware install programs (Anonymous 13, 2007). In another study, AOL and the National Cyber Security Alliance found that 91 percent of respondents did not even know they had spyware on their PCs (AOL/NSCA, 2005). Spyware software can monitor keystrokes, report back file information to the "mother" company, or do more malicious acts on one's PC. Many Spyware companies sell the information they collect to data aggregators. Data aggregators also obtain information from public sites for marriage, legal, driving, property ownership, and other situations to build even more complete dossiers on individuals. Their clientele are both legitimate businesses and questionable entities who use the data unbeknown to the 1st or 2nd parties from which it emanated.

The nebulous cloud with fuzzy boundaries identifies the last category: 5th-party data invaders. This category of 5th-party users, are unintended, unwanted, and often unethical and/or illegal users of vendor data operating out of bad faith, malice, or grave negligence (cf. Sherman, 2007). Fifth-party data users obtain data without permission or knowledge of their sources, which may be 1st, 2nd, 3rd or 4th parties (ACLU, 2003; Albrecht & McIntyre, 2004; Carlson, 2006; CNet, 2006; Stanley & Steinhart, 2003). People who steal computers and who leak names, addresses, and, for example, financial information, are in this category (Zeller, 2005).

Fifth parties are active. From ChoicePoint's famous identity theft scam in February, 2005 through December, 2006 there were 438 thefts, hacks, or leakages of consumer information of which 335 organizations reported losses over 181 million individual accounts with social security information (Anonymous 9, 2007; Dunham, 2006; PRC, 2007; Reuters, 2006; Scalet, 2006). The 103 organizations either not reporting or not including SSNs, would approximately double the number of transgressions (Anonymous 9, 2007). In the first three months of 2007, the number of compromised SSNs approximately doubled to 360 million as losses and leakages continue (PRC, 2007).

These problems are not unique to the U.S. In 2007, The Commission of the European Communities began an effort to create polices on cyber-crime because of "growing involvement of organized crime groups in cyber-crime" (CEC, 2007, pg. 2). One significant difference is that in the EU, many issues that are 5th party in the U.S. are criminalized and prosecuted (CEC, 2002). Many countries are experiencing increasing transgressions of all types (Denning & Baugh, 1997; Dolya, 2007; Gouldson, 2001; Hempel & Töpfer, 2004; HRW, 2006; ICAS, 2005; Kane & Wall, 2005; McCullagh, 2005A, 2005B; McMillan, 2006; Meller, 2006; Newitz, 2004; Woo, 2006; Wright et al., 2006).

Emerging technologies threaten to change the scope of privacy issues again from relating to transactions to relating to constant, unanticipated surveillance and the concomitant sharing of that data with virtually the world. Data mining and business intelligence software allow heretofore unprecedented abilities to combine and permute information from multiple sources that provide not just product usage and contextual information but information on household individuals, their usage patterns, and their life styles. This is not a new thought. The ACLU published its *RFID*

Position Statement in 2003 with an impressive, international list of signers (ACLU, 2003). Yet, organizations promulgating *new technology* use, such as the Internet Home Alliance and its members, provide only the sanguine view of RFID and its uses, ignoring the privacy issues completely (IdTechEx, 2007; IHA, 2005).

New Technologies Challenge Personal Information Privacy (PIP)

Three technologies further will reduce personal privacy in the coming 10 years if nothing is done to stem the wholesale collection and sale of personal information. The technologies are radio frequency identification chips (RFID), geographical positioning systems (GPS), and smart motes.

These three technologies were selected because each is in a different stage of maturation, but each promises to change privacy issues and extend challenges to individuals in protecting their personal information. Rogers (1985) defined an S-curve of innovation that projects market growth over time (See Figure 2). GPS, introduced in 1978, and imbedded in all U.S. cell phones, is also a maturing industry for hand-held GPS with a U.S. market expected to reach $22 billion in 2008 and a global market about double at $60 billion (David, 2003; ETRI, 2005). Therefore, GPS is toward the top of the diffusion growth curve and represents a relatively mature technology. RFID, developed in the 1940s, is still finding its market. While it

Figure 2. S-curve of innovation and emerging technologies

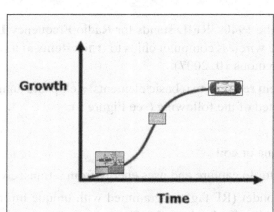

Figure 3. RFID chip

has had significant press, primarily because of privacy concerns, the technology is still in a growth phase, represented in the figure as mid-way up the S-curve. Smart motes enjoy limited commercialization and are still under development. As such, they are the least mature technology and are about at the beginning growth inflection point on the S-curve.

Each technology is described in the next section. Then, privacy issues are described. The state of remedies for the potential transgressions is described next along with the status of current approaches. Finally, future needs are defined for further development of solutions to problems arising from these technologies.

RFID

Developed in the 1940s, RFID stands for **R**adio **F**requency **ID**entification, a technology that use wireless computer chips to **track items at a distance** (Anonymous 5, 2002; Anonymous 10, 2007).

An RFID system requires two basic elements: a chip and an interrogator. An RFID chip is composed of the following (see Figure 3):

- An antenna or coil

- A capacitor to capture and uses energy from a transceiver

- A transponder (RF tag) programmed with unique information (Anonymous 2, 2007; Alien Technology, 2007).

Figure 4. RFID capabilities. Adapted from Anonymous 5 (2002) and IDTechEx (2007)

	Active RFID	Passive RFID
Communication Range	300+ Feet	< 10 Feet
Tag Collection	• 1,000s tags • Over 7 acres • Moving at 100 MPH (reduces the rate)	• 100s tags • < 10 Feet • < 3 MPH
Sensor Capability	• Continuous monitoring and recording • Sensor input • Date/time stamps sensor events • Amenable to hostile environments	• Reader powered to read and send sensor value • No date/time stamp
Data Storage	• 128KB read/write data storage • Search/access capabilities • Re-programmable	• 128 bytes data storage
Media	• Plastic or other durable media	• Paper, file or other printable media
Startup Cost	• Reader - $800 • Tags - $50	• Reader - $400 • Printer - $1, 600 • Tags - < $.05

The interrogator is a powered radio frequency transceiver that, in a separate device gives power to passive RFID in the form of radio waves. For passive RFID, transceivers are slow (see Figure 4), reading about 20 items from less than 10 feet in about three seconds (Anonymous 5, 2002). Active RFID transceivers contain a battery, memory, and ability to continuously monitor and record sensor inputs. They are re-programmable and vulnerable to viruses and software attacks (Miller, 2006; Ricker, 2006). Transceivers for active RFIDs that can be as small as 2x3 inches are installed in thousands of door portals and can read data from thousands of tags a minute, from 300+ feet (100 meters), moving at 100 mph (Anonymous 5, 2002). Active RFID are amenable to hostile environments such as ship cargo holds, deserts, or warehouses.

Prices of RFID chips have steadily dropped for the past 10 years and, with the development of RFID printers, the price is now under $.03 for a passive chip. The antenna on printed chips use conductive ink and are virtually invisible (Anonymous 10, 2007; IdTechEx, 2007; McCarter, 2006; McGrath, 2006).

RFID chips range from passive to active[1]. *Passive* RFID does not transmit until a reader "requests" data from a chip, has no energy source imbedded in the chip, and is limited to reading from about 10 feet (three meters). *Active* RFID transmit continuously and are readable by any reader within 30 meters, about 90 feet. RFID are used in every conceivable product including metals, liquids, textiles, plastics, pharmaceuticals, and others. For instance, they are imbedded in children's pajamas, robots to guard playgrounds, and even shaving gear (Alien Technology, 2007; Gilbert, 2005; IDTechEx, 2007; Olsen, 2007, Sullivan, 2005).

The global market for RFID is huge and growing, including governments and businesses in every industry. Sales are predicted to hit $1 Trillion by 2012 (IdTechEx, 2007; McCarter, 2006; McGrath, 2006). The price of RFID chips has been falling between 5 percent and 10 percent a year for six years (Murray, 2006), enticing new users every year. Many experts predict a world with RFID chips "incorporated into … everyday objects … wherein virtually everything is networked through the Web" (Murray, 2006; Stibbe, 2004).

The new generation of RFID chips coming on the market contains electronic product codes (EPC), which are a 96-bit code capable of uniquely identifying everything on the planet (EPC Global, 2005; Stibbe, 2004). And, there are some people who think that recording everything about a person may have some use (Bell, 2004).

RFID is not all bad. RFID can "accelerate, simplify, and improve the handling of data" (Schuman, 2006, p2). Repetitive counting tasks, such as taking a physical inventory, morph from onerous, backbreaking, days-long work to a walk down each aisle. Shrinkage, the euphemism for stolen, lost, or otherwise missing goods, transforms from a rising percentage of retail costs to almost a thing of the past, simply by placing RFID sensors at all ingress/egress points. In addition, shoplifters who might "hide" goods on their person while they checkout other goods will be discovered and charged for the items. Traffic jams are reduced by toll tags, and transit tickets. Luggage at airports or containers in shipping yards are easily identified and experience speedier processing with embedded RFID. Similarly, transactions are speeded by Speed Pass® and other smart cards with embedded RFID, as is identification and return of stray animals that have been "chipped." These clearly are desirable outcomes of RFID use for corporations and society.

Global Positioning Systems

The next technology that threatens privacy, global positioning system technology (GPS), is available as stand-alone devices or imbedded in devices such as cell phones and autos. Ivan Getting envisioned GPS in the 1950s while he was a researcher at Raytheon Corporation working on systems for guided missiles. Getting left Raytheon and started his own company where he realized his dream for GPS in the 1960s (Anonymous 12, 2007).

Figure 5. Trilateration example

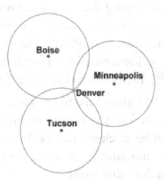

GPS is enabled by a constellation of 27 earth-orbiting satellites, 24 of which are in active operation at any one time. Each satellite circles the globe twice a day with orbits arranged so that at any time, anywhere on earth, there are at least four satellites "visible" in the sky. A GPS receiver is a device that locates at least three satellites to determine its distance to each and use this information to deduce its own location (Anonymous 1, 2007; Brain & Harris, 2007).

Location identification is based on a mathematical principle called trilateration. Trilateration is the location of a single point in space relative to its distance from three other known points. The GPS receiver calculates location and distance from each of the satellites by timing how long it takes a signal to come from each. Figure 5 shows how the location of Denver is found by plotting its location along with known device locations at Boise, Tucson, and Minneapolis. By computing the difference in time from each satellite to each known point, an exact fourth point (Denver in Figure 5) is identified accurately to within ten feet (Anonymous1, 2007; Brain & Harris, 2007). GPS can tell you how far you have traveled, how long you have been traveling, your current and average speeds, and the estimated time of arrival at current speed. Further, a "bread crumb" trail showing where you have traveled is available to track your trip. GPS tracking data can be stored inside the unit, or sent to a remote computer by radio or cellular modem. Some systems allow the location to be viewed in real-time on the Internet with a web-browser (Anonymous 1, 2007; Brain & Harris, 2007).

Enhanced 911 (E-911) telephone service required that, as of October, 2001, GPS locators be installed in every cell telephone in the U.S. and able to be read by operators when cell calls to 911 are made. E-911 enables location-based commerce (L-comm) to help phone companies recoup the cost of E-911 service. Using L-comm, one might program his phone to call when he's within two blocks of a Starbucks. Stores will be able to push advertisements to people in the area for special sales. Or, retailers might track how many cars pass their location and how many stop, without letting the car passengers know they are being watched (Said & Kirby, 2001). Location tracking requires that an RFID tag be placed on the object to be tracked. Then, the GPS receiver locates the object. Together, RFID and GPS enable location identification of anything on earth. The RFID identifies the individual, the GPS tracks them (PRC, 2006).

On the positive side, E-911 allows the finding of cars under water, children stranded with only a phone, and so on. E-911 also makes stolen goods a thing of the past because everything can be tracked. Yet, as the PC, PDA, RFID, GPS, telephone, and fast Internet access miniaturize into one pocket-sized device the last vestiges of PIP location information, disappear.

Smart Motes

Now we turn to the technology that has implications not just for household privacy but industrial espionage and loss of privacy in everything for everyone everywhere: *Smart motes*.

Smart motes, also known as smart dust, will eventually be sand speck-sized sensors, or "motes" each of which is a "complete, wireless subsystem," running TinyOS, and outfitted with an antenna connector, serial interface, analog inputs, and digital

Figure 6. Smart mote on a U.S. penny (Kahn & Warnecke, 2006)

inputs and outputs (dustnetworks.com, 2006). Currently they are highly miniaturized micro-electromechanical devices (MEMs) with imbedded intelligence that pack wireless communication in the digital circuitry (Anonymous 8, 2003; Culler & Mulder, 2004; Warneke & Pister, 2004).

"Each mote digitizes the data collected by an attached sensor and uses an onboard radio to send it in packet form to neighboring motes. Motes are compact, ultra low-power, wireless network devices that provide modular connections to a wide range of sensors and actuators. The unique low-power capabilities of Smart Mesh enable network topologies where all motes are routers and all motes can be battery-powered" (dustnetworks.com, 2006).

Smart motes are already used in energy and military applications but they have similar capabilities to RFID with the added benefit that they can be engineered to adhere to desired surfaces (see Figure 6), imbedded invisibly in paint, aerosoled into a situation, ingested by humans and animals, reprogrammed dynamically from "home," and report "in" to "home" by piggybacking through any handy wireless network. Thus, motes have infinite capacity to invade and erode privacy.

The smart mote on a penny in Figure 6 evidences the current state of the art. Capable of sensing an area $11.7mm^3$ and itself a miniscule $4.8mm^3$ in volume, the "Berkeley mote" is solar powered with bi-directional wireless communication and sensing. From university lab to commercialization took about four years but the demand for these small devices is going to be boundless when they become a few millimeters smaller and a few centimeters more powerful.

Smart motes are a form of nanotechnology that will be the width of a few strands of hair and cost less than $5 each to create. Smart motes are sprayable, paintable, ingestible mechanisms that form self-organizing, intelligent, networks programmed to perform some task, usually surveillance of some type. In addition to obvious problems with organizational security, they can remove any vestige of personal privacy as well. If inhaled, motes might even report on the inner health of individuals (Anonymous 7, 2004; Anonymous 11, 2006; Requicha, 2003; Warneke & Pister, 2004).

If collected data are reported back to a "database integration" company that matches credit and demographic information with IRS, INS, personal movement, medical, biogenetic, financial, and household information and magnitude of the privacy losses becomes clear.

Threats

Threats to PIP relate to all three of the exemplar technologies. The privacy concerns fall into several different categories:

- Invisibility (ACLU, 2003; Anonymous 4, 2006; Chromatius, 2006; Coffee, 2004; PRC, 2003; Rosenzweig et al., 2004; Stanley & Steinhart, 2003)
- Massive data aggregation (ACLU, 2003; Faber, 2007; OECD, 2000, 2003, 2006; Owne et al. 2004; PRC, 2003; Said & Kirby, 2001; Stanley & Steinhart, 2003)
- Individual tracking and profiling (Chestnut, 2006; Gibbons et al., 2003; OECD, 2006; PRC, 2003; Rosenzweig et al., 2004; Saponas et al., 2006; Stanley & Steinhart, 2003)
- Theft (Coffee, 2004; OECD, 2006; Konidala et al., 2005)
- Data corruption and infrastructure threats (Faber, 2007; Konidala et al., 2006; Mohoney, 2006; Naraine, 2006; OECD, 2000; 2003; 2006)
- Health risks (Albrecht & McIntyre, 2004; Singer, 2003).

RFID has been written about more than the other two technologies and, therefore dominates the threat discussion. However, the threats presented apply to all three of the technologies. Each privacy concern is discussed next.

Figure 7. RFID tages can be embedded anywhere and are invisible. http://www.revenews.com/wayneporter/archives/EPC-RFID-TAG.jpg

Invisibility

Consumers have no way of detecting imbedded RFID which can be as small as the dot on the letter "i". RFID are capable of being "printed" with virtually imperceptible antennae that are becoming historic artifacts anyway (see Figure 7).

Because transceivers (RFID readers) can be imbedded in building, road, street corner, traffic light, container, truck, ship, aircraft, or other infrastructures, RFID are being read everywhere. In supermarkets, the door portals contain RFID readers that can identify the shopper through smart cards; then, floor sensors track movements while hidden cameras, microphones, and heat sensors monitor the shopping experience. The individual shopper, if not already identified, is identified at check out either via loyalty card or payment methods if not cash. Thus, RFID and the other surveillances have led to eavesdropping concerns (Albrecht & McIntyre, 2004).

GPS devices are more visible than RFID but cell phone GPS is not visible and users forget they are being tracked as the technology blends into daily use (PRC, 2006). Motes, especially ingested, painted, or implanted ones, are invisible and may be unknown recorders of corporate actions, troop strengths, or medical states (Chromatius, 2006; Kitchener, 2006; Singer, 2003; Williams, 2006).

Data Aggregation

Once data is collected, it can be matched to credit card transactions, and other demographic information. Third party data users of PIP aggregate data from many sources now: click streams, personal movements, health, or biological data, and criminal, court proceeding, genealogical, transaction, or financial history (Conger et al., 2005).

RFID is the first tracking technology to allow snapshots of movements for products like clothes, appliances, medicine, and food. By linking these with the existing dossiers on individuals, privacy further erodes.

As GPS and motes mature and report all whereabouts, privacy is retained only for non-computing (and non-TV, non-iPod) actions in one's home. It is only a matter of time before all genetic markers and DNA information are aggregated with the rest to form a complete record of humans and their activities.

Aggregation, per se, is the enabler of other problems: Who has access and what they do with it. The next items address these issues.

Figure 8. Calvin Klein RFID Label cryptome.org/mystery/calvin-closeup.jpg

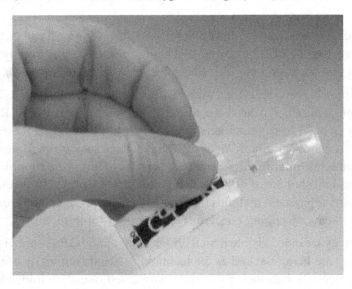

Figure 9. Spy Coin from http://a.abclocal.go.com/images/wjrt/cms_exf_2005/features/sci_tech/cia_spy_coin200.jpg

Individual Tracking and Profiling

The same capabilities that solve some business problems, like shrinkage and taking inventory, allow any person or company with an RFID reader to "spy" on individuals' behavior, clothes, and so on. Like the label in Figure 8, RFIDs can be invisible to the naked eye, washed, dried, and still function, and continue sending their information for years (Albrecht, 2002; Albrecht and McIntyre, 2004; Anonymous, 14, 2007; OECD, 2000, 2003, 2006; PRC, 2003).

Table 2.

Year	Incident
2000	DOD and the FBI sought to develop "real-time" Internet intrusion devices "without becoming intrusive" and accompanying database to fight network intrusions (Seffers, 2000, pg 1).
2002	The Total Information Awareness (TIA) program begins in Defense Advanced Research Projects Agency (DARPA) as six+ projects to collect information from Internet and phone sources to create a 360° view of individuals and their relationships with others. The six projects were: **Genesys** – to build a database to hold all of the collected information **"TIDES:Translingual Information Detection, Extraction and Summarization"** to populate the database with eMail, transaction and other digital information (DARPA, 2002, p. 11) **"EARS: Effective Affordable Reusable Speech to Text"** to support phone or other audio recordings and convert them to digital text (DARPA, 2002, p. 11) **"EELD: Evidence Extraction and Link Delivery"** to analyze and extract potentially illegal activities from integrated data from TIDES and EARS (DARPA, 2002, p. 12). **"WAE: Wargaming the Asymmetric Environment"** for bio-surveillance (DARPA, 2002, p. 13) **"GENOA 11: [for] collaborative response"** to frame questions integrating the above through a query engine (DARPA, 2002, p. 14) As of 2002, an initial version of TIA was in operation. The goal of TIA, according to DARPA's Office of Information Awareness, "is to revolutionalize ... U.S. ability to detect, classify, and identify foreign terrorists and decipher their plans" (Waller, 2002, p. 3). The system was called a "self-made public-relations disaster" (Waller, 2002, p. 1) that was likened to Orwell's *1984* and the Nazi Gestapo. Major newspapers also sounded alarms (Waller, 2002). The ACLU described the project as providing "government officials with the ability to snoop into all aspects of our private lives without a search warrant or proof of criminal wrongdoing" (ACLU, 2003; Stanley & Steinhart, 2003). In February, 2003, Congress, as part of an omnibus bill, banned TIA funding pending further explanation of scope, purpose, and access to TIA and a privacy assessment impact statement (Waller, 2002). The ACLU, EPIC, and other privacy organizations mounted an anti-TIA campaign that was partly successful. TIA as a government project disappeared ... but was successfully outsourced to a data aggregator that developed and deployed the database for DOD (ACLU, 2003; Waller, 2002).
2005	Lisa Myers, NBC news correspondent, reported on Department of Defense (DOD) collection of "domestic intelligence that goes beyond legitimate concerns about terrorism or protecting U.S. military installations" (Myers, 2005, p. 2). One field in the database contained the official assessment of incident threat with at least 243 non-threatening, legal incidents, such as a Quaker meeting in Florida, stored along with legitimate threats (Myers, 2005).
2006	Donald Rumsfeld, then Secretary of Defense, sponsored the multi-year development of the Joint Advertising, Marketing Research and Studies (JAMRS) database of "the largest repository of 16-25 year-old youth data in the country, containing roughly 30 million records" (JAMRS.org, 2005). "DOD was in violation of the Federal Privacy Act for over two years" (Ferner, 2005, p. 1) while JAMRS was under development and for numerous uses, contractor non-disclosure, and data disclosure violations (Rotenberg et al., 2005).

continued on following page

Table 2. continued

Year	Incident
2006	The National Security Agency (NSA) was found to have amassed "tens of millions" of phone call records since 2001 with "the agency's goal 'to create a database of every call ever made' within" the U.S. (Cauley, 2006, pg1). Ostensibly to identify terrorists, NSA has "gained a secret window to the communication habits" of about 200 million Americans that included identifying information (Cauley, 2006, p. 1). The NSA actions violated the Foreign Intelligence Surveillance Act (FISA) of 1978 that was developed to protest U.S. citizens from illegal eavesdropping. Under FISA an 11-member court for surveillance warrants must approve all requests. George Bush, U.S. President in 2006, signed an executive order waiving the need for a warrant (Cauley, 2006).
2006	The FBI and Department of Justice (DOJ), asked Google, MSN, AOL, and Yahoo to turn over current files and to retain data on surfing queries and click streams (Ahrens, 2006). Google did not comply and some public debate ensued (Vaas, 2006).
2006	U.S. Government tracks all cell phone calls (UPI, 2006).
2006	In a postal reform bill signed into law in December, 2006, President Bush added a phrase that declared post office rights to open mail "as authorized by laws for foreign intelligence collection" (Memott, 2007) thus, widening the collection of information about U.S. citizens without criminal wrongdoing or legal due process.

But, unlike bar codes, RFID can be customized for each item and can both send and write information, including the credit card information of purchases, frequent shopper IDs, PINs, and so on (See Figure 8– Calvin Klein RFID inside the label).

Related to eavesdropping is the illicit tracking of individuals—employees, friends, or strangers—because it can be done. Illicit tracking is difficult to identify or track since readers are everywhere and which reader led to the illicit activity is difficult to track unless a crime is committed and the perpetrator apprehended with an RFID reader on his person (Denning, 2001; McAfee, 2005; OECD, 2006).

One bizarre example of this was found by the U.S. Department of Defense, which, in 2006, found contractors in Canada had hollowed out quarters with RFID chips in them (See Figure 9). The inference was that the movements of the contractors were traced while they worked in Canada but details of the incident have not been published and claims were retracted by the U.S. Government (Anonymous 6, 2007; Associated Press, 2007; Briandis, 2006; Bronskill, 2007).

In addition, the ACLU alleges that US citizens, post-2001, are "unknowingly becoming targets of government surveillance" (Anonymous 10, 2007). Post-2001 "erosion in protections against government spying and the increasing amount of tracking being carried out by the private sector (which appears to have an unappeasably voracious appetite for consumer information) and the growing intersection between the two" (Albrecht, 2002) have led to the increase in surveillance of all types by all types of organizations and their business partners with whom they share data.

The U.S. Government is one of the most prolific gatherers of data, provoking outcries regularly. The major incidents are summarized in Table 2.

Thus, the U.S. Government is an active and prolific transgressor of data collection and aggregation for purposes of tracking and monitoring everyone in their databases. When public outcries have thwarted public attempts at this collection of data, the agencies outsource or otherwise hide the activities.

Lest one think the U.S. Government is the only transgressor, the International Campaign Against Mass Surveillance, a multi-national consortium sponsored by Canada, Philippines, U.K., and the U.S. with support from over 100 non-profit privacy rights organizations in 35+ nations also opposes European, Australian, South American, African, and Asian uses of RFID, biometric passports, and other means of tracking, data mining, and surveillance that they predict will lead to global surveillance and loss of individual privacy (ICAMS, 2005).

Theft

PIP theft involves two types of transgressions. First is data theft that comes from clandestine RFID readers being built into door portals, highway systems, street corners, and other public places to read the RFID chips that pass by (Faber, 2007). Anyone with a smart card, building radio card, toll tag, and so on is being scanned and read that is, they are being eavesdropped on, daily (OECD, 2006). This hidden eavesdropping is a form of theft enabled by the invisibility of the devices.

For instance, you walk into a mall and have RFID chips read in your Calvin Klein shirt, your Levi's jeans, your Jockey underwear, and your Nike shoes (Albrecht & McIntyre, 2004; Newitz, 2006). Then, you purchase a purse (also with an imbedded RFID chip) and pay for it with your credit card. All of those chips' readings will be matched with your credit card information and used to build, not a profile of your predicted activities, but a dossier of your actual activities.

On the way home, you ride the subway and are jostled by someone who has a hand-held reader in his or her pocket. He scans all of your chips, including those in your smart bank card, and the robber now has all of your information—RFID and identifying—and can steal your identify (OECD, 2006). One study published in the *Washington Post* tracked 112 points of tracking by phone, e-mail, camera, and RFID credit cards, toll tags, and clothing tags (Nakashima, 2007[2]). When RFID are ubiquitous, which is estimated to happen by 2012, we could be tracked as many as 1,000 times per day.

If the person had a cell phone, further tracking of the path between points of rest and the amount of time spent at each location would also have been stored. Further, motes would enrich the data with bio-readings to indicate arousal states, eye movements, or other physical attributes, food ingestion, medical state, plus could have recorded all conversations.

The other type of theft is "cloning" in which the cloner palms a coil that is the antenna for a wallet-sized cloning device, which is "currently shoved up his sleeve. The cloner can elicit, record, and mimic signals from smart card RFID chips. [The cloner] takes out the device and, using a USB cable, connects it to his laptop and downloads the data from the" card for processing (Newitz, 2007, p. 1). The OECD identifies cloning as one of the most serious problems with unprotected RFID since it is virtually undetectable and difficult to trace (OECD, 2006).

One California college student uses an RFID reader about the size of a deck of cards, to scan items and download them to his computer from which he can change prices, walk back through a store and change the prices of desired items (Newitz, 2005). Similar tales of foiling building security based on RFID hotel room keys spoofing, spoofing smart cards with RFID tags, and overriding RFID tag information to obtain, for instance, free gas, and to clone implanted RFIDs all have occurred (Newitz, 2005).

Data Corruption, and Infrastructure Threats

The same methods used in the theft section can be used for more malevolent uses to corrupt data and therefore, create havoc in computer infrastructures around the globe. Active RFID chips suffer a buffer overflow bug, similar to that of Microsoft's operating systems that can be used to inject a virus or obtain the contents of the chip (Ars Technica, 2006). Researchers at a conference demonstrated how to inject malware into RFID chips, thereby disrupting not just chip operation but the readers as well (Naraine, 2006).

Active RFID, GPS, and smart mote operating systems are amenable to viruses and hacks. The RFID used in Netherlands passports was hacked by a high schooler in four hours; this is the same chip used in US e-Passports (Ricker, 2006).

Viruses, injected into the operating system in an active RFID or smart mote network have the potential to cause havoc in the injected environment (Rieback, 2006). For instance, a suitcase contains an active RFID chip that is infected. The chip is read as the traveler enters the airport and promptly infects the airport systems. The infection will spread to all luggage similarly equipped with active RFIDs, and so on, as the virus spreads around the globe (OECD, 2006). Not only are all of the chips in the luggage now unusable but every computer that has read the infected chips also is ruined. The re-programming job involved with such mobility of devices will be endless as infected luggage continues to proliferate and spread the problem. RFID, GPS, and smart motes change the perimeter of the network and, thus, require different security measures (Chromatius, 2006; Rieback, 2006).

Because RFID, GPS, and smart motes all eventually interact with computers, all of the threats posed from one computer to another are present. Denial of Service (DOS) attacks in which the radio frequency channel is jammed with "noise" to prevent communication are added problems in addition to the spoofing, cloning, and viruses discussed above.

Currently the RFID environment is "open" so that all readers are considered authentic and allowed to read a chip. This both gives out the maximum information to the maximum number of readers, but also opens the chip to being read, spoofed, cloned, and so on by unauthorized sources. Malicious RFID reading might become a new form of corporate espionage that is carried out by employees who simply carry an RFID jammer or spoofer, and so on in a pocket at work.

In addition to buffer overflow problems discussed above, spurious data attacks that take advantage of poorly coded database queries, for instance, are an additional source of vulnerability. These vulnerabilities reside not only in the RFID chip-reader interface, but also in the RFID reader, RFID middleware interface, any interfaces with EPC software, and any EPC connectivity (Konidala et al., 2006). There are technical responses to each of these threats, none of which are present in current RFID designs.

As nanotechnology techniques become more sophisticated, smart motes will get both smaller and smarter. Eventually, they will be reprogrammable "bot" armies that are global, self-reproducing and capable of currently unimaginable intelligence (Anonymous 4, 2006; Brenner, 2006; Pelesko, 2005; Singer, 2003; Warneke and Pister, 2004; Warneke et al., 2001; Williams, 2006). In addition, most intelligence won't be used against just individuals, it will be turned against corporations and governments as well (Singer, 2003).

Health Threats

RFID readers, GPS phones and motes all emit electromagnetic energy over the airwaves and cover areas as large as six square acres (Albrecht & McIntyre, 2004). Further, readers are installed and operational in walls, floors, doorways, shelving, cars, security, and payment devices with RFID slated for release in clothing, refrigerators, medicine bottles and other everyday objects imminently (Albrecht & McIntyre, 2004, pg 51). Yet, as of January, 2007, there is no published research on electromagnetic energy impacts on human health and well-being (OECD, 2006).

Therefore, the jury is out on whether or not RFID, GPS, motes, or other similar devices will prove harmless to us or not.

As mote technology matures, their ability to manipulate life forms will come about and wreak new kinds of havoc (Pelesko, 2005; Singer, 2003; Warneke et al., 2001). Someone who is able to detect motes' presence might also be able to re-purpose them for destructive uses. Millions of motes, working together, might be able to take over the execution of, for instance, government or nuclear facilities, or research computers, reprogramming them to any end.

Solutions

The solutions are corporate self-regulation, legislation and legal remedies, and technical controls. Each is discussed in this section followed by an assessment of their effectiveness to date.

Corporate Self-Regulation

No industry likes legislated regulation so companies always profess to be able to self-regulate. Several groups have developed guidelines for self-regulation, making it easier on companies not to have to develop their own (Grant, 2006). One group, The Center for Democracy and Technology, issued standards for corporate self-regulation, recommending that:

- Vendors should notify customers of RFID tags in items and tell them how, if possible, to turn off the tags
- For vendors that collect personally identifiable data, the vendor should "disclose how that data will be employed"
- Vendors should provide "'reasonable' access to information collected"
- Vendors should notify consumers of RFID presence before completing a transaction (All Gross, 2006 p.1).

In 2005, Electronic Product Code Global (EPC Global), the standards organization the created the EPCglobal 96-bit code for RFID, proposed industry self-regulatory guidelines that include:

- Notices on packages of RFID tagging
- Education of consumers to recognize EPC tags
- Choice information about discarding, removing, or deactivating RFID chips in products.
- Record use, retention, and security guidelines propose that the RFID chips not "contain, collect, or store any personally identifiable information." (All OECD, 2006, pg. 24)

Legislation

Legislative means of regulating RFID exist in Europe via Directives 94/46/EC and 2002/58/EC and the US via Section 5 of the FTC Act (OECD, 2006). Plus, the OECD's 1980 *Guidelines on the Protection of Privacy and Transborder Flows of Personal Data* contains eight principles that also apply to RFID privacy:

1. Collection limitation should be limited and with consumer consent
2. Data quality should be maintained. Data should exist for a single purpose and be destroyed afterward.
3. Purpose for data collection should be specified to consumer before the transaction, and data collection, is completed
4. Usage limitations recommend no sharing or disclosure without consumer consent
5. Security safeguards should protect against loss and unauthorized access, modification or disclosure.
6. Openness should be provided to allow consumers to know who controls the data and all aspects of its storage, maintenance and use.
7. Individuals have rights to open access to all information collected about them.
8. Accountability, in the form of a "Data Controller" responsible for compliance to the guideline should be maintained.

While there have been fines and some interdiction for RFID violations, they are after the fact and largely, ineffective. The OECD guidelines are strictly followed because of EU legislation for transborder data flows, but not for RFID or other clandestine data collection.

In addition, the Asia-Pacific countries and Europe have comprehensive privacy laws that cover most situations in which data collection, data aggregation of the collected data, and use of collected data all apply. The U.S. has a mélange of laws that react to specific situations rather than a comprehensive privacy strategy.

Legal Protection

In response to "technological changes in computers, digitized networks, and the creation of new information products," privacy law attempts to protect "against unauthorized use of the collected information and government access to private records" (BBBOnLine, No date p. 1). Thirty-four states have notification laws (Wernick 2006). Typically, the state laws cover combinations of an individual's name with unencrypted data items ranging from social security number to DNA profile. However, statutes exclude information available to the public in federal, state or local records. California created a State Office of Privacy Protection in 2000 and has enacted laws that protect citizens' privacy across many facets of their lives. State regulations, for example, include limits to retrieval of information from automobile "black boxes" (California Department of Consumer Affairs 2006, p. 1), disclosure of personal information on drivers' licenses, protection of confidentiality of library circulation records, and bans on embedding social security numbers on "a card or document using a bar code, chip, magnetic strip…" (p. 3). The State also defines a "specific crime of identity theft" (p. 4).

Similarly, U.S. Federal privacy laws afford privacy protection of cable subscriber information, drivers' license and motor vehicle registration records, "prohibits persons from tampering with computers or accessing certain computerized records without authorization" require protection of medical records and so on (BBBOn-Line, No date p. 3).

Legal recourse is also available under some conditions that are more abstract than, for example, protecting disclosure of specified transactions. To enact a transaction, the individual discloses personal information based on an assumption of trust in a specific relationship with the recipient of the data. A *tort of breach of confidentiality* offers legal recourse when that trust is broken (Cate, 2007; Solove 2004, 2006).

The problem is that although many statutes address privacy protection in many facets of individuals' lives, governments have the power to "trump" those laws (Smith, 2004; Stanley, 2004). Once data integration occurs in the context of a short-term emergency, such as ferreting out terrorists, individual privacy cannot be restored. In fact, known transgressions of HSA by the government have led to records of innocent parties being propagated through generations of federal databases of suspected terrorists (Gellman, 2005).

The EU has the most actionable and protected privacy laws in the world. The European Union Directive on Data Protection of 1995 protections include, for instance,

- "Personal information cannot be collected without consumers' permission, and they have the right to review the data and correct inaccuracies.
- Companies that process data must register their activities with the government.
- Employers cannot read workers' private e-mail.
- Personal information cannot be shared by companies or across borders without express permission from the data subject.
- Checkout clerks cannot ask for shoppers' phone numbers." (Sullivan, 2006)

Each of the 26 EU countries has adopted its own laws, some of which vary from the above recommendations, however, all provide basic individual privacy rights that protect individuals from corporations. Further, the EU law has been duplicated with fewer limitations in Australia and many Asian countries as privacy rules were adopted by the Asia-Pacific Economic Cooperation (APEC). Both sets of laws are more comprehensive, seeking to be positive in supporting individual privacy rights rather than, as in the U.S., reactive and piecemeal (Sullivan, 2006). In addition, in the U.S., it is generally believed that citizens distrust the government more than corporations and that, that distrust has caused the piecemeal law adoptions and general erosion of basic privacy rights (Sullivan, 2006).

In spite of the legal protections in Europe, personal privacy is threatened (Meller, 2006) and government surveillance systems are being deployed throughout whole countries, such as England and France (Wright et al., 2006). Further, other countries are experiencing increasing numbers of 4th and 5th party transgressions (Chatterjee, 2006; Woo, 2006).

Technical Controls

Finally, there are potential technical solutions such as

- Disabling RFID during the check-out process
- Signal encryption (Konidala et al., 2006)
- A "privacy bit" on each RFID chip that would enforce only legitimate readers access to tag information (OECD, 2006; Konidala et al., 2006)

- Develop a consumer-worn, privacy enhancing technology to block reading of hidden RFID in clothing (OECD, 2006).

Konidala et al. (2006) developed a detailed report on all of the vulnerabilities of RFID at each stage of the technology and their interactions—six stages in all. They further detailed technical mitigations of each risk for each level of technology.

Thus far, these technologies have proven too costly or beyond the technical capability of current RFID technology without sacrificing size, weight, or cost in the process.

A temporary reprieve may come in industry because of the sheer volume of data.

Consider the scenario where a major retail chain will be tagging all its goods in all its stores, at the single item level. The number of tagged items in this scenario can easily reach 10 billion or more. This means that the data identifying the 10 billion items amounts to 120 gigabytes (10 billion x 12 bytes per tag). If these items were read once every 5 minutes somewhere in the supply chain, they would generate nearly 15 terabytes of tracking data every day (120 gigabytes x 12 times per hour x 10 hours per day). That's 15 terabytes of additional data generated by one retail chain every day. Using this formula, 10 major retailers tagging and tracking every item will generate 150 terabytes of data. This is bigger than the estimated 136 terabytes of data from 17 million books in the U.S. Library of Congress. (West et al., 2005)

This reprieve will not help with governments who can raise taxes to fund their data gathering projects.

Assessment of Control Effectiveness

The reality of all of these solutions is that Internet technology capabilities, "frequent shopper" cards, RFID reporting, and GPS have whetted organizations' appetites for data such that organizations are no longer content with transactional information. Now, organizations desire the "ubiquitous understanding of on- and off-line consumer purchase behavior, attitudes and product usage" afforded through these technologies (Albrecht, 2002). From a practical perspective one has to ask whether we really "need to know where [a product] is every five seconds in your supply chain" (Schuman, 2006, p. 2). So far, companies have answered "yes" in resounding numbers.

The first solution to privacy threats, corporate self-regulation, is not being used (Culnan, 2003; Schwaig et al., 2005). Evidence amasses of corporate transgressions of the innocence and trust of ordinary shoppers. For instance, Gillette and Proctor and Gamble imbedded cameras, microphones, heat sensors, RFID, and other technology into store shelves to be alerted when shoppers lifted an item from a shelf. Company employees recorded and monitored the shopping behavior (Albrecht and McIntyre, 2004). Similar stories have been published about similar incidents at Tesco's in England and other parts of Europe (OECD, 2006). Companies clearly are not self-regulating.

Legislative regulation, at least in the U.S., loses credibility when U.S. Government organizations—DOD, FBI, DOJ, and the post office—amass significant information about everyone in the U.S. (Ahrens, 2006; Cauley, 2006; DARPA, 2002; Ferner, 2005; Seffers, 2000; Stanley & Steinhart, 2003; Waller, 2002). Similarly, China uses search engine records to build a legal case against suspected subversives (Goodman, 2005). The Council of Europe, in 2000, mandated that member countries "have domestic laws requiring (Internet) service providers to cooperate in both the collection of traffic data and the content of communications" (Taylor, 2004).

Some research suggests "pay for data" programs for industry (Laudon, 1996) or "pay for privacy" programs for individuals (Alba et al., 1997). Both of these models bear further investigation for social acceptability and implementation issue resolution. Further, the allegation that privacy can be good for business is worth future research consideration (cf. Poneman, 2006). If providing improved 1st party privacy can drive profits for 2nd parties, then privacy will move to being a priority without legislation or other coercion.

Technical controls appear to be the most effective solution but control implementation is at executive direction and executives balance their desire for consumer information against collection of that information that violates consumer privacy. At the moment, the privacy side of the balance equation appears to be losing.

The most effective legislation seems to be a technical solution to problems, such as buffer overflow. With legislated technical solutions, manufacturers and software developers would be legally responsible for their software transgressions and would, therefore, be able to be fined and/or sued upon problem occurrences. Instead, without legislated technical solutions, the same errors proliferate through generations of shoddy software and provide the basis for many 4th and 5th party invasions.

Conclusion

Most of the transgressions relating to new technologies are extensions of other transgressions for which the discussions of ethics and proper behavior started long ago. Emerging technologies make those discussions more urgently needed or privacy will be a thing of the past for all but the few who live off the grid.

Of possible solutions to privacy issues, corporate self-regulation and legislative regulations are unlikely to be effective. Technology controls, while articulated and appearing complete have not been implemented to date. Legislated technical solutions and responsibility appear to have the most potential for a lasting solution.

References

ACLU (2003). *RFID position statement of consumer privacy and civil liberties organizations*, American Civil Liberties Union (ACLU)., November 30.

ACLU (2003). *Total information compliance: The TIA's burden under the Wyden amendment, a preemptive analysis of the government's proposed super surveillance program*. American Civil Liberties Union (ACLU)., May 19.

Ahrens, F. (2006). Government, Internet firms in talks over browsing data. *Washington Post*. June 3, p D3

Alba, J., Lynch, J., Weitz, B., Janiszewski, C., Lutz, R., Sawyer, A. & Wood, S. (1997). Interactive home shopping: Consumer, retailer, and manufacturer incentives to participate in electronic marketplace. *Journal of Marketing, 61*, 38-53.

Albrecht, K. (2002). Supermarket cards: The tip of the retail surveillance iceberg. *Denver University Law Review, 79*(4, 15)., 534-554.

Albrecht, K. and McIntyre, L. (2004). RFID: The big brother bar code, *ALEC Policy Forum, 6*(3)., pp 49-54.

Alien Technology (2007, January 10). *RFID tags*. retrieved from http://www.alien-technology.com/products/rfid-tags/

Anonymous 1 (2007). *Global positioning system*. Wikipedia.

Anonymous 2 (2007). *Radio frequency identification*. Wikipedia.

Anonymous 3 (2007). *Smart card*. Wikipedia.

Anonymous 4 (2006). *Smart dust*. Wikipedia.

Anonymous 5 (2007). *Part I: Active and passive RFID: Two distinct, but complementary, technologies for real-time supply chain visibility.* Retrieved from http://www.autoid.org/2002_Documents/sc31_wg4/docs_501-520/520_18000-7_WhitePaper.pdf

Anonymous 6 (2007). *Pocketful of espionage: Beware the spy coins.* CNN. Retrieved from http://www.cnn.com/2007/US/01/11/spy.coins.ap/index.html

Anonymous 7 (2004). *Heterogeneous sensor networks.* Intel. Retrieved from http://www.intel.com/research/exploratory/hetergeneous.htm

Anonymous 8 (2003, June 11). What is smart dust, anyway? *Wired Magazine,* pp. 10-11.

Anonymous 9 (2007). *Data loss database.* Retrieved from http://attrition.org/data-loss/

Anonymous 10 (2007). *What is RFID?* Retrieved from http://www.spychips.com/what-is-rfid.html

Anonymous 11 (2006, August 22). SmartDust & ubiquitous computing. *Nanotechnology News.* Retrieved from http://www.nanotech-now.com/smartdust.htm

Anonymous 12 (2007). *Famous inventors: GPS.* Retrieved from http://www.famous-inventors.com/invention-of-gps.html

Anonymous 13 (2007, May 11). Google searches web's dark side. *BBC News.* Retrieved from http://news.bbc.co.uk/2/hi/technology/6645895.stm.

Anonymous 14 (2007). *What is a smart card?* Retrieved from http://computer.howstuffworks.com/question322.htm

AOL/NCSA (2007, December). *AOL/NCSA Online Safety Study.* AOL and the National Cyber Security Alliance. Retrieved from http://www.staysafeonline.info/pdf/safety_study_2005.pdf

APEC (2005). *APEC Privacy Framework.* Asia-Pacific Economic Cooperation (APEC).. Retrieved from www.ag.gov.au/.../$file/APEC+Privacy+Framework.pdf

Associated Press (2007, January 10). *There's an undercurrent of espionage in that currency: Canadian coins with transmitters planted on U.S. defense contractors, baffling both countries.*

Attrition.org (2007, March 3). *Data Loss Archive and Database (DLDOS)..* Attrition.org. Retrieved from http://attrition.org/dataloss/.

BBBBOnLine (2008). *A Review of Federal and State Privacy Laws.* BBBBOnLine, Inc. and the Council of Better Business Bureaus, Inc. Retrieved from http://www.bbbonline.org/UnderstandingPrivacy/library/fed_statePrivLaws.pdf

Bell, G. (2004). A personal digital store. *Communications of the ACM, 44*(1)., 86- 94.

Brain, M. and Harris, T. (2007, January). *How GPS Works.* Retrieved from http:// electronics.howstuffworks.com/gps.htm

Brenner, S. (2006, March 19). Bugs and dust. *Cybercrim3.* Retrieved from http:// cyb3rcrim3.blogspot.com/2006/03/bugs-and-dust.html

Briadis, T. (2006). *U.S. warns about Canadian spy coins.* Physorg.com. Retrieved from http://www.physorg.com/news87716264.html

Bronskill, J. (2007, January 14). *Spy coin caper loses currency.* Ocnus.net. Retrieved from http://www.ocnus.net/artman/publish/article_27531.shtml

California Department of Consumer Affairs (2006, February 14). *Privacy Laws.* California Department of Consumer Affairs Office of Privacy Protection. Retrieved from http://www.privacy.ca.gov/lawenforcement/laws.htm.

Carlson, C. (2006, February 1). Unauthorized sale of phone records on the rise. *eWeek.*

Cate, F. H. (Forthcoming). The failure of fair information practice principles. In *Consumer protection in the age of the ' information economy.'*

Cauley, L. (2006, May 11). NSA has massive database of Americans' phone calls. *USA Today.* Retrieved from http://www.usatoday.com/news/washington/2006-05-10-nsa_x.htm.

CEC (2002). *Creating a safer information society by improving the security of information infrastructures and combating computer-related crime.* Council of the European Communities (CEC).. Retrieved from http://europa.eu.int/ ISPO/eif/InternetPoliciesSite/Crime/CrimeCommEN.html#1.Opportunities %20and%20Threats%20in%20the%20Information%20Society

Chatterjee, S. (2006, October 3). India BPOs under scanner after TV channel exposes data leak. *International Business Times.* Retrieved from www.ibtimes. com/.../nasscom-kiran-karnik-hsbc-data-privacy-cyber-crime-channel-4-bpo-call-center.htm

Chen, Y.-H. and Barnes, S. (2007). Initial trust and online buyer behavior. *Industrial Management and Data Systems, 107*(1)., 21-36.

Chestnut, A. (2006, March 9). Cell phone GPS tracking-privacy issues, *eZine Articles*, Retrieved from http://ezinearticles.com/?Cell-Phone-GPS-Tracking---Privacy-Issues&id=159255.

Cheung, C.M.K. and Lee, M.K.O. (2004/2005). The asymmetric effect of Web site attribute performance on Web Satisfaction: An empirical study. *E-Service Journal, 3*(3)., 65-105.

Cheung, C.M.K., Chan, G.W.W., and Limayem, M. (2005). A critical review of online consumer behavior: Empirical research. *Journal of Electronic Commerce in Organizations, 3*(4)., 1-19.

Chromatius (2006, February 19). Dust: A ubiquitous surveillance technology. *Blog Critics Magazine.* Retrieved from http://blogcritics.org/archives/2006/02/19/111529.php

Clarke, R. (1999). Internet privacy concerns confirm the case for intervention. *Communications of the ACM, 42*(2)., 60-66.

CNET News (2006). *Three workers depart AOL after privacy uproar.* Retrieved on August 23, 2006, from http://news.com.com/Three+workers+depart+AOL+after+privacy+uproar/2100-1030_3-6107830.html

Coffee, P. (2004, April 19). Privacy concerns dog RFID chips, *eWeek.*

Conger, S. & Loch, K. (1995). Ethics and computer use. *Communications of the ACM, 38*(12)., 30-32.

Conger, S., Mason, R.O., Mason, F., and Pratt, J.H. (2005, August). The connected home: Poison or paradise. In *Proceedings of Academy of Management Meeting.* Honolulu, HI.

Conger, S., Mason, R.O., Mason, F.. Pratt, J.H. (2006, December 10). Legal sharing, shadow sharing, Leakages—Issues of personal information privacy have changed. In *Proceedings of IFIPS 8.2 OASIS Meeting.* Milwaukee, WI.

Culler, D.E., and Mulder, H. (2004, August 2). *Sensor Nets/RFID.* Intel. Retrieved from http://www.intel.com/research/exploratory/smartnetworks.htm.

Culnan, M. (2000).. Protecting privacy online: is self-regulation working? *Journal of Public Policy & Marketing, 19*(1)., 20-26.

Culnan, M.J., & Armstrong, P. (1999). Information privacy concerns, procedural fairness, and impersonal trust: An empirical investigation. *Organization Science, 10,* 104-115.

Culnan, M.J. (1993). How did they get my name? An exploratory investigation of consumer attitudes toward secondary information use. *MIS Quarterly, 17*(3). 341-363.

DARPA (2002). *DarpaTech 2002 Symposium: Transforming fantasy.* U.S. Defense Applied Research Projects Agency.

David, L. (2003, November 5). *Satellite navigation: GPS grows up, market lifts off.* Space.com. Retrieved from http://www.space.com/businesstechnology/technology/satcom_gps_overview_031105.html.

Denning, D. (2001). *Is cyber terror next?* Social Science Research Council. Retrieved from http://www.ssrc.org/sept11/essays/denning.htm

Denning, D. and Baugh, W. (1999). Hiding crimes in cyberspace. *Information, Communication and Society, 2*(3)., 251-276.

Dictionary.com (2007). *Definitions of Privacy.* Retrieved from http://www.dallas-news.com/sharedcontent/dws/bus/stories/092306dnbushp.7a661b5.html.

Dillon, G. & Torkzadeh, G. (2006). Value-focused assessment of information system security in organizations. *Information Systems Journal, 16,* 293-314.

Dinev, T. & Hart, P. (2006). An extended privacy calculus model for E-commerce transactions. *Information Systems Research, 17*(1)., 61-80.

Dolya, A. (2007, April 18). *Internal IT Threats in Europe 2006,* CNews.ru. Retrieved from http://eng.cnews.ru/cgi-bin/oranews/get_news.cgi?tmpl=top_print_eng&news_id=246325

Doolin, B., Dillon, S., Thompson, F. & Corner, J. (2005). Perceived risk, the internet shopping experience and online purchasing behavior: A New Zealand perspective. *Journal of Global Information Management, 13*(2)., 66-88.

Drennan, J., Mort, G. & Previte, J. (2006, January-March). Privacy, risk perception, and expert online behavior: An exploratory study of household end users. *Journal of Organizational and End User Computing, 18*(1)., 1-22.

Dunham, W. (2006, May 22). Personal data on millions of U.S. veterans stolen. *Computerworld.* Retrieved from http://www.computerworld.com/action/article.do?command=viewArticleBasic&articleId=9000678.

Dustnetworks.com (2006). *Technology overview.* Retrieved January 10, 2007, from http://dustnetworks.com/about/index.shtml

EPC Global (2005, September). *Guidelines on EPC for consumer products.* Retrieved from at http://www.epcglobalinc.org/public/ppsc_guide/

EU (1995). *Directive 95/46/EC of the European Parliament and of the Council of 24 October 1005 on the protection of individuals with regard to processing of personal data and on the free movement of that data.* Council of the European Union (EU)..

Faber, P. (2007, January 9). RFID strategy—RFID privacy and security issues. *Industry Week.* Retrieved from http://www.industryweek.com/ReadArticle.aspx?ArticleID=13371

Ferner, M. (2006, February 4). Pentagon database leaves no child alone. *Counterpunch.* Retrieved from http://www.counterpunch.org/ferner02042006.html

Gallivan, M.J. & Depledge, G. (2003). Trust, control and the role of interorganizational systems in electronic partnerships. *Information Systems Journal, 13,* 159-190.

Gaudin, S. (2007, April 11). *Security breaches cost $90 to $305 per lost record.* Information Week. Retrieved from http://www.informationweek.com/shared/printableArticle.jhtml?articleID=19900022

Gauzente, C. (2004). Web merchants' privacy and security statements: How reassuring are they for consumers? A two-sided approach. *Journal of Electronic Commerce Research, 5*(3)., 181-198.

Gefen, D., Karahanna, E. & Straub, D. (2003). Trust and TAM in online shopping: An integrated model. *MIS Quarterly, 27*(1)., 51-90.

Gellman, B. (2005, November 6). *The FBI's secret scrutiny.* The Washington Post, A01.

Gibbons, P., Karp, B., Ke, Y., Nath, S., and Seshan,S. (2003, October-December). IrisNet: An architecture for a worldwide sensor web, *Pervasive computing, 2*(4).,22-33.

Gilbert, A. (2005, July 8). *Will RFID-guided robots rule the world?* CNet News. com. Retrieved from http://news.com.com/2102-7337_3-5778286.html.

Goodman, P.S. (2005, September 11). *Yahoo says it Gave China Internet data.* Washing Post Foreign Service, A30. Retrieved from http://www.washingtonpost.com/wp-dyn/content/article/2005/09/10/AR2005091001222.html

Goss, G. (2006, May 1). *RFID standards released IT by vendors, privacy groups.* News Service.

Gouldson, T., (2001, July 27). Hackers and crackers bedevil business world, *Computing Canada, 27*(16), 13.

Greenaway, K. & Chen, Y. (2006). Theoretical explanations for firms information privacy. *Journal of the Association for Information Systems-Online, 6*, 1.

Hempel, L., & Töpfer, E. (2004, August). *CCTV in Europe.* Center for Technology & Society and UrbanEye.net.

Hoffman, L.J., Lawson-Jenkins, K., and Blum, J. (2006). Trust beyond security: An expanded trust model. *Communications of the ACM, 49*(7), 94-101.

Hoffman, T. (2003, March 24). Smart dust: mighty motes for medicine, manufacturing, the military and more. *Computerworld.*

Holmes, A. (2006, March 25). The Profits in Privacy, *CIO Magazine, 19*(11), 3. Retrieved from http://www.cio.com/archive/031506/privacy.html

Horton, M. (2005, February 9-10). *The future of sensory networks.* Xbow.com. Retrieved from http://www.xbow.com

HRW. (2006). *The race to the bottom: Corporate complicity in Chinese Internet censorship.* Human Rights Watch (HRW). Retrieved from http://www.hrw.org/reports/2006/china0806/china0806webwcover.pdf, 2006

Hutcheson, R. (2006, October 17). *U.S. Government has long history of abusing personal information.* Common Dreams News Center. Retrieved June 26, 2007, from http://www.commondreams.org/headlines06/0513-04.htm

ICAMS (2005, April). *The emergence of a global infrastructure for mass registration and surveillance.* International Campaign Against Mass Surveillance (ICAMS). Retrieved from http://www.i-cams.org/ICAMS1.pdf

IDTechEx (2007, January 12). *The RFID Knowledgebase.* IDTechEx. Retrieved from http://rfid.idtechex.com/knowledgebase/en/nologon.asp

Internet Home Alliance (IHA) (2005). *Industry summaries.* retrieved from http://www.internethomealliance.org/resrch_reports/industry_summaries.asp

JAMRS.org (2005). *Joint advertising market research & studies.* Retrieved from http://www.jamrs.org/

Kahn, J.M., and Warneke, B.A. (2006, August 22). Smart dust and ubiquitous computing. In *Nanotechnology Now.*

Kane, J. & Wall, A. (2005). *Identifying the links between white-collar crime and terrorism.* U.S. Department of Justice.

Ke, G. S., and Karger, P. A. (2005, November 8). *Preventing security and privacy attacks on machine readable travel documents (MRTDs).* IBM Document RC 23788.

Kitchener, G. (2006, March 16). *Pentagon plans cyber-insect army.* BBC News. Retrieved from http://www.bbc.co.uk,/2/hi/americas/480342.stm

Konidala, D., Kim, W-S., and Kim, K. (2006). *Security assessment of EPCglobal architecture framework.* (White Paper #WP-SWNET-017). Daejeon, Korea: Auto-ID Labs.

Laudon, K. (1996). Markets and privacy. *Communications of the ACM, 39*(9), 92-105.

Lazarus, D. (2006, June 21). *AT&T rewrites rules: Your data isn't yours.* San Francisco Chronicle. Retrieved on July 9, 2007, from http://sfgate.com/cgi-bin/article.cgi?file=/chronicle/archive/2006/06/21/BUG9VJHB9C1.DTL&type=business

Lichtblau, E. (2006, September 25). *Europe panel faults sifting of bank data.* The New York Times.

Liptak, A. (2006, August 2). *U.S. wins access to reported phone records.* The New York Times.

Loch, K., & Conger, S. (1996). Evaluating ethical decision making and computer use. *Communications of the ACM, 39*(7), 74-84.

Malhotra, N., Kim, S. & Agarwal, J. (2004). Internet users' information privacy concerns (IUIPC): The construct, the scale, and a causal model. *Information Systems Research, 15*(4), 336-355.

McAfee. (2005). *Virtual criminology report: North American study into organized crime and the Internet.* McAfee, Inc. Retrieved from www.softmart.com/mcafee/docs/McAfee%20NA%20Virtual%20Criminology%20Report.pdf

McCarter, C. (2006, January 19th). *RFID Market $2.71Bn in 2006 rising to $12.35Bn in 2010.* RFIDTimes.org. Retrieved from http://rfidtimes.org/2006/01/rfid-market-271bn-in-2006-rising-to.html

McCullagh, D. (2005a, April 19). *New RFID travel cards could pose privacy threat.* C/Net. Retrieved from http://www.news.com/2102-1028_3-606574.html

McCullagh, D. (2005b, January 13). *Snooping by satellite.* C/Net. Retrieved from http://www.news.com/2102-1028_3-5533560.html

McGrath, D. (2006, January 26). *RFID market to grow 10 fold by 2016, firm says.* EE Times. Retrieved on June 3, 2007, from http://www.eetimes.com/news/latest/showArticle.jhtml?articleID=177104240

McKnight, H., Choudhury, V., & Kacmar, C. (2004). Dispositional and distrust distinctions in predicting high and low risk internet expert advice site perceptions. *E-Service Journal, 3*(2), 35-59.

McMillan, R. (2006, August 6). *Defcon: Cybercriminals taking cues from Mafia, says FBI.* Computerworld Security. Retrieved from http://www.computerworld.com/action/article.do?command=viewArticleBasic&taxonomyName=cybercrime_hacking&articleId=9002230&taxonomyId=82

Meller, P. (2006, May 30). *Officials downplay EU data privacy concerns.* NetworkWorld.com, IDG News Service. Retrieved from http://www.networkworld.com/news/2006/053006-officials-downplay-eu-data-privacy.html.

Memott, M. (2007, January 4). *Bush says feds can open mail without warrants.* USA Today. Retrieved from http://blogs.usatoday.com/ondeadline/2007/01/bush_says_feds_.html

Miller, P. (2006). *German hackers clone RFID e-passports.* Retrieved from http://www.engadget.com

Mohoney, D. (2006, September 1). *Same threats, different technology.* MRT Magazine. Retrieved from http://mrtmag.com/mag/radio_threats_different_technology/

Mutz, D. (2005). Social trust and e-commerce: Experimental evidence for the effects of social trust on individuals' economic behavior. *Public Opinion Quarterly, 69*(3), 393-416.

Myers, L., Pasternak, D., Gardella, R., and the NBC Investigative Unit (2005, December 14). *Is the Pentagon spying on Americans?* MSNBC. Retrieved from http://www.msnbc.msn.com/id/10454316/

Nakashima, E. (2007, January 16). *Enjoying technology's conveniences but not escaping its watchful eyes*. Washington Post.

Naraine, M. (2006, March 15). *Dutch researchers create RFID malware*. eWeek.

Newitz, A. (2006, November 30). *Nike + IPod = Surveillance*. Wired Magazine. Retrieved from http://www.wired.com/science/discoveries/news/2006/11/72202

Newitz, A. (2004). *The RFID hacking underground*. Wired Magazine, *13*(12). Retrieved from http://www.wired.com/wired/archive/14.05/rfid_pr.html

OECD (2000). *Guidelines on the protection of privacy and transborder flows of personal data*. Organization for Economic and Co-operation and Development (OECD).

OECD (2003). *Privacy online: policy and practical guidance*. Organization for Economic and Co-operation and Development (OECD).

OECD (2006). *Report of cross-border enforcement of privacy laws*. Organization for Economic and Co-operation and Development (OECD).

Ohkubo, M., Suzuki, K., & Kinoshita, S. (2005). RFID privacy issues and technical challenges. *Communications of the ACM, 48*(9), 66-71.

Olsen, S. (2007, January 9). *RFID coming soon to scooters, diapers*. ZDNet. Retrieved from http://www.zdnet.com.au/news/hardware/soa/RFID_coming_to_scooters_diapers/0,130061702,339272981,00.htm?ref=search

Owne, E. et al. (2004, October 29). *GPS—Privacy Issues*. M/Cyclopedia. Retrieved from http://wiki.media-culture.org/au/index.php/GPS_-_Privacy_Issues

Pelesko, J. A. (2005, July 24-27). Self assembly promises and challenges. In *Proceedings of International Conference on MEMS, NANO and Smart Systems 2005* (pp 427-428). IEEE.

Poneman, L. (2006, July 15). *Privacy is good business*. CIO Magazine.

PRC. (2003, November 20). *PFID Position statement of consumer privacy and civil liberties organizations*. Privacy Rights Clearinghouse (PRC). Retrieved from http://www.privacyrights.org/ar/RFIDposition.htm

PRC. (2006, October). *When a cell phone is more than a phone: Protecting your privacy in the age of the super-phone*. Privacy Rights Clearinghouse (PRC). Retrieved from http://www.privacyrights.org/fw/fw2b-cellprivacy.htm

PRC (2007, February 24). *A chronology of data breaches*. Privacy Rights Clearinghouse (PRC). Retrieved from http://www.privacyrights.org/ar/ChronDataBreaches.htm

Requicha, A. (2003, November). Nanorobots, NEMS, and NanoAssembly. *Proceedings of the IEEE, 91*(11), 1922-1933.

Reuters (2006, September 26). *GE: Laptop with data on 50,000 staffers stolen*. Reuters News Service.

Ricker, T. (2006). *Dutch RFID e-passport cracked—US next?* http://www.engadget.com

Rieback, M. Crispo, B., and Tanenbaum, A. (2006). RFID malware: Truth vs. myth, *IEEE Security and Privacy, 4*(4).70-72.

Rogers, E. (1995). *Diffusion of innovations* (4th Edition). New York: The Free Press.

Rosenzweig, P., Kochems, A. and Schwartz, A. (2004, June 21). *Biometric technologies: Security, legal and policy implications*. The Heritage Foundations. Retrieved from http://www.heritage.org/research/homelanddefense/lm12.cfm

Rotenberg, M., Hoofnagle, C., Kapadia, D., Roschke, G. (2005, July 15).*The pentagon recruiting database and the privacy act* (Memo). Electronic Privacy Information Center.

Said, C. and Kirby, C. (2001, March 19). *GPS cell phones may cost privacy*. San Francisco Chronicle.

Saponas, T.S.,Lester, J., Hartung, C., and Kohno, T. (2006, November 30). *Devices that tell on you: The Nike+iPod sport kit.* (Working paper University of Washington). Retrieved from http://www.cs.washington.edu/research/systems/privacy.html

Scalet, S. (2006, February 3). *The never-ending Choicepoint story*. CSO. Retrieved on June 26, 2007, from http://www.csoonline.com/alarmed/02032006.html

Schuman, E. (2006, February 27). *The RFID hype effect*. EWeek.

Schwaig, K., Kane, G. C., & Storey, V. C. (2005). Privacy, fair information practices and the fortune 500: the virtual reality of compliance. *SigMIS Database, 36*, 49-63.

Seffers, G. (2000, November 2). *DOD database to fight cybercrime*. Federal Computer Week. Retrieved from http://www.fcw.com/fcw/articles/2000/1030/web-data-11-02-00.asp

Sherman, T. (2007, May 10). *'New strain' of terrorism: Hatched in the U.S.* Newark Star-Ledger.

Singer, M. (2003, October 24). *Smart dust collecting in the enterprise.* Retrieved from http://siliconvalley.internet.com/news/

Smith, G. (2004, August 23). *Police to seek greater powers to snoop.* Globe and Mail. Retrieved from http://www.theglobeandmail.com/servlet/Page/document/v5/content/subscribe?user_URL=http://www.theglobeandmail.com%2Fservlet%2Fstory%2FRTGAM.20040823.wxpolice23%2FBNStory%2FNational%2F&ord=2967516&brand=theglobeandmail&force_login=true

Smith, H. (2004). Information privacy and its management. *MIS Quarterly Executive, 3*(4), 201-213.

Smith, H., Milberg, S., & Burke, S. (1996). Information privacy: Measuring individuals' concerns about organizational practices. *MIS Quarterly, 20*(2), 167-196.

Solove, D. J. (2004). *The Digital Person.* NYU Press.

Solove, D. J. (2006, January). A Taxonomy of Privacy. *University of Pennsylvania Law Review. 154*(3). 477-560.

Stanley, J. and Steinhart, B. (2003, January). *Bigger monster, weaker chains: The growth of an American surveillance society.* American Civil Liberties Union.

Stanley, J. (2004, August). *The surveillance industrial complex: How the American government is conscripting businesses and individuals in the construction of a surveillance society.* American Civil Liberties Union.

Stibbe, M. (2004, February). *Feature: Technologies that will change our lives.* Real Business. Retrieved from http:// www.realbusiness.co.uk/ARTICLE/FEATURE-Technologies-that-will-change-our-lives/1035.aspx

Sullivan, B. (2006, October 19). *La difference' is stark in EU, U.S. privacy laws.* MSNBC. Retrieved from http://www.msnbc.msn.com/id/15221111/

Sullivan, L. (2005, July 18). *Apparel maker tags RFID for kid's pajamas.* Information Week, p.26.

Swire, P.P. (1997). Markets, self-regulation, and government enforcement in the protection of personal information. *Privacy and Self-regulation in the Information Age* (pp. 3-20). Washington, DC: US Department of Commerce.

Takahashi, D. (2007, January 30). *Demo: aggregate knowledge knows what you want to buy.* San Jose Mercury News. Retrieved from www.mercextra.com/blogs/takahashi/2007/01/30/demo-aggregate-knowledge-knows-what-you-want-to-buy/

Taylor, G. (2004). *The Council of Europe cybercrime convention: A civil liberties perspective.* Electronic Frontier Australia. Retrieved from http://www.crime-research.org/library/CoE_Cybercrime.html

UPI (2006, May 11). *Report: NSA tracking all U.S. phone calls*. GOPUSA.com. Retrieved on May 11, 2006, from http://www.gopusa.com/news/2006/May/0511_nsa_phonesp.shtm

Vaas, L. (2006, January 25). *Government sticks its fingers deeper into your data pie*. eWeek Magazine. Retrieved from http://www.eweek.com/print_article2/0,1217,a=170019,00.asp

Waller, J.M. (2002, December 24). *Fears mount over 'total' spy system: civil libertarians and privacy-rights advocates are fearful of a new federal database aimed at storing vast quantities of personal data to identify terrorist threats—Nation: homeland security*. Insight Magazine. Retrieved from http://www.findarticles.com/p/articles/mi_m1571/is_1_19/ai_95914215

Warneke, B., Last, M., Liebowitz, B., Pister, K.S.J. (2001). Smart dust: Communicating with a cubic-millimeter computer. *Computer*, *34*(1), 44-51.

Warneke, B.A. & Pister, K.J.S. (2004, Feb. 16-18). An ultra-low energy microcontroller for smart dust wireless sensor networks. In *Proceedings of the Int'l Solid-State Circuits Conf. 2004* (ISSCC 2004). San Francisco. Retrieved on June 26, 2007, from www-bsac.eecs.berkeley.edu/archive/users/warneke-brett/pubs/17_4_slides4.pdf

Wernick, A.S. (2006, December). Data theft and state law. *Journal of American Health Information Management Association*, 40-44.

West, Andrew C., Smith, C. D., Detwiler, D. J. , and Kaman, P. (2005, November). *Trends in Technology*. (AGA CPAG Research Series. Report #3).

Westervelt, R. (2007, February 23). *Data breach law could put financial burden on retailers*. SearchSecurity.com.

Williams, M. (2006, March/April). The knowledge: biotechnology's advance could give malefactors the ability to manipulate life processes—and even affect human behavior. MIT Technology Review. Retrieved from http://www.technologyreview.com/Biotech/16485/

Woo, R. (2006, July 6). *Privacy crises in Hong Kong and how the privacy commissioner is dealing with them*. Paper presented at the Privacy Laws and Business Conference, Cambridge, England. Retrieved from http://www.pcpd.org.hk/english/files/infocentre/speech_20060705.pdf

Wright, D. Ahoenen, P., Alahuhta, P., Daskala, B., De Hert, P., Delaitre, S., Friedewald, M., Gutwirth, S., Lindner, R., Maghiros, I., Moscibroda, A., Punie, Y., Schreurs, W., Verlinden, M., Vildjiounaite, E. (2006, August 30). Safeguards in a world of ambient intelligence. *Fraunhofer Institute Systems and Innovation Research*.

Zeller, T., Jr. (2005, May 18). *Personal data for the taking*. The New York Times.

Endnotes

1   There are actually five classes of RFID, dumb passive, passive with some functionality and/or encryption, semi-passive which use broad-band communication, active which communicate via broadband and peer-to-peer and with both tags and readers, and active which can give power to the three passive classes and communicate wirelessly. (Sensitech, http://www.sensitech. com/pdfs/Beyond_Passive_RFID.pdf , 2003).

2   The article reported 74 points of tracking but it forgot the tracking from deleted emails—another 38.

Chapter XII

Digital Democracy:
Democracy in the Light of Information and Communication Technology

Anza Akram A., Management Consultant, USA

Abstract

The purpose of the chapter is to discuss the effects of information and communication technologies on democracy and focuses on the driving forces, citizen and technology, to understand the effects and future implications. The research is based on literature review and uses informative approach to analyze the existing practices in electronic democracy. It inquires the relationship between the theories in communications and democracy, and analyzes the interaction with the citizens from Athenian and the Orwellion perspectives in Politics. It proposes a framework to identify and analyze the driving forces and the issues related to the digital democracy. The resultant effects are important to study as they play a major role in shaping society and uncovering the issues related to direct democracy through integrated technologies. The future of democracy has privacy, security and legal implications but the enlightened citizens, compatible infrastructure and governess bodies will help in eliminating the drawbacks of direct democracy.

Introduction

Government plays an important role in the development of democracy and spends billions of dollars every year in information and communication technology (ICT). The Federal government alone spends over $25 billion annually on IT systems and services to decrease the gap between government and citizens (United States General Services Administration, n.d.). In 1993, the White House formed the Information Infrastructure Task Force (IITF) to articulate and implement the Administration's vision for the National Information Infrastructure (NII) (United States Department of Justice Computer Crime and Policy Program, n.d.).

The benefits of the NII claimed by the Center for Civic Networking are to create a smarter country that provides less costly, efficient government; have well-informed citizens that result in eliminating poverty; and promoting life-long learning (The Public's Library and Digital Archive, n.d.). According to the estimation of Computer System Policy project, NII will create as much as $300 billion annually in new sales across a broad range of industries (The Public's Library and Digital Archive, n.d.). Besides, all these claims and promises, the effects of ICT on politics and democracy are still a question to many experts where the conflict of interest occurs between the two.

This paper analyzes the effect of ICT issues like security and privacy on politics and democracy and predicts the future of democracy in 2008 as by then the ICT will be experimented, used, and experienced in various areas of government bodies and the citizens and the governess bodies will be more aware of the ICT usages and the issues related to the digital democracy. The discussion also includes the concept of tele-democracy and driving forces behind it and anchors examples of the usage of ICT in the public interest and points out the social, privacy and security implications in the present and in the future.

Definition of Tele-Democracy

Experts describe a democracy facilitated by the ICT as "Tele-democracy." Tele-democracy originates a system that takes an initiate to educate citizens by providing an access to databases (Grosswiler, 1998; Schwartz, 1992); promotes discussion and electronic community meetings between advocates or politicians and citizens (Becker, 1993; Betts, 1992; Igbaria, Shayo, Olfman, 1999; Schwartz, 1992). It facilitates electronic voting systems (Betts, 1992; Schwartz, 1992), and directs electronic discussion between citizens and thus, promotes better understanding of issues and differences among different cultures (Croce, 1993; Igbaria et al., 1999).

Perspectives in Tele-Democracy

In Politics, two perspectives are discussed at length on Tele-democracy, the Athenian and the Orwellion perspective. The Athenian perspective advocates that technologies will eliminate the representations from the hierarchy of democracy and direct democracy will predominate in the future. In contrast to, the Orwellian perspective portrays a negative role of technology. It argues that government will control and dominate citizens permanently. They predict that due to the easy and direct access to citizens, the interference of government will increase and democracy will be replaced by an "electronic cloak of darkness that gives the illusion of closeness" (Grosswiler, 1998).

To understand the concept of tele-democracy and its evolution, it is worthwhile to discuss the human theories of communication and theories of democracy. According to human communication theory, humans interact when they communicate (Hacker, 1996). In the technology age, humans communicate using computer networks. Computer networks are considered to be a two-way interactive communication system because of its ability to send and receive data. In politics most of the communication is considered mass communication, which provides a one-way channel of political information dissemination, from leaders to a mass. Discussion on networks and democracy rely on the same concept, that is, a linear model of human communication. Critics also argue that a two-way network communication system is not necessarily an interactive system. In an interactive system, citizens are encouraged to share their opinion and talk, thus, creates equilibrium of communication between leaders and citizens (Hacker, 1996). If the interaction is not present between the networks, it is, then, just another source of sending information from one sender to many receivers and justly is not an effective way of generating knowledge to understand the depth of issues to produce positive results.

In democracy theories, four theories of democracies are closer to the views about tele-democracy (Hacker, 1996). (1) The classical democratic theory is fundamental in ancient Greek that talks about direct participation in speech and debate. (2) The classical pluralism theory assumes that a spokesperson represents everyone in a democratic society. (3) The elite pluralism assumes that people in the lower class do not have enough knowledge or concern to participate in political issues and

Figure 1. Democracy model

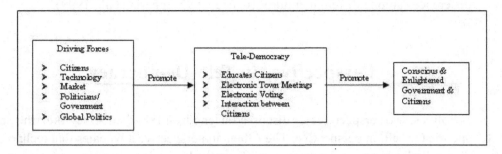

policies. (4) Critical pluralism theory assumes that in capitalist states technologies favor to those who have capital more than to those who do not.

The above-mentioned theories incorporate a need for a system, which supports the citizen's needs and provides them an opportunity as an active participant in the process of democracy. In some critics' view, tele-democracy presently, is closer to critical pluralism theory, while in my opinion it is a combination of both critical pluralism and classical pluralism theory. This study explores the role of information technology plays in solving the issues related to above theories and addresses various issues that evolve due to its participation in the tele-democracy.

The model in Figure 1 shows a framework for tele-democracy. This framework introduces the environment of tele-democracy and covers the essential stipulations affecting the process. It takes into consideration different theories' assumptions and represents a model, which covers the conceptual constructs to promote a well aware citizen that can represent herself and himself even in the presence of a leader. This model is used to identify and study the driving forces and their issues.

Driving Forces

The driving forces of tele-democracy have been arguably the government, politicians, more enlightened citizens, technology, communities, and global political pressures. In some experts' viewpoints, the major driving force behind democracy is technology. However, we cannot ignore the importance of awareness of information power between today's citizens. The roles of driving forces are discussed in the following sections:

Citizens

The usage of computers, computer competency and information literacy is dramatically increasing in citizens. New ICT is able to attract the involvement of citizens in the political process who felt neglected, frustrated and betrayed in the past. Exposure to technology at a young age in Schools is creating a new generation of computer and information literate (Igbaria et al, 1999). According to a Gartner (1999) Dataquest survey of 16,500 U.S. households, 55 percent of voting-age American has Internet access from home, work, school or libraries. This figure was expected

Figure 2.

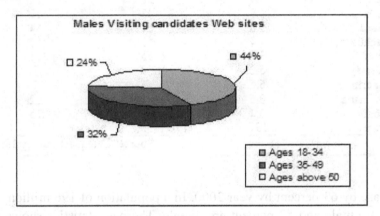

Figure 3.

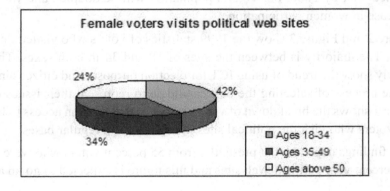

Table 1.

Early Primary Caucus States	# of voters in State (Millions)	# of online voters (percentages)	# of online voters who visit political sites
Iowa	1.9	50	14
New Hampshire	1.0	60	4
Delaware	0.8	64	5
South Carolina	2.6	45	19
North Dakota	0.6	37	10
California	21.9	63	15
Connecticut	2.8	63	7
D.C.	0.4	62	25
Florida	10.7	55	19
Georgia	4.9	58	12
Maine	0.9	43	10
Maryland	5.0	61	14
Massachusetts	4.4	55	11
Missouri	3.7	55	11
New Jersey	6.0	59	7
New York	6.6	41	7
Rhode Island	0.6	41	12
Vermont	0.4	65	15
All States	196	55	12

Source: Dataquest Survey 1998

to increase by 63 percent by year 2000. In a population of 196 million voters, 48 percent are male and 52 percent are female. The past statistics shows that from the population of 13.2 million voters, who visit political candidates' Web sites, 71 percent are males and 29 percent are females. The increasing trend in the figures predicts that by 2008, our voter's population will be doubled and we will see an increase in women participation.

Figure 2 and Figure 3 show the 1999 statistics of voters who visited Political Web sites. The majority is between the ages of 18 and 34 in both sexes. The statistics clearly show the trend of using ICT for election purposes and citizens involvement in the process of selecting the best candidate to represent their issues effectively. Table 1 shows the breakdown of voters by states that have an access to Internet and the voters who visit the political sites in each state on regular bases.

The findings depicted that presently, from 55 percent voters who were Web users, 12 percent visit political Web sites and this figure is expected to go up as the Election Day will come closer. The November 7, 2000, an Election Day, 70 percent of voting-age adults were expected to have Internet access. Since 1999, citizens have used electronic voting machine system to caste their vote.

Technology

Information communications and technology now are seen as essential parts of the social and political framework of society. Global and local usage of the Internet has confirmed that to enhance an effective democratic process lower cost, ease of access and open architecture plays a major role (Berman & Weitzner, 1997; Calhoun, 1998). It enables users to access distributed databases, value-added networks, and supports novelty of ideas, information and diverse opinion with complete anonymity (Iwas, 1997).

The increase in capacity of storage and high broadband makes possible video conferencing between the politicians and citizens to exchange opinions, ideas and discussion (Weintraub, 1993). Thus, ICT improves citizens' participation by providing each individual an access to their leaders. Unlike, radio and television (Simon, 1991), ICT does not have restrictions of time, space and channels. On the Internet, the addition of a new Web page does not require an elimination of another Web page (Berman & Weitzner, 1997). In short, since the creation of a task force the developments in bringing the government message through the virtual interaction are noticeable and worth the time and money spent by the previous and present government. The ease of usage and accessibility to the information is an integration of software and hardware that is a combined effort of government and private companies.

Communities

The extensive demand of technologies has made the cost of ICT hardware and software affordable. In the process of the creation of virtual communities, technology's infrastructure is becoming a part of other wiring system in a new housing and commercial development (hotels, resorts, and airport). This trend is guiding a living style where computers will be seen as an essential part of our life, like other utilities. The usage of ICT is giving rise to virtual-learner-communities who are learning through new technologies like "distance learning." Today's new communities are providing distance-learning facilities to teach programs such as parenting and mentoring to residents through their community centers that is convenient and cost effective for both parties. The media of interaction is a high-speed Internet (combination of high-speed networks and large capacity databases), which provide multimedia interaction to educate themselves in the programs that can be a source of income in the future.

Politicians/Government

Politicians are citizens who lead the entities and put forward strategies to solve the entities' national and international issues. Government governs the entities and is elected by the entities of the governing bodies. Government and politicians are also realizing a power of ICT and are participating actively to make a direct contact to the citizens. They are eager to use the technologies as a rational mean to find and satisfy the needs of citizens (Nordin, 1991). Unengaged and uninformed voters have created a government that neither knows nor implements the public's will. This situation has created a frustration at both ends. In the future, government is eager to access approximately 250 million citizens and spend billions of dollars annually to ensure more educated and knowledgeable citizens at less expense. Some politicians such as Steve Forbes and Al Gore initiated in providing their own Web sites and are communicating directly with voters and later followed by other politicians and government institutions to create the similar interface with the public. Their Web sites provide their bio, speeches, policy issues they support and other releases.

Global Politics

Global politics with the help of ICT is creating a global democracy where citizens of global communities are working together regardless of any physical boundaries. Governments and politicians worldwide are concerned about the impact of technologies and information flow to their power and control of countries. Previous experiences in the world have shown that the effect of technologies is not only on a national level but it is also spreading across other boundaries (Naisbitt, 1994). In ideal situation, when all the other factors are kept constant, technologies are the most effective weapon ever used in global issues. The Internet has been and is being used to call international attention to the struggle on issues like Iraq, Afghanistan, Bosnia, and Yugoslavia, and plays a major role in linking governments on every continent.

Governments and politicians are starting to realize the implications of collapsed global boundaries and are working together to establish a more effective and calm virtual environment. Besides, putting together the infrastructure for the global telecommunication system, the policies and regulation are also coming to place for tackling the problem of communication gap between international communities.

In 1995, an independent body of the G7 governments (Canada, France, Germany, Great Britain, Italy, Japan, and the United States) established the Global Information Infrastructure Commission (GIIC) for a period of three years, to fill the gap in international communications policy and regulation (Ferguson, 1998). Russia joined the GIIC in 1997 and is now called G8. The government of 20 other countries has also joined the organization to initiate a collaboration in developing an infrastructure that support a common interest (Liguori & Lorantffy, 2000). The G8 motivates and invites other countries and individuals from all over the world to join them in their efforts of global democracies.

Recent Practices

To understand the issues of ICT the study examines the recent practices in various areas and participating bodies. Government is making every effort to keep a free flow of information between themselves and the citizens. The task force of National Information Infrastructure (NII) is working on improving the equitable delivery of government information to the taxpayers who paid for its collection at a fair price. Besides, the NII task team efforts are to decrease a gap between Americans who have information and who do not have information. The later sections discuss the examples of ICT (The Public's Library and Digital archive, n.d.).

Government Information Dissemination

The Emergency Planning and Community Right-to-Know Act of 1986 established a Toxic Release Inventory (TRI) database, which required industries to report their estimated total releases of toxic chemicals to the environment. The Environmental Protection Agency has used a variety of means for making the data available to the public, including a collaborative effort involving the agency, the nonprofit community, and philanthropy. This effort involved making the TRI available through an online service called RTK NET (the Right-to-Know Computer Network), operated by OMB Watch and Unison Institute. As a result of the TRI program, EPA and industry developed the "33/50" program, in which CEOs set a goal of reducing their pollution by 33 percent by 1992 and 50 percent by 1995. Because of RTK NET's success, the EPA is seeking to expand the information available on the service.

Table 2. Other examples of projects on Tele-Democracy (Dutton, 1992)

Communication Task	Systems Employed	Applications	Examples
Broadcasting	Touch screen, multimedia PC	Multi-lingual kiosks	24-hour City Hall, Hawaii Access, LA project
Transaction	Automated teller machines	Welfare and Medicaid transaction	Proposals at the state and federal level
Access to Public Records	Dial-up electronic bulletin boards	Public, government, community information	Santa Monica's PEN, PARIS/PALS Pasadena
Interpersonal communication	Electronic mail	Citizens complaints, inquiries, requests	Santa Monica's PEN
	Computer conferencing & bulletin boards	Electronic forums on public issues	Santa Monica's PEN, NYCENET
Surveying & Monitoring	Computer assisted dialing & interviewing	Opinion polling	Political campaigns
	Audience response systems	Voting & polling from the home	QUBE system in Columbus, Ohio

Universal Accesses and Distance Learning

In the city of Harlem, where 40 percent of the residents live below the poverty line, NII deployed fiber optic cable. New York City was exploring the use of interactive video conferencing between community rooms in housing projects and government offices, schools, and New York corporations. These facilities could be used to teach parenting to teenage mothers, and promote mentoring programs between inner city youth and employees of New York corporations.

Electronic Town Meeting

President Bill Clinton used teleconferencing to take his ideas on health care to citizens in St. Paul, Minnesota.

Table 2 illustrates various other projects government has implemented to increase the participation of citizens.

Issues in Tele-Democracy

The analysis of present practices and usages in various government and non-government areas shows the sensitivity of implementation of the technology in the area of democracy. Digital democracy model helps in studying the issues around the identified driving forces. The issues related to the implementation of interactive democracy are discussed in sections below.

Social Issues

Among United States total population of approximately 250 million, 90 million adults do not have literacy skills. Nationwide 25 percent of students no longer complete high school and this percentage increases to 57 percent in large cities (United States Census Bureau, n.d.). To enjoy a true and robust democracy, Americans must be educated and trained. Though technology alone cannot eliminate an issue of uneducated and untrained population, studies have shown that computer-based instruction is cost-effective, enables 30 percent more learning in 40 percent less time at 30 percent less cost (United States Census Bureau, n.d.). In year 2002 high school graduates increase to 84.1 percent as compare to in 1990 where 75.2 percent graduated (United States Census Bureau, n.d.). Although the literacy ratio is increasing, the increment over the period is still disappointing. The registered voting population in 2000 was approximately 200 thousands and the actual voting percentage for Presidential election year was 63.9 percent and for Congressional election year 54.7 percent, (United States Census Bureau, n.d.). Whereas, in 2004 the turnout was 59 percent among those eligible to vote that was 4.8 percent higher than the 2000 election (McDonald, 2004). This raises an issue of the true democracy, as not all citizens are aware of their rights and available incentives to live a decent life and be an active member of the society.

Taylor et al. (2005) argued that e-government social design view of the UK and Netherlands is implemented on both national and international levels to consider the changing relationship between the government and the citizen. The national social design takes into consideration of involvement of different government organization maintaining relevant database and claiming the ownership of the databases information, and thus, are responsible for the authentication of the information and the authentication of the citizens. The international access to the e-government has also different levels of service provisions and is dependent upon the role the international citizen playing in using the information in addition to their relationship with the government.

Some experts fear that the consequences of a privatized information infrastructure will increase inequality between information haves and have-nots, or information rich and poor. To ensure that benefits of access to information will be distributed equitably and democratically, NII is being used to bring Americans together. Government exploited the educational applications of computers and networks. They are implementing NII to promote collaborating learning between students, teachers, and experts; take virtual field trips and access on-line digital libraries. Despite all the claims, critics are still skeptical about the future participation of uneducated proportion of population. The experts fear that a gap between educated and uneducated, rich and poor will increase.

Privacy Issues

Telecommunication will open new ways of communication and thus, will increase the issues of privacy. Due to government's involvement in new ways of reaching citizens, their surveillance is the major threat (Friedland, 1996). Furthermore, ICT also encourages adequate recognition of the structures of power that lie behind the machines and the Web, which in return provide an attractive challenge to the computer hackers to destroy those structures. The privacy of information is still a huge issue in the information economy. The recent privacy problem in electronic voting systems through touch-screen voting machine (like ATM) has raised the critics', states' and other law makers' concern about the legal implications and the future usage of the voting machines in certain states. Moreover, the state is also mandating a print copy of each vote caste for the records as a backup. In California, the Riverside County Supervisors voted against these restrictions and voted to take legal action against the Secretary of State (Associated Press, 2004).

Akram (2006) studied the privacy issues and explains the concepts "as a richness of intensity a person encounters when the boundaries he or she defines are intentionally crossed and uninvited scrutiny threatens the safety." The four main dimensions of individual's concerns about organizational information privacy practices identified by Smith et al (1996) and studied by other researchers like Akram (2006), are collection, unauthorized secondary use, improper access, and errors. Privacy issues with the electronic democracy challenge these dimensions of privacy and systems like Direct recording electronic (DRE) system, internet voting, punch card voting, and lever voting machine raise issues like public viewing, verification, usage of data, duplications, alteration or deletions of record (The National Committee for Voting Integrity, 2006).

Security Issues

The driving forces behind the security issues are government, citizens, and technologies. The major concern in security is the authentication of a person. Authentication is a mean of identifying a person identity through various types of documents or electronic measurements. The various ways of authentications are digital signature, finger printing, retina scanning, DNA, voice recognition, drivers license, passport, SSN, PIN numbers and passwords provided by the authorized service providers. Taylor, Lips, and Organ (2005) argue that technical design view of the UK and Netherlands e-government is to implement authentication within the system that provides a single point of access between the government and the citizens. The technical design is based upon a central Internet-based e-authentication facility to access different type of information from the government. The individuals provide their personal information to the provider of the authentication system and receive a user ID and pass word to clear the authentication requirements. The system is close to digital signature system and does charge a fee to access information. The authentication service provider certifies the authentication or trustworthiness of the user. The system has various levels of authentications for accessing different types of information (Taylor et al., 2005).

Political sites in U.S.A. has implemented authentication to assure a better two way electronic information exchange that can guarantee the integrity of the site, information, and the citizen. The usage and testing of other type of user interfaces like direct recording electronic (DRE) voting system, internet voting, punch card voting, and lever voting machine have brought forward issues like lack of transparency, inadequate testing of software, vulnerability to fraud, recalibration, cryptography, authentication, hacking, cyber attack, equipment problems, and lack of auditing (The National Committee for Voting Integrity, 2006). Due to the unreliability of e-democracy, various federal government and private organization such as Help America Vote Act (HAVA), U.S. Election Assistance Commission (EAC), Technical

Guidelines Development Committee (TGDC), The National Committee for Voting Integrity (NCVI) and National Institute of Standards and Technology (NIST) (The National Committee for Voting Integrity, 2006) have been established to come up with a social, logical and technical design of the tele-democracy.

Issues in 2008

The issues in 2008 will not be so different from today's issues or issues of five years ago due to the technologies advancement that bring more complication in dealing with the information exchange issues and lack of understanding of the processes that assure a legitimate control. Moreover, because of an increase in the usage of technologies, privacy and security issues will be the major concerns. The present practices of implementing technology will give more control to the machines resulting in decisions that will be based upon the compatibility of technologies than the citizens and will raise the e-democracy compatibility. The initial prediction was done in 1999 for the year 2004 and the observed facts depicted the issues of privacy and security violence as a major concern and are still found to be the great concern of electronic communication systems in 2004 and thus, are resulted in legal actions against government entity by informed citizens. Regardless of government's efforts in fulfilling the gaps, the large amount of dollar amount will be spent on settling these issues like physical records, legal fees, expertise, existing hardware and software problems, and introduction of technologies. Shortages of lawyers who have understanding of both politics and technology will affect the number of pending cases.

Information increase in government databases, which store the citizens' private and public data, will increase the interference from politicians, government and other sources (hackers). The government and politicians will have a direct access to the citizens' and they will have more and better ways of manipulating the citizens and the system and vice versa. Despite of G8 present role, global political boundaries will shrink, and global interference of powerful countries towards powerless countries will grow in developing the international information infrastructure.

The isolation of democracy will increase and will become an electronic threat with the introduction of wireless and microwave technologies. Presently, a new era of electronic terrorism is opening a challenging front for our governess bodies to fight war against these unknown electronic forces where no one needs batches and physical security clearances and each have power to fight very efficiently and effectively to achieve their hidden and declared agendas. The harm is not only monetary but also life threatening and a life and death are only a wave of thought away from the sender and have no geographical boundaries.

Future of Democracy

In a country like United States, the next five years are crucial in shaping the future of electronic democracy. The driving forces of democracy demand effective information and technology infrastructure. The awareness and participation of citizens in 2008 will increase and the complicated government and high cost of information in the past will be replaced by more Internet access interfaces. Ease of usage and lower cost of information will encourage citizens to access information more frequently and the systems will be more controlled and monitored by the government and non-government entities to ensure the integrity of the political system.

The Internet will be the major source of support of democratic activities. Electronic town meetings on local, state, and national level will increase as more communities' value-networks and high-speed telecommunication media integration will transpire. Public information sources will be more common and intelligent agents will be more popular to answer the citizens' questions. Participation of voters will increase, as there will be software that is more powerful available. Telecommuting will increase citizens' participation in elections. The percentage of Democratic party member voters will grow in numbers. For election registration purposes, the usage of digital signature and on-site electronic fingerprints will be a common practice in most of the states.

The immensity of government will decrease due to more dissemination of information regarding its vital services. The electronic bureaucracy in government will decrease due to flatter organizational structure. New public policies regarding publicly finance elections will be under enormous pressure. The tens of millions of dollars spend on television advertisement on presidential candidates would be given directly to eligible citizens run organizations to spend on presidential candidates' information. The movement to protect the consumer rights will be stronger because the role of the media will be vital in the political process. The citizens will have the right to know more about the media as they do about the government and politicians. The competition between politicians will increase considering less financial burden.

Globalization is the accretion of economic, social and political relations across periphery. To enhance an effective global order, the collective governance between certain countries will increase due to international communication policies and more distributed political power. The worldwide national communications policies will be led by GIIC on a large scale, which will transfer more power to G8. United States, European and Asian countries will be the major players, and the struggle of control and power over the standardization of telecommunication infrastructure will increase.

Due to an increase in the privatization of public broadcasting and state-run tele-communications corporations and more strategic alliances with private enterprise on global level, there will be more competition between companies in providing better services at lower costs.

Conclusion

The present view of e-government represents on the one hand Athenian perspective and support the classical democratic theory. The e-access promotes e-democracy and provides access to the politicians' bio, ideologies, practices, explanation of different issues, and their solutions by just one electronic interface and does provide a substantial knowledge of the country's know-how. The access to debates, related informational databases on issues does stimulate more ideas regarding the solutions of the problems. Regardless of all the sophisticated amenities, elimination of representation is still not possible as representation is a collection of knowledge, people's support, representation's power to make a change and her or his diplomacy in handling issues and political relations and thus, cannot be eliminated from the process of country's political system. Accordingly, the argued facts support classical pluralism theory.

On the other hand, Orewellian perspective does hold its ground. The security and privacy issues demand government, citizen and other private regulatory bodies to closely monitor the e-government processes to save the integrity of the e-democracy. ICT produces data on citizens' private and public lives, but does not provide any promising security measures. The data provides a potential surveillance from the government and from the hackers. The structure behind the Internet though claimed to be decentralized is amazingly centralized and consequently gives more power of control to parties involved behind the scene and thus, demands an effective management and administrative processes that promote ethical electronic structure.

Tele-democracy is bringing a new way of thinking, which is perceptible, bright, curious, deliberate, and dangerous. Society is and will be enthusiastic and surprisingly different as a result. The changes have already started to happen. We are seeing the world with the interactive eye of ICT and are informed through small icons just by a click of a mouse. The images are descriptive and provide visual education of an ideology. Direct democracy will happen in direct participation in the political process not by direct governess of the state or country.

Our society is still centuries away from the sort of country where citizens replace the representatives and technologies represent the President of United States. Our political, social and economic issues are too complex for a common person to understand and solve the country's issues. Moreover, isolated citizens cannot run a complex government; they have to come together under a common umbrella and interact to build the perfect country. Therefore, technologies will permit alliances to gather successively and advertently, around issues that are important to publics and not to the lobbyists.© *2005 updated in 2007*

References

Akram, A.A. (2006). Electronic privacy: Patient concerns. *Communications of the IIMA, 6*(1), 67-82.

Associated Press (2004, May 8). Security first. *The Press Enterprise*.

Becker, T. (1993).Teledemocracy: Gathering momentum in state and local governance. *The Journal of State Government, 66*(2), 14-20.

Berman, J. & Weitzner, D. J. (1997). Technology and democracy. *Social Research, 64*(3), 1313-1319.

Betts, M. (1992). Electronic town meeting a safe vote? (Pilot electronic polling project). *Computerworld, 26*(43), 25.

Calhoun, C. (1998). Community without propinquity revisited: Communications technology and the transformation of the urban public sphere. *Sociological Inquiry, 68*(3), 373-397.

Croce, J. P. (1993). Erosion of mass culture. *Society,* (July/August), 11-17.

Dutton, W. H. (1992). Political science research on teledemocracy. *Social Science Computer Review, 10*(4), 505-522.

Ferguson, K. (1998). World information flows and the impact of new technology. *Social Science Computer Review, 16*(3), 252-267.

Friedland, L. A. (1996). Electronic democracy and the new citizenship. *Media, Culture & Society, 18*(2), 185-212.

Gartner (1999). Gartner Group's dataquest sees pivotal role for Internet in presidential election in 2000. Retrieved January, 2007, from http://www.gartner.com/5_about/press_room/pr19990504a.html

Grosswiler, P. (1998). Historical hopes, media fears, and the electronic town meeting concept: Where technology meets democracy or demagogy. *Journal of Communication Inquiry, 22*(2), 133.

Hacker, L. K. (1996). Missing links in the evolution of electronic democratization. *Media, Culture & Society*, 18, 213-232.

Igbaria, M., Shayo, C., & Olfman, L. (1999). On becoming virtual: The driving forces and arrangements. *ACM*, 27-41.

Iwas. A. (1997). Groupthink and possibility of teledemocracy. *Sociological Theory & Methods 12, 1*(21), 31-46.

Liguori, M. & Lorantffy, N. (2000). The G20 Montreal Ministerial Meeting: Report on Private Sector Involvment, Standards and Codes, Institutional Reform and the Financial Sector. G8 Research Group, University of Toronto, October. U Of T G8 Information Centre. Retrieved on January 2007, from http://www.g8.utoronto.ca/g20/evaluations/ligloroct25.html

McDonald, M. (2004). Voter turnout: The numbers prove that 2004 signal more voter interest. Milwaukee Journal Sentinel, November. Retrieved January 2007, from http://www.brookings.edu/views/op-ed/mcdonald20041127.htm

Naisbitt, J. (1994). *Global paradox*. New York: Willian Morrow and Company, Inc.

Nordin, I. (1991). State, technology, and planning. *Philosophy of the Social Sciences, 21*(4), 458-475.

RTK Network (n.d.). The right-to-know network. Retrieved January 2007, from http://rtknet.org

Schwartz, E. I. (1992).Putting the PC into politics. (Prodigy and CompuServe take a wider role in an evolving teledemocracy). *Business Week*, March 16, n3256, 112-114.

Simon, T. W. (1991). Electronic inequality. *Bulletin of Science, Technology & Society, 11*(3), 144-146

Taylor, J., Lips, M., & Organ, J. (2005). Electronic government: Towards new forms of authentication, citizenship and governance. Authentication, digital signature and PKI issues- Part I Article, November. Retrieved January 2007, from http://www.egov.vic.gov.au/index.php?env=-innews/detail:m1063-1-1-8-s#electronicgovernment

The National Committee for Voting Integrity (2006). Issues: Program areas, November. Retrieved January 2007, from http://www.votingintegrity.org/issues

The Public's Library and Digital archive (n.d.). The national information infrastructure: Benefits and applications of the national infrastructure. Retrieved January, 2007, from http://www.ibiblio.org/nii/NII-Benefits-and-Applications.html

United States Census Bureau (n.d.) American community survey. Retrieved 2004, from http://eire.census.gov/popet/data/national/tables

United States Department of Justice Computer Crime and Policy Program (n.d.). Computer crime and intellectual property sections. Retrieved January, 2007, from http:// www.usdoj.gov/criminal/cybercrime/ccpolicy.html

United States General Services Administration (n.d.). Technology. Retrieved on January, 2007 from http://www.gsa.gov/portal/gsa/ep/home.do?tabId=4

Weintraub, D. M. (1993). The technology connection. (Teledemocracy). *State Legislatures, 19*(6), 44-46.

Chapter XIII

Trust Modeling and Management:
From Social Trust to Digital Trust

Zheng Yan, Nokia Research Center, Finland

Silke Holtmanns, Nokia Research Center, Finland

Abstract

This chapter introduces trust modeling and trust management as a means of manag-
ing trust in digital systems. Transforming from a social concept of trust to a digital
concept, trust modeling and management help in designing and implementing a
trustworthy digital system, especially in emerging distributed systems. Furthermore,
the authors hope that understanding the current challenges, solutions and their
limitations of trust modeling and management will not only inform researchers of
a better design for establishing a trustworthy system, but also assist in the under-
standing of the intricate concept of trust in a digital environment.

Introduction

Trust plays a crucial role in our social life. Our social life is characterized by the trust relationships that we have. Trust between people can be seen as a key component to facilitate coordination and cooperation for mutual benefit. Social trust is the product of past experiences and perceived trustworthiness. We constantly modify and upgrade our trust in other people based on our feelings in response to changing circumstances. Often, trust is created and supported by a legal framework, especially in business environments or when financial issues are involved. The framework ensures that misbehavior can be punished with legal actions and increases the incentive to initiate a trust relationship. The legal framework decreases the risk of misbehavior and secures the financial transactions. With the rapid growth of global digital computing and networking technologies, trust becomes an important aspect in the design and analysis of secure distributed systems and electronic commerce. However, the existing legal frameworks are often focused on local legislation and are hard to enforce on a global level. The most popular examples are email spam, software piracy, and a breach of warranty. Particularly, because legal regulation and control cannot keep pace with the development of electronic commerce, the extant laws in conventional commerce might not be strictly enforceable in electronic commerce. In addition, resorting to legal enforcement in electronic commerce might be impracticably expensive or even impossible, such as in the case of micro payment transactions (Ba, Whinston, & Zhang 1999). This raises the importance of trust between interacting digital entities. People can not assume that the legal framework is able to provide the needed trustworthiness for their digital relationships, for example, for an electronic transaction purpose. It has been a critical part of the process by which trust relationships are required to develop in a digital system. In particular, for some emerging technologies, such as MANET (Mobile Ad Hoc Networks), P2P (Peer-to-Peer) computing, and GRID virtual systems, trust management has been proposed as a useful solution to break through new challenges of security and privacy caused by the special characteristics of these systems, such as dynamic topology and mobility (Lin, Joy, & Thompson, 2004; Yan, 2006; Yan, Zhang, & Virtanen 2003).

Trust is a very complicated phenomena attached to multiple disciplines and influenced by many measurable and non-measurable factors. It is defined in various ways for different purposes and cultures, even though in information technology area. Thereby, it is difficult to have a common definition for this comprehensive concept.

Establishing a trust relationship in digital networking environment involves more aspects than in the social world. This is because communications in the computing network rely on not only relevant human beings and their relationships, but also digital components. On the other hand, the visual trust impression is missing and need somehow to be compensated. Moreover, it is more difficult to accumulate accurate information for trust purposes in remote digital communications where information can be easily distorted or faked identities can be created. The mapping of our social understanding of trust into the digital world and the creation of trust models that are feasible in practice are challenging. Trust is a special issue beyond and will enhance a system security and personal privacy. Understanding the trust relationship between two digital entities could help selecting and applying feasible measures to overcome potential security and privacy risk. From social trust to digital trust, how can trust theory help in designing and implementing a trustworthy digital system? The literature suggests the usage of trust modeling and management. This book chapter aims to help readers understanding trust modeling and management in the emerging technologies. The reader is guided from the creation of a digital trust concept to the deployment of trust models for trust management in a digital environment.

Background

The problem to create trust in the digital environment has led to a number of approaches, for example, expressing and modeling trust in a digital way, evaluating trust in a reputation system, rating agencies, certificate authorities that equip trading partners with certificates as trusted providers and brokers, trustworthy user interface design, and so on. Current academic and industrial work related to trust covers a wide area of interest ranging from such aspects as perception of trust, cryptographic-security enforced trust solutions, trust modeling, and trust management to trusted computing activities.

Perception of Trust Concept (from Social Trust towards Digital Trust)

What is trust and how is trust influenced? We will now examine the most common definitions of trust and start from a classical social trust concept that is supported by a legal framework to a concept for digital processing. Through the study of various definitions of trust, we explain the properties of trust relationships and classify the factors that influence trust.

Definitions of trust. The concept of trust has been studied in disciplines ranging from economic to psychology, from sociology to medicine, and to information science. It is hard to say what trust exactly is because it is a multidimensional, multidiscipline and multifaceted concept. We can find various definitions of trust in the literature. For example, it can be loosely defined as a state involving confident positive expectations about another's motives with respect to oneself in situations entailing risk (Boon & Holmes, 1991). This definition highlights three main characteristics of trust. First, a trust relationship involves at least two entities: a trustor and a trustee, reliant on each other for mutual benefit. Second, trust involves uncertainty and risk. There is no perfect guarantee to ensure that the trustee will live up to the trustor's expectation. Third, the trustor has faith in the trustee's honesty and benevolence, and believes that the trustee will not betray his/her risk-assuming behavior.

Gambetta (1990) defined trust as trust (or, symmetrically, distrust) is a particular level of the subjective probability with which an agent will perform a particular action, both before [we] can monitor such action (or independently of his capacity of ever to be able to monitor it) and in a context in which it affects [our] own action. Mayer, Davis, and Schoorman (1995) provided the definition of trust as the willingness of a party to be vulnerable to the actions of another party based on the expectation that the other party will perform a particular action important to the trustor, irrespective of the ability to monitor or control that other party. These definitions point out another important main characteristic of trust: Trust is subjective. The level of trust considered sufficient is different for each individual in a certain situation. Trust may be affected by those actions that we cannot (digitally) monitor. The level of trust depends on how our own actions are in turn affected by the trustee's actions. Grandison and Sloman (2000) hold an opinion that trust is a qualified belief by a trustor with respect to the competence, honesty, security and dependability of a trustee within a special context.

McKnight and Chervany (2000, 2003) conducted analysis on the trust definitions and noted that trust is a concept hard to define because it is itself a vague term. Looking up the term "trust" in a dictionary may reveal many explanations since it is a cross-disciplinary concept. For example, from the sociologists' point of view, it is related to social structure. From the psychologists' point of view, it concerns personal trait. From the economists' point of view, it is a mechanism of economic choice and risk management. The definitions of trust can be classified based on the consideration of structural, disposition, attitude, feeling, expectancy, belief, intention, and behavior. There are suggestions to evaluate trust with regard to competence, benevolence, integrity, and predictability. But generally, these attributes are only applicable to very narrow scenarios and hard to measure.

Other expressions of trust are targeting at different context and technology areas, for example:

- **Online System:** Online trust is an attitude of confident expectation in an online situation of risk that one's vulnerabilities will not be exploited (Corritore, Kracher, & Wiedenbeck, 2003).
- **Multi Agent System:** In a multi-agent system, trust is a subjective expectation an agent has about another agent's future behavior (Mui, 2003).
- **Software Engineering:** From a software engineering point of view, trust is accepted dependability (Avizienis, Laprie, Randell, & Landwehr, 2004).
- **Ad-Hoc Networks:** For an ad hoc network, trust could be defined as the reliability, timeliness, and integrity of message delivery to a node's intended next-hop (Liu, Joy, & Thompson, 2004).

Denning (1993) emphasizes the importance of assessment for trust in a system, which is of particular importance in the digital environment, where the entities often just have digital artifacts to base their trust judgment on. The current paradigm for trusted computing systems holds that trust is a property of a system. It is a property that can be formally modeled, specified, and verified. It can be "designed into" a system using a rigorous design methodology. Trust is an assessment that a person, organization, or object can be counted on to perform according to a given set of standards in some domain of action. In particular, a system is trusted if and only if its users trust it. Trust itself is an assessment made by users based on how well the observed behavior of the system meets their own standards.

Common to many definitions are the notions of confidence, belief, faith, hope, expectation, dependence, and reliance on the goodness, strength, reliability, integrity, ability, or character of a person or entity. Generally, a trust relationship involves two entities: a trustor and a trustee. The trustor is the person or entity who holds confidence, belief, faith, hope, expectation, dependence, and reliance on the goodness, strength, reliability, integrity, ability, or character of another person or entity, which is the object of trust - the trustee.

Table 1. Factors influencing trust extracted from some definitions of trust

Factors related to trustee's objective properties	competence; ability; security; dependability; integrity; predictability; reliability; timeliness; (observed) behavior; strength
Factors related to trustee's subjective properties	honesty; benevolence; goodness
Factors related to trustor's objective properties	assessment; a given set of standards; trustor's standards
Factors related to trustor's subjective properties	confidence; (subjective) expectations or expectancy; subjective probability; willingness; belief; disposition; attitude; feeling; intention; faith; hope; trustor's dependence and reliance
Context	situations entailing risk; structural; risk; domain of action

Figure 1. Classification of factors that influence trust

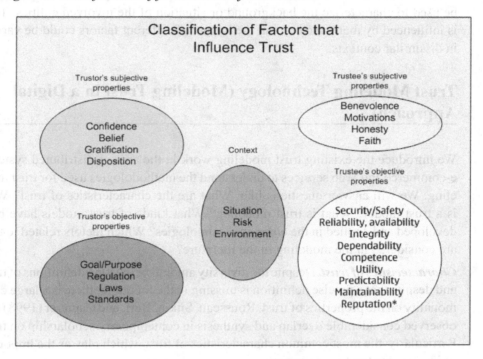

Although the richness of the concept, we can still summarize the subjective and objective factors that are relevant to a decision of trust, as shown in Table 1.

Factors influencing trust. Trust is subjective because the level of trust considered sufficient is different for each entity. It is the subjective expectation of the trustor on the trustee related to the trustee's behaviors that could influence the trustor's belief in the truestee. Trust is also dynamic as it is affected by many factors that are difficult to measure and monitor. It can be further developed and evolved due to good experiences about the trustee. Or it is sensitive to be decayed caused by one or several bad experiences. From the digital system point of view, trust is a kind of assessment on the trustee based on a number of referents, for example, competence, security, reliability, and so on. Trust is influenced by a number of factors. Those factors can be classified into five categories, as shown in Figure 1.

From the digital system point of view, we pay more attention to the objective properties of both the trustor and the trustee. For social human interaction, we consider more about the trustee's subjective and objective properties and the trustor's subjective properties. For economic transactions, we study more about the context for risk management. The context of trust is a very important factor that influences a trust relationship, e.g. the why and when to trust. It specifies any information that can be used to characterize the background or situation of the involved entities. Trust is influenced by many factors, but the impact of different factors could be various in dissimilar contexts.

Trust Modeling Technology (Modeling Trust in a Digital Approach)

We introduce the existing trust modeling work in the area of distributed systems, e-commerce and Web services to understand the methodologies used for trust modeling. We will answer questions like: What are the characteristics of trust? What is a trust model? What is trust modeling? What kinds of trust models have been developed and applied in the emerging technologies? Which factors related to trust are considered in the modeling in the literature?

Characteristics of trust. Despite the diversity among the existing definitions of trust, and despite that a precise definition is missing in the literature, there is a large commonality on the properties of trust. Rousseau, Sitkin, Burt, and Camerer (1998) also observed considerable overlap and synthesis in contemporary scholarship on trust. Particularly, the most common characteristics of trust, which play as the important guidelines for trust modeling are:

a.   Trust is directed: This property says that trust is an oriented relationship between the trustor and the trustee.
b.   Trust is subjective: Trust is inherently a personal opinion. According to the survey conducted by Grandison and Sloman (2000), trust is considered a personal and subjective phenomenon that is based on various factors or evidence and that some of those may carry more weight than others. Trust is different for each individual in a certain situation.
c.   Trust is context-dependent: In general, trust is a subjective belief about an entity in a particular context.
d.   Trust is measurable: Trust values can be used to represent the different degrees of trust an entity may have in another. "Trust is measurable" also provides the foundation for trust modeling and computational evaluation.
e.   Trust depends on history: This property implies that past experience may influence the present level of trust.
f.   Trust is dynamic: Trust is usually non-monotonically changed with time. It may be refreshed or revoked periodically, and must be able to adapt to the changing conditions of the environment in which the trust decision was made.

Trust is sensitive to be influenced due to some factors, events, or changes of context. In order to handle this dynamic property of trust, solutions should take into account the notion of learning and reasoning. The dynamical adaptation of the trust relationship between two entities requires a sophisticated trust management approach (Grandison and Sloman, 2000).

g. Trust is conditionally transferable: Information about trust can be transmitted/received along a chain (or network) of recommendations. The conditions are often bound to the context and the trustor's objective factors.

h. Trust can be a composite property: "trust is really a composition of many different attributes: reliability, dependability, honesty, truthfulness, security, competence, and timeliness, which may have to be considered depending on the environment in which trust is being specified" (Grandison and Sloman, 2000, pp. 3). Compositionality is an important feature for making trust calculations.

Trust modeling. What is a trust model? The method to specify, evaluate and set up trust relationships amongst entities for calculating trust is referred as the trust model. Trust modeling is the technical approach used to represent trust for the purpose of digital processing.

One of the earliest formalizations of trust in computing systems was done by Marsh (1994). In his approach, he integrated the various facets of trust from the disciplines of economics, psychology, philosophy and sociology. Since then, many trust models have been constructed for various computing paradigms such as ubiquitous computing, P2P networks, and multi-agent systems. In almost all of these studies, trust is accepted as a subjective notion by all researchers, which brings us to a problem: how to measure trust? Translation of this subjective concept into a machine readable language is the main objective needed to be solved. Rahman and Hailes (2000) proposed a trust model based on the work done by Marsh (1994). Their trust model focuses on online virtual communities where every agent maintained a large data structure representing a version of global knowledge about the entire network. Gil and Ratnakar (2002) described a feedback mechanism that assigns credibility and reliability values to sources based on the averages of feedback received from individual users.

Regarding the trust modeling, there are various methodologies can be applied for different purposes. Some trust models are based on cryptographic technologies, for example Public Key Infrastructure (PKI) played as the foundation in a trust model (Perlman, 1999). A big number of trust models are developed targeting at some special trust properties, such as reputations, recommendations and risk studied by Xiong and Liu (2004) and Liang and Shi (2005). Seldom, they support multi-property of trust that is needed to take into account the factors like multiple objective factors of the trustee and context. Many trust models have been constructed for various computing paradigms such as GRID computing, ad hoc networks, and P2P systems. Those models use computational, linguistic or graphical methods. For example, Maurer (1996) described an entity's opinion about the trustworthiness of a certificate as a value in the scope of [0, 1]. Theodorakopoulos and Baras (2006) used a two-tuple in $[0, 1]^2$ to describe a trust opinion. In Jøsang (1999), the metric is a triplet in $[0, 1]^3$, where the elements in the triplet represent belief, disbelief, and uncertainty, respectively. Abdul-Rahman and Hailes (2000) used discrete integer numbers to describe the degree of trust. Then, simple mathematic, such as minimum, maximum, and weighted average, is used to calculate unknown trust values through concatenation and multi-path trust propagation. Jøsang and Ismail (2002) and Ganeriwal and Srivastava (2004) used a Bayesian model to take binary ratings as input and compute reputation scores by statistically updating beta probability density functions. Linguistic trust metrics were used for reasoning trust with provided rules by Manchala (2000). In the context of the "Web of Trust," many trust models (e.g., Reiter and Stubblebine, 1998) are built upon a graph where the resources/entities are nodes and trust relationships are edges.

One promising approach of trust modeling aims to conceptualize trust based on user studies through a psychological or sociological approach (e.g., a measurement scale). This kind of research aims to prove the complicated relationships among trust and other multiple factors in different facets. Two typical examples are the initial trust model proposed by McKnight, Choudhury, and Kacmar (2002) that explained and predicted customer's trust towards an e-vender in an e-commerce context, and the Technology Trust Formation Model (TTFM) studied by Li, Valacich, and Hess (2004) to explain and predict people's trust towards a specific information system. Both models used the framework of the theory of reasoned action (TRA) created by Fishbein and Ajzen (1975) to explain how people form initial trust in an unfamiliar entity, and both integrated important trusting antecedents into this framework in order to effectively predict people's trust. For other examples, Gefen (2000) proved that familiarity builds trust; Pennington, Wilcox, and Grover (2004) tested that one trust mechanism, vendor guarantees, has direct influence on system trust; Bhattacherjee (2002) studied three key dimensions of trust: trustee's ability, benevolence and integrity; Pavlou and Gefen (2004) explained that institutional mechanisms engender buyer's trust in the community of online auction sellers. The trust models generated based on this approach are generally linguistic or graphic. They do not quantify trust for machine processing purposes. Therefore, the achieved results could only help people understanding trust more precisely in order to work out a design guideline or an organizational policy towards a trustworthy digital system or a trustworthy user interface. Although little work has been conducted to integrate psychological,

Table 2. Taxonomy of trust models

Criteria of classification	Categories		Examples
Based on the method of modeling	Models with linguistic description		Blaze, Feigenbaum, and Lacy (1996) and Tan and Thoen (1998)
	Models with graphic description		Reiter and Stubblebine (1998)
	Models with mathematic description		Xiong and Liu (2004) and Sun, Yu, Han, and Liu (2006)
Based on modeled contents	Single-property modeling		Xiong and Liu (2004) and Sun, Yu, Han, and Liu (2006)
	Multi-property modeling		Zhou, Mei, and Zhang (2005), Wang and Varadharajan (2005), and Yan and MacLaverty (2006)
Based on the expression of trust	Models with binary rating		
	Models with numeral rating	Continuous rating	Maurer (1996) and Xiong and Liu (2004)
		Discrete rating	Liu, Joy, and Thompson (2004)
Based on the dimension of trust expression	Models with single dimension		Maurer (1996) and Xiong and Liu (2004)
	Models with multiple dimensions		Theodorakopoulos and Baras (2006) and Jøsang (1999)

sociological and technological theories together, we believe, however, the psychological and sociological study results could further play as practical foundations of computational trust—modeling trust for a digital processing purpose,.

Modeling trust in a digital way is important in a distributed digital system in order to automatically manage trust. Although a variety of trust models are available, it is still not well understood what fundamental criteria the trust models must follow. Without a good answer to this question, the design of trust models is still at an empirical stage and can never reach the expectation to simulate social trust to a satisfying degree. Current work focuses on concrete solutions in special systems. We would like to advocate that the trust model should reflect the characteristics of trust, consider the factors that influence the trust, and thus support the trust management in a feasible way.

Despite the variety of trust modeling methods, a common approach can be found in a number of publications regarding computational trust, for example, Xiong and Liu (2004); Theodorakopoulos and Baras (2006); Song, Hwang, Zhou, and Kwok (2005), Liu, Joy, and Thompson (2004), and Sun, Yu, Han, and Liu (2006). This approach is applied by firstly presenting an understanding of the characteristics of trust, principles or axioms, then modeling them in a mathematical way, and further applying the model into trust evaluation or trust management for a specific issue.

Taxonomy of trust models. The trust model aims to process and/or control trust using digital methods. Most of the modeling work is based on the understanding of trust characteristics and considers some factors influencing trust. The current work covers a wide area including ubiquitous computing, distributed systems, multi-agent systems, Web services, e-commerce, and component software. The discussed trust models can be classified into categories according to different criteria, as shown in Table 2.

Current research status. Trust is influenced by reputations (i.e., the public evidence of the trustee), recommendations (i.e., a group of entities' evidence on the trustee), the trustor's past experiences, and context (e.g., situation, risk, time, etc.). Most of work focused on a singular trust value or level calculation by taking into account the previous behavior of the trustee. The reputations, the recommendations and the trustor's own experiences are assessed based on the quality attributes of the trustee, the trust standards of the trustor, and the local context for making a trust or distrust conclusion. A number of trust models support the dynamics of trust. So far, some basic elements of context are considered, such as time, context similarity, and so on. The time element has been considered in many pieces of work, such as Wang and Varadharajan (2005) and Xiong and Liu (2004). For peer-to-peer systems, Sarkio and Holtmanns (2007) proposed a set of functions to produce a tailored trustworthiness estimation, which takes into account factors like age of reputation, value of transaction, frequency of transactions, reputation of the reputation giver, and so on. However, no existing work gives a common consideration on all factors that influence trust in a generic digital environment, especially those subjective factors of the trustor and the trustee, as shown in Figure 1. It is still a challenge to digitally model the subjective factors related to the trustor and the trustee, especially when the trustor or the trustee is a person.

Mechanisms for Trust Management (Applying and Deploying Trust Models)

About the following questions will be addressed in this part: "What is trust management? What does trust management do? Why is trust management needed in the emerging technologies? What is the current research status of trust management?"

As defined by Grandison and Sloman (2000), trust management is concerned with: collecting the information required to make a trust relationship decision; evaluating the criteria related to the trust relationship as well as monitoring and reevaluating existing trust relationships; and automating the process. Due to the amount of data collected and processed in the digital environment, the definition should be extended to accommodate support for automatic processing in order to provide a system's trustworthiness. Yan and MacLaverty (2006) proposed that autonomic trust management includes four aspects and these four aspects are processed in an automatic way:

- **Trust establishment:** The process for establishing a trust relationship between a trustor and a trustee.
- **Trust monitoring:** The trustor or its delegate monitors the performance or behaviour of the trustee. The monitoring process aims to collect useful evidence for trust assessment of the trustee.
- **Trust assessment:** The process for evaluating the trustworthiness of the trustee by the trustor or its delegate. The trustor assesses the current trust relationship and decides if this relationship is changed. If it is changed, the trustor will make decision which measure should be taken.
- **Trust control and re-establishment:** If the trust relationship will be broken or is broken, the trustor will take corresponding measures to control or re-establish the trust relationship.

As we can see from the above, trust management can be achieved through trust modeling and evaluation.

Reputation systems. There are various trust management systems in the literature and practice. A category of large practical importance is reputation based trust management system. Trust and reputation mechanisms have been proposed in various fields such as distributed computing, agent technology, grid computing, economics, and evolutionary biology. Reputation-based trust research stands at the crossroads of several distinct research communities, most notably computer science, economics, and sociology.

As defined by Aberer and Despotovic (2001), *reputation* is a measure that is derived from direct or indirect knowledge on earlier interactions of entities and is used to assess the level of trust an entity puts into another entity. Thus, reputation based trust management (or simply reputation system) is a specific approach to evaluate and control trust.

Reputation schemes can be classified into two different categories depending on what sort of reputation they utilize. Global reputation is the aggregation of all available assessments by other entities that have had interactions with the particular entity, and thus it has an *n-to-1 relationship*. On the other hand, the local reputation of an entity is each entity's own assessment based on past history of interaction with the particular entity, thus it is a *1-to-1 relationship*. This reflects the social situation that a person trusts another one, because "they are good friends."

Several representative P2P reputation systems currently exist, although the list we present is by no means exhaustive. The eBay and PeerTrust systems focus on trust management in securing commodity exchanges in e-commerce applications, as does the FuzzyTrust system by Song et al. (2005). Other systems focus on generic P2P applications such as P2P file sharing and Web service-based sharing platforms.

The eBay (www.ebay.com) user feedback system described by Resnick and Zeckhauser (2002) is by far the simplest and most popular trust-management system, and is specifically tailored for e-auction applications. It applies a centralized database to store and manage the trust scores. Data is open to the general public, so a newcomer can easily obtain a peer score. It's a hybrid P2P system using both distributed client resources and centralized servers. This system tries to be user friendly by providing a limited amount of data to a user, but on the other hand the provided and processed information is not complete and does not provide a "full picture."

Singh and Liu (2003) presented Trustme, a secure and anonymous protocol for trust. The protocol provides mutual anonymity for both a trust host and a trust querying peer. Guha and Kumar (2004) developed an interesting idea about the propagation of distrust. In addition to maintaining positive trust values for peers, the system also allows the proactive dissemination of some malicious peers' bad reputations. Buchegger and Le Boudec (2004) designed a distributed reputation system using a Bayesian approach, in which the second-hand reputation rating is accepted only when it is compatible with the primary rating.

Several universities are working on the research projects involving trust management in P2P applications. Xiong and Liu (2004) developed the PeerTrust model. Their model is based on a weighted sum of five peer feedback factors: *peer records, scope, credibility, transaction context,* and *community context.* PeerTrust is fully distributed, uses overlay for trust propagation, public-key infrastructure for securing remote scores, and prevents peers from some malicious abuses.

Kamvar, Schlosser, and Garcia-Molina (2003) proposed the EigenTrust algorithm, which captures peer reputation in the number of satisfactory transactions and then normalizes it over all participating peers. The algorithm aggregates the scores by a weighted sum of all raw reputation scores. The fully distributed system assumes that pre-trusted peers exist when the system is initiated. It uses majority voting to check faulty reputation scores reported.

Liang and Shi (2005) proposed the TrustWare system (retrieved from http://mist. cs.wayne.edu/trustware.html), a trusted middleware for P2P applications. Their approach consists of two models: the Multiple Currency Based Economic model (M-CUBE) and the Personalized Trust model (PET). The M-CUBE model provides a general and flexible substrate to support high-level P2P resource management services. PET derives peer trustworthiness from long-term reputation evaluation and short-term risk evaluation.

Sherwood and Bhattacharjee (2003) proposed in the Nice project a scheme for trust inference in P2P networks. The trust inference consists of two parts for local trust inference and distributed search. After each transaction, the system generates cookies to record direct trust between peers. It also uses trust graphs to infer transitive trust along a peer chain.

Credence is a robust and decentralized system for evaluating the reputation of files in a P2P file sharing system (Retrieved from http://www.cs.cornell.edu/people/egs/credence/index.html). Its goal is to enable peers to confidently gauge *file authenticity*, the degree to which the content of a file matches its advertised description. At the most basic level, Credence employs a simple, network-wide voting scheme where users can contribute positive and negative evaluations of files. On top of this, a client uses statistical tests to weight the importance of votes from other peers. It allows the clients to share selected information with other peers. Privacy is ensured by not collecting or using any personally identifiable information in any way in the protocol. Each Credence-equipped client is supplied with a unique, randomly generated key pair that is not bound to any personal information for use in cryptographic operations.

Meanwhile, European Union (EU) project SECURE investigated the design of security mechanisms for pervasive computing based on the human notion of trust. It addresses how entities in unfamiliar pervasive computing environments can overcome initial suspicion to provide secure collaboration (Cahill et al., 2003). Another EU project Trust4All aims to build up trustworthy middleware architecture in order to support easy and late integration of software from multiple suppliers and still have dependable and secure operations in the resulting system (Retrieved from https://nlsvr2.ehv.compus.philips.com/).

Requirements of trust for ad hoc networks. More dimensions are needed to secure the communications in wireless mobile ad hoc networks. Balakrishnan and Varadharajan (2005) demonstrated the issues that might creep out in the security design, when a cryptographic technique alone is involved. They also suggested how to counter those issues through the combination of trust management with cryptographic mechanisms. Moreover, they proposed the need to introduce the notion of heterogeneity resource management in the security design to address the divergence among the nodes, which can be taken advantage to diminish the packet drop attacks. To handle the dynamic nature of the medium, the authors proposed that the design of secure mobile ad hoc networks should envisage including trust management as another dimension apart from the cryptographic mechanisms. In addition, inclusion of trust management alone cannot guarantee secure communication due to some persisting issues such as packet dropping. Therefore, the resource should be also considered in order to provide a trustworthy system.

Trust Evaluation Mechanisms (Methodologies for Trust Decision)

Trust evaluation is a technical approach of representing trustworthiness for digital processing, in which the factors influencing trust will be evaluated by a continuous or discrete real number, referred to as a trust value. A trust evaluation mechanism aims to provide supporting information for the actual trust decision of an entity for managing trust. Embedding a trust evaluation mechanism is a necessity to provide trust intelligence in future computing devices.

The trust evaluation is the main aspect in the research for the purpose of digitalizing trust for computer processing. A number of theories about trust evaluation can be found in the literature. For example, Subjective Logic was introduced by Jøsang (2001). It can be chosen as trust representation, evaluation and update functions. The Subjective Logic has a mathematical foundation in dealing with evidential beliefs rooted in the Shafer's theory and the inherent ability to express uncertainty explicitly.

Figure 2. A simple fuzzy cognitive map

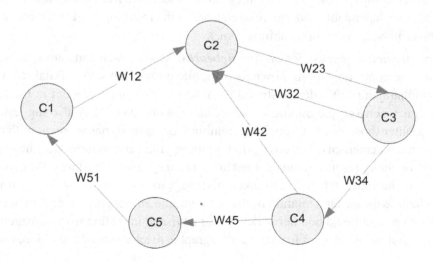

The trust valuation can be calculated as an instance of the opinion in the Subjective Logic. An entity can collect the opinions about other entities both explicitly via a recommendation protocol and implicitly via limited internal trust analysis using its own trust base. It is natural that the entity can perform an operation in which these individual opinions can be combined into a single opinion to allow relatively objective judgment about other entity's trustworthiness. It is desirable that such a combination operation shall be robust enough to tolerate situations where some of the recommenders may be wrong or dishonest. Other situation with respect to trust valuation combination includes combining the opinions of different entities on the same entity together; aggregation of an entity's opinion on two distinct entities together with logical AND support or with logical OR support. (The description and demo about the Subjective Logic can be retrieved from http://sky.fit.qut.edu. au/~josang/sl/demo/Op.html.)

But the Subjective Logic is a theory about opinion that can be used to represent trust. Its operators mainly support the operations between two opinions. It doesn't consider context support, such as time based decay, interaction times or frequency, and trust standard support like importance weights of different trust factors. Concretely, how to generate an opinion on a recommendation based on credibility and similarity and how to overcome attacks of trust evaluation are beyond the Subjective Logic theory. The solutions of these issues need to be further developed in practice.

Fuzzy Cognitive Maps (FCM) developed by Kosko (1986) could be regarded as a combination of Fuzzy Logic and Neural Networks. In a graphical illustration, the FCM seems to be a signed directed graph with feedback, consisting of nodes and weighted arcs. Nodes of the graph stand for the concepts that are used to describe the behavior of the system and they are connected by signed and weighted arcs representing the causal relationships that exist between the concepts, as depicted in Figure 2.

The FCM can be used for evaluating trust. In this case, the concept nodes are trustworthiness and factors that influence trust. The weighted arcs represent the impact of the trust influencing factors to the trustworthiness. These weighted arcs allow putting weight on the trust influencing factors. The FCM is convenient and practical for implementing and integrating trustworthiness and its influencing factors. In addition, Song et al. (2005) made use of fuzzy logic approach to develop an effective and efficient reputation system.

Theodorakopoulos and Baras (2006) introduced Semiring. It views the trust inference problem as a generalized shortest path problem on a weighted directed graph $G(V, E)$ (*trust graph*). The vertices V of the graph are the users/entities in the network. A weighted edge that belongs to E from vertex i to vertex j corresponds to the *opinion* that the trustor i has about the trustee j. The weight function is $l(i,j)$:

$V \times V \rightarrow S$, where S is the opinion space. Each opinion consists of two numbers: the *trust* value, and the *confidence* value. The former corresponds to the trustor's estimate of the trustee's trustworthiness. The confidence value corresponds to the accuracy of the trust value assignment. Since opinions with a high confidence value are more useful in making trust decisions, the confidence value is also referred to as the *quality or reliability* of the opinion. The space of opinions can be visualized as a rectangle (*ZERO_TRUST, MAX_TRUST*) × (*ZERO_CONF, MAX_CONF*) in the Cartesian plane. They don't treat distrust or negative confidence, but these could be accommodated by rescaling S.

A *Semiring* is an algebraic structure $(S, \oplus, \otimes)$, where S is a set, and $\oplus$, $\otimes$ are binary operators. $\oplus$, $\otimes$ are associative and $\oplus$ is commutative. $\oplus$ and $\otimes$ can be used to aggregate opinions along the paths from the trustor to the trustee together. Concretely, $\otimes$ is used to calculate the opinion along a path from the trustor to the trustee, while $\oplus$ is applied to compute the opinion as a function of all paths from the trustor to the trustee. Theodorakopoulos and Baras (2006) gave the formula of $\oplus$ and $\otimes$ regarding path Semiring and distance Semiring.

Sun et al. (2006) presented an information theoretic framework to quantitatively measure trust and model trust propagation in the ad hoc networks. In the proposed framework, trust is a measure of uncertainty with its value represented by entropy. The authors develop four Axioms that address the basic understanding of trust and the rules for trust propagation. Based on these axioms two trust models are introduced: entropy-based model and probability-based model, which satisfy all the axioms. Xiong and Liu (2004) introduced five trust parameters in PeerTrust. By formalizing these parameters, they presented a general trust metric that combines these parameters in a coherent scheme. This model can be applied into a decentralized P2P environment. It is effective against dynamic personality of peers and malicious behaviors of peers.

Digital Management of Trust

Issues, Controversies and Problems

The rapid evolution of the digital environment and emerging technologies creates a number of issues related to trust.

E-commerce. Electronic commerce and services are revolutionizing the way we conduct our personal and organizational business. And this trend will be extended to mobile domain. But it is very hard to build up a long-term trust relationship between all involved parties: manufactures, service providers, application providers, access providers and end users. Different legislation areas and distrust in the applicable legal frameworks of transaction partners make the creation of a trust foundation necessary for the electronic transaction quite challenging. This could be a major obstacle that retards the further development of e-commerce.

Hoffman, Novak, and Peralta (1999) pointed out that the reason more people have yet to shop online or even provide information to Web providers in exchange for access to information is the fundamental lack of faith between most businesses and consumers on the Web. Almost 95 percent of Web users have declined to provide personal information to Web sites when asked because they are not clear how the personal data will be used and they feel there is no way for them to control over secondary use of their personal information (Hoffman et al., 1999). In addition, differently from traditional commerce, uncertainty about product quality, that is, information asymmetry is always a problem for consumers in an online environment (Ba & Pavlou, 2002). Lack of consumer trust is a critical impediment to the success of e-commerce. Ultimately, the most effective way for commercial Web providers to develop profitable exchange relationships with online customers is to earn their trust. Trust thus becomes a vital factor influencing the final success of e-commerce.

Digital distributed networking and communications. On the other hand, new networking is raising with the fast development of Mobile Ad hoc Networks (MANET) and local wireless communication technologies. Boundaries between traditional computers, laptops, mobile phones, Personal Digital Assistants (PDA), and consumer electronics devices dissolve. It is more convenient for mobile users to communicate in their proximity to exchange digital information in various circumstances. However, the special characteristics of the new networking paradigms (e.g., dynamically changed topology) introduce additional challenges on security. The ad hoc networks are generally more prone to physical security threats than conventional networks, due to their lack of any security infrastructure support. Security approaches used for fixed networks are not feasible due to the salient characteristics of the ad hoc networks. The root of the threats is originated from the lack of trust among network nodes.

In addition, new P2P computing technology has emerged as a significant paradigm for providing distributed services, in particular collaboration for content sharing and distributed computing. Generally, a P2P system consists of a decentralized and self-organizing network of autonomous devices that interact as peers. Each peer acts as both client and server to share its resources with other peers. However, this computing paradigm suffers from several drawbacks that obstruct its wide adoption.

Lack of trust between peers is one of the most serious issues, which causes security challenges in the P2P systems. Building up trust collaboration among the system peers is a key issue to overcome, especially in the mobile environment.

GRID computing systems have attracted research communities in recent years. This is due to the unique ability of marshalling collections of heterogeneous computers and resources, enabling easy access to diverse resources and services that could not be possible without a GRID model. The context of GRID computing does introduce its own set of security challenges, as user(s) and resource provider(s) can come from mutually distrusted administrative domains and either participant can behave maliciously.

User-device or user-system interaction. Most current digital systems are designed based on the assumptions that the user trusts his/her device fully; or the user has to trust a service provider. Generally, the current systems are not designed to be configured by user with regard to their trust preferences. As can be seen from the above study, trust evaluation based management technology has been proposed to overcome the challenge of trust and security in distributed systems and Internet e-commerce. However, the human-machine interaction in order to support trust management, especially in mobile domain, has still many open research questions. Embedding personal criteria of trust regarding different events into the device or system requires interaction between the end user and his/her devices. This would require friendly user interface for the device to collect useful information for trust evaluation and present the evaluation results in a comprehensive manner to the user. It also provides a technical challenge to design an effective trust management system that is light weight with regard to memory management, process observation and data mining.

Privacy support. User data privacy is hard to control once the personal data is released into digital format. New customized services require detailed user information like location, preferences or general behavior profiles. People expect such a privacy control service that only trusted parties can get specified personal information. The user-friendly administration of this control is a tough challenge especially for the mobile systems with a limited user interface even through taking into account the latest privacy visualization approaches for the mobile environment (Hjelm & Holtmanns, 2006).

How to solve these issues described above depends on better understanding of trust, trust modeling and management technologies.

Solutions and Recommendations

Solutions for the trust issues of e-commerce. Trust management is introduced to evaluate trust for reduced risk. Tan and Thoen (1998) specified a generic model of transaction trust for e-commerce as party trust supplemented with control trust. It provides a generic model of transaction trust for e-commerce. This model is based on separating the mostly subjective party trust and mostly objective control trust. The transaction trust consists of the sum of the party trust and the control trust. If the level of the transaction trust is not sufficient, then the party trust should be possibly complemented by the control trust in order to reach a required level. This theory was further developed to build up online trust between trading parties in a first trade situation through a trust matrix model.

Manchala (2000) described metrics and models for the measurement of trust variables and fuzzy verification of transactions. The trust metrics help preserve system availability by determining risk on transactions. Several variables (such as cost of transaction, transaction history, customer loyalty, indemnity, spending pattern, and system specific) on which trust depends are used to define trust. These variables in turn influence actions taken by a transacting entity (e.g., verification, security level decision, and authorization). Certain parameters, such as time and location, modify trust actions. In addition, Manchala pointed out that the existing e-commerce protocols have not been equipped with mechanisms to protect a vendor from a customer who makes a fraudulent payment or a customer from a vendor who supplies low quality or garbage goods. In other words, these protocols need to be equipped with suitable trust mechanisms and they should be strengthened by adding a non-reputable context to the transaction protocol. In an e-commerce transaction, mutual trust should exist between a vendor and a customer with several intermediaries involved in the transaction. In practical scenarios, eBay, for example, offers a safeguard service, that ensures the payment and the satisfactory delivery of the goods, but this service is not without costs.

The game theory-based research lays the foundation for online reputation systems research and provides interesting insight into the complex behavioral dynamics. Most of the game theoretic models assume that stage game outcomes are publicly observed. Online feedback mechanisms, in contrast, rely on private (pair-wise) and subjective ratings of stage game outcomes. Dellarocas (2003) introduced two important considerations, the incentive for providing feedback and the credibility or the truthfulness of the feedback.

Khare and Rifkin (1998) presented pragmatic details of Web-based trust management technology for identifying principals, labeling resources, and enforcing policies.

It sketched how trust management might be integrated into Web applications for document authoring and distribution, content filtering, and mobile code security. By measuring today's Web protocols, servers, and clients, the authors called for stakeholders' support in bringing automatable trust management to the Web.

The reputation systems play an important role to evaluate the trustworthiness of transaction parties. A number of reputation systems and mechanisms were proposed for online environments and agent systems. Pujol, Sanguesa, and Delgado (2002) applied network flow techniques and proposed a generalized algorithm that extracts the reputation in a general class of social networks. Jøsang and Ismail (2002) and Jøsang and Tran (2003) developed and evaluated the beta reputation system for electronic markets by modeling reputation as posterior probability given a sequence of experiences. Among other things, they showed that a market with limited duration rather than infinite longevity of transaction feedback provides the best condition. Sabater and Sierra (2002) proposed the Regret system and showed how social network analysis can be used in the reputation system. Sen and Sajja (2002) proposed a word-of-mouth reputation algorithm to select service providers. Their focus was on allowing querying agent to select one of the high-performance service providers with a minimum probabilistic guarantee. Yu and Singh (2000) developed an approach for social reputation management and their model combines agents' belief ratings using combination schemes similar to certainty factors. The reputation ratings are propagated through neighbors. Zacharia and Maes (2000) proposed an approach that is an approximation of game-theoretic models and studied the effects of feedback mechanisms on markets with dynamic pricing using simulation modeling.

A few proposals specifically attempted to address the issue of quality or credibility of the feedback. Chen and Singh (2001) differentiated the ratings by the reputation of raters that is computed based the majority opinions of the rating. Adversaries who submit dishonest feedback can still gain a good reputation as a rater in a method simply by submitting a large amount of feedback and becoming the majority opinion. Dellarocas (2000) proposed mechanisms to combat two types of cheating behaviors when submitting feedbacks. The basic idea is to detect and filter out the feedbacks in certain scenarios using cluster-filtering techniques. The technique can be applied into feedback-based reputation systems to filter out the suspicious "fake" ratings before an actual aggregation. Miller, Resnick, and Zeckhauser (2002) proposed a mechanism, based on budget balanced payments in exchange for feedbacks, which provides strict incentives for all agents to tell the truth. This provides yet another approach to the problem of feedback trustworthiness. However, such a mechanism is vulnerable to malicious collusion. The development of effective mechanisms for dealing with collusive manipulations of online reputations systems is currently an active area of research.

On the other side, Salam, Iyer, Palvia, and Singh (2005) explored a framework to highlight the importance of nurturing consumer trust in the context of e-commerce. In particular, the authors pointed that the technical approaches to establish credibility and integrity are necessary but not sufficient for creating the long-term trusting relationships between consumers and online businesses. Web vendors must align both their long-term and short-term relationships with consumers and develop interventions to inspire consumer beliefs that affect their attitudes, intentions, and dependence, and ultimately their willingness to spend money. The Web vendors must address the factors affecting different belief classes to establish the trustworthiness of their organizations. They need a long-term approach to manage trust and generate a positive consumer experience from each and every Internet transaction. Quite a number of studies attempted to seek trust building factors and their relationships in order to propose guidelines or policies for designing a trustworthy e-commerce solution, for example, Jones, Wilikens, Morris, and Masera (2000); Rutter (2001); McKnight et al. (2002); Li et al. (2004); Gefen (2000); Pennington, Wilcox, and Grover (2004); Bhattacherjee (2002); and Pavlou and Gefen (2004). As we can see from the above, technologies and policies are in parallel influencing and enhancing trust management.

Solutions for distributed systems. Trust modeling and management can be applied to enhance security, dependability and other quality attributes of a system or a system entity. Main usage of trust management can be summarized below:

- Detecting malicious entity in a system;
- Helping in decision making in system processing;
- Selecting the best entity from a number of candidates, for example, selecting the best route node or the best path in MANET;
- Benefiting on system optimization. For example, if an entity is trusted, some procedures can be saved, which could benefit the efficiency of a system.
- Improving Quality of Services through applying trust management technology in a system.

So far, the trust evaluation and management technology have been studied and developed in many areas, such as distributed systems: P2P, Ad hoc, GRID, e-commerce, Web services, and software engineering. For example, P2P library, resource management in GRID, security enhancement in GRID computing, trusted Ad hoc routing and component software system configurations. We have introduced many of them in Section 2.3.

Tajeddine, Kayssi, Chehab, and Artail (2005) proposed a comprehensive reputation based trust model for distributed system. This approach requires that a host asks about the reputation of a target host that it wants to interact with. It calculates a reputation value based on its previous experiences and the gathered reputation values from other hosts, and then it decides whether to interact with the target host or not. The initiator also evaluates the credibility of hosts providing reputation values by estimating the similarity, the activity, the popularity, and the cooperation of the queried host. Moreover, each host uses different dynamic decay factors that depend on the consistency of the interaction results of a certain host.

Common opinions can be summarized based on the literature study. For a distributed system, trust modeling and evaluation can be used for improving system security and reliability. The trust of a trustor on a trustee is based on the trustor's past experience in the same or similar context, and recommendations or reputations generated from the experiences of other system entities. The contributions of the recommendations and the trustor's experiences to the trust value calculation are influenced by their age or time. The recommendations' contribution is also influenced by such factors as the trustor's opinion on the recommenders, distance (e.g., hops between the trustor and the recommender in ad hoc networks), and so on. Taking some detailed examples of policies for trust evaluation:

- Trust value is no bigger than trust value generated by trustor's experiences or recommendations;
- Latest information from experiences and recommendations will contribute more the calculation of trust value.

Furthermore, we summarize the factors considered in trust modeling:

- Recommendations, reputations, feedback from other entities (based on their experiences)
- Personal or local experience and its influencing factor (e.g. the time of the experience)
- Trust (credibility) on recommendations/reputations of the trustor
- Context factors (e.g. time, distance, transaction context, community context)
- Policy factors, i.e. the trustor's standards with regard to trust (e.g. accepted level of recommendations)

The above factors are generally aggregated through weighting. The weighting has some dependencies, for example, similarity, activity, popularity, and cooperation of a certain entity.

However, most modeling aims to support trust evaluation for decision making. Little considers trust control or management, for example, how to maintain trust for a period of time based on the evaluation. Trust management is more than trust evaluation, especially in an open computing platform, where autonomic trust management is becoming an important research topic.

Solutions for user-device or user-system interaction. A number of trusted computing projects have been conducted in the literature and industry. For example, Trusted Computing Group (TCG) defines and promotes open standards for hardware-enabled trusted computing and security technologies, including hardware building blocks and software interfaces, across multiple platforms, peripherals, and devices. TCG specified technology enables more secure computing environments without compromising functional integrity, privacy, or individual rights. It aims to build up a trusted computing device on the basis of a secure hardware chip—Trusted Platform Module (TPM). In short, the TPM is the hardware that controls the boot-up process. Every time the computer is reset, the TPM steps in, verifies the Operating System (OS) loader before letting boot-up continue. The OS loader is assumed to verify the Operating System. The OS is then assumed to verify every bit of software that it can find in the computer, and so on. The TPM allow all hardware and software components to check whether they have woken up in trusted states. If not, they should refuse to work. It also provides a secure storage for confidential information. In addition, it is possible for the computer user to select whether to boot his/her machine in a trusted computing mode or in a legacy mode.

eBay, Amazon, and other famous Internet services show the recommendation level of sellers and products based on the feedback accumulated. Credence employs a simple, network-wide voting scheme where users can contribute positive and negative evaluations of files. On top of this, a client uses statistical tests to weight the importance of votes from other peers. And finally, Credence allows clients to extend the horizon of information by selectively sharing information with other peers.

In order to design a trustworthy system, a number of user studies provide results on how to design a trustworthy user interfaces, especially for the recommendation systems. For example, Herlocker, Konstan, and Riedl (2000) studied explanation's aid on user trust regarding Automated Collaborative Filtering (ACF)—a technological recommendation approach based on the similarity of interest). It addressed explanation interfaces for the ACF systems—*how* they should be implemented and *why* they should be implemented. It presented that experimental evidence shows that providing explanations can improve the acceptance of the ACF systems.

As we have discussed, trust is a subjective topic. A system is trusted if and only if its users trust it. But little work practiced to formalize user-device or user-system interaction in order to extract the user's standards, as well as adaptively provide information about trust status to the user, particularly if the device is portable with a limited screen.

Privacy support. Trust modeling and management can not only enhance security, but also support privacy. The term *privacy* denotes the ability of an entity to determine whether, when, and to whom information is to be released. With the trust modeling and evaluation, it is helpful to determine above "whether," "when," and "to whom." However, it lacks discussion on how to enhance privacy through trust management in the literature.

Limitations and Further Discussion

Trust modeling and management remain an active research area in recent years. Trust is today's fashion in security (Gollmann, 2007). However, many interesting research issues are yet to be fully explored. We summarize some of them for interested readers.

As discussed above, it lacks a widely accepted trust definition across multiple related disciplines. This could cause a comprehensive trust model missing in the literature. Perhaps it is impossible to have such a model that can be applied in various situations and systems. Diverse definitions could make normal people confused. This would make it hard for them to understand a trust management solution.

Secondly, it lacks general criteria to assess the effectiveness of a trust model and a trust management solution in the literature. Why is a trust model trustworthy? Why and how is a trust management system effective? Most of the existing work overlooked these issues and missed discussions about them. In addition, new attacks or malicious behaviors could also destroy a trust management system. Current prove is still based on empirical and experimental study.

Thirdly, the literature lacks discussions on the competence of trust management. That is when and in which situation trust is possibly or impossibly managed. This is a very interesting and important issue worth our attention, especially for autonomic trust management.

Finally, from the practical point of view, some important issues such as trust/reputation value storage (Li & Singhal, 2007), usability of a trust management system, what is the proper settings of a user's policies for trust decision, and how to extract these policies in a user-friendly way need further exploration.

Future Trends

Herein, we provide insights about future and emerging trends on trust modeling and management.

An Integrated "Soft Trust" and "Hard Trust" Solution

Theoretically, there are two basic approaches for building up a trust relationship. We name them "soft trust" solutions and "hard trust" solutions. The "soft trust" solution provides trust based on trust evaluation according to subjective trust standards, facts from previous experiences and history. The "hard trust" solution builds up the trust through structural and objective regulations, standards, as well as widely accepted rules, mechanisms and sound technologies. Possibly, both approaches are applied in a real system. They can cooperate and support with each other to provide a trust-worthy system. The "hard trust" provides a guarantee for the "soft trust" solution to ensure the integrity of its functionality. The "soft trust" can provide a guideline to determine which "hard trust" mechanisms should be applied and at which moment. It provides intelligence for selecting a suitable "hard trust" solution.

An integrated solution is expected to provide a trust management framework that applies both the "hard trust" solution and the "soft trust" solution. This framework should support data collection and management for trust evaluation, trust standards extraction from the trustor (e.g., a system or device user), and experience or evidence dissemination inside and outside the system, as well as a decision engine to provide guidelines for applying effective "hard trust" mechanisms for trust management purposes.

In addition, how to store, propagate and collect information for trust evaluation and management is seldom considered in the existing theoretical work, but is a relevant issue for deployment. Human-device interaction is also crucial to transmit a user's trust standards to the device and the device needs to provide its assessment on trust to its user. These factors influence the final success of trust management.

Autonomic Trust Management

There is a trend that all the processing for trust management is becoming autonomic. This is benefited from the digitalization of trust model. Since trust relationship is dynamically changed, this requires the trust management should be context-aware and intelligent to handle the context changes. Obviously, it does not suffice to require the trustor (e.g., most possibly a digital system user) to make a lot of trust related decisions because that would destroy any attempt at user friendliness. For example, the user may not be informed enough to make correct decisions. Thus, establishing trust is quite a complex task with many optional actions to take. Rather trust should be managed automatically following a high level policy established by the trustor. We call such trust management autonomic. Autonomic trust management automatically processes evidence collection, trust evaluation, and trust (re-)establishment and control. We need a proper mechanism to support autonomic trust management not only on trust establishment, but also on trust sustaining. In addition, the trust model itself should be adaptively adjusted in order to match and reflect real system situation. Context-aware trust management and adaptive trust model optimization for autonomic trust management are developing research topics (Campadello, Coutand, Del Rosso, Holtmanns, Kanter, Räck, Mrohs, & Steglich, 2005; Yan & Prehofer, 2007).

Cross-Domain Benefit

We can estimate that trust management will not only benefit security, but also other properties of the system, such as privacy, usability, dependability and Quality of Services. Combining trust management with other management tasks (e.g., resource management, power management, identity management, risk management and fault management) or applying it into other areas could produce cross-domain benefits. The outcome system will be a more intelligent system to help users managing their increasing amount of digital trust relationships, while providing also good performance.

Conclusion

This chapter firstly introduced the perception of trust in the literature. Based on the various definitions of trust, we summarized the factors influencing trust and the characteristics of trust. The trust modeling for digital processing is actually based on the understanding of trust, the influencing factors of trust and its characteristics. From a social concept, trust has become a digital object that can be processed. The research on trust modeling, trust evaluation and trust management that have been conducted in the area of distributed systems and e-commerce was presented. The latest trust management systems model trust using mathematical approaches. Thus, it is possible to conduct digital trust management for the emerging technologies.

Current research on trust modeling mostly focuses on the theoretic study based on empirical and experimental results. It lacks experiences in practice. Most of existing deployed solutions are special system driven. The support of a generic solution for trust management, which also benefits other system properties, is usually not considered. In addition, the user-device interaction with regard to trust management is a topic that needs further study. There are still many interesting research issues requiring full investigation.

Regarding the future trends, we believe an integrated solution is very promising that combines traditional security solution with newly developed trust evaluation based management together. This integrated solution should handle trust management in an automatic way and cooperate with other technologies to offer a better system performance.

References

Aberer, K., & Despotovic, Z. (2001). Managing trust in a peer-to-peer information system. *Proceedings of the ACM Conference on Information and Knowledge Management (CIKM)*, USA, 310–317.

Abdul-Rahman, A., & Hailes, S. (2000). Supporting trust in virtual communities. *Proceedings of the 33rd Hawaii International Conference on System Sciences*, 6007.

Avizienis, A., Laprie, J. C., Randell, B., & Landwehr, C. (2004). Basic concepts and taxonomy of dependable and secure computing. IEEE Transactions on Dependable and Secure Computing, 1(1), 11–33.

Azzedin, F., & Muthucumaru, M. (2004). A trust brokering system and its application to resource management in public-resource grids. Proceedings of the 18th International Symposium on Parallel and Distributed Processing, April, 22.

Ba, S., & Pavlou. P. A. (2002). Evidence of the effects of trust building technology in electronic markets: Price premiums and buyer behavior. *MIS Quarterly, 26*(3), 243–268.

Ba, S., Whinston, A., & Zhang, H. (1999). Building trust in the electronic market through an economic incentive mechanism. *Proceedings of the International Conference on Information Systems*, 208–213.

Balakrishnan, V., & Varadharajan, V. (2005). Designing secure wireless mobile ad hoc networks. Proceedings of the 19th International Conference on Advanced Information Networking and Applications (AINA 2005), March, Vol. 2, 5–8.

Bhattacherjee, A. (2002). Individual trust in online firms: scale development and initial test. *Journal of Management Information Systems, 19*(1), 211–241.

Blaze, M., Feigenbaum, J., & Lacy, J. (1996). Decentralized trust management. *Proceedings of IEEE Symposium on Security and Privacy*, May, 164–173.

Boon, S., & Holmes, J. (1991). The dynamics of interpersonal trust: Resolving uncertainty in the face of risk. In R. Hinde & J. Groebel (Eds.), *Cooperation and prosocial behavior*, pp. 190-211. Cambridge, UK: Cambridge University Press.

Buchegger, S., & Le Boudec, J. Y. (2004). A robust reputation system for P2P and mobile ad-hoc networks. *Proceedings of the 2nd Workshop Economics of Peer-to-Peer Systems.*

Cahill, V. et al. (2003). Using trust for secure collaboration in uncertain environments. IEEE Pervasive Computing, 2(3), 52–61.

Campadello, S., Coutand, O., Del Rosso, C., Holtmanns, S., Kanter, T., Räck, C., Mrohs, B., & Steglich, S. (2005). Trust and privacy in context-aware support for communication in mobile groups. *Proceedings of Context Awareness for Proactive Systems (CAPS) 2005,* Helsinki, Finland.

Chen, M., & Singh, J. P. (2001). Computing and using reputations for internet ratings. *Proceedings of 3rd ACM Conference on Electronic Commerce.*

Corritore, C. L., Kracher, B., & Wiedenbeck, S. (2003). Online trust: Concepts, evolving themes, a model. *International Journal of Human-Computer Studies, Trust and Technology, 58*(6), 737–758.

Dellarocas, C. (2000). Immunizing online reputation reporting systems against unfair ratings and discriminatory behavior. *Proceedings of the 2nd ACM Conference on Electronic Commerce.*

Dellarocas, C. (2003). The digitization of word-of-mouth: promise and challenges of online reputation mechanism. *Management Science, 49*(10), 1407-1424.

Denning, DE. (1993). A new paradigm for trusted systems. *Proceedings of the IEEE New Paradigms Workshop.*

Fishbein, M., & Ajzen, I. (1975). *Beliefs, attitude, intention, and behavior: An introduction to theory and research.* Addison-Wesley, Reading, MA.

Gambetta, D. (1990). *Can we trust Trust? Trust: Making and breaking cooperative relations.* Oxford: Basil Blackwell.

Ganeriwal, S., & Srivastava, M. B. (2004). Reputation-based framework for high integrity sensor networks. *Proceedings of the ACM Security for Ad-Hoc and Sensor Networks*, pp. 66–67.

Gefen, D. (2000). E-commerce: The role of familiarity and trust. *Omega 28*(6), 725–737.

Gil, Y., & Ratnakar, V. (2002). Trusting information sources one citizen at a time. *Proceedings of the 1st International Semantic Web Conference,* Italy, June.

Gollmann, D. (2007). Why trust is bad for security. Retrieved May 2007, from http://www.sics.se/policy2005/Policy_Pres1/dg-policy-trust.ppt

Grandison, T., & Sloman, M. (2000). A survey of trust in Internet applications. *IEEE Communications and Survey, 4th Quarter, 3*(4), 2–16.

Guha, R., & Kumar, R. (2004). Propagation of trust and distrust. *Proceedings of the 13th international conference on World Wide Web*, ACM Press, pp. 403–412.

Herlocker, J. L., Konstan, J. A., & Riedl, J. (2000). Explaining collaborative filtering recommendations. *Proceedings of the 2000 ACM conference on Computer supported cooperative work.*

Hjelm, J., & Holtmanns, S. (2006). Privacy and trust visualization. Computer Human Interaction - CHI 2006 Conference Proceedings and Extended Abstracts, ACM Press, Montréal, Canada.

Hoffman, D. L., Novak, T. P., & Peralta, M. (1999). Building consumer trust online. *Communications of the ACM, 42*(4), 80–87.

Jones, S., Wilikens, M., Morris, P., & Masera, M. (2000). Trust requirements in e-business - A conceptual framework for understanding the needs and concerns of different stakeholders. *Communications of the ACM, 43*(12), 80–87.

Jøsang, A., & Ismail, R. (2002). The beta reputation system. *Proceedings of the 15th Bled Electronic Commerce Conference*, June.

Jøsang, A. (1999). An algebra for assessing trust in certification chains. *Proceedings of the Networking Distributed System Security Symposium.*

Jøsang, A. (2001). A logic for uncertain probabilities. *International Journal of Uncertainty, Fuzziness and Knowledge-Based Systems, 9*(3), 279–311.

Jøsang, A., & Tran, N. (2003). Simulating the effect of reputation systems on e-markets. *Proceedings of the First International Conference on Trust Management.*

Kamvar, S. D., Schlosser, M. T., & Garcia-Molina, H. (2003). The EigenTrust algorithm for reputation management in P2P networks. *Proceedings of the 12th International World Wide Web Conference.*

Kosko, B. (1986). Fuzzy cognitive maps. *International Journal Man-Machine Studies, 24*, 65–75.

Khare, R., & Rifkin, A. (1998). Trust management on the World Wide Web. *First Monday 3*(6).

Li, H., & Singhal, M. (2007). Trust management in distributed systems. Computer, 40(2), 45–53.

Li, X., Valacich, J. S., & Hess, T. J. (2004). Predicting user trust in information systems: a comparison of competing trust models. Proceedings of the 37th Annual Hawaii International Conference on System Sciences,.

Liang, Z., & Shi, W. (2005). PET: a PErsonalized Trust model with reputation and risk evaluation for P2P resource sharing. Proceedings of the 38th Annual Hawaii International Conference on System Sciences, January, pp. 201b–201b.

Liu, Z., Joy, A. W., & Thompson, R. A. (2004). A dynamic trust model for mobile ad hoc networks. Proceedings of the 10th IEEE International Workshop on Future Trends of Distributed Computing Systems (FTDCS 2004), May, pp. 80–85.

Lee, S., Sherwood, R., & Bhattacharjee, B. (2003). Cooperative peer groups in NICE. *Proceedings of the IEEE Conf. Computer Comm. (INFOCOM 03)*, IEEE CS Press, pp. 1272–1282.

Lin, C., Varadharajan, V., Wang, Y., & Pruthi, V. (2004). Enhancing GRID security with trust management. Proceedings of the IEEE International Conference on Services Computing (SCC 2004), pp. 303–310.

Manchala, D.W. (2000). E-commerce trust metrics and models. *IEEE Internet Computing, 4*(2), 36-44.

Marsh, S. (1994). *Formalising trust as a computational concept*. (Doctoral dissertation, University of Stirling, 1994).

Maurer, U. (1996). Modeling a public-key infrastructure. *Proceedings of the European Symposium of Research on Computer Security, LNCS,* Vol. 1146, pp. 325–350.

McKnight, D. H., & Chervany, N. L. (2000). What is Trust? a conceptual analysis and an interdisciplinary model. *Proceedings of the 2000 Americas Conference on Information Systems (AMCI2000). AIS,* August, Long Beach, CA.

McKnight, D. H., Choudhury, V. & Kacmar, C. (2002). Developing and validating trust measures for e-commerce: An integrative typology. *Information Systems Research, 13*(3), 334-359.

McKnight, D. H., & Chervany, N. L. (2003). The meanings of trust. UMN university report. Retrieved December 2006, from http://misrc.umn.edu/wpaper/WorkingPapers/9604.pdf

Mayer, R. C., Davis, J. H., & Schoorman, F. D. (1995). An integrative model of organizational trust. *Academy of Management Review, 20*(3), 709–734.

Miller, N. H., Resnick, P., & Zeckhauser, R. J. (2002). *Eliciting honest feedback in electronic markets.* KSG Working Paper Series RWP02-039.

Mui, L. (2003). *Computational models of trust and reputation: agents, evolutionary games, and social networks.* Doctoral dissertation, Massachusetts Institute of Technology.

Pavlou, P. & Gefen, D. (2004). Building effective online marketplaces with institution-based trust. *Information Systems Research, 15*(1), 37–59.

Pennington, R., Wilcox, H. D. & Grover, V. (2004). The role of system trust in business-to-consumer transactions. *Journal of Management Information Systems, 20*(3), 197–226.

Perlman, R. (1999). An overview of PKI trust models. *IEEE Network, 13*(6), 38–43.

Pujol, J. M., Sanguesa, R. & Delgado, J. (2002). Extracting reputation in multi-agent systems by means of social network topology. *Proceedings of the First International Joint Conf. Autonomous Agents and Multiagent Systems.*

Reiter, M. K., & Stubblebine, S. G. (1998). Resilient authentication using path independence. *IEEE Transactions on Computer, 47*(12), 1351–1362.

Resnick, P., & Zeckhauser, R. (2002). Trust among strangers in Internet transactions: Empirical analysis of eBay's reputation system. In M. Baye, (Ed.), *Advances in applied microeconomics: The economics of the Internet and e-commerce, 11,* 127–157.

Rousseau, D. M., Sitkin, S. B., Burt, R. S., & Camerer, C. (1998). Not so different after all: A cross-discipline view of trust. *Academy of Management Review, 23*(3), 393–404.

Rutter, J. (2001). From the sociology of trust towards a sociology of "e-trust". *International Journal of New Product Development & Innovation Management, 2*(4), 371–385.

Sabater, J., & Sierra, C. (2002). Reputation and social network analysis in multi-agent systems. *Proceedings of the First International Joint Conference on Autonomous Agents and Multiagent Systems.*

Salam, A. F., Iyer, L., Palvia, P, & Singh, R. (2005). Trust in e-commerce. *Communications of the ACM, 48*(2), 73–77.

Sarkio, K., & Holtmanns, S. (2007). Tailored trustworthiness estimations in peer to peer networks. To appear in International Journal of Internet Technology and Secured Transactions IJITST, Inderscience.

Sen, S., & Sajja, N. (2002). Robustness of reputation-based trust: Boolean case. *Proceedings of the First International Joint Conference on Autonomous Agents and Multiagent Systems.*

Singh, A., & Liu, L. (2003). TrustMe: Anonymous management of trust relationships in decentralized P2P systems. *Proceedings of the IEEE International Conference on Peer-to-Peer Computing,* pp. 142–149.

Song, S., Hwang, K., Zhou, R., & Kwok, Y. K. (2005). Trusted P2P transactions with fuzzy reputation aggregation. IEEE Internet Computing, 9(6), 24–34.

Sun, Y., Yu, W., Han, Z., & Liu, K. J. R. (2006). Information theoretic framework of trust modeling and evaluation for ad hoc networks. IEEE Journal on Selected Area in Communications, 24(2), 305–317.

Tan, Y. & Thoen, W. (1998). Toward a generic model of trust for electronic commerce. *International Journal of Electronic Commerce, 5*(2), 61–74.

TCG, Trusted Computing Group, Trusted Platform Module - TPM Specification v1.2, 2003. Retrieved May, 2006, from https://www.trustedcomputinggroup.org/specs/TPM/

Theodorakopoulos, G., & Baras, J.S. (2006). On trust models and trust evaluation metrics for ad hoc networks. IEEE Journal on Selected Areas in Communications, 24(2), 318–328.

Tajeddine, A., Kayssi, A., Chehab, A., & Artail, H. (2005, September). A comprehensive reputation-based trust model for distributed systems. Proceedings of the Workshop of the 1st International Conference on Security and Privacy for Emerging Areas in Communication Networks, pp. 118–127.

Wang, Y., & Varadharajan, V. (2005). Trust2: developing trust in peer-to-peer environments. Proceedings of the IEEE International Conference on Services Computing, Vol.1, July, pp. 24–31.

Guo, W., Xiong, Z., & Li, Z. (2005). Dynamic trust evaluation based routing model for ad hoc networks. Proceedings of International Conference on Wireless Communications, Networking and Mobile Computing, Vol. 2, September, pp. 727–730.

Xiong, L., & Liu, L. (2004). PeerTrust: Supporting reputation-based trust for peer-to-peer electronic communities. IEEE Transactions on Knowledge and Data Engineering, 16(7), 843–857.

Yan, Z., & MacLaverty, R. (2006). Autonomic trust management in a component based software system. *Proceedings of 3rd International Conference on Autonomic and Trusted Computing (ATC06), LNCS,* Vol. 4158, September, pp. 279–292.

Yan, Z., & Prehofer, C. (2007). An adaptive trust control model for a trustworthy software component platform. *Proceedings of the 4th International Conference on Autonomic and Trusted Computing (ATC2007), LNCS,* Vol. 4610, pp. 226-238.

Yan, Z. (2006). A conceptual architecture of a trusted mobile environment. *Proceedings of IEEE SecPerU06*, France, pp. 75–81.

Yan, Z., Zhang, P., & Virtanen, T. (2003). Trust evaluation based security solution in ad hoc networks. *Proceedings of the Seventh Nordic Workshop on Secure IT Systems (NordSec03)*, Norway.

Yu, B., & Singh, M.P. (2000). A social mechanism of reputation management in electronic communities. *Proceedings of the Seventh International Conference on Cooperative Information Agents.*

Zacharia, G., & Maes, P. (2000). Trust management through reputation mechanisms. *Applied Artificial Intelligence, 14*(8), 881-908.

Zhou, M., Mei, H., & Zhang, L. (2005). A multi-property trust model for reconfig-
uring component software. Proceedings of the Fifth International Conference
on Quality Software QAIC2005, September, pp. 142–149.

Zhang, Z., Wang, X., & Wang, Y. (2005). A P2P global trust model based on recommendation. *Proceedings of the 2005 International Conference on Machine
Learning and Cybernetics,* Vol. 7, August, pp. 3975–3980.

Chapter XIV

Security, Privacy, and Politics in Higher Education

Dan Manson, California State Polytechnic University, USA

Abstract

This chapter introduces the interrelationships of security, privacy and politics in higher education. University curriculum politics are ingrained through organizational structures that control faculty hiring, retention, tenure, and promotion, and self-governance policy bodies such as academic senates and faculty curriculum committees that control curriculum approval and implementation. Compounding the politics of curriculum are different constructs of security and privacy, with security viewed as a technical issue versus privacy as a legal and organizational issue. The author believes that multiple disciplines must learn to work together to teach the constantly changing technical, scientific, legal, and administrative security and privacy landscape. While university "ownership" of security and privacy curriculum may create new political challenges, it has the potential to help limit competing faculty, department and program politics.

Introduction

Since the first Internet worm was launched in 1988 by a Cornell graduate computer science student, higher education academics and administrators have struggled to address computer security and privacy issues while teaching and using information technology. In 1989, the American Council of Education (ACE) noted that universities "have an unusual concentration of people with computer expertise and the freedom and incentive to explore frontier technologies" (Elliott, 1988). Since then, the use of Internet-enabled technology in academia has increased exponentially, in fact "economic growth has been dominated by investments in information technology and higher education" (Jorgenson, 2003).

Reflecting societal and industry needs, information technology continues to be ingrained into the fabric of higher education. Internet access, electronic mail, and personal computing devices have become "mission critical" to university administrators, faculty, staff, and students. At the same time, there are growing academic concerns over internal and external compromise of computing resources and exposures of sensitive and confidential information, and industry needs for graduates that can address these issues in government and industry.

These concerns and needs raise the following question. What are the political issues that universities face in improving security and privacy on the campus and in the curriculum? It is the perspective of this chapter that the politics of security and privacy issues in higher education revolve around the following areas:

- **Technology:** The pervasive use of computer and Internet technology used in higher education today.
- **Policy:** The development, implementation and enforcement of security and privacy policies in higher education.
- **External environment:** The growth of security incidents in higher education, application of security and privacy legislation to higher education, development of government and academic accreditation of information assurance programs, and need for graduates with knowledge of computer security and privacy domains.
- **Curriculum:** The growth of security curriculum in higher education, and corresponding political and other factors involved in higher education developing, implementing and teaching information assurance curriculum.
- **Synergy:** The opportunities in combining academic and administrative resources in creating a higher education environment that supports teaching and practicing of computer security and privacy.

The objectives of this chapter involve a discussion of the above issues, the politics of higher education, and how an interdisciplinary approach may assist in reconciling related security, privacy and political issues and support a coherent cohesive set of offerings across the curriculum.

Background

There is a fundamental difference between security and privacy. Security involves freedom from risk, which can be defined as "the possibility that a threat is capable of exploiting a known weakness" (Schou, 2007). Privacy involves freedom from unwanted intrusion, better known as confidentiality, the "need to restrict access to information or data" (Schou, 2007). Security involves control of infrastructure. Privacy involves control of personal information. Security is usually viewed as a technical issue, privacy as a legal and organizational issue. As Table 1 shows, the constructs of security vs. privacy involve different goals.

In curriculum, security may be considered more within the domains of Computer Science and Engineering. Privacy may be viewed more within the domains of Business, Management, and Law. For example, a course covering operating systems security is primarily technical and would likely be taught by Computer Science, while a course on information systems policy centers around legal and administrative issues would more likely be taught by Business. There are opportunities for crossover between these areas. One example is computer forensics, which has significant technical, scientific, legal, and business components. However, if computer forensics is taught in computer science without input from law and business, the legal and business components may not be emphasized. Another example is Web development, which has security, design, programming, and database components. Again, a Web development course in business may not provide enough emphasis on security in UNIX

Table 1. Security vs. privacy constructs

Security	Privacy
Technical	Legal and Organizational
Infrastructure	Information
Availability and Integrity	Confidentiality
Process	Consequence
Organizational protection	Individual protection

or Linux Web environments. In these and other cases, there can be advantages to a cross-functional approach to teaching security and privacy.

University curriculum politics are ingrained through organizational structures that control faculty hiring, retention, tenure, and promotion, and self-governance policy bodies such as academic senates and faculty curriculum committees that control curriculum approval and implementation. New curriculum requires approval by multiple university levels and must meet guidelines for accreditation and certification. Curriculum change must be considered part of an overall campus and community environment.

At an overall level, university curriculum is driven by faculty interests, student attraction, campus resources, and funding support. Curriculum input is provided by faculty based on their knowledge and beliefs about curriculum. Most faculty members aspire to teach courses in specific areas that they have developed expertise in through years of teaching and research. For example, once faculty members are experts in teaching a programming environment or systems methodology course, they may lack incentive to focus on security or privacy issues in that course or develop a new course focusing on security and privacy in these areas. Even more likely to do so are faculty members who do not interact with other disciplines. There is little incentive for Computer Science and Business faculty to collaborate in teaching and curriculum development. Computer Science and Business are seen as separate disciplines, even though security and privacy cut across these disciplines. Cryptography may be viewed as more theoretical by Computer Science, or more of a management issue by Business. Both approaches are valid, but are not likely to be integrated.

Students tend to be attracted to courses that meet specific degree requirements, so a required programming course will attract many more students than an elective in cryptography. Courses are often taught based on enrollment, so a low enrollment elective course in secure programming may be offered but not taught. These degree requirements also must satisfy general education, college and department needs, which can limit opportunities for new or cross-discipline security and privacy courses.

Curriculum development is both top down and bottom up. At the top level, curriculum is driven by academic degree programs. Degree programs consist of courses that can involve multiple prerequisites, and therefore may not be taken by students from more than one college or department. Each college and department has their own curriculum committee and process. Faculty members on these committees develop proposals for new courses and requests to change or replace existing courses. When new courses are proposed, they normally include a catalog description, required background or experience, expected outcomes, text and readings, minimum student material, minimum college resources, course outlines, instructional methods, and evaluation of outcomes. Each of these components must be approved by department, college and university academic senate levels, which has political implications.

Institutional goals influence where security and privacy curriculum is based (Spafford, 1998). Today, skill sets are necessary to staff the information security workforce (Bishop, 2005). Information Assurance (IA) is a broad topic, spanning many areas in computer science, criminology and business management. One of the first and most important curriculum considerations is in which department the curriculum is located. Computer Science programs may be housed in Science, Mathematics, Engineering, or interdisciplinary programs. Business may feel they "own" courses than cover information security issues related to Sarbanes-Oxley, Gramm-Leach-Bliley and other information security related legislation. Computer Science may feel they "own" courses that cover operating systems. Engineering may feel they "own" courses that cover software engineering. Law may feel they "own" courses than deal with privacy issues. Competing needs for students may limit opportunities for a cross-discipline approach to these courses.

The curriculum process is complicated and made more political by time to implement, need to consult under shared governance, and budget allocation using FTE (Full Time Equivalent) students. FTE is calculated by the number of students taking courses in a specific program. Especially for public universities, FTE can determine how much funding an academic program receives. When a program declines in number students, program budgets are likely to be reduced.

Within a university curriculum decisions and policies are driven by curriculum cycles that involve departments, colleges or schools, campuses, and university systems. Consultation can also be a political factor during curriculum development. Consultation occurs when an academic program believes another program may have interest in their curriculum proposal. Consultation is recommended in all cases in which a unit has some reason to think that another unit may have interest in their curriculum proposal. Often, consultation outcomes are influenced by academic program budget allocation based on the number of number FTE students enrolled in program courses. An example is when a computer science program currently teaches an operating systems course, and an information systems program wants to teach a new course on system administration. The computer science program may see the system administration course as a threat to their existing FTE base, and voice concerns over the new course. A disagreement during consultation can result in impasse, which is usually resolved at the Dean's or higher level.

Technology

The increased reliance on information technology and Internet use in higher education over the last 15 years has been dramatic. A 2006 national survey of undergraduate students revealed "97.8 percent of respondents own a personal computer; virtually all students use the Internet on a regular basis, and owning a computer, in most cases a laptop computer, has become a prerequisite for attending higher education" (Salaway, 2006).

A 2006 report revealed that "more that 25 percent of higher education institutions did not communicate computer security awareness on a regular basis to faculty, students, or staff" (Caruso, 2006). At the same time, a report on IT campus security viewed computer security education and awareness programs as potentially "the most single effective way to sensitize the campus community to security needs and responsibilities" (Boes, 2006). Students report "more expertise in use of online library resources, presentation software and spreadsheet software over computer security skills" (Salaway, 2006). Students are likely to be more concerned with technology use than security. As one security professional stated "I don't believe user education will solve problems with security because security will always be a secondary goal for users" (Evers, 2006).

Policy

Security and Identity Management was recently ranked "as the number one IT-related issue in terms of its strategic importance to academic institutions" (Dewey, 2006). During the same time period, "colleges and universities accounted for more than one-third of publicly reported information security breaches" (Cate, 2006). Higher education faces an ongoing battle between their historical openness and need to provide adequate information protection. "Institutions face a tenuous balance between the need to expand information access and the requirements to protect information assets from unauthorized and inappropriate use" (Dewey, 2006). Many universities believe other IT priorities and corresponding lack in funding inhibit effective implementation of security and identity management (Yanosky, 2006). Moreover, developing, implementing, and enforcing effective computer security and privacy policy is about more than effective technology. IT security is also a cultural issue, and academia has a responsibility to foster a culture of security through curriculum and responsible campus IT use (Davidson, 2005). Higher education responsibility for IT security involves many stakeholders. Senior administration officials, centralized and departmental IT staff, students, faculty, and other end users all have a role to play (Boes, 2006). A recent survey of 492 higher education institutions revealed that the two top barriers to IT security in higher education are a lack of resources and an academic culture that values openness and autonomy (Caruso, 2006). "Higher education institutions frequently implement new technologies and systems paying little attention to privacy and security implications" (Cate, 2006). Existing and new security and privacy legislation affecting higher education impose obligations to create and maintain effective security and privacy practices (Adler, 2006).

External Environment

Led by government initiatives and a growing job market for graduates with computer security skills, over the last 10 years universities have significantly increased the number of course offerings covering security and privacy. At the same time, software makers continue to point to inadequate security training at colleges and universities as reasons software continues to be plagued with security flaws. According to Mary Ann Davidson, chief security officer at Oracle, "Unfortunately, if you are a vendor, you have to train your developers until the universities start doing it" (Lemos, 2005). One reason for this disconnect is a traditional approach of computer science curriculum to focus on computer programming languages, computer architecture, and the design and application of computer algorithms. In these cases, computer science may involve teaching concepts more than practice.

Synergy

With the increase in security and privacy curriculum in higher education, and the increased attention to university security and privacy requirements, there is a tremendous opportunity for academics to help universities practice what they teach. A clear need exists for those teaching and practicing IT in higher education to collaborate.

In 2006, the EDUCAUSE/Internet2 Computer and Network Security Task Force and the National Cyber Security Alliance sponsored the first annual Computer Security Awareness Student Video contest. In 2006 the contest included 62 video submissions from 17 universities; in 2007 56 video submissions were made from

24 universities (EDUCAUSE Security and Network Security Task Force, 2007). Many universities also use student internships, projects and competitions to support campus security efforts.

Future Trends

What are the future and emerging trends for security and privacy in higher education? A recent report on changes in information security education concluded that future work "should focus on specifying recommended topics, courses, and sequence Information Security Assurance curricula appropriate for particular degrees" (Hentea, 2006). One example of this is the Masters Degree in Digital Forensics now offered by Central Florida University (Craiger, 2007). The degree helps avoid political academic program turf issues previously mentioned by "leveraging existing courses in several disciplines, including engineering technology, computer science, chemistry, criminal justice and legal studies" (Craiger, 2007). Relevant courses in non-technical disciplines should be considered as a way to integrate information assurance into an overall curriculum.

In developing a theory of interdisciplinary studies, Newell (2001) stated "the appropriate focus of interdisciplinary study is on specific complex systems and their behavior."

Effectively teaching security and privacy is an ongoing challenge because they are complex issues. At the beginning of this chapter, security and privacy constructs were shown to include information, infrastructure, and organizations, components of complex systems. Security and privacy need to be understood in the context of a complex system. Complex systems require a multidimensional approach. Security and privacy curriculum is too important to be left to the whims and politics of competing groups in higher education. A holistic view of security and privacy in higher education requires support from multiple disciplines. No one program can cover the broad, constantly changing technical, scientific, legal, and administrative security and privacy landscape. In the future we may see university level degrees in information assurance, encompassing security and privacy curriculum across multiple disciplines. University "ownership" of security and privacy curriculum may create new political challenges, but can limit competing faculty, department and program politics.

Conclusion

In 2003, The National Strategy to Secure Cyberspace services stated that higher education institutions are subject to security exploits because "they possess vast amounts of computing power and allow relatively open access to those resources" (The National Strategy to Secure Cyberspace, 2003, p. 55). The same report viewed higher education as providing "best practices for IT security" and "model user awareness programs and materials" (The National Strategy to Secure Cyberspace, 2003, p. 56). This chapter has discussed challenges and opportunities for security and privacy in higher education from the administrative and academic viewpoint. With greater collaboration between academia and administrative campus entities, and a multi-disciplinary approach within academia, higher education can be viewed as a key part of addressing current and future security and privacy issues.

References

Adler, M. P. (2006). A unified approach to information security compliance. *EDUCAUSE Review , 41*(5), 47-59.

Bishop, M. F. (2005). Centers of academic excellence: A case study. *IEEE Security and Privacy, 3*(1), 62-65.

Boes, R. C., Cramer, T., Dean, V., Hanson, R., & McKenna, N., (2006). Campus IT security: Governance, strategy, policy, and enforcement. *EDUCAUSE Center for Applied Research,.2006*(17), 1-13.

Caruso, J. B. (2006). *Key findings: Safeguarding the tower: IT security in higher education 2006.* EDUCAUSE Center for Applied Research.

Cate, F. H. (2006). The privacy and security policy vacuum in higher education. *EDUCAUSE Review, 41*(5), 18-29.

Craiger, P. P. (2007). Master's degree in digital forensics. *Proceedings of the 40th Hawaii International Conference on System Sciences – 2007*, p. 6. Waikloloa, Hawaii: Hawaii International Conference on System Sciences.

Davidson, M. A. (2005). Leading by example: The case for IT security in academia. *EDUCAUSE Review*, 14-21.

Dewey, B. I., & DeBlois, P. B. (2006). Top 10 IT issues 2006. *EDUCAUSE Review, 41*(3), 58-79.

EDUCAUSE. (2007). EDUCAUSE. Retrieved January 20, 2007, from EDUCAUSE: http://www.educause.edu/about

EDUCAUSE Security and Network Task Force (2007). Retrieved May 27, 2007 from http://www.educause.edu/SecurityVideoContest2006/7103 and http://www.educause.edu/SecurityVideoContest2007/10955

Elliott, R. (1988). Information security in higher education. CAUSE The Association for the Management of Information Technology in Higher Education.

Evers, J. (2006). Security expert: User education is pointless. Retrieved January 19, 2007, from CNET news.com: http://news.com.com/Security+expert+User+education+is+pointless/2100-7350_3-6125213.html

Hentea, M. D. (2006). Towards changes in information security education. *Journal of Information Technology Education, 5*, 221-232.

Jennings, R. E. (1972). The politics of curriculum change. *Peabody Journal of Education*, 295-299.

Jorgenson, D. W. (2003). Growth of US industries and investments in information technology and higher education. *Economic Systems Research*, 279-325.

Kvavik, R. B. (2006). *IT security in higher education: A sea change.* EDUCAUSE Annual Conference. Dallas Texas: EDUCAUSE Center for Applied Research.

Lemos, R. (2005). Software firms fault colleges' security education, February 16. Retrieved January 15, 2006, from http://news.com.com/2100-1002_3-5579014.html

Newell, W. H. (2001). A theory of interdisciplinary studies. *Issues in Integrative Studies*, 19, 1-25.

Salaway, G. K., Katz, R. N., Caruso, J. B., & Kvavik, R. B. (2006). *The ECAR study of undergraduate students and information technology, 2006.* Volume 7. EDUCAUSE Center for Applied Research.

Schou, C., & Shoemaker, D.,(2007). *Information assurance for the enterprise: A roadmap to information security.* McGraw-Hill-Irwin.

Spafford, E. (1998). *Teaching the big picture of InfoSec*. Colloquium on Information Systems Security Education.

The National Strategy to Secure Cyberspace, (2003). The White House. Retrieved July 23, 2007 from http://www.whitehouse.gov/pcipb/

Yanosky, R. S. & Salaway, G. (2006). *Identity management in higher education: A baseline study.* Volume 2. Boulder, Colorado: EDUCAUSE Center for Applied Research.

About the Contributors

Ramesh Subramanian is the Gabriel Ferrucci professor of computer information systems at the School of Business, Quinnipiac University in Hamden, Connecticut. Dr. Subramanian received a PhD in computer information systems and an MBA from Rutgers University, NJ. He also holds a Post Graduate Diploma (Hons) in management from XLRI – School of Business and Human Resources, Jamshedpur, India, and a Bachelor of Applied Sciences from Madras University, India. Dr. Subramanian's research interests include information systems strategy, technology and culture, cross cultural issues, security, historical and philosophical underpinnings of IS/IT, digital asset management, e-commerce, peer-to-peer computing and IT education. He has published and presented several papers in these areas. His edited book *Peer-to-Peer Computing: The Evolution of a Disruptive Technology* (co-editor B.D. Goodman) was published by IGI Global (formerly Idea Group Publishing) in 2005. Prior to his current appointment, Dr. Subramanian has held the following positions: senior software engineer, IBM's Advanced Technology Lab (Southbury, CT); associate professor of MIS (tenured), College of Business and Public Policy, University of Alaska, Anchorage; instructor of computer science, Computer Science Department, Rutgers University, NJ; member, technical staff, Database Research District, Bell Communications Research, Morristown, NJ. Dr. Subramanian is currently a visiting professor of information systems at the Indian Institute of Technology Madras. He is a recipient of the Fulbright Senior Researcher Grant for 2007-2008.

* * *

Yolande E. Chan is a professor and E. Marie Shantz research fellow in MIS at Queen's University, Canada. She holds a PhD from the University of Western Ontario, an MPhil in management studies from Oxford University, and SM and SB degrees in electrical engineering and computer science from MIT. Prior to joining Queen's, she worked with Andersen Consulting (now Accenture). Currently she serves as director, The Monieson Centre. Dr. Chan conducts research on information privacy, knowledge management, strategic alignment, and information systems performance. She has published her findings in journals such as *Information Systems Research, MIS Quarterly Executive, Journal of Management Information Systems, Journal of the Association for Information Systems, Journal of Strategic Information Systems, Information & Management, IEEE Transactions on Engineering Management* and *The Academy of Management Executive.* Dr. Chan is a member of several journal editorial boards and is an officer of the Association for Information Systems.

Amita Goyal Chin is an associate professor in the Information Systems Department at Virginia Commonwealth University. She received a BS in computer science and an MS and PhD in information systems, The University of Maryland at College Park. Her research focuses primarily on database technology and its applications in information systems. She has been investigating new approaches in data models for text representation and document databases, for this area may contribute to information delivery vehicles beyond the World Wide Web. She is also pursuing innovative solutions for managing data quality in database systems. Additionally, Dr. Chin has combined her information technology experience with her classroom skills to experiment with new teaching technologies and methodologies.

Madhu V. Ahluwalia is a PhD student in the Department of Information Systems, University of Maryland, Baltimore County (USA). Her current research interests include privacy preserving data mining and data warehousing. She has presented a paper entitled "Preserving Privacy in Mining Association rules" at the Second Secure Knowledge Management Workshop (SKM), Brooklyn, New York.

Anza Akram A. completed an MBA in finance from Pakistan. She also received an MBA in MIS and a PhD in MIS. Her professional experience is in banking, healthcare organization, and government. Her research work is on privacy, security, teledemocracy, DSS, and KMS. She worked as a lecturer in California State University, San Bernardino, California and University of California Riverside, California. Formerly, she also taught as a part time faculty in Community Colleges. Presently, she is involved in consulting in the areas of strategic planning and management information systems and writing a book on organization structures.

Ian Allison is a professor and head of computing at The Robert Gordon University. After graduating he spent 10 years working in global technology and financial organisations. He holds a PhD from University of Warwick and is a chartered engineer. His research and teaching focus on IS management and development issues drawing together engineering and organisational perspectives.

Roger Clarke has been principal of Xamax Consultancy Pty Ltd, in Canberra, Australia, since 1982. He is also a visiting professor in the Cyberspace Law & Policy Centre at the University of N.S.W., a visiting professor in the E-Commerce Programme at the University of Hong Kong, and visiting fellow in the Department of Computer Science at the Australian National University. His consultancy work focusses on strategic and policy aspects of e-business, information infrastructure, and dataveillance and privacy. He holds degrees in information systems (MIS) from UNSW, and a doctorate in IS from the ANU.

Sue A. Conger is on the faculty of the University of Dallas where she manages both IT and IT service management programs (1st in the U.S.). She is the author of three books, *The New Software Engineering*, 1994; *Planning and Designing Effective Web Sites* (with Richard O. Mason), 1997; and *Process Mapping & Management*, forthcoming. Dr. Conger's research focuses on innovative uses of IT and emerging technologies and privacy issues relating to emerging technologies. Dr. Conger has an extensive consulting practice, which draws on her work experiences in the information systems field.

Aryya Gangopadhyay is an associate professor of information systems at the University of Maryland, Baltimore County (USA). His current research interests include privacy preserving data mining, data cube navigation, and data mining in healthcare and eco-informatics. He has authored and co-authored three books, many book chapters, numerous papers in journals such as *Decision Sciences, VLDB journal, Decision Support Systems, IEEE Transactions on Knowledge and Data Engineering*, as well as presented papers in many national and international conferences.

Martin Grossman is an assistant professor in the Department of Management at Bridgewater State College. Dr. Grossman received a DBA in information technology management, a master's degree in international busienss from Nova Southeastern University and a BS in computer systems from Florida Atlantic University. He has over 20 years of IT experience in the aviation and communications industries. Dr.

Grossman's current research interests include knowledge management, e-learning and technology innovation.

Silke Holtmanns received a PhD in mathematics from the University of Paderborn (Germany), Department of Computer Science and Mathematics. She is a principal member of the research staff at Nokia Research Center since 2004. Before she was working in Ericsson Research Lab Aachen (Germany) as a master research engineer and at the University of Paderborn as a scientific assistent. She has more then 30 publications and is rapporteur of six 3GPP security specifications and reports and involved in various standardization activities. Her research activities involve trust, privacy, identity management and mobile application security.

Frederick Ip holds a Master of Science in management science, a Bachelor of Commerce and a Bachelor of Arts in computing from Queens University. He is intrigued by technology and its impact on business optimization and human social interaction. His scholastic interests include strategy, innovation and knowledge management. He currently works as a business analyst and programmer developer at LYNXDev Inc. serving Canadian Financial Institutions.

Yue Liu is a PhD candidate at the Norwegian Research Centre for Computers and Law in University of Oslo. Her current research focuses on the biometric technology and privacy protection issues. She is an editor for the legal column of *ERCIM News*, and a research assistant at the Oslo University. Liu is admitted to the National Bar of China. Her education includes an LLM in technology and law from Stockholm University and an MA in international human rights law from Oslo University. She received her LLB from Sichuan University, China. She was a legal consultant for the China National Petroleum Corporation and an attorney in a law firm.

Dan Manson is a professor at California State Polytechnic University, Pomona (Cal Poly Pomona). Manson teaches Internet security and computer forensics in the College of Business Administration Computer Information Systems and Master of Science in Information Systems Auditing programs. From September 2003 to March 2005 and again in 2006, Manson served as the campus information security officer for Cal Poly Pomona. He is involved with several professional organizations, including the Information Systems Security Association, InfraGard, the Information Systems Audit and Control Association and High Tech Crime Investigation Association.

Richard V. McCarthy is a professor of information systems management in the School of Business at Quinnipiac University, Hamden, CT. Dr. McCarthy received a DBA in IT management from Nova Southeastern University, a Master in Business Administration from Western New England College and a BS in management information systems from Central Connecticut State University. He has nearly 20 years of IT management experience in the insurance and manufacturing industries and holds a CPCU designation. His current research interests include enterprise architecture, information systems strategy and knowledge management.

Alok Mishra is an associate professor of computer and software engineering at Atilim University, Ankara Turkey. He had his PhD in computer science (software engineering) besides dual master's degrees in computer science & applications and human resource management. His areas of interest and research are software engineering, information system, information & knowledge management and object oriented analysis & design. He had extensive experience of distance and online education related to computers and management courses. He has published articles, book chapters and book-reviews related to software engineering and information system in refereed journals, books and conferences including *International Journal of Information Management, Government Information Quarterly, IET-Software, Lecture Notes in Computer Science, Behaviour and Information Technology, Public Personnel Management, European Journal of Engineering Education, International Journal of Information Technology and Management.*

Sushma Mishra is a PhD candidate at in the Information Systems Department, Virginia Commonwealth University. She received a master's degree in business administration from the International Management Institute, India. Her research interests are in the area of information systems security, regulatory impact on IT, audit issues and systems development methodologies.

Bernd Carsten Stahl is a reader in critical research in technology in the Centre for Computing and Social Responsibility, De Montfort University, Leicester, UK. His interests cover philosophical issues arising from the intersections of business, technology, and information. This includes the ethics of computing and critical approaches to information systems. He is editor-in-chief of the *International Journal of Technology and Human Interaction* (IGI Global).

Craig Strangwick is systems manager for ABC Awards, a national awarding body in the UK. He holds a master's degree in business information technology and is a member of the British Computer Society. Craig has worked as a systems developer in pharmaceuticals, logistics, and more recently the education sector, implementing business systems, intranets & extranets, e-commerce applications and CRM. Current projects include developing on-screen testing and electronic portfolios for the vocational education sector.

W. John Thomas is a professor of law and director of the Health Law Program at Quinnipiac University School of Law. His publications address topics ranging from international pharmaceutical regulation, health policy, juvenile justice, juvenile mental health treatment, to pharmaceutical advertising. Professor Thomas has spoken on these topics at law conferences around the world. He is currently at work on a book, to be published by Centerstream Publishing, LLC, concerning the unsung women who worked for the Gibson Guitar Company during WWII.

Zheng Yan holds two master's degrees from Xi'an Jiaotong University, China and National University of Singapore, respectively. She received her licentiate degree at the Helsinki University of Technology. She will defend her doctoral dissertation about trust management for mobile computing platforms in 2007. Zheng is a senior member of research staff at the Nokia Research Center, Helsinki. Before joining in the NRC in 2000, she worked as a research scholar at I2R and software engineer at IBM SingaLab, Singapore. She first-authored more than 20 paper publications. Her research interests are trust modeling and management; trusted computing; trustworthy software, applications and services; usable security/trust and DRM.

Index